KEYWORDS
FOR TODAY

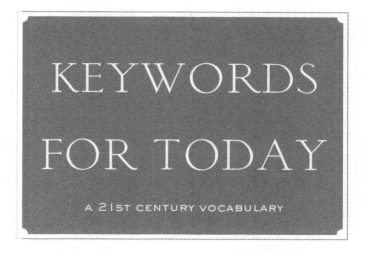

KEYWORDS FOR TODAY

A 21ST CENTURY VOCABULARY

THE KEYWORDS PROJECT

EDITED BY

COLIN MACCABE

HOLLY YANACEK

OXFORD
UNIVERSITY PRESS

OXFORD
UNIVERSITY PRESS

Oxford University Press is a department of the University of Oxford. It furthers
the University's objective of excellence in research, scholarship, and education
by publishing worldwide. Oxford is a registered trade mark of Oxford University
Press in the UK and certain other countries.

Published in the United States of America by Oxford University Press
198 Madison Avenue, New York, NY 10016, United States of America.

© Oxford University Press 2018

Library of Congress Cataloging-in-Publication Data
Names: MacCabe, Colin, editor. | Yanacek, Holly, editor.
Title: Keywords for today : a 21st century vocabulary : the keywords project /
edited by Colin MacCabe and Holly Yanacek.
Description: New York, NY : Oxford University Press, 2018. |
Includes bibliographical references and index.
Identifiers: LCCN 2018013234 (print) | LCCN 2018030170 (ebook) |
ISBN 9780190636586 (updf) | ISBN 9780190636593 (epub) |
ISBN 9780190636579 (pbk. : alk. paper)
Subjects: LCSH: English language—21st century—Glossaries, vocabularies, etc. |
English language—Etymology.
Classification: LCC PE1680 (ebook) | LCC PE1680.K47 2018 (print) |
DDC 428.1—dc23
LC record available at https://lccn.loc.gov/2018013234

3 5 7 9 8 6 4

Printed by Webcom, Inc., Canada

Contents

History of the Keywords Project

The **Keywords Project** is a radically collaborative, cross-institutional, and cross-disciplinary research initiative sponsored by the University of Pittsburgh, Jesus College Cambridge, and the academic journal *Critical Quarterly*. Over the past decade, the members of the Keywords Project have worked to update Raymond Williams's classic *Keywords* for the 21st century and new generations of readers.

As the Keywords Project concludes, the membership list includes some who have left the Project and others who joined while work was already underway, but all have contributed to the substance of this volume and of the website (http://keywords.pitt.edu/):

Sylvia Adamson, Emeritus Professor of Linguistics and Literary History, School of English, University of Sheffield

Kathryn Allan, Senior Lecturer in the History of English, University College London

Susan Z. Andrade, Associate Professor of English, University of Pittsburgh

Jonathan Arac, Director of the Humanities Center at the University of Pittsburgh

Jennifer Davis, Faculty of Law and Fellow of Wolfson College, University of Cambridge

Alan Durant, Professor of Communication in the School of Law, Middlesex University, London

Philip Durkin, Deputy Chief Editor of the *Oxford English Dictionary*

Matthew Eagleton-Pierce, Senior Lecturer in International Political Economy, SOAS University of London

Stephen Heath, Fellow of Jesus College, Cambridge, and Keeper of the Old Library

Colin MacCabe, Distinguished Professor of English and Film, University of Pittsburgh

Seth Mehl, Research Associate, School of English, University of Sheffield

Arjuna Parakrama, Senior Professor of English, University of Peradeniya, Sri Lanka

Kellie Robertson, Associate Professor of English, University of Maryland

Holly Yanacek, Assistant Professor of German, James Madison University

In addition to these fourteen members of the Keywords Project, *Keywords for Today* brought together over twenty participants in University of Pittsburgh graduate seminars. More information about the seminar directed by Jonathan Arac and Colin MacCabe may be found in *Critical Quarterly* (2016), along with a sample of the students' work; some others appear as part of this volume, and yet others appear on the website. These are the students and the words they worked on: Samuel Allen, *Public*; Amanda Awanjo, *Trans*; Sagnika Chanda, *Man*; Evan Chen, *Gentrification*; Max Ginsberg, *Authority*; Joshua Graber, *Social*; Sylvia Grove, *Artificial*; Treviene Harris, *Privilege*; Kaitlyn Haynal, *Access*; Adam Hebert, *Occupy*; Artan Hoxha, *Fundamental*; Nicholas Marsellas, *Respect*; Sarah Mejia, *Digital*; Alexandra Ouyang, *Security*; Lauren Posey, *Gender*; Sarah Schaefer, *Love*; Tetyana Shlikar, *Network*; Leonardo Solano, *Diaspora*; Nicholas Stefanski, *Future*; Marina Tyquiengco, *Appropriation*.

Introduction

Key is a very old word in English with the simple sense of an instrument designed to be inserted into a lock and turned. Over time it has developed a whole range of figurative uses, and in its sense of "a solution or explanation for a problem" it undoubtedly informed Raymond Williams's choice of the term **keywords** to name the set of words for which he began to write glosses in the 1950s. These **keywords** helped to solve both a very particular and a very general problem with which he was wrestling in that decade. The particular problem was the meaning of *culture*. In 1948 T. S. Eliot had published *Notes towards the Definition of Culture*. Eliot was widely considered both as the greatest of living poets and the most important of literary critics, but his message was unambiguously conservative. If you valued culture, then you had to abandon the desire for a classless society, because culture could only be produced by a class-stratified society. As a socialist, Williams had struggled against these arguments, and he found his solution, almost by chance, in the *Oxford English Dictionary*: the dictionary's history of this complex word *culture* allowed him both to place Eliot's argument within a development and also to find in that development alternative arguments, which linked the fullest form of culture to the fullest growth of democracy in a classless society. Eliot's definition of *culture* effectively restricted it to the arts, but the dictionary revealed that this sense of the word dated back no further than the late nineteenth century. Earlier meanings of the word stretched back a further century, and they focused on a general process of intellectual, spiritual, and aesthetic development. Those earlier senses led Williams to his own formulation of *culture* as "a whole way of life." By this means he could value the solidarity that he understood to be the great cultural value of the working class into which he had been born, while he could also value those artistic productions to which Eliot had limited the sense of the word.

The *OED* not only provided a very specific answer to the particular problem of *culture*, it also provided the best evidence for the very slow and complicated process of social change which Williams was trying to understand in the 1950s. This had a deeply personal level, explored in his semi-autobiographical novel *Border Country*, but it was also a pressing political problem for anyone who agreed with Marx's analysis of the centrality of class struggle but who rejected Lenin's call for violent and sudden revolution. As Williams tracked his **keywords** across the matrix of the *OED* and his own reading, he revealed those slow movements of consciousness composed both of material progress and mental reflection, which he christened "the long revolution." This revolution made the development of the forms of communication from newspapers to television, from the book to the standard language a crucial element in the development of a fully democratic society. Williams's decade of work in the 1950s produced, in addition to his novel, two massively influential books: *Culture and Society* and *The Long Revolution*. He also produced his glossary of **keywords**, but his publisher, citing the cost of extra pages, refused to include it as an appendix to *Culture and Society*.

Williams published *Keywords*, as a stand-alone book, two decades later in 1976. By then he was no longer an adult education teacher but a university professor at Cambridge, and Lenin's call for a short and sudden revolution had found a new audience in the politicized students of Western universities. **Keywords**, with its long perspective of linguistic change, makes an implicit argument against any such sudden revolution. Williams's work, and the long revolution for which he argued, was deeply rooted in the experience of the postwar years and a moment of great political optimism concerning the possibility of social change. That change would take many decades and generations to reach its final conclusion, but all Williams's work evinces this fundamental political optimism. Today, the universal coverage provided by the British National Health Service remains the most visible evidence of that moment.

The Keywords Project to update Williams's work took shape in the first decade of the 21st century, when it appeared to many that a Labour government in London and a Democratic administration in Washington had largely abandoned the ambition to achieve a more equal society and when the false dawn of the 1960s and its promise of liberation had degenerated into a host of competing identity politics. The members of the Keywords Project could loosely be described as of the left, but it was not politics that propelled us through a decade of writing new entries.

Political imperatives drove Williams to language, but intellectual admiration drove the Project. *Keywords* had pioneered a new way to tell the history of English. That history now needed updating. We all hope that this work will be politically illuminating, but the politics must emerge from the linguistic analysis.

The Keywords Project began over fifty years after Williams had done the bulk of this work. In this period, political and technological change had thrown up new words and had rendered others obsolete. Indeed, even Williams's title was not immune from this process. When Williams selected **keyword** as his name for those lexical items that concentrated political and cultural disagreement, the word also had a specialist meaning related to indexes and catalogues. That specialist use of **keyword**, after Williams's death, came to designate a word entered as a search term in a database or search engine. That term has become so important in our digital world that we had to consider whether we should try to find a new name for what we were doing to update Williams's vocabulary. We decided against such a radical step because there is little chance of confusing the two meanings. Williams's and our use of **keyword** is rooted in the widespread non-technical use of **key** in such familiar phrases as *key witness* and *key concept*.

Williams never makes explicit his criteria for what constitutes a **keyword**; they grow out of his general research project. In deciding which words to discard from Williams's list and which to add, we had to make his criteria explicit. First, they must be words current in social and political debate, and that currency must stretch beyond academic contexts. *Alienation* was one of Williams's words that failed this test. One could argue for its continuing philosophical and political importance as a word that articulates together the individual and the social, but its frequency of use has declined very sharply; in the 1960s there was no doubt that it was a **keyword**, but now it no longer functions in widespread debate. However, frequency is not the only criterion. Both *mentor* and *debt* were words we considered adding because they are much used now, but their philological histories show little complexity, and we do not find several meanings active together in any contemporary use of the words. The best characterization of a **keyword** is a word that both bears a complex meaning rooted in centuries of social history and also features that complexity in current debate. In focusing on these **keywords**, we follow Williams in viewing language not as a shared understanding but rather as a site of division, with the crucial twist that some of the most crucial divisions are masked by the **keywords** themselves. They seem to suggest a single meaning, where in fact there are many competing semantic elements. A very good example of this is the **keyword** *democracy*, where what is meant by "rule of the people" oscillates constantly between notions of representative parliamentary democracy and more direct forms of popular rule, ranging from referendums to workers' representation on company boards. In a volume claiming to represent crucial terms for the early 21st century, one might reasonably expect to find many versions of *cyber* and *digital*. We have not, however, chosen words on the basis of their mere ubiquity. Instead, following the principles articulated in Williams's own Introduction, we have sought to identify words that could be used in virtually antithetical ways by individuals or social groups with very different social agendas, concepts whose meaning is contested in some crucial way.

Setting out to update *Keywords* was not simply a question of adding recent developments to the some forty of Williams's entries that were still current and of replacing some eighty-five of his words that had faded into history with newer words from the political and social debates of our time. We also believed that the huge databases and powerful search engines now available would enable us to broaden the base of Williams's work. The long revolution continues in the digital revolution, and in the study of vocabulary and the lexicon, the most obvious new resource has been the emergence of ever larger corpora of (largely written) English, especially contemporary written standard US and British English. (Appendix 1 provides a survey of the sources we used.) Such corpora make it possible to obtain a snapshot of the "typical" behavior of a word (in the types of source that they are compiled from). In studying a word, you let the software generate a summary of the usual patterns of collocation shown by a word—e.g., which other words a noun typically occurs beside, or which verbs it is typically the object of—and then analyze this summary to discover what it reveals about the word's semantics. *Collocate* proved such an important technical term that we have not purged it from our entries, which we had hoped to keep completely free of specialized linguistic or lexicographic terminology. Yet collocation patterns and analysis of frequency are not the best instruments for investigating many of the questions this book most cares about: often, our entries focus on fine nuances of meaning and connotation, which emerge from close reading of significant texts. The interaction and intertwining of language with culture and society form the core of this book, and investigating this necessarily involves stepping beyond corpus data abstracted from a word's original contexts of use. In establishing the discrimination and interaction of meanings, we have found, like Williams, that our most important tools have been the *OED* and our own reading and frames of intellectual reference.

Williams's *Keywords* grew from an individual intellectual and political project; *Keywords for Today* brought together some dozen individuals differentiated by age, gender, class, and nationality, as well as over twenty participants in University of Pittsburgh seminars. This multiple and multiply differentiated authorship of the entries is evident even when the entries have been subjected to the most rigorous standardization by collaborative editing. Something certainly is lost as we miss the unified tone and manner of Williams's entries, but something also is gained in the different range of readings and references. What unifies both *Keywords* and *Keywords for Today* is the method of close reading developed by I. A. Richards and elaborated by William Empson for the reading of complex poetry. Williams's most original contribution came from applying this method to the historical record of the English language. *Keywords for Today* follows in those footsteps.

Williams composed his **keyword** entries at a time when the national press in England enjoyed its period of greatest dominance, and *Keywords* can be understood as assuming the discursive dominance of such a national press. The challenge to this dominance posed by the new technology of television had not yet become clear in Williams's lifetime, because public service broadcasting in Britain preserved and enlarged the discursive space that Williams explored. However, since his death in 1988, the breaking of the public service remit for British television in the 1990s and even more importantly the growth of the Internet have fundamentally altered the public discursive space. In 1990, research showed that the vast majority of the population, after leaving formal education, used writing only to make lists (as the telephone had very largely usurped the role of letter writing); however, the next twenty years saw an explosion of writing. By e-mailing, texting, blogging, and tweeting, written language burgeoned in ways that redefine our conceptions of public and private and that may even end by abolishing entirely the press which provided a central focus for Williams.

Such considerations threaten to render the very pursuit of a **keywords** project obsolete. The notion of investigating polysemous words whose histories carry clues to sharpening and making more acute social debate may seem to belong to the past. And yet when we look at society, at health, at education, we see in words like *diversity*, *well-being*, and *excellence* a crystallization of social contradictions that seem active in our political debates. We still share Williams's hope that sketching this crystallization may add an extra "edge of consciousness" to contemporary social understanding.

The Keywords Project

How to Read *Keywords for Today*

TYPES OF HEADWORDS IN THIS VOLUME

Standard font (e.g., IDENTITY)
   Completely new entries written by Keywords Project members
Bold font (e.g., DEMOCRACY)
   Words in Raymond Williams's *Keywords* with recent developments
Bold italic font (e.g., SEXUALITY)
   New entries that replace entries in Williams's *Keywords*

IN-TEXT AND END-OF-TEXT
CROSS-REFERENCES

Raymond Williams used cross-references in his original *Keywords* in order to remind readers of the "many necessary connections" between his analyses of particular words.

Following Williams, cross-references to other words in *Keywords for Today* are provided within the text and at the end of each entry in small caps (e.g., See LITERATURE, REALISM).

CITATION PRACTICE

FOR SECONDARY SOURCES

In the era of fake news, it is more vital than ever that every argument is properly sourced so that any reader may pursue the discussion to its roots. However, to use unnecessary scholarly apparatus would be against all that Raymond Williams embodied.

At the core of each entry in this book is dialogue between the history of each word as presented in the *OED* and our own readings in social and cultural history. Unless otherwise noted, the different senses of each word are cited from the *OED*, and, following Williams, quotations followed by a name and date only, or a date only, are often illustrative examples cited in the *OED*. Quotes from other sources that are not cited in the *OED* are only identified if they cannot be searched easily on Google. For the rest, scholarly marking of author name, title, and date indicate their importance for the argument. This follows Williams's practice in the original *Keywords*: references are part of the discourse. The ease of searching on Google was the criteria used to prune Williams's original according to his own principles.

Abbreviations

The following abbreviations are used in the text.

fw   immediate forerunner of a word, in the same or another language.

rw   ultimate traceable word, from which "root" meanings are derived.

C   followed by numeral, century (C19: nineteenth century).

eC   first period (third) of a century.

mC   middle period (third) of a century.

lC   last period (third) of a century.

a   (before a date) *ante*, before, not later than.

c   (before a date) *circa*, approximately.

AN   Anglo-Norman

ME   Middle English (*c*1100–1500).

OE   Old English (to *c*1100).

F   French

mF Medieval French

oF Old French

Gk Classical Greek

IE Indo-European

It Italian

L Latin

mL Medieval Latin

vL Vulgar Latin

OED *The Oxford English Dictionary.*

KEYWORDS
FOR TODAY

ABSTRACT

Abstract comes from Latin *abstractus*: this is the past participle of the verb *abstrahere*, to draw from, and the elements it is composed of are *abs*, from, and *tractus*, drawn. It enters English from lC14 as past participle and then adjective: "[the authors] of whom thys presente cronicle is abstracte" (1475). With the formation of **abstract** as a verb, **abstracted** eventually replaced **abstract** as participle. The senses of **abstract** and the noun **abstraction** (second half of C15) follow from the Latin etymology, involving ideas of withdrawing, removing, separating from: *c*1550, "He dois chestee [rebuke] them, be the abstractione of . . . superfluite"; 1690, "The more abstract therefore we are from the Body, . . . the more fit we shall be both to behold, and to indure the Rays of the Divine Light."

Such **abstraction** could have a more secular context: 1660, "Justice must have . . . abstraction from all affections of love, hate, or self-interest." It could also refer to mental inattention: 1509, "Theyr mynde abstract, nat knowynge what they say." This sense has become common, usually with more or less negative connotations. Charles Dickens talks cheerfully of his "habit of easy self-abstraction" (1867), but **abstract** in Iris Murdoch's *A Severed Head* (1961) indicates failure of expression or feeling: "she spoke in an abstract tone"; "the abstractedness of his bond [with his lover]." Joseph Conrad's *The Shadow Line* (1917) exemplifies the habitual opposition of **abstract** and *concrete*: the command of a ship "is an abstract idea," which the encounter with its "concrete existence" makes real—"concreting the abstract sentiment." From eC19 there is a use of **abstraction** to mean theft: "He robs nothing but the revenue—an abstraction I never greatly cared about" (Charles

Lamb, 1828); **abstracting electricity** is a criminal offense in British law (the offense with which computer hackers were initially charged).

The *OED* cites an occurrence of "a noun abstract" by 1398, and the characterization of certain nouns as **abstract**, denoting an idea, quality, or state, or *concrete*, denoting an individual particularity, is established in grammar and logic by C17: "Let it be considered whither it be a Noun Abstract or Concrete" (Zachary Coke, 1653). A similar distinction is made from that time with regard to numbers: "some are said to be abstract, and some concreate" (Thomas Blundeville, 1594). For John Locke in his *Essay Concerning Human Understanding* (1690), **abstraction** is the process "whereby ideas taken from particular beings become general representatives of all of the same kind." The existence, or not, of such representatives or "abstract ideas" concerned British empiricist philosophers in accounting for knowledge as derived from the senses, and **abstraction** was taken generally as epistemologically fundamental, "the first in order of the scientific processes" (Alexander Bain, *The Senses and the Intellect*, 1855).

Though **abstract** is not an entry in Raymond Williams's *Keywords*, it is very much a key word in his writing. Most *Keywords* words are **abstract** nouns of Latin provenance, and come from what Williams calls "the vocabulary of learning and power." **Abstraction** could be regarded as a defining *human* capacity—for Locke "the power of abstracting" marked "a perfect distinction between Man and Brutes" but also a *social* one related to class and education: "the Vulgar have not such Logical Heads, as to be able to Abstract subtile Conceptions" (Robert South, 1690). For George Orwell, "many necessary abstract words" were class-identified and so rejected by the working class as "public-schoolish" (Orwell, *The English People*, 1947). Williams's stated intention in *Culture and Society*, from which *Keywords* derives, was to give people confidence in using such words.

Abstract appears regularly in *Keywords* to describe this class of word: *communications* is "the abstract general term" in C19 for "roads, canals, railways." It is also often distinguished from *general: society* is "our most general term for the body of institutions and relationships within which a relatively large group of people live" *and* "our most abstract term for the condition in which such institutions and relationships are formed." The distinction is important for Williams's treatment of his keywords, critically seen as frequently involving a hardening into abstraction. *Progress* as "forward movement" has no necessary ideological implication. There is, however, an ideological abstraction of this movement as "a discoverable historical pattern," linked to similarly abstracted and ideologically deployed formulations of *civilization* and *improvement*. **Abstract** is essential to *Culture and Society*'s analysis of modes of thought abstracted from a society's "whole way of life"—thinking not governed by attention to social reality and historical process leads "very quickly to abstraction and unreality." *Culture and Society* itself was later faulted by Williams for "a degree of abstraction from history," and Williams used this self-criticism to make an important distinction between *ideology* and *hegemony*. Marx attacked "the abstract categories of 'individual' and 'society,' " and attacked ideology as "abstract and false thought," yet Marxism could itself fall too easily into abstraction. Hegemony goes beyond "abstracted ideology," refuses "to equate consciousness with the articulated formal system which can be and ordinarily is abstracted as 'ideology,' " and understands "a wider area of reality than the abstractions of 'social' and 'economic' experience" (Williams, *Marxism and Literature*, 1977).

Tocqueville noted a predilection for "abstract expressions" in "democratic languages," and a tendency "to sublimate into further abstraction the abstract terms of the language": "an abstract term is like a box with a false bottom: you may put in it what ideas you please" (*Democracy in America*, trans. H. Reeve, 1840). **Abstract** and **abstraction**, indeed, have been key words in arguments over democracy, notably as regards its dependence on abstracting from the concrete realities of the individuals within it—democracy as "a dense abstract mass of somebody elses" (Wyndham Lewis, 1927). Recent feminist thought has opposed **abstract individualism**: the masking of individual histories and cultural experiences with "abstract notions of equality" (Marie A. Failinger, 2007). Arguments here crystallize around *liberalism*, perceived as viewing "individual human beings as social atoms, abstracted from their social contexts" (Marilyn Friedman, 1989).

The first decades of C20 saw an important concern with **abstraction** in LITERATURE and ART. "Go in fear of abstractions"—poetic images "should be 'concrete' " (Ezra Pound, 1913); this at the same time as the emergence of **abstract art**, or art moving away from figurative traditions. *OED* has an instance of **abstract painting** from 1851, then **abstract canvas**, 1915; **abstraction** as opposed to *realism*, 1909; and **abstract expressionism**, 1922. **Abstract** here indicates a crisis of REPRESENTATION, running parallel with arguments about political—democratic—representation. On the one hand, there is a movement against abstraction, for a language of the concrete in place of a worn-out language of "abstract counters" (T. E. Hulme, 1909); on the other, abstraction is presented as a throwing off of conventional forms, a struggle for new vision, new language (Virginia Woolf wants a cinema of "abstractions," 1926; and she attempts in *To the Lighthouse* "the most difficult abstract writing," 1927).

The history of **abstract** shows not so much substantial shifts in meaning as shifts in the value attached to Locke's "power of abstracting." This is evident in the ways in which the last two hundred years or so have seen the word given both negative and positive values; this above all in thinking about the individual and society, rights and equality—the very focus of *Keywords* and of Williams's work overall.

See ART, REPRESENTATION

ACCESS

The use of **access** has increased considerably in English in the last fifty years at the same time as its once current medical meanings have become effectively archaic. This increase is directly related to its use in relation to both disability and computing, but these uses are intertwined with a set of political debates in which **access** is interpreted as an important right. Contemporary questions of **access** often mobilize contradictory ideological assumptions, and **access** has become a key term in debates ranging from law to medicine to education.

Etymologically, **access** is derived from both French and Latin with the root word being the classical Latin *accessus*, which is a noun covering a very wide range of movement from approach or visit to the rising of the tide or the blowing of the wind. As Norman French *accesse* or Middle French *acces,* it emerges in C13 as an attack or onset of an illness: the body is invaded by a "strong access of fever." With this sense it enters English at the beginning of C14: "[Tymon] in a strong acces was of a feuere" (*c*1300). It soon developed an important figurative use signaling the onset of a powerful EMOTION: "an axcess of soule" (*c*1384), "þacces of anguych" (*c*1400). Thus, in 1815, "In a fresh access of jealousy, [he] plunged a dagger into her heart." This figurative meaning is important into C20 but is now rare, if not archaic.

Much of **access**'s importance in the past fifty years is its ability to switch between very concrete meanings and very vague ones. Thus **access** can refer to a physical point of entry or to its digital equivalent, but it can also imply a set of RIGHTS or PRIVILEGES that come with this entry. This emphasis on rights and privileges was stressed in the selection of **Access** as the brand name for the first credit card in the UK to challenge the Barclaycard in 1972. The brand disappeared when it was taken over by MasterCard in 1996, but the ambiguities of the word continue to make it a potent articulator of political promise.

Its most direct political role has been in the disability movement that developed out of the wider Civil Rights movements of the 1960s. In a series of developments of the past fifty years, **access** has been a key term to refer to the attempts to integrate disabled people into a physical world that until then had ignored their needs. In 1968 the US Congress passed the Architectural Barriers Act (ABA) that required federal facilities to become **accessible** to people with disabilities. Significantly, when it was realized that this act required a regulatory body, the name chosen in 1973 was Access Board, which was charged with "Full Access and Inclusion for All." The UK Disability Discrimination Act of 1995 gave rights "to use and access services."

At the same time, **access** became an important term in efforts to democratize television so that people outside the television industry could enjoy the possibility of producing television programs. The important use of **access television** was very short lived as technological developments in the recording, editing, and broadcasting of sound and image meant that the aims of access television were realized on an unimaginable scale even if the broadcasting outlets remain largely in state or commercial ownership. You could call YouTube **access television**, but technology and language have moved so fast that it is not clear that younger speakers of the language would recognize this use at all.

Access's connection with computing and telecommunications has been more durable, and a host of compounds have appeared in recent decades: **access provider** (1983), **access code** (1955), and **access time** (1979). **Access** has also been the rallying cry of the digital **open access** movement, which took off in the late 1990s as the Internet encouraged and enabled a low-cost means of distributing content and knowledge, characterized by the rise of blogs, content-sharing forums, and other social media platforms. The **open access** movement argues that all research online should be freely **accessible**, and its utopian vision is well articulated by *Wikipedia* founder Jim Wales: "imagine a world in which every single person on the planet is given free access to the sum of all human knowledge." A specialist use, anticipating the Internet use, is its development as a term in library science referring to unrestricted **access** for readers to the shelves on which a library's books and other publications are kept—"the principle of open access" (*The Library*, November 1894).

The vagueness of **access** enables the utopian vision of **open access** to ignore those who lack the education to benefit from it. This ambiguity of **access** is written deep into its history. From lC14 there are uses of **access** which link admission to right and thus suggest that to gain **access** is to enjoy some entitlement. This sense clearly emerges in mC16: "the one has access to the legal maintenance; the other is cast upon peoples benevolence, and burdensome to their private purse."

This vagueness about what constitutes **access** surfaces in many political debates. Thus, the debates about health provision in the United States often use *availability, affordability*, and **accessibility** as confusing synonyms. For some, equal **access** entails guarantee of availability of medical supplies and resources. Others argue that equal **access** should ensure equal use for equal need and that the question of the external factors that affect the understanding of that availability is a crucial part of providing a FAIR provision of health care. The way that **access** semantically implies that entry or admittance also provides entitlement has made it a very much used term in debates about education and culture. The LEGITIMATE demand for **access** can often mask inconvenient facts about the difficulty of fully benefiting from the cultural or educational INSTITUTION to which **access** is being demanded.

Access plays a central role in two of the most important political movements of recent years. It was a key argument of the movement for same-sex MARRIAGE that same-sex couples should have **access** to all the benefits enjoyed by differently sexed couples. More recently, the question of **access** to appropriate bathrooms has become a key demand of the TRANSGENDER movement. **Access**, however, with its constant promise that entry will provide satisfaction, proliferates from banks which offer **instant access** accounts to Maya Angelou's statement that "the most called-upon prerequisite of a friend is an accessible ear." **Access** hesitates in its senses between potential for use and actual achievement. In a society that combines an ideology of EQUALITY with ever greater inequality, **access** often hides what is **inaccessible**.

See EQUALITY, FAIR, PRIVILEGE, RIGHTS

ANIMAL

The word **animal** used to refer to a living organism is a borrowing from French and Latin that enters English in lC14, where it joins C13 *beast* and lC14 *creature*, both of which similarly refer to living organisms. In early uses, **animal** can encompass humans: "man is animal and hors is animal, and so of oþer bestes" (a1398); "undyr *animal* beyn conteynt all mankynd, beist, byrd, fowll, fish serpent, and all other sik thingis" (a1522). That last quotation separates *mankind* from *beast*, a word that could likewise in the first instance include humans: "Al þing þat haþ lif and felynge is y-clept a beste" (a1387). Application to humans is made explicit with some distinguishing qualification: "a man or woman, which be reasonable beastes" (1547);

"reasonable" evoking the traditional division of the soul into three parts: vegetative, animal, and rational, with humans alone possessed of the latter. The use of *beast* in respect to humans came increasingly to indicate negative *beastlike* characteristics that pervert our essential humanity when we should rather "exalt the man and depress the beast in us" (1667). The adjective *beastly* exemplifies the movement from a relatively straightforward designation of **animals** other than humans to an emphasis on what is *beastlike* in the latter. Humans may be "beastly witted" or "beastly foolish" (1561), lacking the sense and intelligence that should distinguish them from humans; just as they may give in to "beastly desires of inordinate lust" (1567). The word *creature*, which had a first, now obsolete sense of the created universe, of creation—"the bigynnynge of creature" (c1384)—is initially bound up with the account of God creating "every living creature that moveth" (Genesis 1:21, King James Bible, 1611); "all creatures great and small," in the words of the popular Victorian hymn "All Things Bright and Beautiful" (1848). Like *beast, creature* includes the human being, the creature above all others, "the master work": "a creature who not prone/And brute as other creatures, but endued/With sanctity of reason" (*Paradise Lost*, 1667). Used for an individual, *creature* is qualified by a descriptive term: "a ful comely creature" (c1400), "a sorweful creature," "this ravishing creature" (2007). The current main use of **animal** to refer to living organisms *other* than man is from lC16. The range of organisms to which it is applied varies, though, as *OED* notes, it frequently designates mammals, as opposed to birds, reptiles, fish, etc.; with distinctions made regarding habitat: **land-animal, water-animal, sea-animal**. The **human animal** (1495) is indeed an **animal** but special, above all others—"the paragon of animals" (1616).

Human beings by definition possess HUMANITY (c1384), the quality of being human, which also has meanings referring particularly to qualities, of kindness, goodness, fellow-feeling. The later **animality** appears in eC17 with the meaning, now rare, of **animal nature**, vital power of LIFE—"Lifesomeness or animality" (1674), along with that of **animal** characteristics as distinct from human ones. Unlike the first, this second meaning opposes **animality** to *humanity*; it follows "the Dictates of Flesh and Blood" (1726) and is largely seen in men—since "In woman, humanity, as contradistinguished to animality . . . has attained its zenith" (1836). The same neutral/negative shift occurs with **animal**, moving from simple designation of living organisms to lC16 emphasis on people or peoples lacking the qualities of humanity: "sick monstruous animals . . . the cruell cannibals, [who] feids on flesch of men" (?1590–1); "he is only an annimall, only sensible in the duller partes"

(1598). "Campbell is an absolute animal. Scum like him should never be allowed to walk the streets" (2004). A positive human-animal reality is expressed by **animal spirit** (*a*1425), referring first to a supposed vital agent responsible for sensation and movement that runs through the body from the brain: "spirit animal dwellith in the brayne" (*a*1500). From lC17 the plural, **animal spirits**, draws figuratively on this idea of animal vitality to mean courage, vivacity, possibly excessive liveliness in a person: "[in young people] A Spring-tide of Animal Spirits easily overflows the judgement before it's grown up" (1701); *Pride and Prejudice*'s Lydia Bennet has "high animal spirits" (1813).

The understanding of **animal** and of the kind and nature of the many species the word includes has shifted over the centuries and has been a matter of much recent debate and cultural-political action regarding the boundaries between *human* and **animal**, animals and humans. Common law distinguished between *ferae naturae* and *mansuetae naturae*, animals wild and tame. A division conventionally assumed today is among **wild animals**, **domestic animals** (such as cattle, horses, sheep, pigs, poultry, reared for human purposes), and *pets*. The word *pet* is a C16 borrowing from Scottish Gaelic *peata* used of a lamb or other animal reared by hand; Samuel Johnson's *Dictionary of the English Language* definition is: "A lamb taken into the house, and brought up by hand" (1755). The current meaning of an animal domesticated and kept for pleasure or companionship is recorded from eC18, as is **animal companion** (1731). The continuing increase in the number of *pet lovers* in eC20 produced *pet shops, pet food*, and an industry providing for all requirements until death—*pet cemetery*.

Pets are a special case of the human recognition of animals, given names and included within their owner's domestic life and space (the German for *pet* is *Haustier*, "house animal," the French is *animal de compagnie*, "animal companion"; these languages, along with many others, have no equivalent word for the special intimacy of *pet*, distinct from **animal**). Indicatively, *pet* became a term of affection used of humans, women and children especially: "*Pet* . . . a fond designation for a female favourite" (1825); "Do you know, pet, it seems almost a dream . . . that we have been married" (1849).

The relation between *human* and **animal** has been central to many of the most important debates in recorded history. **Animal sacrifice** was perhaps the most important public argument that divided Christian and pagan in the later Roman Empire. The status of **animal slaughter** is central to Hinduism and many versions of Buddhism. The moral status of animals has become a central issue for modern

Western times since Jeremy Bentham's oft-cited assertion of the moral status of animals as grounded in their capacity to suffer: "The question is not, Can they *reason*? nor, Can they *talk*?, but, Can they *suffer*?" (1781). Concern for **animal welfare** (1828) and opposition to **animal cruelty** (1809) knew substantial development in C19: New York passed the first US state law against animal cruelty in 1828; the UK passed its first Cruelty to Animals Act in 1835. It should be noted that **animal cruelty** means both cruelty *to* animals and cruelty *of* animals, the latter also subject to legislation in respect of the danger they may represent and the damage they may cause; the UK Dangerous Wild Animals Act (1976) is one example.

The UK Animal Welfare Act (2006) works with a definition of **animal** as "a vertebrate other than man" capable of experiencing pain or suffering; the earlier US Animal Welfare Act (1966) defines **animal** for its purposes by listing the warm-blooded animals it concerns and those it excludes. Different pieces of legislation deal with different species of animals in respect to the particular matters with which they are concerned, such as conditions for scientific **animal experiment** (1770). What counts as an **animal**, however, for legal and other protection has been increasingly posed from lC19 in terms of **animal rights** (1875) and **animal liberation** (1970). The former has brought debates as to whether animals, not possessed of self-consciousness, could fulfill duties and RESPONSIBILITIES that RIGHTS entail; the latter as to which animals are selected for liberation and what their liberated state would be. At an extreme, *speciesism* (1970) was coined to name "the widespread discrimination practised by man against other species."

Modern debates and controversies about the ETHICAL treatment of animals, along with questions, there from the beginning in the history of the word **animal**, concerning the position of the **human animal** *as animal*, have given **animal** its presence in contemporary discourse. This is at a time when developments in artificial intelligence and robotics are recasting how we may have to think about *human* and **animal**.

See HUMANITY, LIFE, NATURE, RIGHTS

APPROPRIATION

Although **cultural appropriation**'s centrality in eC21 has yet to be fully documented in the *OED*, it is a key term for cultural debate on contemporary university campuses. In April 2016 one could count over 40,000 tags on Instagram and nearly 100,000 conversations featuring the term on Facebook. Nor is this popularity limited to so-cial media. While barely featuring before the late 1980s, its frequency in print has increased dramatically in the past twenty years. Further evidence of its particular importance for universities was that the student members of the Keywords seminar of 2016 overwhelmingly voted **appropriation** the most important of the keywords that the seminar was discussing. **Cultural appropriation** relates to a whole series of terms with which it overlaps, including *acculturation, hybridity, assimilation, cultural exchange*, and *cultural interaction*, words related to the mass movement of peoples since the colonial period. It is also related to much older and more central words like AUTHENTICITY, COMMUNITY, IDENTITY. It is a crucial term in contemporary debates about the importance of cultural identity and the complexity of its formation.

Appropriation enters the language in lC14 from the late Latin *appropriare*, derived from *proprius*, the Latin adjective for "own," and linked etymologically to PROPERTY and proper, among others. **Appropriation**'s first sense in the *OED* is "The making of a thing private property," with an increasing emphasis that this private property is now one's own. There are early uses that refer to taking land to endow religious institutions, and a related sense is written deep into the polit-ical process in both the UK and the US where **Appropriation Bills** move money from tax income to government expenditure. Indeed the strong economic con-notation of **appropriation** is attested by the fact that **misappropriation**'s dom-inant meaning, from its entry into the language in C18, is misuse of funds. **Appropriation** develops from the Latin verb and has a strong meaning of action, while the closely related adjective **appropriate** has the sense of a state. This gram-matical difference leads to the very different valences that these two words have had on college campuses in C21. **Appropriate** is secure in the proper, while **appro-priation** destroys the very notion. There has been no strong relation between these different senses from C15 on.

The Marxist tradition displays a use which may be echoed in contemporary debate. For Marx, the **appropriation** of surplus value was the key form of exploi-tation in CAPITALISM, and **appropriation** thus grounds the very definition of an economically unjust system. If this sense may provide some of the background for contemporary usage, it is art history and not political economy that is the key dis-course for its contemporary importance. **Appropriation** as an artistic technique is first described by the artist and writer John La Farge in 1895 and the *OED* glosses it as follows: "The practice or technique of reworking the images or styles contained in earlier works of art, esp. (in later use) in order to provoke critical re-evaluation of well-known pieces by presenting them in new contexts, or to challenge notions of individual creativity or authenticity in art." New York's Museum of Modern Art (MoMA) defines **appropriation** as "the intentional borrowing, copying, and alteration of preexisting images and objects," citing the work of Andy Warhol and Robert Rauschenberg as examples.

In the 1980s and in the context of debates in media and cultural studies around so-called **appropriation artists, cultural appropriation** began to gather force as a term. Perhaps the most famous example of **appropriation art** was Sherrie Levine's re-photographing the famous Depression-era Walker Evans photographs and titling the results *After Walker Evans*. The debates around Levine and other artists' work led to a dropping of the term **appropriation artists; appropriation** migrated through debates in media and cultural studies into **cultural appropriation**. A crucial context for these debates was the growing importance of notions of **cultural property** first recorded in the *OED* in 1898 and recognized in a UNESCO convention of 1954 with a further protocol in 1999.

There is no founding text or manifesto for this focus on **cultural appropriation,** and the difficulty of defining cultures as limited and autonomous entities makes it impossible to set out a rigorous definition. There are, however, two constant examples: the relations between dominant white American culture and black African American culture, on the one hand, and Native American culture, on the other. A favorite illustration is the use of blackface in music halls where white performers appeared with the exaggerated features of African Americans. The ideological purpose of this mimicry was to demean and disparage black culture and to emphasize the power differentials within American society which oppressed African Americans. Some see **cultural appropriation** as more ambivalent or dialectical in character, as sketched in Eric Lott's *Love and Theft* (1993), a title then appropriated by Bob Dylan in 2001.

Another illustration of what is meant by **cultural appropriation** is the use of toys described as Indian war bonnets in children's play. Here the offense is that the clothing being imitated is rich in symbolic and ritual meanings for the Native Americans, who are simply and offensively ignored in the production and marketing of these children's toys.

Perhaps the single most famous example because it combined cultural and economic **appropriation** was the case that pitted Urban Outfitters, the clothing manufacturers, against the Navajo Nation. Urban Outfitters, which had previously used both the traditional Palestinian headscarf and the Hindu elephant god Ganesh as models for clothing, marketed a whole range of products under the name Navajo. The Navajo Nation took a court action, claiming that Urban Outfitters was unlawfully using the Navajo name.

These examples and others are what underlie definitions of **cultural appropriation**, such as the following from *The Concise Oxford Companion to English Literature*: "a term used to describe the taking over of creative or artistic forms, themes, or practices by one cultural group from another. It is in general used to describe Western appropriations of non-Western or non-white forms, and carries connotations of exploitation and dominance." However, the practices described here—which could also be labelled "borrowing," "influence," "adaptation," "translation," "imitation"—have been central to the techniques of literary modernism (typified by Eliot's collaging of other writers' texts in *The Waste Land*, Pound's imitation of Chinese poetic forms in *Cathay*, and Joyce's use of Homeric plot and polyglot wordplay in *Ulysses*).

Much of the force of the arguments around **cultural appropriation** seems to come from the word **appropriation** itself. The word is in criminal law a term for theft, as in the UK Theft Act of 1968, which has as its "basic definition of theft" the dishonest **appropriation** of property belonging to another, with the intention of permanently depriving the other of it. Its strong sense of "taking" something from someone else and making it your own means that questions of economics and power are immediately in play. Many uses and connotations of the word CULTURE work in the other direction, producing an area of activity divorced from politics and economics, but **appropriation** immediately reintroduces both.

The concept of **cultural appropriation** is often criticized for positing notions of cultures as homogenous, autonomous, and not subject to historical change. It is also criticized for refusing to allow identifications and explorations outside one's own culture. However, its contemporary importance does not simply reside in the questions of power and exploitation that are written into its etymological history, but as importantly on its emphasis on the emotional reaction of those whose cultures have been appropriated. The inflection of culture by both power and emotion makes **cultural appropriation** such a powerful key phrase.

See CULTURE, IDENTITY, PROPERTY

ART

The original general meaning of **art**, to refer to any kind of skill, is still active in English. But a more specialized meaning has become common, and in **the arts** and to a large extent in **artist** has become predominant.

Art has been used in English from C13, fw *art*, oF, rw *artem*, L—skill. It was widely applied, without predominant specialization, until 1C17, in matters as various as mathematics, medicine, and angling. In the medieval university curriculum the **arts** ("the seven arts" and later "the LIBERAL arts") were grammar, logic, rhetoric, arithmetic, geometry, music, and astronomy, and **artist**, from C16, was first used in this context, though with almost contemporary developments to describe any skilled person (as which it is in effect identical with **artisan** until 1C16) or a practitioner of one of the **arts** in another grouping, those presided over by the seven muses: history, poetry, comedy, tragedy, music, dancing, astronomy. Then, from 1C17, there was an increasingly common specialized application to a group of skills not hitherto formally represented: painting, drawing, engraving, and sculpture. The now dominant use of **art** and **artist** to refer to these skills was not fully established until 1C19, but it was within this grouping that in 1C18, and with special reference to the exclusion of engravers from the new Royal Academy, a now general distinction between **artist** and **artisan**—the latter being specialized to "skilled manual worker" without "intellectual" or "imaginative" or "creative" purposes—was strengthened and popularized. This development of **artisan**, and the mC19 definition of *scientist*, allowed the specialization of **artist** and the distinction not now of the *liberal* but of the **fine arts**.

The emergence of an ABSTRACT, capitalized **Art**, with its own internal but general principles, is difficult to localize. There are several plausible C18 uses, but it was in C19 that the concept became general. It is historically related, in this sense, to the development of CULTURE and *aesthetics*. Wordsworth wrote to the painter Haydon in 1815: "High is our calling, friend! Creative Art." The now normal association with *creative* and *imaginative*, as a matter of classification, dates effectively from 1C18 and eC19. The significant adjective **artistic** dates effectively from mC19. **Artistic temperament** and **artistic sensibility** date from the same period. So too does **artiste**, a further distinguishing specialization to describe performers such as actors or singers, thus keeping **artist** for painter, sculptor, and eventually (from mC19) writer and composer.

It is interesting to notice what words, in different periods, are ordinarily distinguished from or contrasted with **art**. **Artless** before mC17 meant "unskilled" or "devoid of skill," and this sense has survived. But there was an early regular contrast between **art** and *nature*: that is, between the product of human skill and the product of some inherent quality. **Artless** then acquired, from mC17 but especially from 1C18, a positive sense to indicate spontaneity even in **art**. While **art** still meant skill and *industry* diligent skill, they were often closely associated, but when each was abstracted and specialized they were often, from eC19, contrasted as the separate areas of imagination and utility. Until C18 most sciences were **arts**; the modern distinction between *science* and **art**, as contrasted areas of human skill and effort, with fundamentally different methods and purposes, dates effectively from mC19, though the words themselves are sometimes contrasted, much earlier, in the sense of "theory" and "practice" (see THEORY).

This complex set of historical distinctions between various kinds of human skill and between varying basic purposes in the use of such skills is evidently related both to changes in the practical division of labor and to fundamental changes in practical definitions of the purposes of the exercise of skill. It can be primarily related to the changes inherent in capitalist commodity production, with its specialization and reduction of use values to exchange values. There was a consequent defensive specialization of certain skills and purposes to **the arts** or *the humanities* where forms of general use and intention which were not determined by immediate exchange could be at least conceptually abstracted. This is the formal basis of the distinction between **art** and *industry*, and between **fine arts** and **useful arts** (the latter eventually acquiring a new specialized term, in TECHNOLOGY).

The **artist** is then distinct within this fundamental perspective not only from *scientist* and *technologist*—each of whom in earlier periods would have been called **artist**—but from *artisan* and *craftsman* and *skilled worker*, who are now *operatives* in terms of a specific definition and organization of work. As these practical distinctions are pressed, within a given mode of production, **art** and **artist** acquire ever more general (and more vague) associations, offering to express a general *human* (i.e., non-utilitarian) interest, even while, ironically, most **works of art** are effectively treated as commodities and most **artists,** even when they justly claim quite other intentions, are effectively treated as a category of independent *craftsmen* or *skilled workers* producing a certain kind of marginal commodity.

RECENT DEVELOPMENTS

The frequency of the word **art** has remained relatively steady in English since its high point in lC18. However, in the last half-century compounds have proliferated. **Pop art** (1957), for which the most prominent names were Andy Warhol and Roy Lichtenstein, appropriated images from commercial and popular CULTURE into the world of art, marking in practice the refusal to distinguish between ELITE and popular culture that was the theoretical base of cultural studies. **Conceptual art** (1967) and **performance art** (1971) both challenged the status of the art object: **conceptual art** focused on the ideas that underpinned the art object and **performance art** on the moment of its consumption. Both could be considered as extreme reactions to the contradiction that Williams noted between the ambition of art to transcend the commodity form and its reality as a marginal commodity. **Computer art** (1969), **video art** (1970), and **digital art** (1978) are different attempts to capture artists' efforts to utilize the new MEDIA. Finally, **public art** (1982) marks a new emphasis on **art** that is located outside the space of gallery exhibition. While the history of **public art** is as old as the history of statuary, only recently has emphasis fallen on the geographical and political possibilities of work that incorporated its setting into its significance and found its audience in the aleatory choice of passing spectators rather than a self-selected gallery audience.

All these compounds mark a desire to expand and challenge the notion of **art**, often characterized as elite, while still retaining an appeal to **art** as offering a privileged ACCESS to a world of transcendent VALUE. The contradictions of these arguments do not in any way detract from, indeed may fundamentally constitute, their force.

See ABSTRACT, APPROPRIATION, ARTIFICIAL, CREATIVE, CULTURE, ELITE, TECHNOLOGY

ARTIFICIAL

The word **artificial** is currently employed in the fields of nutrition, marketing, technology, medicine, and more, and is often evoked with a broad range of ethical undertones that speak to its contested meaning. It was borrowed into English in mC15, partly via AN and mF *artificial,* from Latin *artificiālis* "made or contrived by art," in some medieval sources also "prescribed by art, scientific," "skilled, artistic, involving craftsmanship." In C15 in English **artificial** was first deployed to describe physical objects, as seen in Caxton's translation of *Eneydos,* "to destroye soo artyfycyall a werke" (1490), and also systems or situations brought about by human skill or intervention. **Artificial** could also indicate the acquired intellectual reasoning of an individual, such as Thomas Elyot's 1531 definition of rhetoricians as "artificiall spekers." While as early as 1475, the meaning of **artificial** could coincide with that of the modern word *artifice,* as in "cunning, seeking to deceive," during the scientific Renaissance of mC15 to mC17, **artificial** generally lauded the progression of human scientific, artistic, and intellectual achievements. Well into C19 the term could designate something that was skillfully crafted or a person who was untrustworthy. Coleridge can praise the "artificial" writing of Shakespeare and Milton, a poetry so well-crafted that one cannot remove a single word without destroying its effect (1833), while a religious writer can lament how unsuspecting men are "caught and drawn into evil by political and artificial men" (*Family Prayer Book,* 1868).

Since the terms *natural* and **artificial** are mutually constitutive—the first definition for **artificial** in the *OED* is "opposed to natural"—**artificial**'s connotations depend heavily upon the way that the *natural* is constructed. From eC15 to C17, the two words predominantly described the physical relationship between objects, such as John Lydgate's *c*1425 depiction of the embalming of Hector's body with "bawme natural" running into it through "pipes artificial." Frequent collocations with **artificial** from lC16 onward evoke the restoration of the human body with **artificial eyes, ears, teeth,** and **legs.** In eC21, this particular definition of **artificial** maintains currency; **artificial heart,** for example, is one of the most common collocations in contemporary American English.

However, the increasing proximity between that which was perceived to be *natural* and its **artificial** imitations provoked rising levels of anxiety from mC16 onward. Originally, the two were similar but distinguishable in physical and intellectual contexts, such as William Bullein's 1558 judgment, "Artificiall women . . . haue more beastlines then beuty" or John Rastell's 1564 challenge that readers "plaie the foole with a foole . . ., that he may beholde his artificiall wysedome." **Artificial**'s connotation of interpersonal deceptiveness was enhanced—as expressed by Edward Stillingfleet in 1679, "the most artificial men have found it necessary to put on a guise of simplicity and plainness"—and extended to all social relationships. In his influential 1750 essay, "Discourse on the Arts and Sciences," Jean-Jacques Rousseau declared,

Before art had molded our behavior, and taught our passions to speak
an artificial [*apprêté*] language, our morals were rude but natural
[*naturelles*] . . . men found their security in the ease with which they could
see through one another, and this advantage, of which we no longer feel
the value, prevented their having many vices.

Throughout the Industrial Revolution of mC19, the dominant meanings of **artificial**
split between connoting concrete scientific and TECHNOLOGICAL advancements—
including **artificial fertilizer, artificial blood, artificial insemination,** and **artificial satellite** (first cited from 1883 and thus far predating Sputnik 1)—and
indicating interpersonal duplicity. The tension between **artificial** and *natural* still
resonates in the significant crossover found between these definitions in C20 and
C21, in which people, objects, science, and deceit are blurred.

Early debates regarding **artificial additives** in processed foods attest to this
complexity. The contemporary concern regarding the healthfulness of **artificial
additives** in processed foods began during the Progressive Era (1890–1920) when
consumers learned that saccharin, an **artificial sweetener** from lC19, had been
used in place of sugar in carbonated beverages. Public outcry identified danger
to the physical body as the primary concern, as well as threats to the familial
and social order, as indicated in the accusation of Alfred McCann that saccharin
was "as false a scarlet as the glow of health transferred from the rouge pot to the
cheek of a bawd." Despite the rise in popularity in mC20, during which **artificial
sweeteners** occupied the intersection of progressivity, health, and science, the instability of these relationships is displayed in their eC21 reversal. Global food and
beverage giants—including Pepsi-Cola and its 2014 product line "Pepsi-Cola Made
with REAL Sugar"—have shifted production and marketing in response to the opposition of the concepts *nature/natural, real(ity), transparency,* and *health* to the
notions *illusion,* **artificial,** and *harm.* Used in the grammatical subject of recent
headlines such as "Artificial flavors are making you hate healthy food," the term **artificial** is no longer perceived to be a mere descriptor of duplicity: unperceived and
unperceivable, **artificial** connotes the very agent of that deception.

Contemporary anxieties regarding **artificial intelligence** follow a similar trajectory in which the social order is perceived to be threatened by scientific and
technological systems that are indistinguishable from human bodies and minds.
While the term **artificial intelligence** was coined by John McCarthy in 1955, the
anxieties surrounding it date back to eC19 in which tales, such as Mary Shelley's

1818 *Frankenstein,* pit *mechanical* creations against the ORGANIC social order. Today, the word *natural* pairs with *human* and **artificial** with *deceit*, especially in relationship to the female body; in *The Guardian*'s 2015 list of the top twenty **artificial intelligence** films of the century, five—including Alex Garland's *Ex Machina* (2015) and Spike Jonze's *Her* (2013)—gender **artificiality** and *deceit* as feminine.

The advent of **artificial intelligence** (AI) has only intensified discussions about the ethical problems that the adjective marks. The increasing automation of even complex tasks through AI has resulted in significant economic and social change. While there are economic benefits (cheaper production costs, medical advances), there are also significant social disruptions (the loss of manufacturing jobs, information monopolies). Techno-optimists such as Daniel Dennett who are involved with attempting to create a humanoid agent (or co-agent) argue that these projects give us insight into just what human consciousness is; that is, the **artificial** helps us to understand better the biological.

While **artificial** can often denote an imitative or deficient copy, the term can also be invoked with an optimistic even utopian spirit, particularly in the domains of science and medicine. From C18, the development of **artificial languages** was intended to allow for easier communication among a diversity of speakers. From the early modern period, **artificial limbs** have replaced or supplemented body parts. Today, **artificial satellites** orbit around our planet and send us information about ones much farther away. The rise of experimental laboratory biology, including experimental embryology, biochemistry, and genetics, have led to a rise in technologies such as **artificial life, artificial selection,** and **artificial chromosomes.**

In considering the long history of **artificial,** one sees that the poles of this argument remain constant even as the specifics of the argument shift over time. Each society values (or devalues) the **artificial** depending on how it defines ART as opposed to NATURE. Finally, there remains a constant tension between those who are uneasy with certain technological innovations (designating them **artificial**), as opposed to those who see utopian promise in mankind's ability to exceed nature through **artifice.**

See ART, NATURE, ORGANIC, TECHNOLOGY

AUTHENTIC

Borrowed in C15, from French (*autentic*) and Latin (*authenticus*), **authentic** appears to have been polysemous from the beginning; but many of its early senses—"legally valid," "authorized," "authoritative"—are mutually reinforcing, and many early contexts make it difficult or pointless to distinguish among them.

A good vantage point for tracking the emergence of today's complexities is the entry for **authentic** in Samuel Johnson's *Dictionary of the English Language* (1755), which looks both backward and forward in the history of the word's meaning.

> **Authentick** adj. [*authenticus*, Lat.] That which has every thing requisite to give it authority, as an *authentick* register. It is used in opposition to any thing by which authority is destroyed, as *authentick*, not *counterfeit*. It is never used of persons.

Johnson starts with a generalized definition and "an authentic register" is an example intelligible in all periods of the word's use. Modern readers, however, probably interpret it as an instance of what the *OED* labels "now the usual sense" signifying "genuine," whereas the default C16 interpretation would have been "legally valid because duly authorized by the relevant religious or secular authority." In the first of Johnson's illustrative quotations, John Milton reserves **authentic** for the divine source of AUTHORITY, reaching back to its more distant ancestor, the Greek *authentēs*, the first author and creative origin: "one who does things with his own hand, an absolute master, an autocrat."

> URIEL, for thou of those seav'n Spirits that stand
> In sight of God's high Throne, gloriously bright,
> The first art wont his great authentic will
> Interpreter through highest Heav'n to bring,
> Where all his Sons thy Embassie attend.

By 1755, the divine and regal power bases of **authenticity** had been secularized into the secular warranty that C18 called "good authority" (Chesterfield, 1739). Johnson's choice of *counterfeit* as the defining antonym of **authentic** expresses the anxieties of a period that developed a mass market for texts and material artifacts and coined the terms *authorship* and *connoisseurship* for its regulators. Market value depended on **authentic** authorship, and connoisseurship was the—somewhat unreliable— method of establishing **authenticity**. C18 literary critics were much troubled by questions of forgery (as with Macpherson's Ossian, Chatterton's Rowleie, Ireland's

Shakespeare) and the artworks brought back from Italy by amateur-connoisseur Grand Tourists too often proved bogus.

By lC18, another strand in the modern sense-range of **authentic** became salient, prompting Johnson to enlarge his 1755 entry to include the sense "not fictitious." This may not seem very different from "not counterfeit," but in fact it marks an important shift in the notion of what is "requisite to give authority," displacing the criterion of attested authorship with adherence to "matters of fact, as they really happened" (Richard Watson, 1796). One impulse towards redefinition may have been the spate of C18 autobiographical and travel writings entitled **Authentic** Accounts/Narratives/Memoirs, etc. The problem was that while some of these accounts were written to satisfy natural science's demand for "authentic facts and unquestionable evidence" (*Geographical Magazine*, 1782), others fed the growing appetite of circulating libraries and their readers for the imaginary worlds of the novel. The scientists' desire for empirical facts coincided with the educationalists' fear of fictitious fictions. The perils (especially for women) of failing to distinguish fiction from fact became a key issue of the period, viewed comically in Austen's *Northanger Abbey* (1817), more tragically in Flaubert's *Madame Bovary* (1856) and its descendants.

For the *New English Dictionary* (1885) and *OED1* (1933) truth-to-fact was "the prevailing sense" of **authentic** and in eC20, the distinction between "matters of fact" and the novel was reinforced by the coinage of the genre label *non-fiction*. But that very coinage implies that fiction was assuming the status of the norm, and by mC20 the fact-fiction distinction was sufficiently blurred to legitimize the use of **authentic** for both the factual reporting of warfare and its fictional but verisimilitudinous representation. *OED* lists "The latest authentic reports of the progress of the war" (1944) alongside "a tense story of sea warfare. . . . The mess-room talk is most authentic" (1958). This blurring of boundaries licensed the new fusion genres of *docu-drama* and *non-fiction novel* (or *faction*) in the 1960s and *reality TV* shows in the 1990s. C21 has radicalized the fusion with the controversial coinages *alternative facts* and *post-truth*.

A similar (con)fusion has overtaken Johnson's distinction between **authentic** and *counterfeit*, as witness such collocations as **authentic reproduction**. Recent editions of *Merriam-Webster Student Dictionary* offer its young readers just two current senses for **authentic**:

1: being really what it seems to be: <*authentic* examples of Hopi jewelry>
2: made to be or look just like an original <*authentic* colonial costumes> <*authentic* French-style mustard>

These definitions are virtually antonymic: (1) = "what it seems to be"; (2) = "*not* what it seems to be"; and the contradiction clearly signals that the word in its most frequent contemporary uses is being pulled in opposite directions by its users. Arguably, **authentic** has become a go-to term in the language of advertising precisely because sense (2) exploits the resonances of sense (1), evoking consumers' desire for "the real" and their value for particular ethnic origins or geographical provenances. The ambiguity becomes an overt site of contestation in the domains of law (see BRAND) and identity politics (see APPROPRIATION), where battles have raged over, e.g., what can legally be called champagne or who can legitimately wear cornrow hairstyles.

While subverting the antonymic distinctions that Johnson set up, modern usage has added a strand of meaning that he had not envisaged. His 1755 entry declares that **authentic** is "never used of persons." This is factually inaccurate. But earlier examples typically occur in specialized legal contexts (referring, for instance, to a notary) and Johnson may have ignored such uses, in line with his policy of excluding technical terms from his dictionary. The non-technical application of **authentic** to persons begins in eC20, when traditional questions about the **authenticity** of documents and artifacts were supplemented by questions about the subjective world. The *OED* attests "authenticity of the emotions" from 1910, closely followed by the 1915 example, "I wanted to shake him into being a man, some one who would bear me off, or make tremendous and authentic love" (which, surprisingly, comes from *Good Housekeeping* rather than D. H. Lawrence). This person-orientated strand of meaning was given a theoretical foundation and extension in Heideggerian existentialism and (particularly after World War II) in the polemical and literary works of Sartre, de Beauvoir, and Camus. The French existentialists developed a line of argument dating back at least to Johnson's contemporary, Rousseau—for whom society and its processes of education and enculturation deformed personal development. De Beauvoir's analysis of the **inauthentic** identity internalized by women was particularly important to the 1970s FEMINIST movement, as it directed attention not only to negative stereotypes of woman ("the weaker vessel") but also to ostensibly positive ones ("ministering angel"): "the altruism of women is merely the inauthenticity of the feminine person carried over into behaviour" (Germaine Greer, 1970). Camus's *L'Etranger* (1942) was perhaps even more influential: its cultural misfit could be transposed to a wide range of contexts, for example, the alienated black intellectual of Richard Wright's *The Outsider* (1953) and the alienated teenager of

J. D. Salinger's *Catcher in the Rye* (1951), whose use of *phony* popularized a colloquial equivalent of **inauthentic**.

Despite its non-colloquial register, **inauthentic** shows a steep rise in frequency
in lC20, coinciding—not coincidentally—with similar peaks in the frequency of
IDENTITY and *autonomy* and the appearance of EXPERIENCE, *voice*, and *self* among
authentic's common collocates. The goal of finding and defending **authentic** identity shapes the rhetoric of many of the shared-interest groups designated by themselves or others as distinct COMMUNITIES and competing for social recognition. At
the individual level, the rejection of social conformism in favor of *autonomy* finds
expression in such formulae as "that's what I do" or WYSIWYG ("what you see is
what you get"), an acronym borrowed from computing as a hallmark of personal
authenticity.

As early as 1977, Cyra McFadden's *The Serial* satirized the conversion of existentialist philosophy into contemporary moral slang: "the really authentic thing to do
was to act on your impulses," suggesting that being "really authentic" had already
become a social prescription and a social asset. In subsequent decades, the cultivation of **authenticity** (sometimes now called "the **authenticity** cult") has moved into
self-help manuals (such as James Park's *Becoming More Authentic*, 1983) and thereafter into the curriculum of management and leadership courses. There is a historical irony here: the existentialist hero was socially marginalized by his quest for
truth-to-self; the new **authentic** individual is seen as a natural leader and winner,
as in actor Tom Hiddleston's description of Shakespeare's character Henry V. "What
distinguished him, above all, were his qualities as a leader: his courage, his rhetoric,
his authenticity, his self-sacrifice. 'We few, we happy few, we band of brothers'"
(*Radio Times*, July 2012). But what does **authenticity** mean in this context?

An article titled "Mitt Romney: S#*! Authentic People Say" forecasts Romney's
defeat in the presidential election and ascribes it to his failure to transfer his tell-
it-how-it-is management skills to the political context. He is urged to "let go of the
fear of offending people and embrace his authentic side" by imitating "the great
philosopher Popeye" because "authentic people give you some version of 'I yam
what I yam, and that's all what I yam'" (*Reuter's*, March 9, 2012). A picture emerges
of the **authentic** leader as the maverick outsider who is nonetheless one of a "band
of brothers" and fundamentally "like everyone else," i.e., authentically *human*.
Correspondingly, C21 political discourse has thrown up a striking new antonym
for **authentic**, replacing *unlicensed, counterfeit, fictitious, inauthentic* with *robotic*, a
term applied to the losers in US presidential elections (Romney in 2012; Clinton in

2016) and UK general elections (Miliband in 2015; May, metaphorically "the loser" in 2017).

The historical trajectory of **authentic** has drawn it variously into the semantic orbits of its etymological relatives AUTHORITY, *author*, and *autonomy*. But Johnson's general definition holds good throughout. To be **authentic** is still to possess "everything requisite to give authority." What has changed is the perceived source of authority, devolving from the autocratic institutions of Church and State to the self-determining individual citizen. But why has the word itself survived this process of democratization? Why is the high-register **authentic** preferred in so many contexts when its contrast terms are colloquial, e.g., *fake, phony*? The *Longman Dictionary of Contemporary English* advises its users that "in everyday English, people usually say that something is *real* or *the real thing* rather than authentic." But perhaps there's a residual authoritativeness in the Latinate form of **authentic**, or a semantic persistence of the Greek *authentikós* from *authentes*, which Milton invoked to describe God. After all, Popeye's "I yam what I yam" is a distant echo of the divine declaration of autonomous identity: "I Am that I Am."

See APPROPRIATION, ARTIFICIAL, AUTHORITY, BRAND, COMMUNITY, IDENTITY, LITERATURE, REALISM

AUTHORITY

The Latin noun *auctoritas*, from which English **authority** is complexly derived through varieties of medieval French, has a wide range of meanings: right of ownership, sanction, approval, resolution, advice, right or power to authorize, leadership, authoritativeness, weighty testimony, precedent, example, prestige, personal influence, esteem, repute. These meanings blend in and out of each other in a particularly complex history in which **authority** plays a key role in regard to both knowledge and power.

Its first established medieval sense, derived from mF *authorité*, is an "authoritative book or passage of text accepted as a source of reliable information," a definition that was carried into its first appearance in English in eC13. **Authority**, in its earliest use, was most commonly synonymous with the Bible and notions of **biblical authority**, in mC13 "God's authoritative or potestative power," in which God was **author** (defined in the *OED* as both writer and creator), the Bible His **authority**.

Early uses of **authority** were frequently references to scripture, as in eC13 "Nothing must be sought contrary to the rule of the supreme authority . . ." from Ancrene Riwle, as well as lC14 "For auctorite of holi writte telliþ vs . . ." from Bartholomaeus Anglicus. This **authority** of the Bible began to disperse over other books, and to cite something as **an authority** became a common way to signify the reliability of a TEXT, such as this C16 example from Sir Thomas More: "Hys fyrst authorite be these words of saynte Austyne in hys fyftieth sermon." This use has carried over into the present, and uses of **authority** similar to the lC20 use in the journal *Rhetorica*, "This dictionary is the authority for the orthography of the edition," remain common in contemporary discourse.

From eC14 **authority** began to refer to individuals with particular claim to legitimated knowledge, as in an **authoritative opinion**, in which an OPINION gains special status because of its relation to legal or scholarly knowledge, a meaning with direct links to eC19 *expert*, or one regarded as an **authority** on a certain subject. Phrases such as "to have it on good authority" and "on the authority of" have become standard. All such **authority** is, however, from the Renaissance on, provisional. As Galileo says in eC17, "In questions of science, the authority of a thousand is not worth the humble reasoning of a single individual," signifying the increase in emphasis on the importance of human reasoning and experimental method over the citing of written texts or even relying on acknowledged experts.

However, if **authority** weakened in relation to knowledge, it strengthened in relation to power, and from C16 onward it is a key political term in a sense that the *OED* defines as "power or right to give orders, make decisions, and enforce obedience." This sense develops in relation to arguments about theories of divine right, as in, "According to theories of divine right, the authority of monarchs is ordained by God and acquired through heredity" (*Encyclopedia of American Religion and Politics*). It is a key term, however, in the assertion of Parliament's rights in England during the Civil War, "The Supreme Autoritie of the Nation, the Parlament of the Common-wealth of England," 1652. Perhaps even more telling is its occurrence in the Supremacy Clause of the US Constitution, which refers to the "Authority of the United States." From lC19 onward, this **authority** of the state begins to proliferate as numerous **authorities—municipal authority, education authority, local authority, port authority**—and **the authorities** becomes a collective noun embracing a range of state bodies.

In this steady development of the power and presence of the STATE, one can detect two countervailing tendencies over the past two centuries; the first wished to increase the **authority** of the state until it dominates every aspect of life, and at the other end of the spectrum, there was a questioning of **authority** in all its forms. This is most evident in the explicitly anarchist arguments of Michael Bakunin and his followers and a refusal to accept any state whatsoever. However, the general questioning of **authority** is less a matter of explicitly anarchist politics and much more the result of the thoroughgoing investigation and interrogation of forms of **authority** across the full range of social sciences: psychology, sociology, anthropology.

In eC20, forms of both fascist and communist governments adopted positions so **authoritarian** that a new term was coined to describe them: **totalitarian**. If these totalitarianisms have been defeated, the rise of the executive power of the state means that authoritarianism is seen as a constant danger, as in a 2014 *Washington Times* article which states, "If Mr. Obama follows through on his threat . . . to ignore Congress and to implicitly emulate the style of authoritarian governments . . . we are in for a rough couple of years," and, more recently, in a 2016 *Washington Post* article regarding supporters of presidential candidate Donald Trump: "Watch out, the authoritarians are coming!"

If the number and power of state-related authorities seem to increase relentlessly, it is also the case that since World War II there has developed an increasingly powerful set of anti-authoritarian discourses. In 1954 Hannah Arendt asked, "What Is Authority?" but lamented that "authority has vanished from the modern world," noting that for the first time in recorded history the **authority** of a parent over a child was being contested. This anti-authoritarianism peaked in the 1960s when a worldwide cultural movement (for which "hippie" is an inadequate description) found a global political cause in opposition to the war in Vietnam. Yet the sixties also saw a proliferation of **authority figures**. This phrase first occurs in 1948 and is glossed by the *OED* as "any person regarded as having authority"; it applies to a government agent, a policeman, an educator, or a parent.

While the role of **authority** and its limits seem clearly defined with relation to knowledge (even allowing for increasingly strident challenges from the far right on climate change and evolution), questions of the LEGITIMACY and necessity of **authority** in the political and personal realm are more fraught and confused than ever. If the need for the authorities becomes ever more pressing in relation to violence in all its varying manifestations, from the domestic to the international, the basis of that **authority**—legal, political, moral—becomes ever more contested.

See LEGITIMATE, STATE, TEXT

BLACK

"Black is beautiful" was one of the key phrases of the 1960s. Much of its force came from a syntactic ambiguity. On the one hand, **black** was the adjective that denoted a color; on the other it was, from the introduction of chattel slavery in the Americas, the noun used to name humans of African descent. Both color and humans were celebrated in a slogan that attempted to eradicate the negative cultural and ideological meanings generated by Enlightenment classifications and the Atlantic slave trade.

Both Latin and Old English had two words for **black**, *ater* and *niger* in Latin, *blaec* and *sweart* in Old English. Although by early Modern English **black** was the only color word, the other three survive in different forms. *Sweart* specialized into Modern English *swarthy*, where it means a dark color (especially of complexion) that is tawny rather than **black** itself. *Niger* is the root word for *Negro* and its derivatives. *Ater* survives as the root for the words atrocity and atrocious, which designate acts as particularly and excessively violent and indicates how easily the color acquires pejorative metaphorical meanings.

This is evident from Old English, where both *blaec* and *sweart* had metaphorical connotations ranging across the spectrum of "sombre, gloomy, miserable, ill-omened, evil, sinful, foul, hateful." This development continued in Middle English. In *Middle English Dictionary* (*MED*) examples, Chaucer describes his hero Troilus as "Ibounden in the blake bark of care" (1385) and describes a suffering heart as "bare of blis, and blake of hewe" (1375). More moralistic texts speak of "Fals-Semblant . . . Ryght blak withynne and whit withoute" (1425) or "my sinnes grete and blake" (1425), and **black** is explicitly associated with the Devil in this example from 1450: "they shall be quyt by Blackberd or Whyteberd, that ys to sey, by God or the Devyll."

The *OED* suggests that such negative connotations proliferated in the following two centuries and conjectures that this is "probably connected in part with negative cultural attitudes towards black people prevalent in the context of the Atlantic slave trade." A notable example is the pejoration of the phrase **black man**. The *OED* quotations before C16 illustrate only literal uses (i.e., referring to skin color) without derogatory implications: "In hote londes cometh forth blake men and browne" (1398); "Ethyopia the londe of blak men" (1482). By contrast, quotations from lC16 onward recruit the negative connotations of the ME figurative uses of **black**, and **black man** is directly identified with the "bogeyman" or "the Devil" in the following examples: "Some entertain conference with God or his Angels, others conceit themselves bewitched or that a black man or Devil perpetually accompanies them" (1656); "I send the Goblins . . . the nightbats, . . . the black men" (1658).

While the slogan "black is beautiful" challenges directly the notion of white as beautiful, it is engaged in two other linguistic contests. On the one hand, **black** is an alternative to *Negro*, which comes into English in C16 via Spanish and Portuguese from the Latin *niger*. While this Latin etymology is also at the root of the most hate-filled and offensive word in the English language, *nigger*, it is *Negro* that becomes the term of rational classification which the Enlightenment uses and which many abolitionists used as a less offensive and more scientific word than **black**. It was, moreover, the word that Lyndon Johnson used as president of the United States in the mid-1960s as he enacted his historic Civil Rights legislation. The most important word, however, that **black** contests semantically is *colored*. The *OED* states, "*Coloured* was adopted in the United States by emancipated slaves as a term of racial pride after the end of the American Civil War. It was rapidly replaced from the late 1960s as a self-designation by *black* and later by *African-American*, although it is retained in the name of the National Association for the Advancement of Colored People. In Britain it was the accepted term for black, Asian, or mixed-race people until the 1960s."

For members of the **Black Power** movement, *colored* was an offensive euphemism, and it quickly ceded ground to **black**. **Black**'s increasing positive value was not simply a revaluing of racial characteristics. Both in modernist art and even more importantly, post–World War I fashion, **black** became a favored color. Already in C19 **black** had become the most prestigious color for male dress, but until the 1920s in a tradition dating back to Roman times, women only wore **black** for mourning.

The enormous revolution in fashion, which made **black** central to the female wardrobe, is often associated with Coco Chanel, who claimed that from 1920 she had formed the ambition to dress all women in **black** and who in 1926 said, "A woman needs just three things; a black dress, a black sweater, and, on her arm, a man she loves."

"Black is beautiful" can thus be read as inflecting RACE with fashion, and this inflection is also evident in the term *Afro-American*. There was no item of the African body more vilified than hair, and the decision to wear hair in an Afro or natural style was perhaps the most important image of a revaluation of race and beauty. Jesse Jackson's presidential campaign of 1988 saw *African American* displace all other generic descriptions in a political context, but **black** remains an important adjective in relation to culture in general and music in particular. Ever since the popularity of jazz in the 1920s, black taste has been a significant element in mainstream culture. The **Black Power** movement of the 1960s inaugurated an era in which the culture and language of young black Americans has been the most fertile element in global Anglophone culture, from vocabulary to dress to music. However, this cultural dominance has not been replicated in the economic and social spheres, where black Americans have been continuously disadvantaged, from employment to education to rates of incarceration.

A recent development particularly associated with the rise of hip-hop music in the 1980s is the use of "nigga" as a positive term among black people. It should be noted that the written forms of this positive use usually contest the dominant spelling, as with the gangsta rap group Niggaz wit Attitudes. The use of a pejorative term as a badge of honor is not limited to this word. In *The Satanic Verses* (1988), the narrator explains his use of a hostile Christian name Mahound for the prophet Mohammed: "To turn insults into strengths, whigs, Tories, Blacks all chose to wear with pride the names they were given in scorn." Nigger is unlike these other examples because despite these positive uses, the word remains irredeemably negative in the mouths of white people.

Since the 1980s, proponents of identity politics in the United States have sought to replace **black** as a description with *people of color*. This formulation has the political advantage of including all those who are not white, but it suffers from the fact that it is not evident that non-politicized individuals recognize themselves in these inclusive descriptions. There was an earlier attempt in Britain in the 1970s to include both Asians and African Caribbeans under the new description "Black British." While the term found a ready response from African Caribbeans, it was never accepted by any but the most politically active Asians. A further difference in British English was that *colored*, which had been the polite usage to describe **black** people up until the 1960s, very quickly turned into an offensive term used only by those opposed to immigration and integration.

The entire vocabulary of color in relation to ethnic and racial difference and their articulation with political and economic exploitation is both ridiculous (white people are not white, black people are rarely black) and deadly serious.

See RACE

BRAND

Use of the word **brand** as both a noun and a verb has massively increased in frequency since the end of C19, and particularly over the past thirty years. The derived noun **branding** has seen an even more meteoric rise in frequency of use over a similar period. Although **brand** has had, and still has, a number of meanings, it appears incontrovertible that its present ubiquity derives from its place in the language of MARKETING and consumption.

The word **brand** or *brond* is to be found in Old English, and also in other Germanic languages, such as Old Frisian, Middle Dutch, and Old Norse. As a noun, the general meaning of **brand** is the act, means, or result of burning; some of its uses within this general category are now more or less archaic or obsolete. In the Old English epic poem *Beowulf*, the word signifies burning or destruction by fire. The modern uses of **brand** derive from the mark made by burning flesh with a hot iron. This was not only a way of marking the ownership of livestock (particularly cattle), but also a punishment for criminals, so that **brand** often conveys "the idea of disgrace; a stigma, a mark of infamy." In Britain the last criminal sentence of **branding** was handed down at the Old Bailey in 1789, but **branding** continued to be used on slaves in the US until 1865, and the tattooing of concentration camp inmates has been referred to as **branding**.

The remaining, now more pervasive, meanings of **brand** given in the *OED* relate to the process of production and marketing. A **brand** may be: "A trademark, whether made by burning or otherwise. (Applied to trademarks on casks of wine or liquors, timber, metals, and any description of goods except textile fabrics)"; and "A particular sort or class of goods, as indicated by the trademarks upon them." As a verb, **to brand** means: "To mark indelibly, as a proof of ownership, as a sign of quality, or for any other purpose"; and, "To apply a trademark or brand to (a product); to promote (a product or service) on the basis of a brand name or design."

The first meaning of a **brand** given here, as both noun and verb, was already recognized in the 1883 Trade Marks Act, which gave specific protection to **brands** as marks that were "printed, impressed, or woven" into goods. However, it was quickly recognized that there was little practical difference between a *trademark* and a **brand**, both serving as indications of origin; and the word **brand** was dropped from that Act as constituting simply a subspecies of trademark. Indeed, unlike a *registered trademark*, there is no legal definition of a **brand**, either in the US or in the UK, even though the words *trademark* and **brand** are used interchangeably, including by the judiciary.

But it is the second meaning of **brand**, both as noun and verb, which gives the word its present ubiquity. While **brands** were originally used to differentiate goods in an era of mass production, it became clear that these **brands** could develop meanings and associations that could be of value and could be both managed and developed. While **brands** and **branding** are being used and developed from eC20 on, it is only since the 1950s that they have become a major focus of interest. Beginning in the 1920s but gathering speed in the postwar era comes a slew of compounds: **brand-image** (1958), **brand-name** (1922), **brand leader** (1967), **brand extension** (1966), **brand awareness** (1950), and **brand identity** (1927).

Brands are now an integral part of balance sheets. Perhaps the most famous **brand** in the world is Apple. The Apple word and apple symbol were first used on computers; but Apple now claims that its **brand** is about "lifestyle; imagination; liberty regained; innovation; passion; hopes, dreams and aspirations; and power-to-the-people through technology." These wider meanings have no obvious reference to computers, and have allowed what is called the **brand** to be transferred to other products apart from computers, most recently a watch. The resulting **brand-transferability** may give a **brand** enormous VALUE, quite beyond any particular material goods on which it is placed: the Apple **brand**, for example, is now the most valuable in the world and has **brand equity** of approximately 250 billion dollars.

An enormous **branding industry** has grown up to create, maintain, and enhance the value of **brands**. Whereas **brands** originally identified a product, now a **brand** is itself the product of this industry. Companies exist that specialize in creating **brands** and **brand strategies**, in order to enhance **brand building** or

brand positioning. A multitude of books explain how to **brand,** with titles such as *Designing Brand Identity* or *The Science and Art of Branding;* and there is a Museum of Brands in London, as well as an Institute of Brand and Innovation Law. However, it would be wrong to think that **brands** are created and used solely by businesses to promote their own products. Characterization as a **brand** is often an attribution made by others to describe the characteristics of a person or thing: for example, an individual may be described as having a particular **brand** of humor; and some people may parlay these personal attributes into a valuable **brand.**

In contemporary society, the words **brand** and **branding** are used not only in the context of commerce. They are also increasingly deployed to explain political and social concerns, such as the "brand of jihadism" promulgated by the Islamic State of Iraq and the Levant (ISIL/IS) (BBC, June 30, 2014). In an article titled, "How to fight the Islamic State's 'brand appeal,'" one analyst described IS as "one of the world's most powerful brands" (*Washington Post,* May 12, 2015). While it is unclear from such an account whether IS deliberately sought to become a **brand,** others have ascribed a conscious **branding strategy** to the group, a strategy that consists, among other things, of its use of product placement, social media, and a nurturing of "celebrity warriors" such as Jihadi John (*Independent,* March 9, 2015). It has also been claimed that the IS "black flag" **brand** has been placed on merchandise including watches and T-shirts, as well as more importantly on UN food parcels, as a way of imposing the IS "brand across the region" (*Int'l Business Times,* February 10, 2015). Still other commentators have likened IS to a franchise, in which loosely affiliated groups adopt the IS **brand** to enhance their own LEGITIMACY, much like the franchising undertaken by well-known fast food chains. Indeed, a recent study for the US Department of Homeland Security titled "The Islamic State of Iraq and the Levant: Branding, Leadership Culture and Lethal Attraction" concluded that the "organizational legitimacy" of ISIS has been achieved through "a unique combination of the strong leadership style, strategic branding, and consistent message," summarized in the report as "ISIL Sells Success."

The increasing significance of the words **brand, branding,** and **to brand** marks how fully we have become a CONSUMER society. In the case of IS, a social and political movement that might once have been explained by its ideological appeal to a particular class or other social group on the basis of its political program, perhaps supported through use of propaganda, has been reconceptualized as a **brand manager** that attracts followers (presumably, consumers) through its **brand appeal.**

Small wonder that when one **brand analyst** (Sophie Devonshire, on *BBC Today*, May 28, 2015) was asked to discuss the likelihood of FIFA changing its ways as a result of withdrawal of **brand sponsorship**, she concluded that anything was possible, as "brands have the power to change the world."

See BUSINESS, CONSUMER, MARKET, PROPERTY, VALUE

BUSINESS

Across its complex semantic history, the term **business** has been used in a wide range of discourse with a wide variety of meanings. For example, it has denoted both professional and official activity and unwanted interference; efficiency and also disorder; and it has had slang uses signifying traditionally taboo activities including sex and bodily functions. In modern times, the most frequent sense relates to trade and commerce, but the limits of what might be referred to as **business** are not always clear. The term often triggers uneasiness when it is applied to professional spheres that were not always conceived of in this way: labelling something as a **business** implies that financial gain is its ultimate end, and arguably de-emphasizes other kinds of value and meaning.

Etymologically, **business** is derived from two native morphemes, the adjective **busy** and the suffix -*ness*, and all three forms are found from Old English onward. Many of the earlier meanings of **business** that have become obsolete reflect this derivation, and *OED* groups these together under the general definition "the quality or state of being busy." The earliest attested sense, "anxiety, solicitude, care; distress, uneasiness," reflects one of the meanings of **busy** that is also obsolete, and the *OED* evidence suggests this is mainly found in religious writings. C14 sees uses that are more closely related to current meanings of **busy**, such as "diligent labor," "application or commitment to a task or purpose; industry," and slightly later, "activity, briskness, motion." These shade into senses that refer positively to attitudes and approaches, such as "eagerness" and "care, attention," but by C14 conflicting meanings are also attested that are closer to present-day English *fuss* or *trouble*. The *OED* sense, "mischievous or interfering activity; prying, officiousness" is obsolete, but the same meaning survives in **busybody** and is suggested by expressions like **mind your own business** and **none of your business**. The tension in the way activity and industriousness are viewed, either in a positive or negative light, is still latent in many compounds and derivatives: for example, while **business acumen** and a **business ethic** tend to be positive, adjectives like **business-minded** and **business-like** can imply ruthlessness or a lack of EMPATHY.

By C18, **busy** and **business** had separated formally and semantically. Competition between earlier and later senses of **business** led to the re-coining of a noun in *-ness* that is more transparently connected with the adjective form, both in its spelling, **busyness,** and its trisyllabic pronunciation. This form has taken over meanings relating to the state or condition of being **busy** in various senses. Current uses of **business** therefore tend to relate to a second strand of meaning attested from lC14 onward, which *OED* defines as: "Something with which a person is busy or occupied." This includes a number of fairly general senses like "a pursuit or occupation demanding time and attention," first attested in lC14. The way in which this sense leads to, but is different from, current uses is pointed up by a line from Daniel Defoe's 1725 work *The Complete English Tradesman*, which asserts that "Trade . . . ought to be follow'd as one of the great businesses of life." **Business** is also used as a mass noun in the same sense from around the same time, and it is at this point that it becomes an antonym of *pleasure*, and begins to imply professional activity. However, it retains general meanings such as "a duty, part, or role" or "matters demanding attention" (**the business of the day**), as well as specific, narrowed senses restricted to particular registers, such as "work done by an animal" and in theater "action on stage (as distinguished from dialogue)." A number of markedly negative senses also survive: **a sad/sorry/bad business** or **the whole business** is used of situations regarded as regrettable, and **business** can also refer to a complex or cumbersome material object or, worse, defecation (in the phrase **do [one's] business**). On the other hand, something described as (**looking**) **the business** is impressive and superior, and this is a relatively late semantic development in lC19. The multiplicity of meaning of **business** is often exploited, for example in slogans such as "Business is our business" (*Politico*) or "Our business is the business" (AgencyQ).

By far the most frequent use in modern times is the mass noun use emerging in C15 that relates to trade and commerce. Often this sense of **business** is modified to denote a particular kind of money-generating activity, such as **the music business,** and it is itself hugely productive as a modifier of other nouns.

A minority of these have been around for several centuries, such as **business affair**, but most date from C19, including **business model** and **business plan**, or later; one of the most recent is **business guru** from the late 1960s. It can also modify an adjective, as in **business-critical**, first attested in 1986. Despite the dominance of the term, and the count use of **business** to denote "a commercial entity" (since C18), the limits of its reference are not always clear. **Business** entities include cooperatives, partnerships, and sole-traders, but the CORPORATION is the dominant type of organization. A usual purpose of corporations is the generation of profit, and it is perhaps this characteristic that has led to tensions about what can and should be regarded as a **business** in a modern CAPITALIST society. Institutions such as universities and charities, which have come under increasing pressure to be self-sufficient or maintain profit margins, are required to have **business plans** and often to engage with **big business**, but many involved in these sectors feel that this is an uncomfortable position that conflicts with their traditional values and aims. The academic Milton Greenberg explores an "often-heard campus expression" in an article called "A University Is Not a Business (and Other Fantasies)," but there are multiple examples of the same expression, **x is not a business**, used of bodies and institutions as diverse as teaching, the church, and the government, as well as more ABSTRACT entities like the US presidency and public health.

Business has a complex relationship with partial synonyms such as *trade, commerce,* and *industry*; all of these overlap but are narrower and have different associations. For example, being **in business** is different from being *in trade*, although this expression is probably slightly dated by now, and a **businessman** (or **business person**) is regarded very differently from a *tradesman*. It seems significant that the UK Department of Trade and Industry was replaced by the Department for Business, Enterprise and Regulatory Reform in 2007, and ultimately by the Department for Business, Skills and Innovation in 2009 (when the latter merged with the Department for Innovation, Universities and Skills). **Business** is also the term that refers to trade and related activity as an academic discipline, and to its centers of study (**business schools**). The technical register of the sector itself is **businessese** (first attested in 1921) or **business-speak** (1973); both are marked as frequently depreciative in *OED*.

See BRAND, CAPITALISM, CONSUMER, CORPORATE, ENTERPRISE

CAPITALISM

Capitalism as a word describing a particular economic system began to appear in English from eC19, and almost simultaneously in French and German. **Capitalist** as a noun is a little older; Arthur Young used it, in his journal of *Travels in France* (1792), but relatively loosely: "moneyed men, or capitalists." Coleridge used it in the developed sense—"capitalists . . . having labour at demand"—in *Table-talk* (1823). Thomas Hodgskin, in *Labour Defended against the Claims of Capital* (1825), wrote: "all the capitalists of Europe, with all their circulating capital, cannot of themselves supply a single week's food and clothing," and again: "betwixt him who produces food and him who produces clothing, betwixt him who makes instruments and him who uses them, in steps the capitalist, who neither makes nor uses them and appropriates to himself the produce of both." This is clearly the description of an economic *system*.

The economic sense of **capital** had been present in English from C17 and in a fully developed form from C18. Chambers *Cyclopaedia* (1727–51) has "power given by Parliament to the South-Sea company to increase their capital" and definition of "circulating capital" is in Adam Smith (1776). The word had acquired this specialized meaning from its general sense of "head" or "chief": fw *capital*, F, *capitalis*, L, rw *caput*, L—head. There were many derived specialist meanings; the economic meaning developed from a shortening of the phrase "capital stock"—a material holding or monetary fund. In classical economics the functions of **capital**, and of various kinds of **capital**, were described and defined.

Capitalism represents a development of meaning in that it has been increasingly used to indicate a particular and historical economic system rather than any economic system as such. **Capital** and at first **capitalist** were technical terms in any economic system. The later (eC19) uses of **capitalist** moved toward specific functions in a particular stage of historical development; it is this use that crystallized in **capitalism**. There was a sense of the **capitalist** as the useless but controlling intermediary between producers, or as the employer of labor, or, finally, as the owner of the means of production. This involved, eventually, and especially in Marx, a distinction of **capital** as a formal economic category from **capitalism** as a particular form of centralized ownership of the means of production, carrying with it the system of wage-labor. **Capitalism** in this sense is a product of a developing bourgeois society; there are early kinds of **capitalist** production but **capitalism** as a system—what Marx calls "the capitalist era"—dates only from C16 and did not reach the stage of **industrial capitalism** until 1C18 and eC19.

There has been immense controversy about the details of this description, and of course about the merits and workings of the system itself, but from eC20, in most languages, **capitalism** has had this sense of a distinct economic system, which can be contrasted with other systems. As a term **capitalism** does not seem to be earlier than the 1880s, when it began to be used in German socialist writing and was extended to other non-socialist writing. Its first English and French uses seem to date only from the first years of C20. In mC20, in reaction against socialist argument, the words **capitalism** and **capitalist** have often been deliberately replaced by defenders of the system by such phrases as "private enterprise" and "free enterprise." These terms, recalling some of the conditions of early capitalism, are applied without apparent hesitation to very large or para-national "public" corporations, or to an economic system controlled by them. At other times, however, **capitalism** is defended under its own now common name. There has also developed a use of **post-capitalist** and **post-capitalism**, to describe modifications of the system such as the supposed transfer of control from shareholders to professional management, or the coexistence of certain NATIONALIZED or "state-owned" industries. The plausibility of these descriptions depends on the definition of capitalism that they are selected to modify. Though they evidently modify certain kinds of capitalism, in relation to its central sense they are marginal. A new phrase, **state-capitalism**, has been widely used in mC20, with precedents from eC20, to describe forms of state ownership in which the original conditions of the definition—centralized ownership of the means of production, leading to a system of wage-labor—have not really changed.

It is also necessary to note an extension of the adjective **capitalist** to describe the whole society, or features of the society, in which a **capitalist** economic system predominates. There is considerable overlap and occasional confusion here between **capitalist** and *bourgeois*. In strict Marxist usage **capitalist** is a description of a mode of production and *bourgeois* a description of a type of society. It is in controversy about the relations between a mode of production and a type of society that the conditions for overlap of meaning occur.

Recent Developments

Capitalism continues as the word to describe the economic system that organizes the majority of the world's resources. **Capital** is generally understood as "assets possessing a monetary value" (*OED*). For Marxists, however, **capital** does not refer to an investment or asset but to a social relation that enables a class of owners to appropriate surplus value from wage laborers and that ensures endless crises of overproduction. The current phase of **capitalism** is often referred to as *neoliberalism*, where neoliberalism refers to dismantling the role of the STATE in the economy and increasing the role of the MARKET. Confusingly, neoliberalism's most important intellectual beginning took place at a 1938 conference where liberal economists gathered to discuss how to allow a greater role for the state in a GLOBAL economy, given that unfettered market economics had been a major contributor to the Great Depression of the 1930s. Its current meaning finds its significant beginnings with the politics of Reagan and Thatcher and its consolidation with the politics of Clinton and Blair.

If the major senses of **capitalism** have known minor changes and inflections, the root word **capital** has seen major developments. Recent changes in usage of **capital** include a sharp rise in frequency of the word with specific modifiers (**social capital, intellectual capital, venture capital, political capital**, and **human capital**) as well as the introduction of new terms (including **diversity capital, emotional capital, knowledge capital**, and **citizenship as capital**). Many of these uses view **capital** as a positive term with the sense of asset or resource as dominant, but there have been important uses within the Marxist tradition which treat **capital** as an exploitative relationship that reproduces CLASS society.

Usage of **social capital** has risen dramatically recently, but the term first appeared in eC19. In its first appearances, as with **capitalism**, **social capital** often referred to an ignoble exploitation of deed or position for personal gain, as in the following:

> . . . a well-drawn character, who makes a sort of social capital out of the pity inspired by a prolonged despondency for the loss of his wife. . . . (*The Literary Churchman: A Critical Record of Religious Publications*, 1859)

Throughout C19, a positive connotation of **social capital** exists as well, as the CRE-ATIVE resources of a shared human COMMUNITY. This usage is codified by Francis Brewster in *The Philosophy of Human Nature* (1851) and by John Bouvier in *Institutes of American Law* (1854); it was much later popularized by Jane Jacobs in *The Death and Life of Great American Cities* (1961). A third sense, as assets shared by a social group, appears in C19 as well, and continues, if infrequently, to the present day. After Marx, in lC19, **social capital** also begins to refer to social groups, such as laborers, as a resource exploited by the powerful for profit.

In *The Forms of Capital* (1983), Pierre Bourdieu reinterprets Brewster's (1851) **social capital** (a group's shared intangible resources) with a strictly negative implicature, and in specifically Marxist terms. Bourdieu identified all forms of power as self-perpetuating and applied Marx's framework for economic **capital** to both **cultural** and **social capital**. These forms of **capital** include the institutionalized social and cultural networks and resources available to some but not others, which perpetuate human power relations. For Bourdieu, **social** and **cultural capital**, like **economic capital**, are leverage used for ultimately self-perpetuating advantage, and thus lead to entrenched inequality and injustice.

Instances of **social capital** increased remarkably from the 1990s to the 2000s. Today, **social capital** continues to be used with various senses. It occasionally indicates monetary assets shared by a society or group. It can indicate workers, or a whole society, seen as a resource to be exploited by the powerful. It can indicate a set of non-financial, intangible resources shared by a group, as a group; this sense often refers to an empowering resource for groups that lack financial **capital**, and hence carries predominantly positive connotations, contrary to Bourdieu. Finally, **social capital** today can indicate an individual's WEALTH of intangible resources derived from her NETWORK of human relationships. Recent writers exploring these last two senses include Robert Putnam and Francis Fukuyama, while the last sense alone occurs largely in relation to popular social networking resources such as Facebook.

Like **social capital**, **human capital** also originated in C19, with senses that reflect similar contradictions to those within **social capital**. **Human capital** can refer to positive, mutually beneficial resources born of shared human interaction, but it can also refer to human beings as a resource to be exploited. More recently, a unique sense seems to have developed in Singapore for **human capital** as a synonym for the fixed, professional term *human resources*. Numerous private, registered staffing corporations in Singapore include the term **human capital** in their official company names. This new usage sparks the question of whether an employee might prefer to be considered a piece of **capital** or a *resource*, and the thought-provoking answer that such preferences can be expected to vary not only among English speakers, but across varieties of English. Other uses of **human capital** continue to exist in Singapore: one Singapore-based firm with **human capital** in its name provides workshops and events for family members looking to connect with each other, a clear reference to **human capital** as mutually beneficial resources born of shared human interaction. Some sort of pragmatic disambiguation is thus likely required when using the term **human capital** in Singapore. It should be noted that **human capital** is an oxymoron from the viewpoint of classical economics for which labor and **capital** are different factors of production.

Does the increased usage of **capital** in various non-economic contexts imply an increasing reduction of social to economic relationships in line with neoliberalism? Or do the positive contemporary usages of **social capital** indicate a semantic shift among speakers, in which **capital** now evokes VALUE in a broad and even humanist sense? The Marxist tradition denies such a shift by asserting that a contemporary positive reading of **social capital** cannot refer to capital at all, as capital is necessarily exploitative. This underlying dichotomy between two usages with two valuations of **capital** and two analytics means that an understanding of **capital** is ever more central to social understanding.

See CLASS, CORPORATE, ENTERPRISE, MARKET, VALUE, WEALTH

CELEBRITY

Celebrity comes into English at the beginning of C15 from Latin *celebritās* meaning "fame," or "the state of being busy or crowded" (there is also the related French *célébrité*). Two important early meanings recorded by *OED* are: "Observance of ritual or special formality on an important occasion; pomp, ceremony" (C15) and "An act of celebrating something; a rite, a ceremony; a celebration." Both are now obsolete, but survived as late as C19. It should be noted that both meanings have strong religious connotations, and it is legitimate to ask whether these meanings contributed to our current usage of **celebrity** as marking a desperate seeking for the sacred in the profane. While there seem no traces of these archaic meanings in current usage, it might be argued that such connotations prompted the initial choice of this word to mark what is a recognizable feature in contemporary life.

More familiar is another meaning also first recorded in C15, "The state or fact of being well known, widely discussed, or publicly esteemed." As *OED* notes, this has gradually developed some much more specific connotations, "personal fame or renown as manifested in (and determined by) public interest and media attention." The first edition of the *OED* ended its equivalent definition by offering a pair of near synonyms, *famousness* and *notoriety*, with very different meanings. The examples presented also stress the way in which **celebrity** is a double-edged term, giving with one hand (well-known) and taking away with the other (for specious reasons). The irony is mildly present in Samuel Johnson's, "I did not find myself yet enriched in proportion to my celebrity" (1751), and with full and exemplary force in Matthew Arnold's comment, "They [Spinoza's successors] had celebrity. Spinoza has fame" (1863). *OED* further observes in a note, "In early use frequently synonymous with *fame*, but later often distinguished as referring to a more ephemeral condition . . . , or as associated with popular as opposed to high culture."

Current usage of **celebrity** meaning "[a] well-known or famous person" is first attested in the *OED* in 1831; its subsequent development is sketched by *OED* with "(now chiefly) *spec*. a person, esp. in entertainment or sport, who attracts interest from the general public and attention from the mass media." An early attestation from 1849 aptly captures **celebrity**'s constant ambiguity: "Did you see any of these 'celebrities' as you call them," the quotation marks presumably call attention to both the novelty of the term and the fact that it confers a status which some think no status at all.

One can sketch out **celebrity**'s rise to fame. First and foremost it denotes a new form of social status that depends neither on rank nor institutional achievement. This social status depends on the development of a PUBLIC sphere largely, at least initially, through a popular press. It is also subject to rapid change: Today's **celebrity** is tomorrow's nobody. Today's nobody is tomorrow's **celebrity**. Such a notion of change seems fundamentally democratic; **celebrity** is a fame that everybody can enjoy. Andy Warhol expressed this element of **celebrity** best with his most famous dictum that "[i]n the future, everyone will be world-famous for 15 minutes."

This "world fame" has a definite necessary condition: the photographic IMAGE. It is not simply that the modern newspaper creates a discursive realm which challenges status embodied in birth or traditional achievement. It is also that one can meet celebrities face to face. Indeed, it might be possible to argue that **celebrity** in a modern sense is not a feature of C19 but of C20, since the most famous celebrities are Hollywood film stars. In the early history of the movies, studios tried to limit the development of stars because of the economic power that stardom delivered to an actor, yet audiences who could see these actors up close decided that they liked some more than others and delivered that economic power accordingly. The most influential academic analysis of this process has been Horkheimer and Adorno's. But for them, **celebrity** and the star system are simply "a cult of personality," in which the star deceptively stands in for the potential of the masses. This Frankfurt School analysis, however, ignores the very active role that audiences play in the creation of celebrities, for which Hollywood still functions as the most complex example.

Hollywood is also where entertainment and INFORMATION first mix in modern terms. By the 1930s, Hollywood was the third-largest news source in the country, with some 300 correspondents. It is revealing to consider why *stars* are not called **film celebrities**. *Star* has none of the crucial ambiguity of **celebrity**. This ambiguity has intensified over the past decade, with the phenomenal success of "reality" television. Now the commerce between **celebrity** and anonymity has become even more explicit, as nobodies become instant **celebrities** on *Big Brother* while on *Celebrity Big Brother* the reverse journey is undertaken.

See IMAGE, INFORMATION, MEDIA, PUBLIC

CIVIL

Civil is a keyword in much contemporary political ideological and legal debate, but it finds much of its semantic force in a series of oppositions: **civil service** is opposed to *military service*, **civil engineer** is opposed to *mechanical* or *chemical engineer*, **civil union** is opposed to *religious union*, **civil law** is opposed to *canon* or *common law*, and these oppositions do not readily lend themselves to description by a strong core sense. At the same time, much of the most important political developments in Western society can be tracked through the changing definitions of **civil society**.

It is derived from both French and Latin and comes into English in C14. The Latin root is *civilis*, of or pertaining to citizens from the noun *civis*, a citizen. *Civilis* has a range of senses, ranging from a citizen's private RIGHTS to the body of citizens or commonwealth, and through this sense of body of citizens it develops the meanings that relate it to POLITICAL and PUBLIC. There is a strong distinction between the **civilian** and the *soldier* and there is a development that relates to behavior: citizen-like, polite, courteous, urbane. These diverse senses all come through into modern English, although there is an early and important development when **civil** is opposed to *ecclesiastical* in the medieval period, a development that is also registered in post-classical Latin.

While modern English continues to retain the sense of **civil** as "courteous and polite," as in "He was barely civil," most of the examples in the *OED* are for archaic or rare uses, and many more modern examples use **civil** not as equivalent to *courteous* but with the much more minimum sense of "not downright rude." One might speculate that the very strong opposition between **citizen** and *soldier* that underpinned these senses has continuously weakened since the classical period to the point that it might be questioned whether many contemporary speakers of English even register the opposition to *military* in the term **civil service**. This undoubtedly has to do with the diminishing social role of the soldier since the Renaissance. But it may also be because of the importance of the phrase **civil war**, both the oldest and one of the most frequent uses of the word **civil**.

In modern English, **civil** most commonly occurs in fixed collocations such as: **civil commotion, civil defense, civil disobedience, civil engineer, civil law, civil liberty, civil list, civil marriage, civil rights, civil service, civil union, civil war,** and **civil wrong**. Given this patterning, it is difficult to identify a single core sense for **civil**. Rather, senses can only be identified by examining context of use (to an even greater extent than seems usual with polysemous words). Although the etymological sense, "of or relating to citizens" and their private rights, can be seen as the root of current senses, these senses have diverged significantly, and it seems unlikely that a clear connection with this sense would be made by all English speakers on the basis of some of the most frequent current uses (e.g., in **civil engineer** or **civil partnership**).

Civil has an important set of political meanings in the collocations **civil liberties, civil rights,** and **civil society**. It is perhaps unsurprising that two of the earliest examples that the *OED* gives for this phrase in both the singular and plural come from the early debates of the C17 political struggle known in Britain as the

Civil War. John Milton in 1644 writes, "When complaints are freely heard, deeply considered, and speedily reform'd, then is the utmost bound of civill liberty attain'd, that wise men looke for" (*Areopagitica*). And four years earlier the plural, "As this plot hath been set on foot for the benefit of strangers, so it will be continued to the weakening of both the Kingdomes the overthrow of our Religion, and civill liberties, to the uttermost of their power" (1640).

From the earliest days of political theory in English, there had been an identification of **civil** with the political STATE, and one can understand these C17 uses as evoking a definition of the state that does not limit it to the monarch. A more radical redefinition comes from Hegel with his attention to those activities of the citizen that belong neither to the FAMILY nor the state but are the result of the interactions of individuals. Hegel calls these activities *bürgerliche Gesellschaft,* which may be translated as either **civil society** or *bourgeois society.* For Marx it is these activities, particularly the economic relations of society, which form the very base of society. Now the state becomes part of society's superstructure and loses, at least for Marxists, its privileged position at the center of political theory and analysis.

The last quotation in the *OED* for this sense is taken from an article published by *Foreign Policy* in 2002: "Working with nonstate actors, such as NGOs, is central to communication with civil societies in other countries (and hence central to influencing their governments)." In fact this quotation uses a new sense of the phrase developed in the Soviet Bloc in the 1970s and 1980s to refer to associations that did not come under the direct control of the state. It was crucial in the struggles against the Eastern European dictatorships, particularly in Poland and Czechoslovakia, but was then adopted by neoliberal theorists to articulate theories of development which underplayed direct state action. It is thus a currently much contested term globally, opposing those who see non-governmental organizations (NGOs) as crucial to developing strong democratic societies against those who argue that such NGOs simply reduplicate the rule of a Western elite.

Civil also retains contemporary political force in the collocation **civil rights**. This term, too, goes back to early political struggles in C17 and the *OED* again finds a quotation from Milton apposite: "The other part of our freedom consists in the civil rights and advanc'ments of every person according to his merit" (1660). If **civil rights** form an element of the arguments that see the final ousting of feudal and absolutist rule, they gain new force in the US in C20 where they refer to rights already established in the Constitution but denied to African Americans. This usage becomes generalized to cover other situations where a group (the Catholics in

Northern Ireland in the 1960s and 1970s, transgender people in Western societies today) is denied rights to which they are entitled.

It is extremely difficult to provide any overall explanation of the functioning of **civil** within contemporary social and political discourse. As part of a collocation it is a key term in a wide array of political struggles from gay marriage to global economic justice. Its ubiquity may be explained by its ability to articulate the individual and the social while bringing little additional semantic content to that articulation.

See FAMILY, PRIVATE, RIGHTS, STATE

CIVILIZATION

Civilization is now generally used to describe an achieved state or condition of organized social life. Like CULTURE with which it has had a long and still difficult interaction, it referred originally to a process, and in some contexts this sense still survives.

Civilization was preceded in English by **civilize**, which appeared in eC17, from C16 *civiliser*, F, fw *civilizare*, mL—to make a criminal matter into a civil matter, and thence, by extension, to bring within a form of social organization. The rw is *civil* from *civilis*, L—of or belonging to citizens, from *civis*, L—citizen. **Civil** was thus used in English from C14, and by C16 had acquired the extended senses of orderly and educated. Hooker in 1594 wrote of "Civil Society"—a phrase that was to become central in C17 and especially C18—but the main development towards description of an ordered society was **civility**, fw *civilitas*, mL—community. **Civility** was often used in C17 and C18 where we would now expect **civilization**, and as late as 1772 Boswell, visiting Johnson, "found him busy, preparing a fourth edition of his folio Dictionary. . . . He would not admit *civilization*, but only *civility*. With great deference to him, I thought *civilization*, from *to civilize*, better in the sense opposed to *barbarity*, than *civility*." Boswell had correctly identified the main use that was coming through, which emphasized not so much a process as a state of social order and refinement, especially in conscious historical or cultural contrast with *barbarism*. **Civilization** appeared in Ash's dictionary of 1775, to indicate both the state and the process. By 1C18 and then very markedly in C19 it became common.

In one way the new sense of **civilization**, from 1C18, is a specific combination of the ideas of a process and an achieved condition. It has behind it the general spirit of the ENLIGHTENMENT, with its emphasis on secular and progressive human self-development. **Civilization** expressed this sense of historical process, but also celebrated the associated sense of modernity: an achieved condition of refinement and order. In the Romantic reaction against these claims for **civilization**, alternative words were developed to express other kinds of human development and other criteria for human WELL-BEING, notably CULTURE. In 1C18 the association of **civilization** with refinement of manners was normal in both English and French. Burke wrote in *Reflections on the Revolution in France*: "our manners, our civilization, and all the good things which are connected with manners, and with civilization." Here the terms seem almost synonymous, though we must note that *manners* has a wider reference than in ordinary modern usage. From eC19 the development of **civilization** towards its modern meaning, in which as much emphasis is put on social order and on ordered knowledge (later, science) as on refinement of manners and behavior, is on the whole earlier in French than in English. But there was a decisive moment in English in the 1830s, when Mill, in his essay on Coleridge, wrote:

> Take for instance the question how far mankind has gained by civilization. One observer is forcibly struck by the multiplication of physical comforts; the advancement and diffusion of knowledge; the decay of superstition; the facilities of mutual intercourse; the softening of manners; the decline of war and personal conflict; the progressive limitation of the tyranny of the strong over the weak; the great works accomplished throughout the globe by the co-operation of multitudes. . . .

This is Mill's range of positive examples of **civilization**, and it is a fully modern range. He went on to describe negative effects: loss of independence, the creation of artificial wants, monotony, narrow mechanical understanding, inequality, and hopeless poverty. The contrast made by Coleridge and others was between **civilization** and *culture* or *cultivation*:

> The permanent distinction and the occasional contrast between cultivation and civilization. . . . The permanency of the nation . . . and its progressiveness and personal freedom . . . depend on a continuing and progressive civilization. But civilization is itself but a mixed good, if not far more a corrupting influence, the hectic of disease, not the bloom of health, and a nation so distinguished more fitly to be called a varnished than a polished people, where this civilization is not grounded in cultivation,

in the harmonious development of those qualities and faculties that characterize our humanity. (*On the Constitution of Church and State,* V)

Coleridge was evidently aware in this passage of the association of civilization with the *polishing* of manners; that is the point of the remark about varnish, and the distinction recalls the curious overlap, in C18 English and French, between *polished* and *polite,* which have the same root. But the description of **civilization** as a "mixed good," like Mill's more elaborated description of its positive and negative effects, marks the point at which the word has come to stand for a whole modern social process. From this time on this sense was dominant, whether the effects were reckoned as good, bad, or mixed.

Yet it was still primarily seen as a general and indeed universal process. There was a critical moment when **civilization** was used in the plural. This is later with **civilizations** than with *cultures;* its first clear use is in French (Ballanche) in 1819. It is preceded in English by implicit uses to refer to an earlier civilization, but it is not common anywhere until the 1860s.

In modern English **civilization** still refers to a general condition or state, and is still contrasted with *savagery* or *barbarism.* But the relativism inherent in comparative studies, and reflected in the use of **civilizations,** has affected this main sense, and the word now regularly attracts some defining adjective: **Western civilization, modern civilization, industrial civilization, scientific and technological civilization.** As such it has come to be a relatively neutral form for any achieved social order or way of life, and in this sense has a complicated and much disputed relation with the modern social sense of *culture.* Yet its sense of an achieved state is still sufficiently strong for it to retain some normative quality; in this sense **civilization, a civilized way of life, the conditions of civilized society** may be seen as capable of being lost as well as gained.

RECENT DEVELOPMENTS

The long development by which a process of cultivation became a general state of being cultivated occurs at the end of C18 as Europe celebrates both its conquest of the globe and its scientific and artistic achievements. **Civilization** provides much of the ideological underpinning for the colonization of the globe by Europe in C19. The catastrophic barbarism of World War I, the development of the social sciences (particularly anthropology and its re-evaluation of questions of barbarity), and the growth of anti-colonial movements means that in C20 **civilization** becomes plural and, certainly within educated discourse, WESTERN **civilization** now simply becomes one **civilization** among others. It also loses its automatic claim to superiority, as is well captured by Gandhi's apocryphal reply to the question, "What do you think of Western civilization?": "I think it would be a good idea."

In its earliest uses, **civilization** is implicitly an alternative to nations and STATES as a way of capturing political realities. Although it is possible to talk of French or English **civilization**, EUROPEAN or **Western civilization** tend to be more frequent collocates in general American and British English corpora. These first uses of **civilization** are linked to notions of religious tolerance and peace.

However, the most important recent development of the term makes RELIGION the key element of a **civilization** and has **civilization** take up the mantle of nations and states as the key organizer of violent conflict. This new use, which contradicts many of the term's earlier peaceful connotations, has a precursor in 1946 when Albert Camus in a radio broadcast talked of the "shock of civilizations," which he saw as opposing the colonizing nations to the colonized. However, it was "the clash of civilizations" that was widely popularized in the 1990s in articles and books by Samuel Huntington. For Huntington, religions define **civilizations** and the opposition between religions, he argued, would provide the motive for violent conflict in C21. Huntington identified eight **civilizations** and their attendant religions, but his notion of a clash of **civilizations** between Christianity and Islam has become a burning political question. Many ultra-right groups have adopted this vocabulary, reworking themes from the long history of conflict between Christianity and Islam, yet others have refused the identification of **civilization** and religion, and more fundamentally have opposed the idea of radically separate **civilizations**. The history of Islam and Christianity is so interlinked that it might make more sense to talk of one **civilization** rather than two.

There can be little doubt that the relation of **civilization** to conflict is among the most vital questions of the contemporary world and that these questions will not find simple answers in the history of words. Yet the history does teach a lesson: a term originally used idealizingly to justify Western supremacy became pluralized as that supremacy foundered in the bloody realities of IMPERIALISM and is now invoked as a practical necessity to justify another version of Western supremacy.

See CIVIL, CULTURE, IMPERIALISM, MODERN, RELIGION, STATE, WELL-BEING, WEST

CLASS

Class is an obviously difficult word, both in its range of meanings and in its complexity in that particular meaning where it describes a social division. The Latin word *classis*, a division according to property of the people of Rome, came into English in 1C16 in its Latin form, with a plural *classes* or *classies*. There is a 1C16 use (King, 1594) which sounds almost modern: "all the classies and ranks of vanitie." But **classis** was primarily used in explicit reference to Roman history, and was then extended, first as a term in church organization ("assemblies are either classes or synods," 1593) and later as a general term for a division or group ("the classis of Plants," 1664). It is worth noting that the derived Latin word *classicus*, coming into English in eC17 as **classic** from fw *classique*, F, had social implications before it took on its general meaning of a standard authority and then its particular meaning of belonging to Greek and Roman antiquity (now usually distinguished in the form **classical**, which at first alternated with *classic*). Gellius wrote: "*classicus . . . scriptor, non proletarius.*" But the form **class**, coming into English in C17, acquired a special association with EDUCATION. Blount, glossing *classe* in 1656, included the still primarily Roman sense of "an order or distribution of people according to their several Degrees" but added: "in Schools (wherein this word is most used) a Form or Lecture restrained to a certain company of Scholars"—a use which has remained common in education. The development of **classic** and **classical** was strongly affected by this association with authoritative works for study.

From 1C17 the use of **class** as a general word for a group or division became more and more common. What is then most difficult is that **class** came to be used in this way about people as well as about plants and animals, but without social implications of the modern kind. (Cf. Steele, 1709: "this Class of modern Wits.") Development of **class** in its modern social sense, with relatively fixed names for particular classes (**lower class, middle class, upper class, working class,** and so on), belongs essentially to the period between 1770 and 1840, which is also the period of the Industrial Revolution and its decisive reorganization of society. At the extremes it is not difficult to distinguish between (i) **class** as a general term for any grouping and (ii) **class** as a would-be specific description of a social formation. There is no difficulty in distinguishing between Steele's "Class of modern Wits" and, say, the *Declaration* of the Birmingham Political Union (1830) "that the rights and interests of the middle and lower classes of the people are not efficiently represented in the Commons House of Parliament." But in the crucial period of transition, and indeed for some time before it, there is real difficulty in being sure whether a particular use is sense (i) or sense (ii). The earliest use that I know, which might be read in a modern sense, is Defoe's "'tis plain the dearness of wages forms our people into more classes than other nations can show" (*Review*, April 14, 1705). But this, even in an economic context, is far from certain. There must also be some doubt about Hanway's title of 1772: "Observations on the Causes of the Dissoluteness which reigns among the lower classes of the people." We can read this, as indeed we would read Defoe, in a strictly social sense, but there is enough overlap between sense (i) and sense (ii) to make us pause. The crucial context of this development is the alternative vocabulary for social divisions, and it is a fact that until 1C18, and residually well into C19 and even C20, the most common words were *rank* and *order*, while *estate* and *degree* were still more common than **class**. *Estate, degree,* and *order* had been widely used to describe social position from medieval times. *Rank* had been common from 1C16. In virtually all contexts where we would now say **class** these other words were standard, and *lower order* and *lower orders* became especially common in C18.

The essential history of the introduction of **class**, as a word which would supersede older names for social divisions, relates to the increasing consciousness that social position is made rather than merely inherited. All the older words, with their essential metaphors of standing, stepping, and arranging in rows, belong to a society in which position was determined by birth. Individual mobility could be seen as movement from one *estate, degree, order,* or *rank* to another. What was changing consciousness was not only increased individual mobility, which could be largely contained within the older terms, but the new sense of a *society* or a particular *social system* which actually created social divisions, including new kinds of divisions. This is quite explicit in one of the first clear uses, that of Madison in *The Federalist* (US, c1787): moneyed and manufacturing interests "grow up of necessity in civilized nations, and divide them into different classes, actuated by different sentiments and views." Under the pressure of this awareness, greatly sharpened by the economic changes of the Industrial Revolution and the political conflicts of the American and French revolutions, the new vocabulary of **class** began to take over. But it was a slow and uneven process, not only because of the residual familiarity of the older words, and not only because conservative thinkers continued, as a matter of principle, to avoid **class** wherever they could and to prefer the older (and later some newer) terms. It was slow and uneven, and has remained difficult, mainly because of the inevitable overlap with the use of **class** not as a specific social division but as a generally available and often ad hoc term of grouping.

With this said, we can trace the formation of the newly specific **class** vocabulary. **Lower classes** was used in 1772, and **lowest classes** and **lowest class** were common from the 1790s. These carry some of the marks of the transition, but do not complete it. More interesting because less dependent on an old general sense, in which the **lower classes** would be not very different from the COMMON *people*, is the new and increasingly self-conscious and self-used description of the **middle classes**. This has precedents in "men of a middle condition" (1716), "the middle Station of life" (Defoe, 1719), "the Middling People of England . . . generally Good-natured and Stout-hearted" (1718), "the middling and lower classes" (1789). Gisborne in 1795 wrote an "Enquiry into the Duties of Men in the Higher Rank and Middle Classes of Society in Great Britain." Hannah More in 1796 wrote of the "middling classes." The "burden of taxation" rested heavily "on the middle classes" in 1809 (*Monthly Repository*, 501), and in 1812 there was reference to "such of the Middle Class of Society who have fallen upon evil days" (*Examiner*, August). *Rank* was still used at least as often, as in James Mill (1820): "the class which is universally described as both the most wise and the most virtuous part of the community, the middle rank" (*Essay on Government*), but here **class** has already taken on a general social sense, used on its own. The swell of self-congratulatory description reached a temporary climax in Brougham's speech of 1831: "by the people, I mean the middle classes, the wealth and intelligence of the country, the glory of the British name."

There is a continuing curiosity in this development. *Middle* belongs to a disposition between *lower* and *higher*, in fact as an insertion between an increasingly insupportable *high* and *low*. **Higher classes** was used by Burke (*Thoughts on French Affairs*) in 1791, and **upper classes** is recorded from the 1820s. In this model an old hierarchical division is still obvious; the **middle class** is a self-conscious interposition between persons of *rank* and the *common people*. This was always, by definition, indeterminate: this is one of the reasons why the grouping word **class** rather than the specific word *rank* eventually came through. But clearly in Brougham, and very often since, the *upper* or *higher* part of the model virtually disappears, or, rather, awareness of a *higher* class is assigned to a different dimension, that of a residual and respected but essentially displaced aristocracy.

This is the ground for the next complication. In the fierce argument about political, social, and economic rights, between the 1790s and the 1830s, **class** was used in another model, with a simple distinction of the **productive** or **useful classes** (a potent term against the aristocracy). In the widely read translation of Volney's *The Ruins, or A Survey of the Revolutions of Empires* (2 parts, 1795) there was a dialogue between those who by "useful labours contribute to the support and maintenance of society" (the majority of the people, "labourers, artisans, tradesmen and every profession useful to society," hence called *People*) and a **Privileged class** ("priests, courtiers, public accountants, commanders of troops, in short, the civil, military or religious agents of government"). This is a description in French terms of *the people* against an aristocratic government, but it was widely adopted in English terms, with one particular result which corresponds to the actual political situation of the re-form movement between the 1790s and the 1830s: both the self-conscious **middle classes** and the quite different people who by the end of this period would describe themselves as the **working classes** adopted the descriptions **useful** or **productive classes**, in distinction from and in opposition to the *privileged* or the *idle*. This use, which of course sorts oddly with the other model of *lower, middle,* and *higher,* has remained both important and confusing.

For it was by transfer from the sense of *useful* or *productive* that the **working classes** were first named. There is considerable overlap in this: cf. "middle and industrious classes" (*Monthly Magazine*, 1797) and "poor and working classes" (Owen, 1813)—the latter probably the first English use of **working classes** but still very general. In 1818 Owen published *Two Memorials on Behalf of the Working Classes,* and in the same year *The Gorgon* (November 28) used **working classes** in the specific and unmistakable context of relations between "workmen" and "their employers." The use then developed rapidly, and by 1831 the *National Union of the Working Classes* identified not so much privilege as the "laws . . . made to pro-tect . . . property or capital" as their enemy. (They distinguished such laws from those that had not been made to protect industry, still in its old sense of applied labor.) In the *Poor Man's Guardian* (October 19, 1833), O'Brien wrote of establishing for "the productive classes a complete dominion over the fruits of their own industry" and went on to describe such a change as "contemplated by the working classes"; the two terms, in this context, are interchangeable. There are complications in phrases like the **laboring classes** and the **operative classes**, which seem designed to separate one group of the **useful classes** from another, to correspond with the distinction between *workmen* and *employers,* or *men* and *masters*: a distinction that was ec-onomically inevitable and that was politically active from the 1830s at latest. The term **working classes**, originally assigned by others, was eventually taken over and used as proudly as **middle classes** had been: "the working classes have created all wealth" (*Rules* of Ripponden Co-operative Society; cit. J. H. Priestley, *History of RCS*; dating from 1833 or 1839).

By the 1840s, then, **middle classes** and **working classes** were common terms. The former became singular first; the latter is singular from the 1840s but still today alternates between singular and plural forms, often with ideological significance, the singular being normal in SOCIALIST uses, the plural more common in CONSERVATIVE descriptions. But the most significant effect of this complicated history was that there were now two common terms, increasingly used for comparison, distinction, or contrast, which had been formed within quite different models. On the one hand *middle* implied hierarchy and therefore implied **lower class**: not only theoretically but also in repeated practice. On the other hand *working* implied productive or useful activity, which would leave all who were not **working class** unproductive and useless (easy enough for an aristocracy, but hardly accepted by a productive **middle class**). To this day this confusion reverberates. As early as 1844 Cockburn referred to "what are termed *the* working-classes, as if the only workers were those who wrought with their hands." Yet *working man* or *workman* had a persistent reference to manual labor. In an Act of 1875 this was given legal definition: "the expression *work man* . . . means any person who, being a labourer, servant in husbandry, journeyman, artificer, handicraftsman, miner, or otherwise engaged in manual labour . . . has entered into or works under a contract with an employer." The association of *workman* and **working class** was thus very strong, but it will be noted that the definition includes contract with an employer as well as manual work. An Act of 1890 stated: "the provisions of section eleven of the Housing of the Working Classes Act, 1885 . . . shall have effect as if the expression *working classes* included all classes of persons who earn their livelihood by wages or salaries." This permitted a distinction from those whose livelihood depended on fees (**professional class**), profits (**trading class**), or property (**independent**). Yet, especially with the development of clerical and service occupations, there was a critical ambiguity about the class position of those who worked for a *salary* or even a *wage* and yet did not do manual labor. (*Salary* as fixed payment dates from C14; *wages and salaries* is still a normal C19 phrase; in 1868, however, "a manager of a bank or railway—even an overseer or a clerk in a manufactory—is said to draw a salary," and the attempted class distinction between salaries and wages is evident; by eC20 the *salariat* was being distinguished from the *proletariat*.) Here again, at a critical point, the effect of two models of **class** is evident. The **middle class**, with which the earners of salaries normally aligned themselves, is an expression of relative social position and thus of social distinction. The **working class**, specialized from the different notion of the *useful* or *productive classes*, is an expression of economic relationships. Thus the two common modern class terms rest on different models, and the position of those who are conscious of relative social position and thus of social distinction, and yet, within an economic relationship, sell and are dependent on their labor, is the point of critical overlap between the models and the terms. It is absurd to conclude that only the **working classes** work, but if those who work in other than "manual" labor describe themselves in terms of relative social position (**middle class**) the confusion is inevitable. One side effect of this difficulty was a further elaboration of classing itself (the period from 1C18 to 1C19 is rich in these derived words: **classify, classifier, classification**). From the 1860s the **middle class** began to be divided into *lower* and *upper* sections, and later the **working class** was to be divided into *skilled, semi-skilled*, and *laboring*. Various other systems of classification succeeded these, notably *socioeconomic group*, which must be seen as an attempt to marry the two models of **class**, and *status*.

It is necessary, finally, to consider the variations of **class** as an abstract idea. In one of the earliest uses of the singular social term, in Crabbe's

> To every class we have a school assign'd
> Rules for all ranks and food for every mind

class is virtually equivalent to *rank* and was so used in the definition of a *middle* class. But the influence of sense (i), **class** as a general term for grouping, was at least equally strong, and *useful* or *productive* classes follows mainly from this. The *productive* distinction, however, as a perception of an active economic system, led to a sense of **class** which is neither a synonym for *rank* nor a mode of descriptive grouping, but is a description of fundamental economic relationships. In modern usage, the sense of *rank*, though residual, is still active; in one kind of use **class** is still essentially defined by birth. But the more serious uses divide between descriptive grouping and economic relationship. It is obvious that a terminology of basic economic relationships (as between employers and employed, or propertied and propertyless) will be found too crude and general for the quite different purpose of precise descriptive grouping. Hence the persistent but confused arguments between those who, using **class** in the sense of basic relationship, propose two or three basic classes, and those who, trying to use it for descriptive grouping, find they have to break these divisions down into smaller and smaller categories. The history of the word carries this essential ambiguity.

When the language of **class** was being developed, in eC19, each tendency can be noted. *The Gorgon* (November 21, 1818) referred quite naturally to "a smaller class of tradesmen, termed *garret-masters*." But Cobbett in 1825 had the newer sense: "so that here is one class of society united to oppose another class." Charles Hall in 1805 had argued that

> the people in a civilized state may be divided into different orders; but for the purpose of investigating the manner in which they enjoy or are deprived of the requisites to support the health of their bodies or minds, they need only be divided into two classes, viz. the rich and the poor. (*The Effects of Civilization on the People in European States*)

Here there is a distinction between *orders* (*ranks*) and effective economic groupings (**classes**). A cotton spinner in 1818 (cit. *The Making of the English Working Class*; E. P. Thompson, 199) described employers and workers as "two distinct classes of persons." In different ways this binary grouping became conventional, though it operated alongside tripartite groupings: both the social grouping (*upper*, *middle*, and *lower*) and a modernized economic grouping: John Stuart Mill's "three classes," of "landlords, capitalists and labourers" (*Monthly Repository*, 1834, 320) or Marx's "three great social classes . . . wage-labourers, capitalists and landlords" (*Capital*, III). In the actual development of capitalist society, the tripartite division was more and more replaced by a new binary division: in Marxist language the *bourgeoisie* and the *proletariat*. (It is because of the complications of the tripartite division, and because of the primarily social definition of the English term **middle class**, that *bourgeoisie* and even *proletariat* are often difficult to translate.) A further difficulty then arises: a repetition, at a different level, of the variation between a descriptive grouping and an economic relationship. A **class** seen in terms of economic relationships can be a category (*wage-earners*) or a formation (**the working class**). The main tendency of Marx's description of classes was towards formations:

The separate individuals form a class only insofar as they have to carry on a common battle against another class; otherwise they are on hostile terms with each other as competitors. On the other hand, the class in its turn achieves an independent existence over against the individuals, so that the latter find their conditions of existence predestined, and hence have their position in life and their personal development assigned to them by their class. . . . (*German Ideology*)

This difficult argument again attracts confusion. A **class** is sometimes an economic category, including all who are objectively in that economic situation. But a **class** is sometimes (and in Marx more often) a formation in which, for historical reasons, consciousness of this situation and the organization to deal with it have developed. Thus:

Insofar as millions of families live under economic conditions of existence that separate their mode of life, their interests and their culture from those of the other classes, and put them in hostile opposition to the latter, they form a class. Insofar as there is merely a local interconnection among these small-holding peasants, and the identity of their interests begets no community, no national bond and no political organization among them, they do not form a class. (*Eighteenth Brumaire of Louis Bonaparte*)

This is the distinction between category and formation, but since **class** is used for both there has been plenty of ground for confusion. The problem is still critical in that it underlies repeated arguments about the relation of an assumed **class consciousness** to an objectively measured **class**, and about the vagaries of self-description and self-assignation to a class scale. Many of the derived terms repeat this uncertainty. **Class consciousness** clearly can belong only to a formation. **Class struggle, class conflict, class war, class legislation, class bias** depend on the existence of formations (though this may be very uneven or partial within or between **classes**). **Class culture**, on the other hand, can swing between the two meanings: *working-class culture* can be the meanings and values and institutions of the formation, or the tastes and life-styles of the category (see also CULTURE).

In a whole range of contemporary discussion and controversy, all these variable meanings of **class** can be seen in operation, usually without clear distinction. It is therefore worth repeating the basic range (outside the uncontroversial senses of general classification and education):

   (i) *group* (objective); social or economic category, at varying levels
   (ii) *rank*; relative social position; by birth or mobility
   (iii) *formation*; perceived economic relationship; social, political, and cultural organization.

Recent Developments

The latest *OED* entry for **middle class** has a first usage of **class** as an economic category: "My parents were of the middle class but reduced to the lowest condition by the war" in 1654, a full century earlier than the Industrial Revolution in which Williams wishes to locate this new meaning. Williams's entry sketches the differing oppositions in which **class** finds its meaning—either as a naming of social rank or as a description of economic position—and how those different definitions overlap and complicate the political arguments in which they are mobilized. The entry ends with a forceful opposition between the meaning of **class** as a social category and the Marxist sense of **class** as a conscious social formation. This distinction between category and formation is now largely historical. The decline in the political importance of **class** analysis can be indicated by the steep decline in the frequency of the phrase **working class** in general corpora, from a high point in the 1970s. As **working class** has declined in frequency, **underclass** has seen a striking increase. While **working class** often contains a notion of political agency, **underclass** implies the inability to organize politically.

The standard Marxist vocabulary of **class** has largely disappeared from left-wing politics. Occupy Wall Street's famous slogan divides the current social and economic order in terms of "the top one percent"/"the 99%." Momentum, a new left-wing pressure group in Britain, uses **working class** only once in its mission statement and that is when it calls for parliamentary candidates "with a wide range of life experiences, especially working class, black, Asian, ethnic minority, LGBT, disabled and women candidates" (May 1, 2017). In this use there is no appeal to **class** as an economic and political force, but only as a subjective experience that needs to be included in political debate. This is a striking example of how identity politics and questions of consciousness have replaced notions of an economic **class struggle**.

At the same time, the term **middle class** has become a key term in electoral politics, particularly in the US, but the sense now is of a social rank that includes everyone except the very rich and the very poor. Indeed, it has become a term that is intended to identify the majority of the population, as in John Prescott's (1997) "We're all middle class now." British English's use of ever more precise social sub-classifications, as in George Orwell's famous "lower-upper-middle class," is disappearing before the ever more generalized use.

See CULTURE, ELITE, OCCUPY, POPULAR, PRIVILEGE

COMMON

Common has an extraordinary range of meaning in English, and several of its particular meanings are inseparable from a still active social history. The rw is *communis*, L, which has been derived, alternatively, from *com-*, L—together and *munis*, L—under obligation, and from *com-* and *unus*, L—one. In early uses these senses can be seen to merge: **common** to a **community** (from C14 an organized body of people), to a specific group, or to the generality of mankind. There are distinctions in these uses, but also considerable and persistent overlaps. What is then interesting is the very early use of **common** as an adjective and noun of social division: **common, the common**, and **commons**, as contrasted with lords and no-bility. The tension of these two senses has been persistent. **Common** can indicate a whole group or interest or a large specific and subordinate group. (Cf. Elyot's protest [*Governor*, I, i; 1531] against **commune weale**, later **commonwealth**: "There may appere lyke diversitie to be in Englisshe between a publike weale and a commune weale, as shulde be in Latin, between *Res publica & res plebeia*.")

The same tension is apparent even in applications of the sense of a whole group: that is, of generality. **Common** can be used to affirm something shared or to describe something *ordinary* (itself ambivalent, related to *order* as series or sequence, hence *ordinary*—in the usual course of things, but also to *order* as rank, social and military, hence *ordinary*—of an undistinguished kind); or again, in one kind of use, to describe something *low* or *vulgar* (which has specialized in this sense from a comparable origin, *vulgus*, L—the common people). It is difficult to date the derogatory sense of **common**. In feudal society the attribution was systematic and carried few if any additional overtones. It is significant that members of the Parliamentary army in the Civil War of mC17 refused to be called **common soldiers** and insisted on *private soldiers*. This must indicate an existing and significant derogatory sense of **common**, though it is interesting that this same army were fighting for **the commons** and went on to establish a **commonwealth**. The alternative they chose is remarkable, since it asserted, in the true spirit of their revolution, that they were their own men. There is a great deal of social history in this transfer across the range of ordinary description from **common** to *private*: in a way the transposition of hitherto opposed meanings, becoming *private* soldiers in a **common** cause. In succeeding British armies, *private* has been deprived of this significance and reduced to a technical term for those of lowest rank.

It is extremely difficult, from 1C16 on, to distinguish relatively neutral uses of **common**, as in *common ware*, from more conscious and yet vaguer uses to mean *vulgar, unrefined*, and eventually *low-class*. Certainly the clear derogatory use seems to increase from eC19, in a period of more conscious and yet less specific class-distinction (cf. CLASS). By 1C19 "her speech was very *common*" has an unmistakable ring, and this use has persisted over a wide range of behavior. Meanwhile other senses, both neutral and positive, are also in general use. People, sometimes the same people, say "it's *common* to eat ice-cream in the street" (and indeed it is becoming **common** in another sense); but also "it's *common* to speak of the need for a *common* effort" (which may indeed be difficult to get if many of the people needed to make it are seen as **common**).

RECENT DEVELOPMENTS

A surprising omission in Williams's entry is the collocation **common sense**, one of the most frequent uses of **common** in modern times. The expression has a long history in English, with *OED* attestations from C16 onward and evidence of use in its current sense by mC17. **Common sense** and **common-sense ideas** are often invoked to justify particular social or political positions, and to present these positions as self-evident and unquestionable; often a view is presented or represented as **common sense** to downplay its controversial nature. In C18, the philosopher Thomas Paine entitled his best-known pamphlet *Common Sense*, and this argued for the independence of the American colonies from Britain, at the time an anti-establishment position. More recently, **common sense** is particularly (though not always) associated with populist right-wing views, and sometimes explicitly or implicitly opposed to positions identified with ELITES. In 2017 US

President Donald Trump described his proposal to ban refugees and residents of several Muslim-majority countries as **common sense**. When this ban was widely opposed by legislators, Trump commented that "[s]ome things are law and some things are common sense." In the UK the 2001 Conservative Party manifesto was titled "Time for Common Sense," and described the party as one "that trusts people instead of government." The introduction concluded with an appeal from leader William Hague, casting him as a man of the people: "I trust the British people. I trust their common sense."

The complicated CLASS meaning of **common** that Williams delineates with great accuracy is fast becoming archaic as many of the class markers that developed in C19 and C20, particularly around speech, have dissolved. However, one of the oldest meanings of **common**, referring to land that local members of a COMMUNITY as a whole could utilize, has seen a spectacular transferred use in the last fifty years. This **common** land, often referred to as **commons**, had been hugely reduced from C16 on by enclosure, and for Williams it had become so unimportant that it is not even mentioned. However, biologists, economists, and anthropologists in the past fifty years have paid increasing attention to resources held in common, challenging the views of C19 economics that such **common** resources are always overexploited by some individuals. The argument that "the tragedy of the commons" would always see selfish individuals taking more than their fair share of a communal resource has been challenged at a variety of theoretical and historical levels. This recent work underpins the massive contemporary use of **commons** (particularly in the phrase **creative commons**) to refer to developments on the Internet of websites that are collectively created and controlled and which stress use rather than exchange value. *Wikipedia* is only the most visible of a host of such sites.

See CLASS, COMMUNITY, ELITE, POPULAR, PRIVATE, PUBLIC

COMMUNICATION

Communication in its most general modern meaning has been in the language since C15. Its fw is *communicacion*, oF, from *communicationem*, L, a noun of action from the stem of the past participle of *communicare*, L, from rw *communis*, L—common: hence *communicate*—make common to many, impart. **Communication** was first this action, and then, from 1C15, the object thus made common: a communication. This has remained its main range of use. But from 1C17 there was an important extension to the *means* of communication, specifically in such phrases as

lines of communication. In the main period of development of roads, canals, and railways, **communications** was often the abstract general term for these physical facilities. It was in C20, with the development of other means of passing information and maintaining social contact, that **communications** came also and perhaps predominantly to refer to such MEDIA as the press and broadcasting, though this use (which is earlier in US than in UK) is not settled before mC20. The **communications industry**, as it is now called, is thus usually distinguished from the *transport industry*: **communications** for information and ideas, in print and broadcasting; *transport* for the physical carriage of people and goods.

In controversy about communications systems and communication theory it is often useful to recall the unresolved range of the original noun of action, represented at its extremes by *transmit*, a one-way process, and *share* (cf. **communion** and especially **communicant**), a common or mutual process. The intermediate senses—make common to many, and impart—can be read in either direction, and the choice of direction is often crucial. Hence the attempt to generalize the distinction in such contrasted phrases as **manipulative communication(s)** and **participatory communication(s)**.

RECENT DEVELOPMENTS

Communication has been transformed in the digital age, and, like MEDIA and TECHNOLOGY, the word **communication** has steadily increased in frequency since mC20. In British English, **comms** has become a familiar short form for the plural noun **communications**, as in the compounds **comms software** and **digital comms**. Prominent collocations now include **communication technology**, **electronic communication(s)**, **mobile communication(s)**, and **digital communication(s)**. The rise of these compound nouns since lC20 suggests that **communication**— whether in the *OED* sense of "interpersonal contact, social interaction" or "transmission or exchange of information, knowledge, or ideas"—now often involves the use of electronic devices. In other words, **communication** in C21 frequently occurs through a screen.

Communication skills, first attested in 1935 according to the *OED*, are "abilities that enable one to communicate effectively with other people, esp. considered as a qualification or asset; (sometimes) *spec.* an aptitude for conveying information and ideas combined with good listening and comprehension skills." In everything from self-help books and articles to academic program descriptions and mission statements, **communication** is cited as one of today's most important skills. However, having good **communication skills** typically implies more than competence in face-to-face, in-person human interaction. Effective **communication** at a distance through social media and other **communication technologies** is now considered integral to the success of businesses and organizations in C21. Today many businesses, organizations, and institutions of higher education feature a **communications office** dedicated to the management of website content, social media, and public relations.

See COMMON, MEDIA, TECHNOLOGY

COMMUNITY

Community has been in the language since C14, from fw *comuneté*, oF, *communitatem*, L—community of relations or feelings, from rw *communis*, L— COMMON. It became established in English in a range of senses: (i) the commons or common people, as distinguished from those of rank (C14–C17); (ii) a state or organized society, in its later uses relatively small (C14–); (iii) the people of a district (C18–); (iv) the quality of holding something in common, as in **community of interests**, **community of goods** (C16–); (v) a sense of common identity and characteristics (C16–). It will be seen that senses (i) to (iii) indicate actual social groups; senses (iv) and (v) a particular quality of relationship (as in *communitas*). From C17 there are signs of the distinction which became especially important from C19, in which **community** was felt to be more immediate than *society*, although it must be remembered that *society* itself had this more immediate sense until C18, and *civil society* (see CIVILIZATION) was, like *society* and *community* in these uses, originally an attempt to distinguish the body of direct relationships from the organized establishment of *realm* or STATE. From C19 the sense of immediacy or locality was strongly developed in the context of larger and more complex industrial societies. **Community** was the word normally chosen for experiments in an alternative kind of group-living. It is still so used and has been joined, in a more limited sense, by **commune** (the French *commune*—the smallest administrative division—and the German *Gemeinde*—a civil and ecclesiastical division—had interacted with each other and with **community**, and also passed into SOCIALIST thought [especially *commune*] and into sociology [especially *Gemeinde*] to express particular kinds of social relations). The contrast, increasingly expressed in C19, between the more direct, more total, and therefore more significant relationships of **community** and the more formal, more abstract, and more instrumental relationships of *state*, or of *society* in its modern sense, was influentially formalized by Tönnies (1887) as a contrast between *Gemeinschaft* and *Gesellschaft*, and these terms are now sometimes used, untranslated, in other languages. A comparable distinction is evident in mC20 uses of **community**. In some uses this has been given a polemical edge, as in **community politics**, which is distinct not only from *national politics* but from formal *local politics* and normally involves various kinds of direct action and direct local organization, "working directly with people," as which it is distinct from "service to the **community**," which has an older sense of voluntary work supplementary to official provision or paid service.

The complexity of **community** thus relates to the difficult interaction between the tendencies originally distinguished in the historical development: on the one hand the sense of direct common concern; on the other hand the materialization of various forms of common organization, which may or may not adequately express this. **Community** can be the warmly persuasive word to describe an existing set of relationships, or the warmly persuasive word to describe an alternative set of relationships. What is most important, perhaps, is that unlike all other terms of social organization (*state, nation, society*, etc.) it seems never to be used unfavorably, and never to be given any positive opposing or distinguishing term.

RECENT DEVELOPMENTS

Community has continued to rise in frequency since the mid-1980s. Its warmly persuasive inflection continues to be caught even in recent coinages like **gated community**, where the social reality of exclusion is obfuscated by the emphasis on a shared social organization. Its ever-growing use particularly in educational contexts (there is scarcely a school, college, or university that does not claim to be a **community**) shows an ever more pressing need to emphasize beliefs that bind the members of an INSTITUTION into a social whole. In this the word may be drawing on its historical resonances in relation to religious **communities**, particularly monastic foundations.

However, Williams's claim that **community** is "never to be used unfavorably" seems exaggerated. Like any group noun, there are instances when it is used unfavorably. Indeed, there is a split built into the word that the *OED* records from C18 which can encourage unfavorable connotations. Like the closely related COMMON, **community** may refer to the whole, or to a part, distinct from the whole, and it may be evaluated negatively by those not belonging to it. With the definite article, **the community** names "the civic body to which all belong; the public; society"; in contrast, with various specifying adjectives, **community** refers to "a group of people distinguished by shared circumstances of nationality, race, religion, sexuality, etc.," such as "the Negro community" (1968), "the gay community" (1983), and "the Shi'ite Muslim community" (1989). This usage extends further, beyond IDENTITY categories to groups "who share the same interests, pursuits, or occupation," such as "the intelligence community" (2001), often felt as a mendacious phrase to cover snoops and spies with the good feelings of intimate interpersonal connection. Yet this usage extends back to "the literary community" (1789) and "the commercial community" (1856), as well as more recently "the ... scientific community" (1969). With their jargons and microsocial codes, such groups may be felt negatively as ghettoes, or criticized yet envied as privileged ELITES.

See CIVILIZATION, COMMON, GLOBAL, IDENTITY, INSTITUTION, NATIONALIST, STATE

CONSERVATIVE

There are few terms that are so different in American and British English. In English **Conservative** most importantly names a political party. It was the name chosen by Robert Peel to re-BRAND the Tory Party, which had been rendered irrelevant by the Great Reform Act of 1832. It was one of the most successful branding exercises of all time. The word had only just started to be used in a POLITICAL register and participates in the formative moment Raymond Williams studied in *Culture and Society*, in which a number of crucial terms, now essential to many forms of public and intellectual discussions, came into use with new or newly shaped or invigorated meanings: such terms as *art, class, culture, democracy, industry, society*. Insofar as Edmund Burke, himself a Whig, not a Tory, is widely held as the "father of modern conservatism," and yet himself did not use the term in any especially vital or complex way, we can recognize that it is in the broad movement asserted against the Revolution in France and its values that **Conservative** became a keyword, and this is its connection to Burke, who so powerfully and influentially argued against the French Revolution. The key decision of Peel was best understood by Benjamin Disraeli, articulated in his novel *Coningsby* (1844): "'A sound Conservative Government,' said Taper, musingly. 'I understand: Tory men and Whig measures.'"

Before being turned to its political uses, it is striking how highly positive was the sense of **conservative**, both as an adjective and as a noun, when Peel appropriated it for his new party. Like the sweetened fruit that as a **conserve** lasts so much longer than untreated ripe fruit does, a **conservative** was a means for conserving and preserving. One of the earliest examples in the *OED* is quite beautiful: "A story is the testimony of tymes, the memory of life . . . a conseruatiue perpetualle to thynges mortalle" (*Polychronicon*, 1475). Before the term is cited in its political sense, this earlier sense was still being used in Robert Southey's *Sir Thomas More*, a work of romantic anti-capitalism. Southey wrote, "The rapid increase of the labouring classes renders education, as a corrective and conservative . . . absolutely needful." Southey here prefigures the often successful alliance between newly enfranchised workers and traditional powers that flourished as "Tory democracy." The *OED* citations for the new political-party uses of the term include John Stuart Mill: "The Conservatives . . . being by the law of their existence the stupidest party" (1861).

Along with the new political usage there also emerged the other most current sense of the term, "A person who conserves or preserves something; (now usually) an adherent of traditional values, ideas, and institutions; an opponent of (social and political) change, a conservative person," along with its associated adjectival sense, "[t]hat conserves, or favours the conservation of, an existing structure or system; (now esp.) designating a person, movement, outlook, etc., averse to change or inno- vation and holding traditional ideas and values, esp. with regard to social and polit- ical issues." The *OED* notes, "Originally almost always with favourable connotations; now usually in more neutral or negative sense. In political contexts . . . often op- posed to *liberal*." This opposition between **conservative** and LIBERAL generates the American usage. It diverged from British usage in lC19, as the Labour Party was formed in England, which gave *liberal* many meanings in opposition to both **con- servative** and SOCIALIST. The failure, unique to the US, to form a workers' party meant that *liberal* in American English covers the whole range of *progressive* and *socialist* views in a way it does not in British English.

Many relatively recent adjectival usages share a sense of **conservative** as *mod- erate* in a generally favorable way. For instance: "Conforming to traditional aes- thetic tastes"; by definition, only an innovative fringe will find this too tame. Then there is the **conservative estimate**, widely favored by all who are not extreme risk- takers. In medicine a more specialized usage points in important directions: "Of treatment: gradual, gentle, or limited in scope or intent," especially in surgery "that involves minimal removal of tissue." This is opposed to the medical sense of *rad- ical*: "*conservative* surgery. By this term, I mean the desire to save all that it is pos- sible to save from excision" (*Lancet*, 1844). The medical historian Roy Porter wrote of the "old-style doctor," who "had a choice between the conservative Hippocratic options (waiting and watching, bedrest, tonics, care, soothing words, calm and hope), or 'heroic' possibilities, including violent purges" (*Blood and Guts*, 2002). Yet in recent years, we are familiar with a political **conservatism** that is in the medical sense *radical*, because it does not favor leaving as is but rather relishes a violent rhetoric of cutting and purging.

The politicization of **conservative** (for a **conservative** was, by original definition, a person who had no politics except tradition) develops in American English and is not well tracked in the *OED*.

What is called **neo-conservatism** has important relations to this development. When Ronald Reagan acted against the air controllers' strike, and Margaret Thatcher against the coal miners' strike, they sought to undermine long-existing institutional structures that organized the lives of large numbers of workers, but they did so in the name of principles that they named as **conservative**. In the wake of Edmund Burke's analytic polemic against the French Revolution, the emergent discipline of sociology established that there were patterns of life, independent of the formal organization of the state or the economy, which largely regulated the ways in which people live with each other—this was the emergence of the analytic category of *society* and the idea that there exist what may be understood as social laws. In contrast, Thatcher argued that "[t]here is no such thing as society. There are individual men and women" (1987). This illustrates the "possessive individualism" which Raymond Williams in the concluding passages for his keywords entry on *liberalism* had named as *the* vice at the core of the concept. To think as C19 liberals thought was now to be **conservative**, and just like those C19 liberals, to be a **conservative** now was to be an ideologue, not in favor of things as they are, but in favor of things as they should be, in accordance with ideas.

It is not surprising, then, that what was in the 1980s called **neoconservatism** got to be called *neoliberalism* in the 1990s, when it marked the policies of the Democrat Bill Clinton and the Labour Party leader Tony Blair. Reagan had asserted, "government is not the solution to our problem; government is the problem"; Clinton, "The era of big government is over." Not much difference. At least to a Canadian source in 1992, the spirit of the age was marked by "free trade, privatization, deregulation, competitiveness, social-spending cutbacks and deficit reduction." This "ensemble" might "be called neo-conservatism, neoliberalism, the free market [etc.]" (*Globe and Mail*, May 1, 1992).

The history of the *OED* citations for these two terms is provocative for current thinking and debates. By eC21, the major distinction between the two terms as applied to current politics was that **neoconservatives** favored an aggressive foreign policy, such as that pursued by President G. W. Bush (exponent domestically of a "compassionate conservatism"), while neoliberals focused more attention on the economy and had favored the euphoria of a supposedly post-national globalization over strongly NATIONALIST foreign policies. Yet most who have used these terms in the last several decades would be surprised to learn from the *OED* that the terms are over a century old, reaching back into the later C19. Barely had C19 germinated *liberalism* and **conservatism** than they began to "neoterize." Lionel Trilling in *The Liberal Imagination* (1950) had influentially asserted that in the US at that moment Mill's view still held: whatever thinking there was, liberals did it. This challenge was taken up by a group that came to be called by the almost oxymoronic title "conservative intellectuals," and by 1955, "Reinhold Niebuhr is to be counted among the 'neoconservatives' of our time, who own kinship with Edmund Burke." Niebuhr, who was a Cold-War Democrat in his politics, is more generally now known as *neo-orthodox*, referring specifically to the character of his Christian beliefs. In the 1970s, **neoconservatives**, especially the group around the new journal *The Public Interest*, were understood as "liberals mugged by reality." The use of the term *mugged* suggested that the continued vigor of the URBAN underclass, its refusal to be pacified and ameliorated by the Great Society, had turned previously hopeful mid-century liberals against government interventionist policies.

The *OED* offers a note on US usage of the term *neoliberal* that might be considered misleading. Supposedly the term is used "to designate a broadly left-wing outlook or political standpoint." This is illustrated by a citation from the *New York Review of Books* (2000): "Historians of the future may see Clinton as a neoliberal, neo-civil-rights radical, taking up Martin Luther King Jr.'s unfinished work toward an economic justice that transcends race." In fact, the context of that sentence contradicts this possible future interpretation. The sociologist Peter Evans and the historian William Sewell locate *neoliberal* as currently used to characterize positions in four areas: in technical economics, as a political ideology, as a guide for policy, and as a "social imaginary." The force of social imaginary means that even those who know nothing of the technical arguments of Milton Friedman may believe that whatever a government does, it does inefficiently or, more largely, that an entrepreneur always does more for others than does a bureaucrat. The core view now joining neoliberals and **neoconservatives** holds that government should get out of the way and leave room for MARKET efficiency and that entrepreneurial CAPITALISM is preferable to the CORPORATE capitalist model that prevailed in the 1950s, that individuals not collectivities are the key, whether as a job-creator or as a worker in one of the created jobs. This view, for example, underlies the change in American higher education that derives from overturning the admissions cartel that had long assured ELITE universities did not use economic incentives to compete for students. The net effect is that some students now get more than they would have but that fewer students can be assisted, except for the very richest institutions, which can use their wealth advantage to gain further on their competitors. The same tendency to amass all the resources at the top end may be found across neoliberal political economy. It explains why, like lC19, eC21 is an era of social Darwinism.

See CAPITALISM, LIBERAL, MARKET, NATIONALIST, POLITICAL, SOCIALIST

CONSUMER

In modern English **consumer** and **consumption** are the predominant descriptive nouns of all kinds of use of goods and services. The predominance is significant in that it relates to a particular version of economic activity, derived from the character of a particular economic system, as the history of the word shows.

Consume has been in English since C14, from fw *consumer*, F, and the variant *consommer*, F (these variants have a complicated but eventually distinct history in French), rw *consumere*, L—to take up completely, devour, waste, spend. In almost all its early English uses, **consume** had an unfavorable sense; it meant to destroy, to use up, to waste, to exhaust. This sense is still present in "consumed by fire" and in the popular description of pulmonary phthisis as **consumption**. Early uses of **consumer**, from C16, had the same general sense of destruction or waste.

It was from mC18 that **consumer** began to emerge in a neutral sense in descriptions of bourgeois political economy. In the new predominance of an organized MARKET, the acts of making and of using goods and services were newly defined in the increasingly abstract pairings of *producer* and **consumer**, *production* and **consumption**. Yet the unfavorable connotations of **consume** persisted, at least until lC19, and it was really only in mC20 that the word passed from specialized use in political economy to general and popular use. The relative decline of *customer*, used from C15 to describe a buyer or purchaser, is significant here, in that *customer* had always implied some degree of regular and continuing relationship to a supplier, whereas **consumer** indicates the more abstract figure in a more abstract market.

The modern development has been primarily American but has spread very quickly. The dominance of the term has been so great that even groups of informed and discriminating purchasers and users have formed *Consumers' Associations*. The development relates primarily to the planning and attempted control of markets which is inherent in large-scale industrial capitalist (and state-capitalist) production, where, especially after the depression of 1C19, manufacture was related not only to the supply of known needs (which *customer* or *user* would adequately describe) but to the planning of given kinds and quantities of production which required large investment at an early and often predictive stage. The development of modern commercial *advertising* (persuasion, or *penetration* of a market) is related to the same stage of CAPITALISM: the creation of needs and wants and of particular ways of satisfying them, as distinct from and in addition to the notification of available supply which had been the main earlier function *of advertising* (where that kind of persuasion could be seen as *puff* and *puffery*). **Consumer** as a predominant term was the creation of such manufacturers and their agents. It implies, ironically as in the earliest senses, the using-up of what is going to be produced, though once the term was established it was given some appearance of autonomy (as in the curious phrase **consumer choice**). It is appropriate in terms of the history of the word that criticism of a wasteful and "throw-away" society was expressed, somewhat later, by the description **consumer society**. Yet the predominance of the capitalist model ensured its widespread and often overwhelming extension to such fields as politics, education, and health. In any of these fields, but also in the ordinary field of goods and services, to say *user* rather than **consumer** is still to express a relevant distinction.

RECENT DEVELOPMENTS

Williams notes that the verb **to consume** was, in its earliest uses, associated with waste and the exhaustion of resources. For example, **consumer** is synonymous with *waster* in a C15 religious treatise that admonished "consumers of sustinans & wastures of ȝowre good" who committed the sin of gluttony (*OED c*1425). Both the verbal and nominal forms take on a more neutral meaning as they become the opposite of, respectively, "to produce" and "producer" in the lexicon of C18 and C19 bourgeois capitalism. As an integral term in the vocabulary of the contemporary

GLOBAL marketplace, **consumer** indicates a certain type of agency (**consumer choice**), even as these choices are increasingly dictated by a relatively small group of multinational corporations and, in some countries, state-run agencies.

Consumer now functions as a lifestyle IDENTITY. We are what we consume. This identity is imagined as universalizing to the extent that it often crosses national, political, and religious lines; it is imagined as collective to the extent that the use of a particular commodity establishes a group identity. The self is extended when one is the kind of person who skydives (experience consumption), drives a 1970s convertible (durable goods consumption), or eats oysters (non-durable goods consumption).

Consumption has long driven politics, from the C17 tulip mania to the C19 opium wars to contemporary petropolitics. As so-called first-world economies shift to be based predominantly on consumption rather than production of goods, the role of the **consumer** grows ever larger. Neoliberalism, which has dominated Western economies over the past decades, has elevated the **consumer** to an independent market actor who makes rational choices on the basis of information such as price or origin. Indeed, it is the assumption of a great deal of EU consumer and competition legislation, that "the average consumer" is "reasonably observant, reasonably well-informed and circumspect." However, others argue persuasively that **consumers** frequently act irrationally, even when given objective information. Behavioral economists assume that much **consumer** behavior is "predictably irrational" (Dan Ariely, 2008). Some scientists make similar assumptions, which has led to the founding of the new field of **consumer neuroscience.** The belief that **consumer choice** is frequently irrational forms the basis for the lucrative business of marketing, which seeks to manipulate **consumer** decision-making. Fundamental to marketing is the assumption that "consumers are just as likely to be driven by emotional cues and non-conscious heuristics as by rational persuasion" (The Marketing Society, 2016).

Partly for this reason, the act of purchasing is thought to demand not just oversight but also safeguards to ensure a FAIR experience. A **consumer advocate** ensures the safety of products and the reliability of services. One of the most frequently found collocations, **consumer protection** implies that the act of consumption is inherently risky: the absolute freedom of contracts and caveat emptor pose a threat to average users or buyers. It is also recognized that there are **vulnerable consumers**, such as the young, who might need additional regulatory protection. To address this perceived threat, the US established a Consumer

Financial Protection Bureau in 2011 that guards citizens against robocalls, unscrupulous mortgage lenders, and combustible mobile phones. The assumption that we all consume even forms the basis of a legal identity in which certain rights and privileges inhere. The US Congress passed a Consumer Bill of Rights under President Kennedy in 1961. Similarly, the EU introduced a Directive on Consumer Rights in 1997, which in its most recent iteration has been implemented in the UK by the 2016 Consumer Rights Act. These legal provisions suggest that certain RIGHTS now inhere in what we buy, rather than who we are; moreover, there is a growing consensus that consumption forms the basis of a legally recognizable identity.

Consumer capitalism is sometimes contrasted with an antecedent *free-market capitalism*. Some have argued that **consumer capitalism** marks a distinct stage of capitalism based on manufactured demand, contrasted with a previous stage where production was based on need. A Marxist would disagree, arguing that the commodity form, in which use values become exchange values, makes consumption central to capitalism from its very beginnings. Indeed, Marx's analysis of the inevitability of crises of overproduction makes hyperconsumption an inevitable stage of capitalism.

There is a transnational assumption that we all consume, perhaps summarized in the widely used term **consumer democracy**. However, we do not all consume equally. One of the dividing lines between first- and third-world countries is the amount and effects of their consumption. Developed economies consume at many times the rate of developing countries, which bear the brunt of the environmental consequences. This asymmetry continues to exert destabilizing political effects across the globe. While the language of **consumer rights** and **consumer protection** suggests that all are equal in their consumption, in reality not all have equal ACCESS to remedies, whether at local or international levels.

See CAPITALISM, IDENTITY, MARKET, RIGHTS, WEALTH

CORPORATE

In contemporary usage, the term **corporate** can connote either "profitable, efficient and disciplined" or "homogenizing, faceless, and bureaucratic." The term's ubiquity in a wide range of phrases, including **corporate affairs**, **corporate influence**, and **corporate culture**, renders it somewhat opaque, as it modifies a seemingly endless array of words denoting commercial activity.

Corporation most commonly refers to a legal entity separate from the persons within it. As such, it is often understood to be an immaterial thing, lacking a physical place of its own. In the words of one legal historian, "the corporation is invisible, incorporeal, immortal; it cannot be assaulted, or beaten or imprisoned." Since the word derives from Latin *corporare* "to embody" and is related to *corpus* "body," the current usage witnesses a semantic dematerialization, which occurred under a variety of ideological pressures brought to bear on the porous line that divides individual from collective, PUBLIC from PRIVATE, and NATURAL from ARTIFICIAL.

Early in its history within English, **corporate** shifts from designating an individual human body to designating a "group-person." In medieval and early modern usage, **corporate** still meant "having a body" or "embodied" in contrast to those things that did not: "Al thinges, aswel . . . visible, as invisible, corporate, as incorporate" (1557).

Alongside this concrete adjectival meaning, the noun **corporation** came to signify a more disembodied associational thinking among religious groups, burgesses, municipalities, and universities. It frequently referred to the collective body of the church, whether earthly or divine. Thomas More asserted that Christ "incorporate[s] all christen folke and hys owne bodye together in one corporacyon mistical" (1534). Gild records show the development of rights granted to the **body corporate** of professional confraternities. Towns, municipalities, and universities **incorporated** in order to protect residents and safeguard privileges. These usages suggest that, while the medieval adjective **corporate** still had a clearly physical sense, the noun began to designate an alliance or collective, a group of people united together in one immaterial body for mutual benefit.

Over the course of C17, **corporate** ceased to mean "bodily." At the same time, the political implications of this shift (from individual body to legally created group-person) were realized. The Corporation Act of 1661 required that no person could hold municipal office unless he had sworn allegiance to the king and had taken communion as administered by the Church of England within the past year. Under this "test act," the loyal servant of the state is defined as a body subsumed in the two larger **corporate** bodies of monarch and church. **Corporation** becomes the rubric under which an identity between polity and persons was forged in C17, a term that stood for the mutually reinforcing prerogatives of church and state well into C19.

As the term **corporate** evolved from denoting a physical body to denoting a disembodied entity, a series of ideological complications ensued. As early as the medieval period, concern was expressed over the ontological status of a **corporation**.

Was it just a name, or was it a person? It is taken for granted today that a **corporation** is an "aggregate of many," yet the idea of the group-person had a complicated path. One problem was that the **corporate** entity both encourages and resists attempts to anthropomorphize it. Though most **corporations** are made up of members guided by a head—a mayor, chancellor, or CEO—the head is not coextensive with the **corporate** body itself. Thus in liability cases the goods of the disembodied **corporation** but not (in most cases) the embodied head are liable for distraint. From C17, this distinction leads to an increasing volume of jurisprudence aimed at defining a private (or "natural") individual in contrast to the "artificial person" of the **corporation**. On account of this evolving legal code, notions of **corporation** significantly influenced notions of personhood from the early modern period forward. As the term **corporate** moved semantically further away from designating actual bodies, its legal impact on those natural bodies arguably increased.

While cities and towns are still said to **incorporate**, the terms **corporate** and **corporation** come to exist almost solely in the domain of commerce and law from lC19. When a business **incorporates**, the process usually precipitates out the personal bodies and possessions of those involved, since the act of **incorporation** is seen to lessen individual RISK in an unknowable MARKET (cf. today's *Ltd* or *LLC*, **limited liability corporation**). By 1915, the House of Lords could confidently assert in a landmark ruling on liability that a **corporation** is a *persona ficta*, "an abstraction . . . [that] has no mind of its own any more than it has a body of its own." Such a view makes conspicuous the oppositions inherent in the term's modern usage: the **corporation** is PUBLIC, perpetual, and lacking a physical existence, while the individual is private, mortal, and locatable. One cannot point to *where* a **corporation** is, nor can one legally point to the individual bodies of those **incorporated** within it.

The expansion of manufacturing industries in lC19 and C20 gave rise to the stereotype of the **corporate man**. Usually defined as college-educated, articulate, and hard-working, he was praised as the engine of modern productivity. At the same time, he was satirized in works such as Sinclair Lewis's *Babbitt* (1922), whose protagonist lacks independence, creativity, and self-understanding. **Corporate** expanded its meaning to become a catchall for any profession where one worked for someone else: "The cowboy is the last of the rugged individualists, the last of the non-corporate man" (*Washington Post*, September 5, 1978, B4/4). The demise of **corporate man** (due to **corporate downsizing**) has been lamented (or applauded) since at least the 1980s, though the term **corporati** (coined in the 1990s) suggests that the rumor of his demise may be greatly exaggerated.

Recent skepticism regarding **corporate** entities has come from a sense that such entities exercise the RIGHTS and PRIVILEGES of personhood but rarely its duties and responsibilities. Similarly unsettling is the act of **corporate ventriloquism** by means of which one voice purports to speak for all but issues from no single speaker. Such anxieties are manifest in the rise of the noun **corporate** (often plural) to describe those who subscribe to the ideological values associated with multinational GLOBAL CAPITALISM. This usage witnesses the term's presence in a new set of arguments, in which the term has become the opposite of *liberal* or *environmentally conscious*. Thus, the "brave Eco-Warrior battle[s] against the corporates who want to build a nasty McDonalds" (2007). This new sense shows the word caught up in continuing debates about the rights of individuals as opposed to group-persons, about what is natural as opposed to artificial, and about what is private as opposed to public.

See CAPITALISM, GLOBAL, MARKET, PRIVATE, PUBLIC, RISK

COUNTRY

Country has two different meanings in modern English: broadly, a NATIVE land and the rural or agricultural parts of it.

The word is historically very curious, since it derives from the feminine adjective *contrata*, mL, rw *contra*, L—against, in the phrase *contrata terra* meaning land "lying opposite, over against or facing." In its earliest separate meaning it was a tract of land spread out before an observer. (Cf. the later use of *landskip*, C16, *landscape*, C18; in OE *landscipe* was a region or tract of land; the word was later adopted from Dutch *landschap* as a term in painting.) *Contrata* passed into English through oF *cuntrée* and *contrée*. It had the sense of native land from C13 and of the distinctly rural areas from eC16. Tyndale (1526) translated part of Mark 5:14 as "tolde it in the cyte, and in the countre."

The widespread specialized use of **country** as opposed to *city* began in 1C16 with increasing urbanization and especially the growth of the capital, London. It was then that **country people** and the **country house** were distinguished. On the other hand **countryfied** and **country bumpkin** were C17 metropolitan slang. **Countryside**, originally a Scottish term to indicate a specific locality, became in C19 a general term to describe not only the rural areas but the whole rural life and economy.

In its general use, for native land, **country** has more positive associations than either *nation* or STATE: cf. "doing something for the country" with "doing something for the nation" or ". . . state." **Country** habitually includes the people who live in it, while *nation* is more abstract and *state* carries a sense of the structure of power. Indeed **country** can substitute for *people*, in political contexts: cf. "the country demands." This is subject to variations of perspective: cf. the English lady who said in 1945: "they have elected a socialist government and the country will not stand for it." In some uses **country** is regularly distinguished from government: cf. "going to the country"—calling an election. There is also a specialized metropolitan use, as in the postal service, in which all areas outside the capital city are "country."

Countryman carries both political and rural senses, but the latter is stronger and the former is usually extended to **fellow-countryman**.

Recent Developments

Williams's characterization of the two very different senses of **country** remains fully pertinent. The way in which **country** functions as a strong affective sense that widens the legal *state* or the political *nation* to include all one's fellow **countrymen** and **women** is there from Mark Antony's speech over Caesar's body in which both friends (a set of personal relations) and Romans (a legal definition) are subsumed in the wider and strongest "countrymen." When E. M. Forster declared that he would rather betray his **country** than his friends, the force of the quote comes from him using the strong collective noun rather than the more juridical terms of *nation* or *state*. The extent to which **country** remains the strongest expression of political COMMUNITY is evident in Nigel Farage's claim the day after the 2016 referendum that "[w]e've got our country back," where replacing *nation* or *state* for **country** would substitute for a noun that includes all listeners, nouns which immediately refer to POLITICAL or legal relationships.

The sense of **country** as opposed to *city* has both become stronger and more contested in the past fifty years. The pejorative **country bumpkin** is now effectively archaic, and the sense of the **country** as a repository of knowledge and wisdom unavailable in the town has become ever stronger. At the same time, the growth of ecological and animal rights movements has led to sharper political divisions, often pitting some of those who live in the **country** against *city* dwellers who are committed to defending and preserving the **countryside**. In England the clearest example of this opposition is in arguments about fox hunting: the vast majority of city dwellers want hunting banned, while significant rural populations want it retained.

The formation of the Countryside Alliance in 1997 was one example of how these sharpened divisions are gaining a political focus.

See COMMUNITY, NATIVE, STATE, URBAN

CREATIVE

Creative in modern English has a general sense of original and innovating, and an associated special sense of productive. It is also used to distinguish certain kinds of work, as in **creative writing, the creative arts.** It is interesting to see how this now commonplace but still, on reflection, surprising word came to be used, and how this relates to some of its current difficulties.

Create came into English from the stem of the past participle of rw *creare*, L— make or produce. This inherent relation to the sense of something having been made, and thus to a past event, was exact, for the word was mainly used in the precise context of the original divine creation of the world: **creation** itself, and **creature,** have the same root stem. Moreover, within that system of belief, as Augustine insisted, "creatura non potest creare"—the "creature"—who has been created— cannot himself create. This context remained decisive until at least C16, and the extension of the word to indicate present or future making—that is to say a kind of making by men—is part of the major transformation of thought which we now describe as the humanism of the Renaissance. "There are two creators," wrote Torquato Tasso (1544–95), "God and the poet." This sense of human creation, specifically in works of the imagination, is the decisive source of the modern meaning. In his *Apologie for Poetrie*, Philip Sidney (1554–86) saw God as having made Nature but having also made man in his own likeness, giving him the capacity "with the force of a divine breath" to imagine and make things beyond Nature.

Yet use of the word remained difficult, because of the original context. Donne referred to poetry as a "counterfeit Creation," where *counterfeit* does not have to be taken in its strongest sense of false but where the old sense of art as *imitation* is certainly present. Several uses of **create** and **creation**, in Elizabethan writers, are pejorative:

> Or art thou but
> A Dagger of the Mind, a false Creation,
> Proceeding from the heat-oppressed Brain. (*Macbeth*)
> This is the very coinage of your Brain:

> This bodiless Creation extasie
> Is very cunning in. (*Hamlet*)
> Are you a God? Would you create me new? (*Comedy of Errors*)
> Translated thus from poor creature to a creator; for now must
> I create intolerable sort of lies. (*Every Man in his Humour*)

Indeed the clearest extension of **create**, without unfavorable implications, was to social rank, given by the authority of the monarch: "the King's Grace created him Duke" (1495); "I create you Companions to our person" (*Cymbeline*). This is still not quite human making.

By 1C17, however, both **create** and **creation** can be found commonly in a modern sense, and during C18 each word acquired a conscious association with ART, a word which was itself changing in a complementary direction. It was in relation to this, in C18, that **creative** was coined. Since the word evidently denotes a faculty, it had to wait on general acceptance of **create** and **creation** as human actions, without necessary reference to a past divine event. By 1815 Wordsworth could write confidently to the painter Haydon: "High is our calling, friend, Creative Art." This runs back to the earliest specific reference I have come across: "companion of the Muse, Creative Power, Imagination" (Mallet, 1728). (There is an earlier use of **creative** in Cudworth, 1678, but in a sentence still partly carrying the older sense: "this Divine, miraculous, creative power.") The decisive development was the conscious and then conventional association of **creative** with *art* and thought. By eC19 it was conscious and powerful; by mC19 conventional. **Creativity**, a general name for the faculty, followed in C20.

This is clearly an important and significant history, and in its emphasis on human capacity the term has become steadily more important. But there is one obvious difficulty. The word puts a necessary stress on originality and innovation, and when we remember the history we can see that these are not trivial claims. Indeed we try to clarify this by distinguishing between *innovation* and *novelty*, though *novelty* has both serious and trivial senses. The difficulty arises when a word once intended, and often still intended, to embody a high and serious claim, becomes so conventional, as a description of certain general kinds of activity, that it is applied to practices for which, in the absence of the convention, nobody would think of making such claims. Thus any imitative or stereotyped literary work can be called, by convention, **creative writing**, and advertising copywriters officially describe themselves as **creative**. Given the large elements of simple ideological and hegemonic reproduction in most of the written and visual arts, a description of everything of this kind as **creative** can be confusing and at times seriously misleading. Moreover, to the extent that **creative** becomes a cant word, it becomes difficult to think clearly about the emphasis which the word was intended to establish: on *human* making and innovation. The difficulty cannot be separated from the related difficulty of the senses of *imagination*, which can move towards *dreaming* and *fantasy*, with no necessary connection with the specific practices that are called *imaginative* or *creative arts*, or, on the other hand, towards *extension, innovation*, and *foresight*, which not only have practical implications and effects but can be tangible in some **creative** activities and works. The difficulty is especially apparent when **creative** is extended, rightly in terms of the historical development, to activities in thought, language, and social practice in which the specialized sense of *imagination* is not a necessary term. Yet such difficulties are inevitable when we realize the necessary magnitude and complexity of the interpretation of human activity which **creative** now so indispensably embodies.

RECENT DEVELOPMENTS

Creative remains a difficult word due to the semantic widening that it has undergone since C18, when it first acquired a conscious association with ART and LITERATURE. The word's rise in relative frequency beginning in eC20 can be attributed to its increasingly broad application to a variety of forms of visual art and writing, even those that one might consider more conventional than innovative. Alongside these positive or neutral applications of the word, there is also a negative sense of **creative**, implying deception, as in the phrase **creative accounting**, "the modification of accounts to achieve a desired end; falsification of accounts that is misleading but not necessarily illegal" (*OED*).

Over the past few decades, **creative** has become strongly linked to BUSINESS and advertising. Many companies now hire a **creative director**, which the *OED* first cites from 1938 and defines as "a person who oversees the creative elements or overall design of an organization's advertising, products, publications, etc." Thus, a **creative director** does not use his or her **creativity** to create art for art's sake, but to sell products or services and develop a company's BRAND IMAGE. Since mC20, the count noun **creative(s)** has also been commonly used to describe individuals who employ their **creativity** in a professional context, frequently for marketing or advertising purposes.

Examples of the **creative industries** include the visual and performing arts, computer software, fashion, music, film, and advertising, but definitions of the **creative industries** vary. Perhaps due to the vagueness of the adjective **creative**, the term **creative industries** itself is contested and sometimes used alongside related terms such as *cultural industries* and **creative economy**. Recently, a growing number of academic publications has noted the impact of the **creative industries** on economic WELL-BEING, especially in countries that have shifted from an industrial economy to a knowledge-based economy. Companies such as Google and Facebook have led the way in designing **creative workplaces** that aim to keep employees happy while improving their productivity and **creative output**.

See ART, BRAND, BUSINESS, IMAGE, LITERATURE

CREDIT

Credit is a key word that straddles the crucial changes that take place from C16 mercantilism (or merchant capitalism) to contemporary post-industrial capitalist political economy through the transformation of the concept's primary meaning from VALUE in general, with an emphasis on the ETHICAL, to a specific technical evaluation of monetary worth. It would not be too much of a stretch to argue that the trajectory of the narrowing meaning of **credit**, together with semantically similar words such as *worth*, reflect the reductive economization of value itself. This is not to suggest that **credit** had no financial connotations in C15: as **creditee** (1541) and **creditor** (?1435) demonstrate, there has been a parallel strand of meaning that related directly to money and finance. Yet, of the two clearly divergent meanings, which coexisted less than easily, it appears that since lC19 the purely economic has become dominant. **Credit**, in this now dominant use, is seen as a euphemism for money specifically, and for WEALTH in general.

Striking evidence for the narrowing and control of the polysemy of this word comes from the adjective **creditworthy**. In C16 and C17, to be **creditworthy** meant to be "deserving to be believed, credible, trustworthy," such as in "reported by credit-worthy writers" (1639). However, by C19, the primary meaning had shifted to "deserving or qualified to receive financial credit," such as, "In the greater number of cases in which parties obtained credit, they did so by attempting to show that they were credit-worthy" (1840). In the latter example, both **credit** and **creditworthy** are specifically financial terms. Derivatives such as **creditworthiness** (lC19) further exemplify this specialization of meaning.

The noun **credit** reached English from Middle French *credit* and Italian *credito*, which was in turn derived from Classical Latin *creditum*. The verb form of the word owes its origin to Latin *crēdit-*, past participial stem of *crēdere*, "to have faith or confidence in, to trust, to believe," also "to entrust, to lend (money) to, to give credit"; this comes ultimately from the same Indo-European base as Sanskrit *śrad*, trust, faith, and Early Irish *creitid*, believes. The word's semantic trajectory from (religious) belief and trust to trustworthiness in general, and then to quantifiable monetary worth clearly reflects the overall shift in emphasis from the extra-economic to the economic coding of value, from use to exchange value.

The general sense of **credit** as a verb—"to accept as true or truthful, give credence to, believe" in someone or something—existed alongside the BUSINESS and financial sense of monetary viability and its corollary, the ability to viably incur debt, from C16 onward. However, this limited financial usage, as well as additional accounting applications, takes center stage from C18 onward, with a corresponding decline in the general use. The *OED* even suggests that two of the more generally positive meanings of **credit** used transitively—"to bring into good repute or estimation" and "to accept as true or truthful"—are now either rare or used negatively.

Thus, while Samuel Johnson could write positively in 1758, "I . . . am content to credit my senses," by C19 all the citations are in negative constructions or express incredulity, as for instance when James Bryce in the *Holy Roman Empire* writes in 1864, "If we may credit Theophanes" or when Charles Gillispie states ". . . he could not credit the Trinity" in 1960. Most explicit is the 1964 citation from the *Listener*: "Governments are more likely to be discredited or credited (if I may revive a neglected use of this positive), through the gossip of civil servants in the Inner Circle of London."

Even the derivative **creditable** no longer carries the C17 meaning of bringing honor and being praiseworthy, as it gradually came to be used in a much weaker sense to signify acceptable, not outstanding, performance. The shift can best be seen as the change from "Whatsoever is just, honest, and Creditable" (1691) to "So, with the bow-oar unmanned, the race began, the crew hopeless of more than a creditable defeat" (1900). Yet, despite this attenuation, **creditable** and its derivatives remain the only consistent non-economic domains of this concept.

Further indication of the relatively recent transformation of **credit** into an almost exclusively financial term is the fact that **discredit**, an antonym formed by addition of the prefix *dis-* in the sense of "with privative sense, implying removal, aversion, negation, reversal of action" still retains an ethical/moral sense, with only one of the four main meanings relating to business and finance. Even here, though, **discredit** has a relatively new and developing financial sense, as in "To discredit the currency was an offence under the Defence of the Realm Act" (1927).

A more telling example is **letter of credit** recorded in mC16, where **credit** is used in the sense of "the quality of being generally believed or credited; reputation for truthfulness, accuracy, or honesty; trustworthiness, credibility." **Letter of credit** is now overwhelmingly confined (except in the specialist diplomatic sense of **accreditation**) to a document written by one bank to another guaranteeing payment on behalf of a customer for a specified quantum of money. Benjamin Franklin famously said, "Remember that credit is money," even though, as Charles Dickens averred, it operates when "a person who can't pay, gets another person who can't pay, to guarantee that he can pay" (*Little Dorrit*).

Credit, both as noun and verb, has now become primarily a monetary term, and its early use, which is closely related to trust, credibility, and credence, has become secondary. In order to serve this newer range of meanings, **credit** has formed a set of exclusively finance-related compounds such as **credit report**, **credit rating**, **credit transfer**, **credit line**, **credit history**, **credit check**, and **credit squeeze** (or **crunch**), which have entered everyday parlance. The need to further nuance and extend these senses of **credit** as, in effect, money, in turn has led to compounding phrases such as **credit card** (1867) into subsidiary compounds such as **credit card company**, **credit card details**, **credit card-sized**, and **credit card number**. The timing is, of course, fundamental; all the compounds have their first recorded use in mC20. However, general corpora indicate that there is a dramatic rise from the 1980s onward, marking the clear links between (economic) **credit** as unbound money and globalization.

Credit is thus a foundational word of our times because it demonstrates the relationship between meaning-making (and making meaning stick), where the material dictates the metaphorical, and yet where no subordinated meaning is entirely lost. Thus, while **credit** as economic and mainly monetary worth dominates, **discredit** still maintains its general use, and **credit** as a transitive verb—used with to, for, or with—has continued its positive general attribution (from mC16 onward) of "a quality, achievement, award, of the conferment of praise, as well as to confirm as true." There is an unintended double-edgedness now in John Dewey's "No man's credit is as good as his money," for on the one hand, **credit** is better than cash, while on the other, it remains entirely outside it.

See BUSINESS, ETHICAL, VALUE, WEALTH

CULTURE

Culture is one of the two or three most complicated words in the English language. This is so partly because of its intricate historical development, in several European languages, but mainly because it has now come to be used for important concepts in several distinct intellectual disciplines and in several distinct and incompatible systems of thought.

The fw is *cultura*, L, from rw *colere*, L. *Colere* had a range of meanings: inhabit, cultivate, protect, honor with worship. Some of these meanings eventually separated, though still with occasional overlapping, in the derived nouns. Thus "inhabit" developed through *colonus*, L to *colony*. "Honor with worship" developed through *cultus*, L, to *cult*. *Cultura* took on the main meaning of cultivation or tending, including, as in Cicero, *cultura animi*, though with subsidiary medieval meanings of honor and worship (cf. in English **culture** as "worship" in Caxton, 1483). The French forms of *cultura* were *couture*, oF, which has since developed its own specialized meaning, and later *culture*, which by eC15 had passed into English. The primary meaning was then in husbandry, the tending of natural growth.

Culture in all its early uses was a noun of process: the tending *of* something, basically crops or animals. The subsidiary *coulter*—ploughshare, had travelled by a different linguistic route, from *culter*, L—ploughshare, *culter*, OE, to the variant English spellings *culter, colter, coulter* and as late as eC17 **culture** (Webster, *Duchess of Malfi*, III, ii: "hot burning cultures"). This provided a further basis for the important next stage of meaning, by metaphor. From eC16 the tending of natural growth was extended to a process of human development, and this, alongside the original meaning in husbandry, was the main sense until 1C18 and eC19. Thus More: "to the culture and profit of their minds"; Bacon: "the culture and manurance of minds" (1605); Hobbes: "a culture of their minds" (1651); Johnson: "she neglected the culture of her understanding" (1759). At various points in this development two crucial changes occurred: first, a degree of habituation to the metaphor, which made the sense of human tending direct; second, an extension of particular processes to a general process, which the word could abstractly carry. It is of course from the latter development that the independent noun **culture** began its complicated modern history, but the process of change is so intricate, and the latencies of meaning are at times so close, that it is not possible to give any definite date. **Culture** as an independent noun, an abstract process or the product of such a process, is not important before 1C18 and is not common before mC19. But the early stages of this development were not sudden. There is an interesting use in Milton, in the second (revised) edition of *The Readie and Easie Way to Establish a Free Commonwealth* (1660): "spread much more Knowledg and Civility, yea, Religion, through all parts of the Land, by communicating the natural heat of Government and Culture more distributively to all extreme parts, which now lie num and neglected." Here the metaphorical sense ("natural heat") still appears to be present, and *civility* (cf. CIV-ILIZATION) is still written where in C19 we would normally expect **culture**. Yet we can also read "government and culture" in a quite modern sense. Milton, from the tenor of his whole argument, is writing about a general social process, and this is a definite stage of development. In C18 England this general process acquired definite class associations though **cultivation** and **cultivated** were more commonly used for this. But there is a letter of 1730 (Bishop of Killala, to Mrs Clayton; cit Plumb, *England in the Eighteenth Century*) which has this clear sense: "it has not been customary for persons of either birth or culture to breed up their children to the Church." Akenside (*Pleasures of Imagination*, 1744) wrote: ". . . nor purple state nor culture can bestow." Wordsworth wrote "where grace of culture hath been utterly unknown" (1805), and Jane Austen (*Emma*, 1816) "every advantage of discipline and culture."

It is thus clear that **culture** was developing in English towards some of its modern senses before the decisive effects of a new social and intellectual movement. But to follow the development through this movement, in 1C18 and eC19, we have to look also at developments in other languages and especially in German.

In French, until C18, **culture** was always accompanied by a grammatical form indicating the matter being cultivated, as in the English usage already noted. Its occasional use as an independent noun dates from mC18, rather later than similar occasional uses in English. The independent noun *civilization* also emerged in mC18; its relationship to **culture** has since been very complicated (cf. CIVILIZA-TION and discussion below). There was at this point an important development in German: the word was borrowed from French, spelled first (1C18) *Cultur* and from C19 *Kultur*. Its main use was still as a synonym for *civilization*: first in the abstract sense of a general process of becoming "civilized" or "cultivated"; second, in the sense which had already been established for *civilization* by the historians of the

Enlightenment, in the popular C18 form of the universal histories, as a description of the secular process of human development. There was then a decisive change of use in Herder. In his unfinished *Ideas on the Philosophy of the History of Mankind* (1784–91) he wrote of *Cultur*: "nothing is more indeterminate than this word, and nothing more deceptive than its application to all nations and periods." He attacked the assumption of the universal histories that "civilization" or "culture"—the historical self-development of HUMANITY—was what we would now call a unilinear process, leading to the high and dominant point of C18 European culture. Indeed he attacked what he called European subjugation and domination of the four quarters of the globe, and wrote:

> Men of all the quarters of the globe, who have perished over the ages, you
> have not lived solely to manure the earth with your ashes, so that at the
> end of time your posterity should be made happy by European culture.
> The very thought of a superior European culture is a blatant insult to the
> majesty of Nature.

It is then necessary, he argued, in a decisive innovation, to speak of "cultures" in the plural: the specific and variable cultures of different nations and periods, but also the specific and variable cultures of social and economic groups within a nation. This sense was widely developed, in the Romantic movement, as an alternative to the orthodox and dominant "*civilization*." It was first used to emphasize national and traditional cultures, including the new concept of **folk-culture**. It was later used to attack what was seen as the "MECHANICAL" character of the new civilization then emerging: both for its abstract rationalism and for the "inhumanity" of current industrial development. It was used to distinguish between "human" and "material" development. Politically, as so often in this period, it veered between radicalism and reaction and very often, in the confusion of major social change, fused elements of both. (It should also be noted, though it adds to the real complication, that the same kind of distinction, especially between "material" and "spiritual" development, was made by von Humboldt and others, until as late as 1900, with a reversal of the terms, **culture** being material and *civilization* spiritual. In general, however, the opposite distinction was dominant.)

On the other hand, from the 1840s in Germany, *Kultur* was being used in very much the sense in which *civilization* had been used in C18 universal histories. The

decisive innovation is G. F. Klemm's *Allgemeine Kulturgeschichte der Menschheit*—
"General Cultural History of Mankind" (1843–52)—which traced human development from savagery through domestication to freedom. Although the American
anthropologist Morgan, tracing comparable stages, used "Ancient *Society*," with a
culmination in *Civilization*, Klemm's sense was sustained, and was directly followed
in English by Tylor in *Primitive Culture* (1870). It is along this line of reference that
the dominant sense in modern social sciences has to be traced.

The complexity of the modern development of the word, and of its modern
usage, can then be appreciated. We can easily distinguish the sense which
depends on a literal continuity of physical process as now in "sugar-beet culture"
or, in the specialized physical application in bacteriology since the 1880s, "germ
culture." But once we go beyond the physical reference, we have to recognize
three broad active categories of usage. The sources of two of these we have already discussed: (i) the independent and abstract noun which describes a general
process of intellectual, spiritual, and aesthetic development, from C18; (ii) the
independent noun, whether used generally or specifically, which indicates a particular way of life, whether of a people, a period, a group, or humanity in general,
from Herder and Klemm. But we have also to recognize (iii) the independent
and abstract noun which describes the works and practices of intellectual and
especially artistic activity. This seems often now the most widespread use: **culture** is music, literature, painting and sculpture, theatre, and film. A **Ministry of
Culture** refers to these specific activities, sometimes with the addition of philosophy, scholarship, history. This use, (iii), is in fact relatively late. It is difficult
to date precisely because it is in origin an applied form of sense (i): the idea of a
general process of intellectual, spiritual, and aesthetic development was applied
and effectively transferred to the works and practices which represent and sustain it. But it also developed from the earlier sense of process; cf. "progressive
culture of fine arts," Millar, *Historical View of the English Government*, IV, 314
(1812). In English (i) and (iii) are still close; at times, for internal reasons, they
are indistinguishable as in Arnold, *Culture and Anarchy* (1867); while sense (ii)
was decisively introduced into English by Tylor, *Primitive Culture* (1870), following Klemm. The decisive development of sense (iii) in English was in 1C19
and eC20.

Faced by this complex and still active history of the word, it is easy to react by
selecting one "true" or "proper" or "scientific" sense and dismissing other senses
as loose or confused. There is evidence of this reaction even in the excellent study

by Kroeber and Kluckhohn, *Culture: A Critical Review of Concepts and Definitions*, where usage in North American anthropology is in effect taken as a norm. It is clear that, within a discipline, conceptual usage has to be clarified. But in general it is the range and overlap of meanings that is significant. The complex of senses indicates a complex argument about the relations between general human development and a particular way of life, and between both and the works and practices of art and intelligence. It is especially interesting that in archaeology and in *cultural anthropology* the reference to **culture** or a **culture** is primarily to *material* production, while in history and *cultural studies* the reference is primarily to *signifying* or *symbolic* systems. This often confuses but even more often conceals the central question of the relations between "material" and "symbolic" production, which in some recent argument—cf. my own *Culture*—have always to be related rather than contrasted. Within this complex argument there are fundamentally opposed as well as effectively overlapping positions; there are also, understandably, many unresolved questions and confused answers. But these arguments and questions cannot be resolved by reducing the complexity of actual usage. This point is relevant also to uses of forms of the word in languages other than English, where there is considerable variation. The anthropological use is common in the German, Scandinavian, and Slavonic language groups, but it is distinctly subordinate to the senses of art and learning, or of a general process of human development, in Italian and French. Between languages as within a language, the range and complexity of sense and reference indicate both difference of intellectual position and some blurring or overlapping. These variations, of whatever kind, necessarily involve alternative views of the activities, relationships, and processes which this complex word indicates. The complexity, that is to say, is not finally in the word but in the problems which its variations of use significantly indicate.

It is necessary to look also at some associated and derived words. **Cultivation** and **cultivated** went through the same metaphorical extension from a physical to a social or educational sense in C17, and were especially significant words in C18. Coleridge, making a classical eC19 distinction between civilization and culture, wrote (1830): "the permanent distinction, and occasional contrast, between cultivation and civilization." The noun in this sense has effectively disappeared but the adjective is still quite common, especially in relation to manners and tastes. The important adjective **cultural** appears to date from the 1870s; it became common by the 1890s. The word is only available, in its modern sense, when the independent noun, in the artistic and intellectual or anthropological senses, has become familiar.

Hostility to the word **culture** in English appears to date from the controversy around Arnold's views. It gathered force in 1C19 and eC20, in association with a comparable hostility to *aesthete* and *aesthetic*. Its association with class distinction produced the mime-word *culchah*. There was also an area of hostility associated with anti-German feeling, during and after the 1914–18 War, in relation to propaganda about *Kultur*. The central area of hostility has lasted, and one element of it has been emphasized by the recent American phrase **culture-vulture**. It is significant that virtually all the hostility (with the sole exception of the temporary anti-German association) has been connected with uses involving claims to superior knowledge (cf. the noun *intellectual*), refinement (*culchah*), and distinctions between "high" art (**culture**) and popular art and entertainment. It thus records a real social history and a very difficult and confused phase of social and cultural development. It is interesting that the steadily extending social and anthropological use of **culture** and **cultural** and such formations as **subculture** (the culture of a distinguishable smaller group) has, except in certain areas (notably popular entertainment), either bypassed or effectively diminished the hostility and its associated unease and embarrassment. The recent use of *culturalism*, to indicate a methodological contrast with *structuralism* in social analysis, retains many of the earlier difficulties, and does not always bypass the hostility.

Recent Developments

Culture has doubled in use over the last four decades, and the complexity and contradictions to which Williams refers have not diminished. One new usage, whereby **culture** simply refers to contemporary **popular culture**, has complicated the arguments still further: "In 15 years culture has moved from the most sublime performances of opera, dance and classical music to street parties, social inclusion, and fun" (*Financial Times*, January 27, 2001). This development, linked to the institutionalization of **cultural studies** as a separate discipline, often goes together with an opposition and hostility to traditional ART, stigmatized as ELITE. However, in anthropology the emphasis on **material culture** remains dominant and in the humanities more generally an emphasis on **culture** may mean an attention to **material culture** or, less specifically, the placing of traditional elite works of art within a more extensive social and historical frame.

    Culture war(s) (1879), a borrowing modeled on the German *Kulturkampf*, has been significant in US English. Used in the late 1920s to describe the developments that had seen urban and rural values diverge, it resurfaced in the last three decades to describe new realities. It was used to describe debates within the humanities which pitted new theoretical approaches against traditional forms of interpretation. Soon, however, it became the shorthand for an argument that traditional or class politics had been displaced by a struggle between differing worldviews in which attitudes toward abortion, homosexuality, gun control, recreational drugs, and similar issues were now the center of political debate.

In general discourse, **culture** has been used to abolish or ignore the conventional distinction between high art and low entertainment. A significant example of this was the *Sunday Times'* decision to rebrand its books and review section "**Culture**" in 1992. In many ways the contemporary uses of **culture** have realized Williams's definition of **culture** as a "whole way of life." At the same time the question of the relations between **material** and **symbolic culture** and the further question of how we are to value the variety of **cultural productions** remain as pressing as when Williams wrote.

See APPROPRIATION, ART, CIVILIZATION, ELITE, HISTORY, HUMANITY, WEST

DEMOCRACY

Democracy is a very old word but its meanings have always been complex. It came into English in C16, from fw *démocratie*, F, *democratia*, mL—a translation of *demokratia*, Gk, from rw *demos*—people, *kratos*—rule. It was defined by Elyot, with specific reference to the Greek instance, in 1531: "an other publique weal was amonge the Atheniensis, where equalitie was of astate among the people. . . . This manner of governaunce was called in greke *Democratia*, in latine, *Popularis potentia*, in englisshe the rule of the comminaltie." It is at once evident from Greek uses that everything depends on the senses given to *people* and to *rule*. Ascribed and doubtful early examples range from obeying "no master but the law" (? Solon) to "of the people, by the people, for the people" (? Cleon). More certain examples compare "the insolence of a despot" with "the insolence of the unbridled commonalty" (cit. Herodotus) or define a government as democracy "because its administration is in the hands, not of the few, but of the many"; also, "all that is opposed to despotic power, has the name of democracy" (cit. Thucydides). Aristotle (*Politics*, IV, 4) wrote: "a democracy is a state where the freemen and the poor, being in the majority, are invested with the power of the state." Yet much depends here on what is meant by "invested with the power": whether it is ultimate sovereignty or, at the other extreme, practical and unshared rule. Plato made Socrates say (in *Republic*, VIII, 10) that "democracy comes into being after the poor have conquered their opponents, slaughtering some and banishing some, while to the remainder they give an equal share of freedom and power."

This range of uses, near the roots of the term, makes any simple derivation impossible. It can, however, be said at once that several of these uses—and especially those which indicate a form of popular class rule—are at some distance from any orthodox modern "Western" definition of **democracy**. Indeed the emergence of that orthodox definition, which has its own uncertainties, is what needs to be traced. "Democracy" is now often traced back to medieval precedents and given a Greek authority. But the fact is that, with only occasional exceptions, **democracy**, in the records that we have, was until C19 a strongly unfavorable term, and it is only since 1C19 and eC20 that a majority of political parties and tendencies have united in declaring their belief in it. This is the most striking historical fact.

Aquinas defined **democracy** as popular power, where the ordinary people, by force of numbers, governed—oppressed—the rich; the whole people acting like a tyrant. This strong class sense remained the predominant meaning until 1C18 and eC19, and was still active in mC19 argument. Thus: "Democracie, when the multitude have government," Fleming (1576); "democratie, where free and poore men being the greater number, are lords of the estate" (1586); "democracy . . . nothing else than the power of the multitude," Filmer, *Patriarcha* (1680). To this definition of the *people* as the *multitude* there was added a common sense of the consequent type of *rule*: a **democracy** was a state in which all had the right to rule and did actually rule; it was even contrasted (e.g., by Spinoza) with a state in which there was rule by representatives, including elected representatives. It was in this sense that the first political constitution to use the term **democracy**—that of Rhode Island in 1641—understood it: "popular government; that is to say it is in the power of the body of freemen orderly assembled, or a major part of them, to make or constitute just Lawes, by which they will be regulated, and to depute from among themselves such ministers as shall see them faithfully executed between man and man."

This final clause needs to be emphasized, since a new meaning of democracy was eventually arrived at by an alteration of the practice here indicated. In the case of Rhode Island, the people or a major part of them made laws in orderly assembly; the ministers "faithfully executed" them. This is not the same as the **representative democracy** defined by Hamilton in 1777. He was referring to the earlier sense of **democracy** when he observed that "when the deliberative or judicial powers are vested wholly or partly in the collective body of the people, you must expect error, confusion and instability. But a representative democracy, where the right of election is well secured and regulated, and the exercise of the legislative executive and judicial authorities is vested in select persons ... etc." It is from this altered American use that a dominant modern sense developed. Bentham formulated a general sense of democracy as rule by the majority of the people, and then distinguished between "direct democracy" and "representative democracy," recommending the latter because it provided continuity and could be extended to large societies. These important practical reasons have since been both assumed and dropped, so that in mC20 an assertion of **democracy** in the Rhode Island sense, or in Bentham's *direct* sense, could be described as "anti-democratic," since the first principle of **democracy** is taken to be rule by elected representatives. The practical arguments are of course serious, and in some circumstances decisive, but one of the two most significant changes in the meaning of **democracy** is this exclusive association with one of its derived forms, and the attempted exclusion of one of its original forms; at one period, its only form.

The second major change has to do with interpretation of *the people*. There is some significant history in the various attempts to limit "the people" to certain qualified groups: freemen, owners of property, the wise, white men, men, and so on. Where **democracy** is defined by a process of election, such limited constitutions can be claimed to be fully **democratic**: the mode of choosing representatives is taken as more important than the proportion of "the people" who have any part in this. The development of democracy is traced through institutions using this mode rather than through the relations between all the people and a form of government. This interpretation is orthodox in most accounts of the development of English democracy. Indeed **democracy** is said to have been "extended" stage by stage, where what is meant is clearly the right to vote for representatives rather than the old (and until eC19 normal English) sense of *popular power*. The distinction became critical in the period of the French Revolution. Burke was expressing an orthodox view when he wrote that "a perfect democracy" was "the most shameless thing in the world" (*Reflections on the Revolution in France*, 1790), for **democracy** was taken to be "uncontrolled" popular power under which, among other things, minorities (including especially the minority which held substantial property) would be suppressed or oppressed. **Democracy** was still a revolutionary or at least a radical term to mC19, and the specialized development of **representative democracy** was at least in part a conscious reaction to this, over and above the practical reasons of extent and continuity.

It is from this point in the argument that two modern meanings of **democracy** can be seen to diverge. In the socialist tradition, **democracy** continued to mean *popular power*: a state in which the interests of the majority of the people were paramount and in which these interests were practically exercised and controlled by the majority. In the liberal tradition, **democracy** meant open election of representatives and certain conditions (**democratic rights**, such as free speech) which maintained the openness of election and political argument. These two conceptions, in their extreme forms, now confront each other as enemies. If the predominant criterion is popular power in the popular interest, other criteria are often taken as secondary (as in the **People's Democracies**) and their emphasis is specialized to "capitalist democracy" or "bourgeois democracy." If the predominant criteria are elections and free speech, other criteria are seen as secondary or are rejected; an attempt to exercise popular power in the popular interest, for example by a General Strike, is described as **anti-democratic**, since **democracy** has already been assured by other means; to claim economic EQUALITY as the essence of democracy is seen as leading to "chaos" or to **totalitarian democracy** or *government by trade unions*. These positions, with their many minor variants, divide the modern meanings of **democracy** between them, but this is not usually seen as historical variation of the term; each position, normally, is described as "the only true meaning," and the alternative use is seen as propaganda or hypocrisy.

Democratic (from eC19) is the normal adjective for one or other of these kinds of belief or institution. But two further senses should be noted. There is an observable use of **democratic** to describe the conditions of open argument, without necessary reference to elections or to power. Indeed, in one characteristic use, freedom of speech and assembly are *the* "democratic rights," sufficient in themselves, without reference to the institution or character of political power. This is a limiting sense derived from the liberal emphasis, which in its full form has to include election and popular sovereignty (though not popular rule) but which often opposes sustained **democratic** activity, such as challenges to an elected *leader* or his policies on other than formal or "appropriate" occasions. There is also a derived sense from the early class reference to the "multitude": to be **democratic**, to have **democratic** manners or feelings, is to be unconscious of class distinctions, or consciously to disregard or overcome them in everyday behavior: acting *as if* all people were equal, and deserved equal respect, whether this is really so or not. Thus a man might be on "plain and natural" terms with everyone he met, and might further believe in free speech and free assembly, yet, following only these senses, could for example oppose universal suffrage, let alone government directed solely to the interests of the majority. The senses have in part been extended, in part moved away, from what was formerly and is probably still the primary sense of the character of political power. Meanwhile *demagogy* and *demagogie*, fw *demagogós*, Gk, rw *demos*—people, *agogós*—leader, *agein*—lead, carried from the Greek the predominantly unfavorable sense, of "irresponsible agitator" rather than "popular leader," in a familiar kind of political prejudice. It was used similarly in English from C17, and cf. *agitator*, first used in the sense of "agent" by soldiers' delegates in the Parliament of 1647–9, but given its derogatory sense mainly from C18.

No questions are more difficult than those of **democracy**, in any of its central senses. Analysis of variation will not resolve them, though it may sometimes clarify them. To the positive opposed senses of the socialist and liberal traditions we have to add, in a century which unlike any other finds nearly all political movements claiming to stand for **democracy** or **real democracy**, innumerable conscious distortions: reduction of the concepts of *election, representation*, and *mandate* to deliberate formalities or merely manipulated forms; reduction of the concept of *popular power*, or government in the *popular interest*, to nominal slogans covering the rule of a bureaucracy or an oligarchy. It would sometimes be easier to believe in democracy, or to stand for it, if the C19 change had not happened and it were still an unfavorable or factional term. But that history has occurred, and the range of contemporary sense is its confused and still active record.

RECENT DEVELOPMENTS

The simple equation of **democracy** with **representative democracy** and with regular elections has, if anything, solidified over the last forty years. In appealing to an alternative **socialist democracy** as a form of power in which the interests of the majority of the people are paramount, Williams continues an argument that dates back to the Soviet Revolution of October 1917. In particular, it evokes Lenin's call for power to pass from the representative Constituent Assembly to workers' councils ("soviets") so that a STATE based on individual citizenship would be replaced by one organized by CLASS power. However, in the Soviet Bloc of **People's Democracies** to which Williams makes explicit reference, "the interests of the majority of the people" were not paramount, and the democratic RIGHTS of FREEDOM of speech and assembly did not exist.

Since the collapse of the Soviet Bloc, even the theoretical opposition between a **socialist direct democracy** and a **liberal representative democracy** has disappeared. **Liberal representative democracy** is widely held to be the optimum form of government in the world today. However, this dominance is accompanied by ever greater discontent with the political ELITES that form in representative democracies and with the dominant role of MEDIA and money in their functioning. In both the United States and Europe, this discontent may explain the marked increase of referendums, which function as a form of **direct democracy**.

While there is no serious questioning of **democracy** as a desirable form of government, there is also remarkably little debate as to what **democracy** might mean other than regular elections, nor even how referendums are compatible with **representative democracy**. This has been particularly evident in debates about the European Union where those who argue that the European Union suffers from a **democratic deficit** in which formal democratic processes lack any substance rarely ask the same questions about national democracies.

See CLASS, COMMON, EQUALITY, FREEDOM, LIBERAL, POLITICAL, POPULAR, RIGHTS, SOCIALIST

DEPRESSION

Depression is a word that names our most common mental illness and the most feared part of the economic cycle. Both of these meanings are relatively recent developments of a word that entered English as a technical term in astronomy in lC14. It is derived from the Latin verb *deprimere* "to press down," and the *OED* gives the most general meaning of the word as "the action of depressing, or the condition of being depressed; a depressed formation; that which is depressed in various senses (Opp to elevation)."

The verb is based on one of the most fundamental of spatial oppositions: that between up and down. This opposition stands at the root of its use in astronomy; in gunnery it means lowering the muzzle below the horizontal; in surgery it names an operation for cataracts; in meteorology, low pressure. There is an associated figurative use that refers to the fact or condition of being brought low, for which the first instance in the *OED* is a set of appositions "aduersite, tribulacion, worldlye depression" from 1531. But the *OED* notes this use as rare.

Depression enters common circulation toward the end of C18 with the meaning of a lowering of economic activity. Its first recorded use in the *OED* is 1793, and in 1819 President Monroe eschewed the then customary word for economic crisis, *panic*, by referring to the contemporary crisis as a **depression**. Although the British economic crisis of lC19 was referred to as the Great Depression, the term crystallized in its use with the publication of Lionel Robbins's 1934 book entitled *The Great Depression*. Curiously enough, and this may be a recurring feature of the word, the economic misery captured by the term was so widely felt and feared that the term no longer has any precise description. The National Bureau of Economic Research, the body charged with measuring and evaluating the American economy, does not use the term, thus ensuring, at least at one level, that we will never again suffer from **economic depression**; however, a drop of more than 10% in productive capacity or a recession lasting more than two years is generally considered a **depression**. In many ways the term has become a historical description; all quotations in the *OED* refer to the worldwide **depression** of the 1930s, which saw an unparalleled fall in productive activity in all the major economies. Frequency of use of **economic depression** tends to fall sharply in use from 1940 onward. Perhaps like *panic* (but unlike *recession*), **depression** as an economic term has run its course. Its related use as a meteorological term, which moves from a fall in the mercury in a barometer to the low atmospheric pressure which causes that fall, is still an absolute constant in the vocabulary of weather forecasters.

The dominant current meaning of **depression** comes latest in the *OED*. The general definition of "The condition of being depressed in spirits; dejection" certainly predates any medical diagnosis. It can be read, for example, in *Daniel Deronda* when George Eliot writes "he found her in a state of deep depression, overmastered by these distasteful miserable memories." But the use of the term as a definite medical diagnosis, "a sign of psychiatric disorder or a component of various psychoses, with symptoms of misery, anguish, or guilt accompanied by headache, insomnia, etc.," is not quoted by the *OED* before 1905.

The medical history is relatively straightforward. The German psychiatrist Emil Kraepelin's life project was to replace diagnosis in terms of symptoms with an understanding of patterns of behavior over time. In particular from 1893 he analyzed *psychosis*, heretofore a singular category, into two subcategories: *dementia praecox* and **manic depression**. Bleuler offered a powerful later reformulation in 1908, because of his objection to the word *dementia*, into a distinction between *schizophrenia* and **manic depression**. For all its difficulties—there is not one symptom that occurs in schizophrenia that cannot occur in **manic depression** and vice versa—this classification prevailed for almost all of C20. The term **depression** displaced the much older term *melancholia*.

Melancholia is part of the theory of the humors that dominated Mediterranean and Western European science from Galen until C19. The body was held to contain a mixture of four liquids: blood, phlegm, yellow bile, and black bile. A preponderance of black bile caused a melancholy mood or disposition. One striking difference between *melancholia* and **depression** is that *melancholy* could be given a positive aspect as a particularly keen appreciation of the changeability of life. Keats's "Ode on Melancholy" summarizes centuries of previous thinking when it claims that "In the very temple of Delight / Veil'd Melancholy has her sovran shrine." But while melancholy entered into a complex set of relationships with the world, based on the interrelated theories of humors, elements, and seasons, **depression** is part of the new world of clinical medicine. Modern odes to **depression** show none of Keats's ambiguity. Contemporary **depression** is unambiguously negative.

In a further development, **depression** becomes one of the defining modern states of being. A literary representation of this can be found in Jonathan Franzen's best-selling *The Corrections* (2001), where one of the leading characters is continuously plagued by the question of whether he is **depressed**. **Depression** has gained such negative overtones and, like the terms *manic* and *mania*, it has been so greatly stigmatized that the more clinical diagnostic term *bipolar disorder* was chosen in 1980 to replace the more emotionally loaded diagnosis of **manic depression** in the *Diagnostic and Statistical Manual of Mental Disorders* (DSM-III). The particular reasons why **depression** has come in and out of linguistic currency are complex, but one could certainly point to a general medicalization of the personality. In this context it may be significant that Freud, an opponent of the medicalization of mental illness, continued to use the older term *melancholia* long after **depression** had established itself as the dominant term.

The economic and psychological senses seem strongly compartmentalized. It is difficult to think of puns or other plays on words (William Empson's test of whether senses are in active relation) that mix the two senses.

DIASPORA

The frequency of the word **diaspora** has increased dramatically in the last thirty years. It has become a key term both to describe the vast movement of peoples that has accompanied contemporary globalization and to consider the key role that migration has played throughout human history. It takes its place in a constellation of words such as *migrant, exile, refugee* that attempt to capture the varying realities of the mass movement of peoples across the globe.

The term originates in relation to the history of the Jewish people. It is the Latin rendering of a Greek word formed from a preposition, "across," and a verb, "to scatter," which is used frequently in the Greek translation of the Hebrew Bible, produced in Alexandria around 250 BCE. Much of the force of the term is that over time it relates to both a literal and metaphorical "scattering" of the Jewish people in the world. Its most fundamental meaning is SPIRITUAL, referring to a punishment that God inflicts on the Jews for their failure to uphold the law, and its single most famous occurrence is Deuteronomy 28:25: "The Lord give thee up for slaughter before thine enemies: thou shalt go out against them one way, and flee from their face seven ways: and thou shalt be a *dispersion* in all the kingdoms of the earth." However, this spiritual punishment is conflated with the geographical dispersion of the Jews, especially the Babylonian captivity after the Jews were defeated by Nebuchadnezzar in 586 BCE and the destruction of the Jewish state by the Romans in 70 CE. **Diaspora** thus refers not only to the geographical condition of the Jewish people but also to their spiritual longing for the land from which they have been exiled.

With this meaning the word enters English in lC17, although it is also used to refer to early Christian communities. Very quickly from mC18 it came to be used for any geographically scattered people linked by nationality, ethnicity, or belief: "I fear not to risque the offence and vociferous repudiations of the disciples of . . . Voltaire and Rousseau. . . . The blaze of this little political diaspora of extravagant and self-opinionated philosophers . . . will . . . go out and evanish" (1794).

This extended sense is not frequent until the 1960s, when it becomes used in political debates about the ties that bind African Americans to Africa: "*Négritude* is claimed . . . equally in Africa and among the Negro diaspora" (1962). This political use feeds into academic debate, and from the 1980s **diaspora** becomes a key term in discussions about IDENTITY, spawning magazines, associations, conferences, and books. There is a constant tension evidenced by many articles on the meaning of **diaspora**, between **diaspora** as a descriptive and as an analytic term. Descriptively the term simply develops the extended use of mC18 and names any geographically scattered people. This very broad meaning is deployed, for example, by the Diaspora social network, which is designed to produce forms of web COMMUNICA-TION and COMMUNITY that bypass privately owned companies and where **diaspora** simply means a non-geographically centered community.

Many argue, however, that **diaspora** has real analytic power in the attempt to understand migrations, and that a set of criteria must be met before the term **diaspora** can be assigned. These criteria include that the original migration is coercive, whether that coercion is physical violence (the Babylonian captivity, the African slave trade), starvation (the Irish Famine and the subsequent migration to the United States), or overwhelming poverty (the Asian Indians who provided so much basic labor throughout the British Empire in C19 or the huge numbers of emigrants working overseas to send money back to their families in today's globalized economy). Some also argue that to count as a **diaspora**, migrants must not only maintain connections (either real or symbolic) to their homeland, but also make a full life for themselves within their new HOME (thus distinguishing **diaspora** from *exile*). Finally, it is argued that there must be links to other migrated communities as well as the homeland. While all of these arguments are important and illuminating in examining the variety of migrant experience, it is extremely doubtful whether they will succeed in displacing the very long established weak extended use of **diaspora**. They do, however, play an important role in elaborating accounts of political and symbolic identity that escape the simplistic and simplifying stereotypes of NATIONALISM.

These recent discussions of **diaspora** have proved of considerable political importance. When Mary Robinson, an academic lawyer, was elected president of Ireland in 1990, she made an explicit commitment that her presidency would include the tens of millions of members of the Irish **diaspora** living outside the Island of Ireland, and in 1995 she gave an address to both houses of Parliament titled "Cherishing the Irish Diaspora." Robinson's explicit ambition was to produce a definition of the Irish nation that did not depend on its borders, and in 1998 the Irish people voted to amend Article Two of its Constitution so that Ireland was no longer defined as one "national territory" and declared that "the Irish nation cherishes its special affinity with people of Irish ancestry living abroad who share its cultural identity and heritage."

Perhaps these academic debates have gained purchase in general discussion because **diaspora** has such firmly established meanings. The inability to fix its meanings in relation to particular theoretical or political arguments allows those theoretical and political arguments to use **diaspora** in such fertile ways.

See COMMUNICATION, COMMUNITY, HOME, IDENTITY, NATIONALIST

DIVERSITY

Diversity is an abstract noun formed on the adjective **diverse**. The adjective was borrowed into Middle English from Latin, along with the (now rare) variant form *divers*. It is typically used to describe populations with internal variation. Although **diverse** seems to have been always able to modify a singular noun, generally some plural population would have been implied. Thus, "she is diverse in her talents" would gloss as "her talents are diverse." Similarly, "her background is diverse" would gloss as "she has a diverse array of experiences in her background." Usages such as these are extremely common today. In addition, the construction "A is diverse from/to B" was used from Middle English onward, through at least to C19, glossed as "A is different from B," though that usage seems less common today. In late Middle English and Early Modern English, it was also possible to use *divers* (but not *diverse*) with the sense "different from, or opposed to what is right, good, or profitable." The *Historical Thesaurus of English* lists over sixty synonyms or near-synonyms for **diverse** since Old English, including *unlike, different,* and *sundry* from ME, and *distinct, disparate,* and *heterogeneous* from Early Modern English.

The term today seems overwhelmingly to be used in relation to human populations with particular types of internal demographic variation. It is not uncommon today, for instance, to refer to **a diverse city**, **a diverse neighborhood**, **a diverse society**, **a diverse student body**, **a diverse profession**, or **a diverse workforce**. In addition, it is quite common to specify how the given population is **diverse**, including by means of such adjective phrases as **racially diverse**, **ethnically diverse**, and **demographically diverse**, or by use of phrases such as nominalized **gender diversity**. Indeed, **diverse** today often implies variation within some notional or standard measure of human demographics. So, when television is **diverse**, this seems often to refer to programming representing human populations with specific types of internal variation: variation in terms of RACE or ethnicity, GENDER, sexual orientation, or ability/disability. **Diverse television**, reflecting this tendency, seems only rarely to refer to variation in terms of genre or other features, rather than population variation. In many instances, **diverse** can accordingly be used in alternation with *multicultural*, and in this way forms part of discourses of social and cultural contact, race, ethnicity, immigration, DIASPORA, and empire. **Diverse** can also be seen to alternate with *vibrant*, used as a term for populations noted for their internal racial or ethnic variation.

In very recent usage, **diverse** has become a descriptor of individuals without explicit reference to any comparator or population, referring instead to individuals showing some "non-normative" or marked characteristics. A **diverse group** can include an individual **diverse member**, for example. This use seems to be evidenced particularly strongly in the spheres of employment and education. It is possible to view the change, linguistically, as related to back-formation, from plural constructions referencing populations with internal variation, including **diverse candidates** and **diverse learners**, to singular constructions referencing the marked variant within the population, including **a diverse candidate** and **a diverse learner**. But while **diversity** of populations is often standardized and quantified (e.g., in measures of increasing or decreasing **diversity** in an elected parliament or city neighborhood), the **diversity** of an individual is not generally represented as quantified or variable, but as something absolute, defined by some assumed demographic benchmark.

The phrase **diverse candidates** refers to a candidate pool, in employment contexts, that exhibits a wide array of features: in particular, a population that contains not only a range of races and ethnicities but also other features, including variation by gender, sexual orientation, or disability. **Diverse candidate** emerges as the related term for a candidate from a minority demographic: that is, the marked or non-normative candidate. **Diverse** in this context seems in some uses a polite alternate for *non-normative*, or "drawn from the minority or underrepresented population." We find guides, for example, advising on "distinguishing yourself as a diverse candidate," while the normative or non-marked candidate within a **diverse** population is not referred to as a **diverse candidate**. The related noun phrase **diverse hire** (referring to a newly hired employee who is **diverse**, representing the minority demographic) is not uncommon in employment discourse and seems to be used similarly to, and in tandem with, **diverse candidate**.

By highlighting a **diverse candidate** and **diverse hire,** non-normative or marked individual attributes and representation of minority demographics may be incorporated into calculations of the value of labor. In fact, such features are used in discussions both for and against particular value associated with the **diverse candidate.** For example, race and disability can become measures of capital when embedded in discussion of "cost-per-diverse-hire"; and they can feature in strategic assessment of commercial advantages or disadvantages in hiring a non-normative or marked candidate. Such employment discourse focuses on the quantum of value of an individual worker with absolute demographic characteristics rather than on the value of a collective population of workers with its internal variation (or **diversity** in another sense). In relating the two, **diversity management** comes to be conceived as an important activity for organizations and businesses. Often supported by **diversity consultants,** such **diversity management** can consist of analyses of the capital value of a **diverse hire,** while also providing **diversity training** for employees who represent majority demographics in how to interact with a **diverse hire** representing a minority demographic.

Use of **diverse learner** has (in a manner similar to **diverse candidate**) also recently become common in pedagogical writing. **Diverse learner** emerges to characterize an individual learner who is non-normative or marked in some way, perhaps by race, ethnicity, gender, age, sexual orientation, or learning disabilities. The term is usually employed, significantly, alongside calls for empowerment of and support for such a non-normative learner. **Diverse learner** might have implied a different kind of relation to a wider population, referring to an individual who had taken an interesting and potentially enriching variety of educational paths. That sense, however, is quite discrete from the more recent **diverse learner** as a non-normative and typically underperforming member of an educational population.

Diverse, then, features importantly in a cluster of discourses representing the relationship between individuals and populations, and so interconnects with changing notions of COMMUNITIES, *collectives,* and *organization* in *society.* The challenge presented by the word reflects an underlying tension it mediates between multiple forms of variation, on one hand, and persistent emphasis on standardization, on the other. **Diversity** increasingly denotes variation in characteristics, lives, and jobs, which is nevertheless often defined against standard demographic measures of populations—which are then themselves subject to variation between *societies, cultures, subcultures,* and *states* in an increasingly interacting and potentially convergent globalized world.

Diversity is a particularly complex word, packing numerous equations of meaning into a single noun and its associated adjective. It is a way in which many of the complexities of multicultural and multiracial societies are both negotiated and obfuscated. Some of the overwhelmingly positive force of the word may derive from its use not in the social, but in the biological realm. The concept of **biodiversity** as the degree of variation of life forms within an ecosystem has mutated from biology into common parlance with incredible speed. As there has been a remorseless decline of biodiversity since the first recorded use of the term in 1985, an increase in **biodiversity** is seen as an unquestionable good.

See COMMUNITY, CULTURE, DIASPORA, GENDER, RACE

ECOLOGY

Ecology is not common in English before mC20, though its scientific use (originally as *oecology*) dates from the 1870s, mainly through translation from the German zoologist Haeckel. There is however one apparently isolated and curiously appropriate use in Thoreau, from 1858. It is from rw *oikos*, Gk—household, with the familiar ending *logy* from *logos*—discourse, thence systematic study. *Economy* shares its reference, with the alternative ending *nomy* (cf. *astronomy*) from *nomia*, Gk—management and *nomos*, Gk—law. *Economy* had developed from its early sense of management of a household (C16) to *political economy* (from F, C16–C17) and to *economics* in its general modern sense from 1C18. **Ecology** (Haeckel's *Ökologie*) developed the sense of *habitat* (a noun for a characteristic living place from C18, from the form of the Latin verb "it lives"), and became the study of the relations of plants and animals with each other and with their habitat. *Ecotone, ecotype, ecospecies* followed in scientific use. In 1931 H. G. Wells saw *economics* as a "branch of ecology . . . the ecology of the human species."

This anticipates important later developments, in which **ecology** is a more general social concern, but at first the commonest word for such concern with the human and natural habitat was *environmentalism*. Actually *environmentalism* had been more specific, as the doctrine of the influence of physical surroundings on development; it was at times associated with Lamarckian as opposed to Darwinian accounts of EVOLUTION. ENVIRONMENT dates from eC19, in the sense of surroundings, as in *environs* (fw *environner*, F—encircle, rw *viron*, oF—circuit); it was extended, as in Carlyle (1827): "environment of circumstances." *Environmentalist* and associated words became common from the 1950s to express concern with *conservation* ("preservation") and measures against pollution. **Ecology** and its associated words largely replaced the *environment* grouping from the late 1960s, continuing but also extending these positions. It is from this period that we find *ecocrisis, ecocatastrophe, ecopolitics,* and *ecoactivist,* and the more deliberate formation of **ecology** groups and parties. Economics, politics, and social theory are reinterpreted by this important and still growing tendency, from a central concern with human relations to the physical world as the necessary basis for social and economic policy.

RECENT DEVELOPMENTS

Ecology was one of the twenty-one words that Raymond Williams added to *Keywords* between 1976 and 1983. In 1976 **ecology** was a relatively new word to describe a political concern with the relations between human society and the ENVIRONMENT. By 1983 it was well established as a significant element in the POLITICAL landscape. In 2016 there are **ecological** or *green* parties in much of the world.

The scientific subject explicitly established by Haeckel in 1866 (but arguably present as an idea, if not a name, for many previous biologists) has grown exponentially since mC20 and, with animal ethology on one side and evolutionary theory on the other, makes up a significant element of contemporary biology. Although concerns about the environment stretch back to the beginning of industrialization, **ecology** made the leap from science to political discourse in the 1960s. The single book most connected to that leap is Rachel Carson's *Silent Spring* (1962), which traced the disastrous effects of pesticides on bird life. Since then, **ecology** has become an ever greater part of political discourse from animal conservation to climate change, and it now figures in almost any major political discussion from national elections to international diplomacy. One crucial date was the establishment in 1971 of Greenpeace, for decades the most visible among what is now a host of charities and organizations devoted to **ecological** concerns. In 1985 the British Ecology Party changed its name to the Green Party and by 2000 most political movements inspired by **ecological** concerns called themselves "Green," although this international movement lacks unanimity about both strategy and tactics.

One striking development in **ecological** thinking is "**deep ecology**," a term coined by Arne Naess in 1973. For Naess, **ecology** must give up any anthropocentric perspectives, inevitably too materialistic and consumer-oriented, in favor of the perspective of the planet itself in which human beings have no special value. Similar in many of its emphases to that section of the animal rights movement which believes that humans have no necessary priority over animals, **deep ecology** is the most radical element within a wide range of political argument that claim to be **ecological**.

Ecology is a word that steadily increased in frequency from 1900 to 1950 but has since mC20 increased even more dramatically. Its uses in science and politics are undoubtedly the two major factors in this astonishing growth, but it has also lent itself to figurative uses, as in **media ecology** or **urban ecology**, in which attention to systematic relationships is seen as more productive of understanding than the concentration on individual elements.

See CONSUMER, ENVIRONMENT, EVOLUTION, NATURE, ORGANIC, SUSTAINABLE

EDUCATION

In the original *Keywords,* Raymond Williams includes a short entry for **educated**, which considers related forms like **uneducated** and **over-** and **half-educated.** These socially sensitive terms reveal class-related tensions, but semantically far more problematic is **education. Education** is recognized by the United Nations as a fundamental human right, which is "essential for the exercise of all other human rights" and "promotes individual freedom and empowerment." Yet it is not always clear what **education** means: the term itself is both polysemous and vague, encompassing concepts from formal instruction and its goals to unstructured "real world" learning.

Education is borrowed into English from Middle French and Latin at the beginning of the early modern period. The earliest example in the *OED* is dated 1527; the first citation for the verb form **educate** is slightly earlier, in 1445, although according to corpora this form is much less frequent than the noun in current British and US English. Etymologically, **education** ultimately comes from Latin *educare*, "to rear, bring up (children, young animals)," related to *ēdūcĕre* "to draw out, lead forth." It is common for writers to refer to the etymology of the term as a justification for their view of the "true" meaning of **education**; for example, the author of one website comments that "[i]t is my belief that the essence of education is a process of drawing forth the best in each human being." In early use, **education** often refers to processes that apply to children. This is still strongly implied in many later uses, although the preceding example, along with current collocations like **adult education** and **continuing education**, shows that it has widened semantically.

In contemporary society, the term **education** is at the center of cultural and political debate, and it is often difficult to pin down its meaning in particular uses. The term is most frequently used with the *OED* sense, "The systematic instruction, teaching, or training in various academic and non-academic subjects given to or received by a child, typically at a school; the course of scholastic instruction a person receives in his or her lifetime," which is attested almost as early as other senses in English (1536). This shows a narrowing from another early use, which refers to the whole process of "bringing up" a child, the formation of character in the widest sense; the current semantic equivalent of this sense is probably *upbringing*. Though its "systematic instruction" sense is more restricted, **education** still covers several shades of meanings that range from strictly academic instruction in a formal (and usually institutional) setting to a process that goes beyond straightforward teaching to encompass what might broadly be called "life skills." Whether consciously or unconsciously, politicians and other public voices often play with the possibilities of the term; a particularly famous British English example is provided in a much recycled speech in 2005 by former Prime Minister Tony Blair:

> Education: the best economic policy, preparing Britain for the future.
>
> Education: the best social policy, helping create a Britain where work and merit, not privilege or class background, decide how far you go.
>
> Education: the best liberator of any human being's potential. Education, education, education, then and now the key to the door of Britain's future success.

In this example, at least two meanings seem to be in play. Earlier in the speech, Blair is very clearly discussing national teaching provision: for example, he talks about "the education system" and "spending on education." In this part of the speech the intended sense is much less clear, and the focus seems to be on what is acquired from the process of **education**. This shows clearly one of the complexities of the meanings of **education**, and the relationship between **education** and **educate** is helpful here; **educate** is always what the teacher does to the pupil, but **education** means both **educating** and **being educated**. However, more than that, in the speech the implication is that **education** is more than simply what is taught or learned from teaching: the term encompasses both the process of being taught and the outcome of *learning* in its broadest sense. *Teaching, training,* and *instruction* can all be used to denote the products of some kind of transfer of knowledge from teacher to pupil, but **education** can be more than a simple accretion of what is taught. The title of the 1980 play by Willy Russell, *Educating Rita*, would have had very different resonances if it had been called *The Education of Rita*, and this alternative title would have shifted the focus away from the lecturer protagonist. It is perhaps because of the semantic range of **education** that there are very few widely used synonyms for **education** in any period in the history of English.

Around lC14 INFORMATION begins to be used with the meaning of **education**, but it soon becomes rare. Other early synonyms like *instruction, erudition,* and CULTURE do not show the same kind of range as **education**, and **education** in its most usual current sense seems to have very little competition synchronically or diachronically after it is borrowed into English. In fact, the modern concept encompassing teaching and learning, and showing all the shades of meaning from social INSTITUTION to personal development, seems to be built around this particular word.

Perhaps because of its vagueness, **education** is very often modified with a preceding noun or adjective that specifies a more restricted meaning, usually relating to the "systematic instruction" sense. **Higher education** tends to be the most frequent by far in both US and UK English, but modifiers referring to other sectors and stages of academic training are also common, including **public** (more frequent in the US), **further** (UK) and **continuing** (US), and **secondary education**. Other very frequent collocations refer to the training provided to particular groups, such as **special** and **teacher education**, and to instruction of a specific type or on a specific topic, such as **physical**, **health**, and **sex education**. Historically, other collocations have had periods of particular importance, and these point up moments of social debate or cultural change: for example, in the period 1910–1940, universal, **compulsory**, and **Negro education** all show significant spikes in usage in US English, while a phrase that is found in only a handful of examples until the 1960s, **environmental education**, shows a huge rise in usage in both US and UK English from the 1990s onward.

A final sense of **education** recorded in some current dictionaries appears in the expressions "an education in itself" and "quite an education"; *The New Oxford Dictionary of English* defines this as "an enlightening experience," and it is often marked as informal or humorous in dictionary entries. This is the opposite of other senses, in that it tends to denote practical rather than formal or theoretical learning; it accounts for uses like the following, where a formal qualification is contrasted with "real education":

> . . . he went to Williams College and graduated in 1972 with an "utterly useless" (his words) degree in psychology. His real education came when he floated around the country post-college, taking blue-collar jobs in nursing homes or sausage factories. . . .

This kind of example shows that the two senses of **education** can be separated: it is possible to have an **education**, i.e., to receive teaching, without really getting an **education**. Similarly, the view of formal academic instruction as potentially over-theoretical means that too much of it can be perceived as detrimental; although it is not desirable to be **undereducated**, a person can also suffer from **overeducation**. In fact, **undereducation** and **overeducation** may also have economic and social consequences: in recent decades they have been discussed in relation to their negative impact on labor markets and their impact on particular ethnic groups.

See CULTURE, INFORMATION, INSTITUTION

ELITE

Elite is an old word which since mC18 has been given a particular social meaning and since eC20 another, related but different, social meaning. **Elite** was originally the description of someone elected or formally chosen, from fw *elit*, oF, from *élire*—elect, from rw *eligere*, L—to choose, whence *electus*, L—chosen, and all the English group **elect, election, electoral**. **Elect** was extended, in C15, from persons formally chosen in some social process to the sense of specially chosen by God (**the elect** in theology and related social thought) and, in a different direction, to "select" or "choice," the most preferred and eminent persons. What in theology or social action had been some kind of formal choice was thus extended to a process of distinction or *discrimination* in which **elect** was often indistinguishable from "best" or "most important." (Many of the words which describe these complicated and overlapping processes—*distinguished* and *preferred*, or *select* and *choice* [adjectives]—show the same complication and overlapping.)

Elect was thus generally equivalent (beyond its specific use for the result of an **election**) to the post-mC18 use of **elite**, and for this general sense was almost invariably preferred. But probably as a result of its controversial theological use, which was specifically distinguished from both social choice and social eminence, the French form was readopted and eventually replaced *elect* in all its general senses as a noun. The verb of course remained, and **elected** and **the elected** came through to describe those formally chosen (except in the residual use of **Bishop-Elect**, **Professor-Elect**, and the like).

Elite, from mC18 but more commonly from eC19, now expressed mainly social distinction by rank, but it was also available for distinction within a group. Compare Byron, 1823: "With other Countesses of Blank, but rank; At once the 'lie' and the 'élite' of crowds" (*Don Juan*, XIII, where the implication is unfavorable and the word is still relatively novel, with some ambiguity about its English pronunciation); "the élite of the Russian nobility" (in translation of a French book, 1848); and "the élite of a comparatively civilized generation" (1880). As it developed along this line, **elite** became virtually equivalent with "best" and was important within the general uncertainty, in the new conditions of C19 society, about other kinds of distinction as expressed in *rank, order,* and CLASS.

It is then not surprising that its emergence in a more specific modern sense is related to conscious arguments about class. This has two main elements: first, the sense that there has been a breakdown in old ways of distinguishing those best fitted to govern or exercise influence by rank or heredity, and a failure to find new ways of distinguishing such persons by formal (parliamentary or democratic) election; secondly, in response to socialist arguments about rule by classes, or about politics as conflict between classes, the argument that the effective formations of government and influence are not classes but **elites**. The first, less formal, sense is represented in C19 by many alternative words—Coleridge's *clerisy,* Mill's *the wisest,* Arnold's *the best* and *the remnant.* The significance in each case is the assumed distinction of such groupings from existing and powerful social formations. In general C20 usage, all these assumptions have found their way into **elite,** though it is characteristic that the word is still often avoided, because of some of its associations (the abstract notions of EXCELLENCE or *standards* are now most often used to express similar or related ideas). The second and more formal sense is effectively introduced in a tendency in social theory deriving from Pareto and Mosca. Pareto distinguished between governing and non-governing **elites**, but also insisted that revolution and other kinds of political change are the result of a former **elite** becoming inadequate or decadent and then being opposed and replaced or overthrown by the new real **elite**, who often claim that they are acting on behalf of a *class*. This conception of **elite** indicates a small effective group which remains an **elite** only by regular circulation and recruitment; the alternative continuities of rank or class prevent the formation or continued effectiveness of a genuine **elite**. The emergence and success of **elites** were seen by Mosca as necessary alternatives to revolutions. Remnants of class-struggle theory then combined with notions of an openly competitive society to produce the notion of **competitive elites**, who are either able groups representing and using competitive or antagonistic social interests, or, more neutrally, alternative able groups who compete for political power. Each of these versions has been applied to modern political parties, and each is a radical revision (not always made conscious) of the supposed general theory of democratic government and especially of representative DEMOCRACY. Such **elites** do not *represent*; they either express or use other interests (whether for their own selfish purposes or not is of course controversial, because proponents of the theory claim that their real purposes, as **elites**, are the necessary best directions of the society as a whole).

Since 1945, attacks on this range of positions have produced the normally unfavorable descriptions **elitism** and **elitist**. Most contemporary uses of these words combine opposition to the informal sense of government or influence by "the best" with opposition to the political and educational procedures designed to produce **elites** in a more formal sense. This is then either (i) opposition to government by a minority or education for a minority, including all the procedures and attitudes consistent with these processes, or (ii) a more general opposition to all kinds of social distinction, whether formally constituted and practiced or not. There is often confusion between these senses, and this can be important in relations between ideas of an **elite** and ideas of a *class* or *ruling class*, where the real social argument seems to be centered. It is significant that there are alternative positive words for an effective political minority in *vanguard* and *cadres*. In some uses these overlap considerably with the more formal sense of **elite**, though there has been a distinction (related to ultimate purposes) between parties of the Right and of the Left (though compare *leadership*, as a group noun, which is used by both). Meanwhile the forgotten etymological association between **elite** and *elected* has a certain wry interest.

Recent Developments

We use **elite** in contradictory ways. Two of the most common collocates are the adjective POLITICAL, where all the examples are negative, and the noun *athlete*, where all the examples are positive. Thus, while any attempt to produce a corps of the best athletes had nearly unanimous assent, any attempt to constitute a top political grouping is unanimously condemned. The attempt to produce **elite** as a category that would supplement class analyses to produce more nuanced political descriptions has all but been lost. Perhaps not surprisingly, both left alternatives for **elite**, *cadre* and *vanguard*, have vanished from use.

　Elite has effectively replaced CLASS as a mobilizer of political hatred. When the British Labour Party largely abandoned any ambition to bring about a more equal society in the 1990s, they replaced a class analysis with a rhetoric against **elites**: everybody can agree in opposing **elites**. Donald Trump's 2016 presidential campaign used this rhetoric even more brazenly. All history and sociology show that **elite** networks will form around power, around money, around knowledge, around beauty and every other precious value. The political question to be asked is how such **elites** are recruited and how they function. The way in which **elite** has over the past fifty years been given an entirely negative political valence means that **elites** are ever less subject to political oversight that would require a more careful analysis.

See CLASS, DEMOCRACY, EXCELLENCE, POLITICAL

EMOTION

Encompassing now far more than its earliest denotation in English of political or social disturbance, the word **emotion** has achieved widespread but specialized use in a variety of technical and professional fields, alongside general currency as an apparent close synonym for *feeling*. The modern complexity of the word arises not only from its range of meanings, but because **emotion** is used increasingly of social practices and exchanges between people rather than exclusively to characterize private mental states. The word also charts a historically complicated interaction between notions of body and mind, commonly in the face of an ideological assumption made about women's predisposition toward feeling rather than reason.

　The origins of English **emotion** lie in part in Middle French *émotion*, which had the meanings of civil unrest, public commotion, movement, disturbance, or an excited mental state. **Emotion** also has an origin in earlier, post-classical Latin *emotio*, signifying displacement, and *emotio mentis*, an agitation of the mind. Earliest recorded use of the word in English dates from mC16, when **emotion** carried a negative connotation and denoted "political agitation, civil unrest; a public commotion or uprising," a meaning that persisted until lC18. Writers of the time quoted in the *OED* used **emotion** in conjunction with other words that communicate disorder: "The great tumultes and emotiones that were in Fraunce betwene the king and the nobilitie" (1562); "during the tyme of the lait troubles and emotioun" (1569); "There were great stirres and emocions in Lombardye" (1579); and "disorder and emotion" (1664).

As shown in the *OED*, around the turn of C16 **emotion** began to acquire new meanings. First, like its root word, *motion*, the term came to represent a generalized concept: it suggested not only civil unrest but any disturbance or movement. The fact that **emotion** still expressed such a disruption into C19 demonstrates that its senses extended but did not at the same time become more neutral. **Emotion** importantly articulated bodily motions such as those of the mouth, pulse, or blood, as well as movements or changes in nature, including wind, thunder, and earthquakes.

Second, toward the end of C16 the term became specialized to denote a migration or movement from one place to another. This sense was short-lived, however, lasting only through to lC17, when **emotion** began to be more commonly ascribed to human mental states. Although the *OED* notes that such early use became obsolete, the influence of this sense on the two major modern senses of **emotion** is unmistakable.

The first contemporary sense of **emotion** is also attested from eC17: "an agitation of mind" or "excited mental state," in this way demonstrating continuity with the earliest English meaning, that of "political agitation." In general terms, the dramatic C17 shift from a social and political to a personal and psychological sense coincides with consolidation of the modern European concept of individualism developing contemporaneously, even though the term *individualism* itself was referred to as "a novel expression" by Alexis de Tocqueville in his *Democracy in America* (1835–40). This sense of agitation of mind expanded subsequently to include "any strong mental or instinctive feeling." The modifier "strong" captures the emerging idea of **emotions** as feelings with gradable intensity and suggests perception of some degree of departure from a usual level of intensity for "normal" feelings. In its second current *OED* sense, also attested from eC17, **emotion** established itself as a mass noun indicating "strong feelings, passion; or instinctive feeling as distinguished from reasoning or knowledge." This sense accentuates a new antithesis between **emotion** and reason, suggesting that **emotion**, supposedly removed from logic or knowledge, is more closely related to intuition and the human sensory apparatus than it is to cognition.

In its main modern sense, **emotion** is often used interchangeably with *feeling*. In technical fields such as psychology, **emotion** studies, and neuroscience, by contrast, scholars go to great lengths to distinguish the two words and the concepts they convey. Since **emotions** are seated in the mind they tend to last longer than feelings, which usually require the presence of a physical stimulus. Although external forces often give rise to **emotions**, internal mental phenomena such as thoughts and memories can also inspire them.

Two adjectival forms, **emotional** (from 1821) and **emotionless** (from 1800), occupy opposite ends of the spectrum and together demonstrate new concern in C19 with methods for quantifying **emotional intensity**. **Emotional** implies an excess of strong, instinctive feelings, and, when used to characterize individuals, describes people who cannot control their feelings or behavior. Since lC18 and eC19, when the human capacity for sensibility was cultivated, **emotions** and the adjective **emotional** have conventionally been associated with femininity. Depending on context, on the other hand, **emotionless** describes either a person who relies on reason rather than passion, or, in a more pejorative sense, a person who is cold and merciless. The unfavorable connotations of both adjectives suggest that lack of conformity to social norms governing the expression of the **emotions**, as much as either particular excess or absence of feeling, is viewed with suspicion.

Emotional variation among individuals is signaled also by **emotional intelligence**, a concept that has gained attention since the 1990s but first appeared in mC19. Reflecting complex changes of meaning also in the word *intelligence*, **emotional intelligence** designates a capacity to experience emotions. Unlike **emotion**, however, which the *OED* defines as removed from reasoning and knowledge, **emotional intelligence** appears by contrast to suggest that one can indeed have the capacity to be aware of, manage, and express emotions in a reasonable and wise manner. The ensuing practice of measuring an **Emotional Intelligence Quotient** (EQ), in the form of a standardized psychological assessment along with the more familiar IQ test, suggests that emotions are increasingly viewed positively in certain social situations. The question remains, nevertheless, whether it is possible to measure a person's ability to understand and respond to emotions, or whether such tests merely judge how far one conforms to socially accepted ways of expressing them.

The emergence of other lC20 terms, including **emotional marketing** and **emotional labor**, suggests that emotions have become commodities. **Emotional**

marketing attempts to understand, predict, and manipulate consumers' emotions for profit, encouraging them to suspend judgment and make impulse purchases. The principles according to which such **emotional marketing** operates build on and emphasize perceived antagonism between **emotion** and reason embedded in the earlier history of **emotion**. Employees are also said to engage in **emotional labor** when their jobs require that they display certain emotions and suppress others. In such contexts emotions may be likened to a PERFORMANCE, particularly if there is a discrepancy between how a person feels and acts. This theatrical aspect of the noun **emotion** also finds expression in the verb form, **to emote**, meaning to "express (excessive) emotion" or to "perform in a dramatic or emotional manner."

Although **emotions** are typically described as mental states, visible signs on the face and body play a critical role in their expression and communication. Facial expressions and bodily movements were first related to **emotional states** by Charles Darwin in *The Expression of the Emotions in Man and Animals* (1872). In this context, influence of the earlier meaning of **emotion**, as movement or bodily motions, most clearly asserts itself, in the (now theorized) link to more modern perspectives.

Emoticon, a portmanteau of **emotion** and icon, first entered the computing world in the 1990s to denote facial expressions formed by keyboard characters used to convey a sender's feelings or intended tone. Such visual representations of **emotional expressions** have now become standardized in digital communications: users employ emoticons conventionally and consistently in order to specify their intended tone or feelings in messages, although idiosyncratic and creative uses are also possible.

Having in its earliest uses been related to physical perception and deployed in contrast with reason, the various senses of **emotion** have absorbed more complex modern understandings of the relationship among **emotion**, cognition, and the sensorium. While the antithesis between feeling and reason is still present in contemporary uses of **emotion**, recent coinages such as **emotional regulation** and **emotional freedom** open up discussion of agency and control, pointing to the further, unexplored significance of emotions in analyses of politics and power relations. These analyses accompany developments in economics and philosophy which make it impossible to maintain a traditional account of rationality that ignores or opposes the emotions; any modern account of rationality must also be an account of the emotions that are an integral part of reasoning.

See EMPATHY, LOVE, PERFORMANCE

EMPATHY

Empathy came into English relatively recently, in eC20, and quickly became a complex word. The concept it denotes first emerged in lC19 aesthetics, but **empathy** now finds itself central to ETHICAL debates and political platforms, as religious leaders, politicians, and humanitarian organizations urge that the characteristics **empathy** denotes should guide public policy and decision-making if just social outcomes are to be achieved. Much of the word's increased complexity arises from efforts to understand it as a general type of "fellow feeling for another," strongly linked to, even interwoven with, older words including *sympathy, pity,* and *compassion.*

The noun **empathy** is probably modeled on Ancient Greek *empátheia,* "physical affection, passion," ultimately from *em-,* in, and *pathos,* feeling. The word was coined in 1909 as an English rendering of the German technical term *Einfühlung,* which literally translates as "in-feeling." Sources cite German philosopher Rudolf Hermann Lotze as the first to use *Einfühlung* in 1858, but the verb form *sich einfühlen* [to empathize] can be traced further back, to Johann Gottfried Herder and Novalis. It was not until lC19, however, that *Einfühlung* gained currency as a key concept in German aesthetics. In Robert Vischer's *On the Optical Sense of Form* (1873), *Einfühlung* refers to the manner in which beholders comprehend an artwork by feeling into it or projecting themselves into its forms. For Vischer and other early **empathy** theorists this process was universal: all humans possess a capacity to empathize continuously by attributing their SOUL and its moods to the inanimate. Due in part to the trend in modernist ART toward abstraction and alienation rather than identification, **empathy** faded from aesthetic discourse during eC20 and the sense of the term broadened, encouraging its use in other fields.

According to the *OED* definition, **empathy** denotes in psychology and aesthetics "[t]he quality or power of projecting one's personality into or mentally identifying oneself with an object of contemplation, and so fully understanding or appreciating it." The seven supporting quotations for this definition in the *OED* span the years 1909 to 1966 and refer specifically to **aesthetic empathy** or *Einfühlung*: "This is, I suppose, a simple case of *empathy,* if we may coin that term as a rendering of *Einfühlung*" (E. B. Titchener, 1909). *OED* follows this with a further sense, namely the interpersonal, psychological sense of **empathy** familiar today: "The ability to understand and appreciate another person's feelings, experience, etc.," with examples from 1946 to the present. An early use outside technical discourse is from Cecil Beaton's journal in 1952 "It is her [*sc.* the Queen Mother's] empathy and her understanding of human nature that endears her to everyone she talks to." In such use of the term, a person empathizes with another human being, not an inanimate work of art or object in nature.

In its most common current sense, **empathy** describes the practice of participating vicariously in the psychological perspective and EMOTIONS of another. The idiom "to put yourself in someone else's shoes" represents the view that **empathy** leads to better understanding of another individual, but different contemporary senses must be distinguished. **Cognitive empathy** is the ability to adopt a different perspective. **Affective empathy**—the capacity to respond appropriately to another's emotions—manifests itself as either empathetic concern for another or self-centered personal distress in response to another's suffering. Each type requires significant work of the imagination in order to "know" and identify with another's experiences. Recent application of **cognitive empathy** to identification with fictional characters demonstrates that **empathy** continues to be important in the aesthetic realm.

Since the **cognitive-affective empathy** distinction is largely unknown outside psychology and philosophy, some users of this cluster of words consider *sympathy, compassion,* and *pity* to be synonymous with **empathy**. The four terms, in their broadest senses, indicate a person's capacity to recognize and share another's feelings; but they have branched in different directions.

After reaching its peak between mC16 and lC17, *compassion*'s prominence dwindled, and of all the related terms it is *sympathy* that has enjoyed the most widespread usage, beginning around 1830. In C16, *sympathy* had denoted "harmony" or "agreement in qualities, likeness, conformity, correspondence" before becoming commonplace during C17 when talking about feelings toward another person. Today, *sympathy* suggests any type of shared feeling, but combinations such as *sympathy pains* and *sympathy card* tend to associate the word with physical pain, loss, and sorrow. In certain contexts only implicitly related to the emotions, *sympathy* and *sympathizer* express support for a political party or cause; for example, workers with no direct grievance against their employer may show solidarity with another group of locked-out or striking workers during a *sympathy strike*.

Although *sympathy, compassion,* and *pity* are close synonyms, **empathy** can convey the sharing of any psychological perspective or emotional state. The distinction between *sympathy* and **empathy** also signifies a difference in perceived depth of shared feeling, as an example cited in the *OED* entry for **empathetic** reveals: "The method . . . condemns the biographer to immerse himself in his subject's mind, to take a view that is more than 'sympathetic,' that is indeed empathetic" (1932).

While regarded in eC20 as a universal impulse in aesthetic contemplation, **empathy** has more recently been subject to attempts to measure and classify it, a trend reflected in a proliferation of derived compounds. Frequently abbreviated to EQ, for example, the **Empathy Quotient** is a self-assessment that aims to determine one's ability to empathize and screens adults for Autism Spectrum Disorders. The term **empath** is also used to describe a person who easily empathizes with others (interestingly it occurs already in the 1950s in science fiction). According to the May 2017 version of the *Wikipedia* article for **empathy**, "The capacity to empathize is a revered trait in society," but terms such as **empathetic sickness** or **empathy fatigue** suggest that too much **empathy** may be detrimental to a person's own health. *Compassion fatigue*, which appears in the online *OED* 2002 draft addition to *compassion*, is defined as "indifference towards the suffering of others . . . , typically attributed to numbingly frequent appeals for assistance, esp. donations." Media analysts have argued that bombarding viewers with decontextualized images of suffering can cause them to experience **empathy fatigue**.

In politics, large-scale social problems have been blamed on lack of **empathy** among citizens. US President Barack Obama frequently decried an "**empathy deficit**" in American society, largely building his 2008 presidential campaign on commitment to promoting **empathy** as a social value. After the controversy that arose when President Obama declared **empathy** one of his criteria in choosing a Supreme Court judge, its emotional overtones seen as potentially distorting the legal system, he restated **empathy** as the "keen understanding of how the law affects the daily lives of the American people."

Public discourse typically aligns **empathy** with *compassion* rather than *sympathy*. The news media, for instance, have applauded Pope Francis for his *compassion* or **empathy** with the poor since his election as leader of the Roman Catholic Church in 2013; in India, an emerging politics of **empathy** has focused on Dalits, people who were traditionally regarded as "untouchable" and who still suffer social stigmatization. For C21 political, religious, or humanitarian discourse, it appears, *sympathy* no longer suffices. Only the deeper sentiment of **empathy** promises to solve social ills, through a process that involves simultaneous recognition and negation of differences between people in order to achieve better mutual understanding.

See EMOTION, ETHICAL, TRAUMA, VICTIM

ENLIGHTENMENT

Kant's question "What is Enlightenment?" has echoed through Western social thought since lC18, receiving many answers and prompting much debate. Kant suggested that the primary characteristic of **Enlightenment** was an intellectual self-reliance that eschewed traditional political and religious AUTHORITY. His faith in the sovereignty of the human rational capacity, a capacity that could independently corroborate the order inherent in the moral world, would become a defining characteristic of modernity, and an object of debate for writers who followed him.

Enlightenment, according to the *OED*, refers both to the process of "bringing someone to a state of greater knowledge, understanding, or insight" and to that subsequent state itself. Early recorded instances appear in C17 religious texts, such as Robert Aylett's allegorical gloss of the Song of Songs: "The Word, without the Spirits enlightenment, Is as good Seede sowne on vntilled ground" (1621). While such attainment can refer to any sort of knowledge, it often carries a spiritual or charismatic charge, as in Buddhism, where it is synonymous with *nirvana*, the SPIRITUAL awareness that releases a person from cycles of rebirth and suffering.

The Enlightenment—with definite article and capitalization—comes to stand for the project of rational and scientific inquiry that characterized C18 Europe. After the German *Aufklärung*, or illumination, it designated an intellectual movement that sought to schematize natural and social knowledge. Following on the Scientific Revolution and the work of Newton in particular, there was a general optimism about the power of human intellect to control NATURE and to improve human life.

What one thinks of the **Enlightenment** often depends on how one interprets the values associated with it. While the unity of the **Enlightenment project** has rightly been questioned by scholars such as J. G. A. Pocock and Jonathan Israel, among others, several strains of social and political thought are usually identified with it. First comes a model of rationalism like Kant's, in which a priori knowledge of the sensible world can serve as a sufficient platform from which to reconcile Newtonian science with traditional morality. While social contract theory had antecedents in C17, **Enlightenment** writers such as Rousseau began to theorize notions of individual and communal consent as the primary basis of political legitimacy. This vision of contractual political affiliation was, in turn, based on an expanded notion of RIGHTS, both natural and legal, that were seen to undergird the sovereignty of the state (in contrast to the monarch). Perhaps the most radical idea to emerge was a confidence in the viability of political pluralism, an optimism that multiple independent constituencies could coexist and could form an alternative to homogenous systems that had little tolerance for dissent or divergent ideologies.

These values were celebrated by many **Enlightenment** writers, but others criticized the philosophical temper of the time as individualistic, even atomistic, marked by an anti-religious empiricism that exacerbated the divide between science and FAITH. The drive to universalize EXPERIENCE, to look for what was common to human nature and then to extract a practical morality from it, was deemed dangerous since it was thought to lead to a moral RELATIVISM. Finally, the increased emphasis on rights was assumed by some to reduce human relations to mere contract, negating a framework of deeper ETHICAL and interpersonal obligation.

The reception of the **Enlightenment** in lC18 and C19 often devolved into a referendum on what a given writer thought about the French Revolution and its conception of human FREEDOM. On its own account, the Revolution attempted to put into practice a political system based on the fundamental equality of all moral agents, to replace monarchy with an experiment in mass DEMOCRACY. On Edmund Burke's more hostile account, by contrast, the achievement of political liberty and anti-authoritarianism was purchased at the cost of traditional mores. When respect for RELIGION and "natural" social distinction was lost, he argued, so too was the reformers' ideal of human EQUALITY. For C20 critics, the referendum is more frequently imagined to be on the idea of modernity itself (along with the teleological notion of progress that is seen to underwrite it). Horkheimer and Adorno lament that the project of the **Enlightenment** remains unfinished, because philosophers put too much stock in an "instrumental rationality"—the twin perils of TECHNOLOGY and bureaucracy—that contributed to the VIOLENCE of C20.

While some still champion the **Enlightenment** values that shaped the modern LIBERAL subject, critics have laid a variety of ills at the **Enlightenment**'s rather broad front stoop: from slavery to colonialism to Nazi genocide. While this critique is certainly valid for writers such as Locke, several **Enlightenment** philosophers (including Spinoza) explicitly reject colonialist models that valued ends over means. Nonetheless, modern critics have insisted that the standard of rational utility instituted by the **Enlightenment** makes it imperative that we continue to ask: whose reason? useful to whom? The flip-side of valuing individuals in terms of their democratic potential or social productivity (rather than birth or other natural endowments) was the tendency to view human bodies as if they were raw materials. In this way, the term's legacy still activates the East-West binary insofar as the colonial project relied on a rhetoric of **enlightening** that encouraged the ventriloquism of an individualistic rights-based liberalism.

Debate over the **Enlightenment**'s legacy was renewed in the wake of 9/11, when some commentators framed the emerging geopolitical situation as a battle between **Enlightenment** secularism and the irrational religious fundamentalism intent on destroying it. Those who did not rally to the **Enlightenment** barricades were dismissed as misguided multiculturalists or postmodern relativists (the latter charge interestingly an echo of charges made against **Enlightenment** thinkers themselves by contemporaries). In such CULTURE wars, the **Enlightenment** "has become an important emotional prop," according to *Guardian* journalist Madeleine Bunting in an article entitled "The Convenient Myth That Changed a Set of Ideas into Western Values" (April 10, 2006). The rhetoric of these culture wars is also found in Islamic sources; a Pakistani editorial lauds the Grand Mufti of Saudi Arabia for preaching that "some elements amongst the Muslims are propagating the ideas of enlightenment and socialism to distort the shape and teachings of Islam." In the last fifteen years, **enlightenment** has become a new code word for tensions between East and West, secularism and faith.

See CULTURE, DEMOCRACY, ETHICAL, EQUALITY, FAITH, FREEDOM, LIBERAL, NATURE, RELATIVISM, RELIGION, RIGHTS, SECULAR, TECHNOLOGY, VIOLENCE, WEST

ENTERPRISE

Enterprise, entrepreneur, and a group of related words have emerged since the 1970s as central terms of a new emphasis in CAPITALIST, especially neoliberal, societies. An overall shift in how we perceive change, opportunity, innovation, and WEALTH creation has already had an impact on the preferred forms of organization by means of which goods and services are produced and delivered. But changes associated with these words are not confined to the traditional BUSINESS sector. When **enterprise** is used in specialized combinations such as **social enterprise** or in collocations such as **enterprise university**, influence extends to INSTITUTIONS previously conceived along very different lines.

Changing meanings of **enterprise** and **entrepreneur** also have an effect on personal value systems, for example in the favorable presumption now typically conveyed by **enterprising person** and **entrepreneurial character**. Precise characteristics of an **entrepreneur**, or of the **entrepreneurial process**, have never, however, achieved any consensual definition. Lack of agreement partly follows from conflicting ideological frameworks within which the words are deployed. While **enterprise** and **entrepreneur** are often used to signify approval (conveying qualities of creativeness or inventiveness), in other circumstances the same terms are used to condemn behavior as opportunistic, exploitative, unethical, unduly competitive, or selfish.

Enterprise and **entrepreneur** derive from a similar route: Old French *entrepris[e]*, past participle of *entreprendre*, "to undertake." Adopted into English from C15, the general, descriptive *OED* sense emerges of "[a] design of which the execution is attempted; a piece of work taken in hand, an undertaking; *chiefly*, and now exclusively, a bold, arduous, or momentous undertaking."

Alongside this general "undertaking" sense, **enterprise** has been used in English in a more specialized, political economy sense from at least eC19. Throughout C19, nevertheless, use of related **entrepreneur** in a broad political economy sense was still often accompanied by reference back to its French roots, as in the *OED* quotation from 1891, "We have . . . been obliged to resort to the French language for a word to designate the person who organizes and directs the productive factors, and we call such a one an *entrepreneur.*" In philosophical writing, that French connection seems to have involved implied reference to Richard Cantillon's (1755) treatment of business judgments exercised in the face of uncertainty as to rewards but with fixed costs: a discussion influential on accounts of **entrepreneurial** activity offered later by Adam Smith, David Ricardo, and Jeremy Bentham.

In C18 and C19 accounts, an **entrepreneur** might still be an owner or proprietor of any small firm, using his or her own capital and operating in a fairly stable MARKET. Only gradually did the difference between general *businessperson* and **entrepreneur** increase in terms of different degrees of RISK, innovation, and tempo of operation. Greater emphasis placed on exploiting opportunities unseen by others, especially in response to uncertain market conditions presented by rapid change, led to emergence of an **entrepreneur** as someone who exploits opportunity in a changing marketplace, often at personal risk, and so as the innovator, initiator, and commercial risk-taker.

The business practices that characterize **enterprise** and **entrepreneurship** were analyzed influentially during C20 by, among others, the Moravian-born American economist J. A. Schumpeter, a major influence on the development during the 1930s and 1940s of **entrepreneurship theory**: a specialized academic field sometimes in tension with the pragmatic, often intuitive and improvisatory approach of many actual **entrepreneurs**.

More recent shifts in **enterprise** and **entrepreneur** are perhaps most closely associated with *OED* sense, "Disposition or readiness to engage in undertakings of difficulty, risk, or danger; daring spirit." This "disposition" sense emerges from the accentuation of risk outlined in the preceding, and introduces the idea of character or personality traits already inherent but not yet developed in earlier senses. This line of development in **entrepreneur** is reflected in modern ideas of **entrepreneurial personality** and commercial instinct. People are praised for showing qualities of a "born entrepreneur," or for engaging in "entrepreneurial decision-making" by following imputed natural inclinations, first illustrated in *OED* with reference to artistic or theatrical work (cf. "impresario"); and attention to the dramatic, sometimes larger-than-life character and lifestyle of the **business entrepreneur** continued into many C20 uses.

The most recent phase of development, from the 1970s onward, can be followed in a range of extensions of meaning reflected in combinations with **enterprise**. **Enterprise zone** began to be used to designate an area of high unemployment and low investment, usually in an inner city, where government encouraged new **enterprise** by granting financial concessions such as tax and rate relief to businesses. In some thinking of the period, such terms presaged an emergent **enterprise culture**, foreseen as an encapsulation of established values of **free enterprise** and **private enterprise**, generalizing policy incentives adopted for urban renewal to all sectors. **Enterprise culture** was also presented as the best way to improve competitive position in GLOBAL commerce. Some uses of **enterprise culture** from the period convey enthusiasm for the vision of individualism, personal achievement, striving for EXCELLENCE, hard work, and assumption of personal RESPONSIBILITY for actions. Others suggest an awkwardness in adopting either the expression or the practice.

One difficulty inherent in a verbal combination like **enterprise culture** is that the phrase brings together potentially conflicting values: that of accentuated individualism (in **enterprise**) and a value inherent in social norms or conventions (in *culture*). Proposed as a basis for social behavior, **enterprise, entrepreneur, entrepreneurial character**, and so on become tangled up not only in how people do business or how services are delivered, but also in more general notions of what constitutes citizenship.

The most challenging verbal combination with **enterprise**, however, is **social enterprise**, which the July 2017 version of the *Wikipedia* article defines as follows: "A **social enterprise** is an organization that applies commercial strategies to maximize improvements in human and environmental well-being—this may include maximizing social impact alongside profits for external shareholders." Rethinking different kinds of organization along these lines has repercussions across many areas of society and CULTURE, including for instance health, arts, and EDUCATION. In education, an **enterprise agenda** can be made part of the curriculum, reflected in a shift toward vocational training to develop **enterprise competencies**. It may also prescribe a form of institutional organization and management. Inevitably, contradictions then surface as regards whether the mission, values of members of staff, and expectation of professional and voluntary contribution are compatible with an **enterprise ethos**. This will be especially the case if that ethos foregrounds risk-taking and a search for market opportunities in delivering what might otherwise be considered a public service.

Little consensus exists on whether theories of **entrepreneurship** have a scientific basis or are primarily a matter of ideological commitment. The connection is also questioned between **entrepreneurship** as a teachable practice or attitude and aspects of social background such as ethnicity, national history, and religion. During a period of recession, debate over **enterprise** and **entrepreneurship** is inflamed by questions about whether aspirations encouraged by ideas of rapid wealth accumulation and risk may lead to social problems associated with exclusion. Different senses of **enterprise** and **entrepreneurship** play a continuing role, too, in changing representations of businesspeople and commercial activity in fiction, cinema, and drama.

See BUSINESS, CAPITALISM, CULTURE, INSTITUTION, MARKET, PUBLIC, RISK, WEALTH

ENVIRONMENT

Environment has become a central term in contemporary debates regarding the relationship between humankind and its surroundings, especially regarding how the two interact (including whether there can be equilibrium in such interaction, whether such interaction is presently damaging but reversible, or whether the planet faces unprecedented GLOBAL danger). The already significant difficulty of engaging in public discussion of such issues is exacerbated by the degree to which the polysemy of the word **environment** and its derivatives reflects but at the same time disguises contested ideas and ideals about the place of humans in the natural and social world.

The word **environment** is borrowed into English from Middle French *environnement*, from *environner* "to surround." The word is first attested in the

OED in a translation of Plutarch's *Morals* in 1603, but only becomes established in English in C18. By the 1720s, **environment** was being used in two senses, each of which reflects its etymological meaning. The first sense, "[t]he action of circumnavigating, encompassing, or surrounding something; the state of being encompassed or surrounded," is already rare in C18 and obsolete after C19. It is the second sense, "[t]he area surrounding a place or thing; the environs, surroundings, or physical context," which leads into the word's present-day meanings that have widened to include both physical and non-physical contexts.

Current uses of **environment** can be split into two branches. The general meaning is that of "the surroundings or conditions in which a person, animal, or plant lives or operates," a sense that encompasses a number of narrower subsenses found from mC19 onward. In these more recent senses **environment** is usually qualified with respect to a specified place or circumstance: the **environment** *of* something or someone, or *type of* **environment**. The inhabitant(s) of an environment, whether implied or specified, are generally living things, including (but not restricted to) humans. In post-C19 scientific use, **environment** is used to refer to what Darwin would have described as the "external conditions" that affect the LIFE, existence, or properties of an organism. Where a particular type of **environment** is intended, an appropriate modifier is used. The most frequent collocates in different periods of this kind of use are telling: the phrases **production environment** and **work environment**, for example, are not common until the 1970s and 1980s, respectively, but are now among the most frequent. Such qualified senses of **environment** imply an interaction between an entity and surroundings or conditions, with many examples showing blurring between technical use in scientific disciplines and more widespread, non-technical use. The derived form **environmental** is found from mC19 onward, in collocations such as **environmental factors** and **environmental causes**, which often have the same connotation of interaction between a physical environment and its contents, with the physical **environment** influencing any living inhabitants.

From around 1930, **environment** begins to be used with an explicitly non-physical meaning, referring to the social, political, and cultural context that shapes a person's behavior and attitudes. The emergence of this sense reflects the rise of behaviorist ideas such as those of B. F. Skinner, who argued that "[i]t is the environment which is 'responsible' for the objectionable behavior [e.g., alcoholism and juvenile delinquency], and it is the environment, not some attribute of the individual, which must be changed" (*Beyond Freedom and Dignity*, 1971, 74). Such use of **environment** is not the beginning of the basic idea that "nurture" is more of a determinant than "nature"; and the related terms **environmentalism** and **environmentalist**, respectively the theory positing the primary influence of environment and a proponent of that theory, are found earlier than **environment** in this sense.

Perhaps the most significant semantic development in **environment** comes in mC20, when **environment** begins to be used without modification but usually with a preceding definite article: as **the environment**. In this instantly recognizable use in contemporary public debate, **environment** refers to the whole natural world, rather than to the immediate physical context of a particular organism. *The Independent* notes, for example, that "Environments . . . keep changing in size," and suggests that in such talk the referent is inevitably "enormously enlarged" (June 25, 2000). First attested in the *OED* in 1948, **the environment** is closely synonymous with *the natural world*, and shares in the positive connotations of the terms NATURE and *natural*, as well as *countryside*. However, **environment** has come to mean more than simply *natural world* or *countryside*. In recent years it has been influenced by the word's earlier meanings, which encompass the notion of interaction between subject and **environment**, so that **environment** now denotes surroundings "esp. as affected by human activity." **Environmental issues** are not simply matters pertaining to the natural world, but issues associated with human behavior; such issues involve a semantic reversal, now foregrounding the impact made by the human inhabitant on its surroundings rather than vice versa. In much of the popular press, this contemporary sense of **environment** has become far more frequent than any other, in part reflecting the fact that it is a term used in the names of many governmental and non-governmental organizations, e.g., the Environment Agency (UK, 1995) and the Environmental Protection Agency (US, 1970). The importance of such bodies and the emergence of *green politics* in the late 1970s as a more mainstream political force reflect a political trend that Williams had already noted in the second edition of *Keywords* (1983) toward "a central concern with human relations to the physical world as the necessary basis for social and economic policy."

That central political concern is nevertheless not consistently expressed in the same terms. In 1983, for example, Williams suggested that "[e]cology and its associated words largely replaced the *environment* grouping from the late 1960s," an apparent replacement, as it seemed to Williams, that appears to have been reversed in recent decades. Indeed, the relationship between **environment** and related words is complex. As a group, *ecology, ecological,* and *ecologist* appear to have more "scientific" connotations than **environment**, **environmental**, and **environmentalist**, which may be why those terms have remained more restricted in their patterns of use. An *ecologist* is typically a qualified professional, whereas an **environmentalist** is as likely to be an enthusiastic amateur; *ecologically sound* appears more precise than **environmentally friendly** or its partial synonym *green*. The **environmental movement** seems to have largely taken over from the earlier *ecological movement*, and **environmental** has increased in other collocations while *ecological* appears to have plateaued. One further difference between the two clusters of terms is that ECOLOGY does not have an everyday sense equivalent to **environment**, and this may be responsible for the growth in frequency and use of **environment**-related terms. There is nevertheless one exception to this tendency: use of the prefix *eco-*, which benefits from being "snappier" than alternatives and is productive in a large number of new forms, including now relatively established *ecotourism* (1992), *eco-warrior* (1987), and *ecofeminist* (1980).

C21 nuances associated with **environment** are not always easy to distinguish. In political and media discourse, speakers often shift between them without acknowledging they are doing so. An example of this can be seen in a 2003 UK newspaper interview with Margaret Beckett, a former UK Secretary of State for Environment, Food, and Rural Affairs, whose first two uses of the word suggest the "natural world" sense, while the third shows a more specific, modified sense:

> The whole environment debate has been seen as either a rural thing or a concern only of the Greens. . . . What is needed now is to mainstream it, and to show the links between social justice, poverty and the environment. We must recognise that poverty goes hand in hand with environmental degradation. If you destroy your environment then you are impoverishing yourself at a later time.

This foregrounds the connection between the natural world in general and the immediate circumstances of individuals. But the connections made between **environment** and social issues blur an important distinction between physical surroundings and non-physical context. In this regard, contemporary use of **environment** shows complications that highlight both the political significance of the word and the intractability of debates in which it has become an essential term.

See ECOLOGY, EVOLUTION, GLOBAL, LIFE, NATURE

EQUALITY

Equality has been in regular use in English since eC15, from fw *équalité*, oF, *aequalitatem*, L, rw *aequalis*, L, from *aequus*—level, even, just. The earliest uses of **equality** are in relation to physical quantity, but the social sense of **equality**, especially in the sense of equivalence of rank, is present from C15 though more common from C16. **Equality** to indicate a more general condition developed from this but it represented a crucial shift. What it implied was not a comparison of rank but an assertion of a much more general, normal or normative, condition. This use is evident in Milton (*Paradise Lost*, XII, 26):

> . . . not content
> With faire equalitie, fraternal state.

But after mC17 it is not again common, in this general sense, until 1C18, when it was given specific emphasis in the American and French Revolutions. What was then asserted was both a fundamental condition—"all men are created **equal**"— and a set of specific demands, as in **equality** before the law—that is to say, reform of previous statutory **inequalities**, in feudal and post-feudal ranks and privileges. In its bearings on social thought, **equality** has two main branches: (i) a process of **equalization**, from the fundamental premise that all men are naturally equal as human beings, though not at all necessarily in particular attributes; and (ii) a process of removal of inherent privileges, from the premise that all men should "start equal," though the purpose or effect of this may then be that they become **unequal** in achievement or condition. There is of course considerable overlap between these two applications, but there is finally a distinction between (i) a process of continual equalization, in which any condition, inherited or newly created, which sets some men above others or gives them power over others, has to be removed or diminished in the name of the normative principle (which, as in Milton's use, brings **equality** and *fraternity* very close in meaning); and (ii) a process of abolishing or diminishing *privileges*, in which the moral notion of **equality** is on the whole limited to initial conditions, any subsequent inequalities being seen as either inevitable or right. The most common form of sense (ii) is **equality of opportunity**, which can be glossed as "equal opportunity to become unequal." (Compare the use of *underprivileged*, where PRIVILEGE is the norm but some have less of it than others, to describe a poor or deprived or even oppressed group.) The familiar complaint against sense (i), that it wishes to bring everybody to a dead level, connects with the positive program of economic equality which, in mC17 England, was the doctrine of the *Levellers*. There is a clear historical break, within both senses, between programs limited to political and legal RIGHTS and programs which also include economic equality, in any of its varying forms. It came to be argued, in eC19, that the persistence of economic inequalities, as in systems of landlord ownership or capitalist ownership of the means of production, made legal or political equality merely ABSTRACT.

Under the influence of arguments derived from the French Revolution, the older English form **equalitarian** was replaced, from mC19, by **egalitarian**, from the modern French form.

The persistence of **equal** in a physical sense, as a term of measurement, has obviously complicated the social argument. It is still objected to programs of economic equality, and even to programs of legal or political equality (though in these now less often), that men are evidently unequal in measurable attributes (height, energy, intelligence, and so on). To this it is replied that what needs to be shown is that the measurable difference is relevant to the particular **inequality**, in a social sense: height would not be, though color of skin has been held to be; energy or intelligence might be, and this is where most serious contemporary argument now centers. Measurable differences of this kind bear especially on sense (ii). They would usually be held, even where real and demonstrated, to be subordinate to sense (i), in which no difference between man, or between men and women, could be reasonably used to give some men power over other men, or, as now critically, over women.

RECENT DEVELOPMENTS

Equality has not increased markedly in frequency in general discourse over the last fifty years. Only recently did it return to its previous high point in lC18 when "Liberty, **Equality**, Fraternity" was the slogan of the French Revolution. However, **Equality** has become written into the law in many countries since the American Civil Rights legislation in the 1960s. Legislation originally designed to deal with discrimination on the grounds of race has been extended to cover other social groupings. Thus, the UK's 2010 **Equality** Act offers broad protection against discrimination based on eight "protected characteristics," including age, disability, gender reassignment, marriage and civil partnership, race, religion or belief, sex, and sexual orientation.

Economic inequality is largely ignored in this equality legislation, which may go some way to explaining why **inequality** has seen a massive increase in use, particularly in the last four decades. While new usages such as GENDER **inequality** and **racial inequality** cover the full range of social, political, and economic relationships, the really striking increase in usage comes in collocations that emphasize the economic: **income inequality**, WEALTH **inequality**, and **economic inequality** itself. This focus on the economic now so predominates that **inequality** without any modifier is taken to mean economic rather than social and political relationships, as in the recent collocation **global inequality**, which has seen a striking rise in usage.

After the global financial crisis of 2007–8, **inequality** became and remains the focus of much political debate. It was the major theme of the Occupy Wall Street movement of 2011 and it now features in many mainstream political debates.

In some regions of the world, including parts of East Africa and South Asia, there is a preference for the term *equity* over **equality**, as in *social equity* and *gender equity* rather than **social equality** and **gender equality**. In American and British English, *equity* generally relates to finance, as in *private equity* or *home equity*, but in other regions, *equity* seems to be preferred, based on the legal meaning of *equity* as "fair" or "just," and an understanding of **equality** as purely quantitative.

See ACCESS, DEMOCRACY, ELITE, FAIR, GENDER, PRIVILEGE, RACE, RIGHTS, WEALTH

ETHICAL

The noun **ethics** enters English in eC15, but until lC16 is found only as a name for Aristotle's treatise; the adjective **ethical** is found from lC14, denoting the topic of Aristotle's and similar works, its first attested use being a reference to "certen ethical Arithmologies drawne out of deuine and prophane auctorities" (1573). In earlier use, these words, borrowings via French and Latin of a word ultimately of Greek origin, stood very much in the shade of Latin-derived *moral* and *morality*, also lC14 borrowings from Latin via French. The terms **ethical** and **ethics**, however, quickly distinguish themselves as more than simply learned synonyms for *moral* and *morality*. The earliest meaning of **ethics** is "a study of, or treatise on, moral principles" (a1425), reflecting the Greek and Latin title of Aristotle's *Ethica*. This use gives rise to an important core meaning: the academic study of morality, or, to put it another way, morality as a topic for systematic analysis. This meaning is reflected in some of the most frequent collocations of **ethical** in contemporary English: **ethical system, ethical principles, ethical standards, ethical code.** All of these reflect a conception of morality as something that can be studied and defined, and although they reflect meanings of **ethical** and **ethics** that have been in existence for centuries, all have increased markedly in relative frequency since lC19. To understand this, we must look at three sense developments shown by the noun **ethics**, as identified by *OED*:

> The moral principles or system associated with a particular leader, thinker, school of thought, or area of enquiry, or with a particular historical period. (1649)

> The moral principles or values held or shown by an individual person. (1749)

> The codes of conduct or moral principles recognized in a particular profession, sphere of activity, relationship, or other context or aspect of human life. (1789)

The first two senses relate to a moral system as manifested by an individual, or in other words, individual morality envisaged as a describable, definable system. This emphasis has important implications for how collocations such as **ethical principles, ethical standards**, or **ethical code** can be applied to an individual's conduct. The third sense development is crucially important for conceptualization of the **ethical** sphere as morality subjected to technical definition and description, within the restricted scope of a particular organization or field of activity.

In addition to these senses there is a post-Holocaust definition of the **ethical**, most strongly associated with the philosopher Emmanuel Levinas, for which **ethics** and the **ethical** is just that which must escape codification or regulation. For Levinas the irreducible basis of ethics is the face-to-face encounter with the Other. This face-to-face encounter for Levinas has all the characteristics of an epiphany, in which we experience both intimacy and distance.

If collocations shown by **ethical** and *moral* are compared in a corpus of contemporary English, those which are most characteristic for **ethical** are **ethical approval, ethical guideline,** and **ethical lapse** (while those for *moral* are *moral courage, moral outrage, moral superiority, moral clarity*). Such collocations highlight the semantic components of measurability and (perceived) objectivity, components that come most obviously to the fore in contemporary uses of **ethical** in corporate social bodies: organizations, whether commercial or non-commercial, governmental or non-governmental, will have an **ethical code** or **ethics code**, with defined **ethical standards** and **ethical guidelines**. Individual conduct will be measured against such defined standards of morality.

In this particular use, the **ethical** is the benchmark of what is acceptable conduct in a particular sphere: what is or is not *moral* may be considered an area where individuals may agree to disagree (and in which academic investigations of **ethics** may or may not be invoked); but, within an organization, what is **ethical** must be agreed if the regulatory mechanisms of that organization are to apply. Definitions of what is **ethical** may well differ between organizations or roles: what is considered **ethical conduct** may differ, for example, for a member of parliament, an investment banker, a university lecturer, or a surgeon. Within each field of activity, individuals are expected to display **ethical conduct** that will reflect sound **ethical judgment**, or they may seek **ethical approval** for a planned action or project. Where someone is perceived to have fallen short of expected standards of conduct **ethical concerns** may be raised. Difficult cases may be judged against the organization's **ethical code** by an **ethics committee**, the decisions of which may have implications for an individual's future position within an organization or within a profession.

In spite of its association with what is measurable and subject to regulation, the word **ethical** is nonetheless still capable, for many people, of encoding highly positive, aspirational connotations. In Britain, New Labour's **ethical foreign policy** was greeted with cynicism by political opponents and was overtaken by events in a very short period of time. But the choice of name was careful: the policy was presented as something moral in a way that could be measured and held to account. Much more successful and enduring has been the lC20 coinage **ethical investment**, embraced by many who feel out of sympathy with mainstream financial CAPITALISM as a way of engaging with financial investment while retaining a concern for environmental or social issues. Such **ethical investment** is also embraced by parts of the world of banking, as a way of offering financial products in a way that is acceptable to a MARKET otherwise distrustful of the CORPORATE world. The connotations of the word **ethical** are important in the success of this compound—the label **ethical investment** suggests a product that will meet, in a measurable way, the age-old aspiration for a form of capitalism that is compatible with morality.

See CULTURE

EUROPEAN

The term **European** may appear semantically simple: **European** means "belonging to Europe" and **Europe** is the name of a continent. Hence the link between the word and a referent in the real world may appear unproblematic. However, in some of its most typical uses, particularly when applied to people, **European** shows a complex interplay of many different strands of meaning.

An ideologically charged term, it moves between the descriptive and prescriptive modes. Historically associated with the privileged status of Western European CULTURE or, more recently, with an attempt to confederate a largely contiguous but disparate group of nation-states, the term alternately elicits praise and blame. **European** has thus become a locus for arguing over definitions of ethnicity, IDENTITY, and sovereignty.

While Medieval Latin *Europa* and Middle English *Europe* were both current as geographical terms, medieval writers wishing to refer collectively to a shared culture among those peoples and nations would be more likely to employ a term such as *latinitas* (or one of its related forms) to designate the political, linguistic, and religious reach of the former Roman Empire and its conquests. As an adjective and a substantive, **European** comes into regular usage only from C16—that is, from the age of seagoing exploration. It is formed on the classical Latin adjective *Eurōpaeus*. The place name **Europe** (Latin *Eurōpa*, Greek *Eurōpē*) goes back to Antiquity, but Greek and Roman conceptions of both the eastward and northern boundaries of Europe were unsettled and hazy. The etymology from the name of Europa, a mythological princess of Tyre courted by Zeus in the form of a bull, is ancient but far from certain.

The meaning history as presented by the *OED* is relatively simple: (i) "Of, relating to, or characteristic of Europe or its inhabitants" (1555), with a subsense from 1714 onward distinguishing specifically continental Europe from Britain, which corresponds to a typical popular use of both **Europe** and **European** in contemporary British English; (ii) "Occurring in, or extending over, Europe" (1575); (iii) "Of or designating a person of European origin or descent living outside the boundaries of Europe" (1666) and various developments of this sense; (iv) "Designating animals and plants native to or originating in Europe," e.g., *European beaver*, etc. (1678); and (v) from 1714 onward various uses relating to notional or prospective unions or associations of European countries, and from 1952 onward referring to the **European Union** and its various precursor organizations. This last

use is dominant in British political discourse, and has given rise to numerous derivative formations such as **Euroskeptic**, but is semantically relatively uncomplicated,
except where it touches on or is colored by other much hazier and much more contentious uses of the word, which lurk behind some of the *OED*'s other definitions.

European has proved a historically durable, if notional, tool of identity for those
wishing to gather under its banner, as well as for those rallying to oppose it. It has
simultaneously been seen as synonymous with an enlightened ideal of political pluralism or with an oppressive colonialism (or both). The adjectival and nominal forms
have traditionally participated in a set of concentric assumptions that are at once
racial (white), religious (Christian), and political (constitutional). The opposite of
European has thus been variously imagined as "Saracen," "New World," "African,"
or "MUSLIM." Edward Said influentially decried what critics have since called the
"Eurocentric universalism" that privileged the European over other categories of
identity and reified perceived divergence from its assumed ideal (white, Christian,
democratic). Postcolonial criticism has explored the ways in which European identity has been structured around a set of binaries (civilized/uncivilized; colonizer/
colonized; rational/irrational; Western/non-Western). In this way, the term marks
both a physical space and a variety of (sometimes competing) metaphysical ideals.

For a modern geographer, the eastward land boundaries of Europe are defined
primarily by the Urals and (between the Black and Caspian Seas) the Caucasus. This
places modern Russia partly in Europe and partly in Asia—a fact of geopolitical importance at least since lC18. Similarly, the narrow water boundary of the Bosphorus
places modern Turkey largely in Asia but partly also in Europe; the situation of
Istanbul straddling the geographical boundary between Europe and Asia provides
an irresistible symbol for the cultural, ethnic, religious, and political complexities of
Europe's southeastern boundaries. Unsurprisingly, divisions of the peoples and nations of Eurasia between **Europe** and Asia frequently reflect uncertainty about the
"**European**" status of Russia or Turkey and their inhabitants, although more than
simply geographical considerations come into play here.

As far as attempts to subdivide Europe into distinct areas are concerned, those
divisions which have an impact on general (as opposed to specialist geographical)
discourse are considerably shaped by cultural, economic, and political factors.
This is particularly evident on the east-west axis, where the old concept of Central
Europe (German *Mitteleuropa*) fell largely into disuse in the mid to late C20 as Cold
War rivalries divided Europe crudely and sharply into a WEST and East; usage today
has once again become more fluid.

Wherever the dividing lines are placed in more or less official use, it is not difficult to see a bias in the deployment of the terms **Europe** and **European** in general Anglophone discourse, which regards nations in the western half of continental Europe as being somehow the most characteristically and prototypically **European**. There is a frequent blurring of the distinctions between the terms **European**, **West European**, and **Western**. This can be seen in part as an inheritance of the geopolitical divisions—and the rhetoric—of the Cold War. It also has much longer and deeper roots. In the Middle Ages, **Europe** and **European** were relatively little used terms in any language (and the adjective **European** did not exist at all in English), but *Christendom* was a core concept, and later conceptions of **Europe** owe a great deal to this. In uses of the term *Christendom* there is again a distinct westward bias, the lands showing obedience to the Roman Catholic Church being regarded as the most prototypical, core part of the European Christian world from an Anglophone perspective. These conceptions remained influential in the aftermath of the Reformation, when **Europe** began to be spoken of much more frequently, conceptualized as being composed most prototypically of the old provinces of the western half of the Roman Empire, very roughly corresponding (with additions of territories never part of the Empire) to the Catholic Christendom of the Middle Ages. Latinity is of course a key common factor here, defining a core **Europe** beside which the Orthodox east has a much less certain status—an uncertainty only reinforced after the fall of Constantinople and the long Ottoman domination of much of Europe's east. In subsequent centuries, supranational intellectual and cultural movements such as the ENLIGHTENMENT and Romanticism have reinforced the central role of the western half of the continent in the development of those forces that have most obviously transcended national boundaries and helped develop a broader sense of cultural identity broadly analogous to that of medieval Christendom. Where empirical discoveries such as the relatedness of the Indo-European language family have seemed to foreground extra-European affiliations, they have been to a certain extent neutralized, as by assuming (almost certainly counterfactually) that the ancient "Aryans" of south Asia must ultimately have originated from Europe. As already noted, an important influence informing contemporary usage is **Europe** (and hence **European**) as a shorthand for the **European Union**. The EU originated in the west of the continent and its most powerful economic and political voices are all broadly west of the Oder-Neisse line. By a simple set of associative steps we see how a linkage **Europe** = EU = (continental) western

Europe is set up, reinforcing and deepening the impression that the core of Europe in cognitive terms is well to the west of its geographical center (itself an interestingly disputed title, with various locations in Lithuania, Hungary, Estonia, and Belarus among the claimants).

In the most characteristic uses of the word **European** to denote ideas and values we can thus see that the equation is not quite so simple as "European = from the continent of Europe"; popular conceptions of the extent and boundaries of Europe may not be the same as geographical ones, and additionally there is a distinct westward geographical bias in what is seen as most prototypically **European**, as a result of numerous different converging cultural and political factors stretching from Antiquity to the economic and political landscape of post–Cold War Europe.

These same factors come into play when **European** is applied to people, with added complications. Firstly, while the population of for instance France or Germany may be accorded the status of **Europeans** in any type of discourse, more uncertainty or controversy may arise in other cases, such as Britain (since in much popular British discourse **Europe** is still conceptualized as beginning on the other side of the Channel), or Russia or other former Soviet republics, or parts of Turkey west of the Bosphorus. Secondly, while populations are mobile and fluid, this reality is often downplayed or denied in conceptualizations of ethnic identity. Here, **European** often acts as shorthand for a complex combination of factors, typically not thought through individually but vaguely apprehended as defining a European: RACE is crucial here, and often **European** is deployed as a means of drawing a distinction between the traditional INDIGENOUS populations of Europe—and especially of its more westerly parts—and any relatively dark-skinned populations seen as belonging indigenously elsewhere. The sinister potential of this can be seen, for instance, in Oswald Mosley's postwar "Europe a Nation" movement: an important factor in the use of **European** in this context is its implicit exclusion of numerous groups seen as non-indigenous, not least Jews. Outside such explicitly racist discourse, the subtle blending of racial and cultural factors in how **European** is applied to people and peoples can generate dangerous ambiguity: to take just two among many different mental configurations, for one speaker, the prototypical **European** may be someone who embraces the principles of the Enlightenment and who resides in, originates from, or identifies closely with the continent of Europe, while for another speaker the prototypical **European** may be white and Christian; and even for a single speaker the same set of considerations may not always be in play.

So far the focus of this entry has been deliberately **Eurocentric** in at least one respect, because it has left until last a usage which the *OED* traces back to the 1660s as both adjective and noun, namely the application of **European** specifically to people living outside Europe. Here we may see a very interesting case of semantic change in action. In earliest use, traders or colonialists living outside Europe will almost invariably have been born there and may well return there (one of the *OED*'s earliest examples in fact comes from a translation of a French text, in which "some of the European Inhabitants of these Islands" renders "nos François"); over the centuries in numerous different colonial and post-colonial contexts this use becomes increasingly a synonym for *white*, applied to people who may well never have visited the continent of Europe and whose most recent ancestors permanently resident in Europe may go back several generations, but who are nonetheless identified as **European**. This is closely linked to use of **European** as a term in attempted schemes of racial classification dating back at least as far as Linnaeus in 1735—although the choice of **European** over, e.g., *white* nonetheless may be seen as in some ways foregrounding cultural factors. This use illuminates the dangerous polysemy of **European**: who or what is conceptualized as **European** differs very much with our perspective, in ways that are seldom rigorously identified or thought through, but which inform and feed upon one another.

The refugee crisis of 2015 and the British vote to leave the European Union in June 2016 have foregrounded the difficulty with which the European Union now confronts both GLOBAL developments and resurgent nationalisms. The dream of Europe providing a transcendent political entity that would transcend the nationalisms of the past and embrace the different ethnicities of the future has never looked more threadbare. Perhaps the greatest challenge that Europe faces is the rise of a xenophobic NATIONALISM. Following the recent political gains of the far right, who are as opposed to the "**European**" as to the "**non-European**," the liberal pluralism that ushered in the European Union era may be as difficult to maintain as its fuzzy internal borders.

See CULTURE, ENLIGHTENMENT, GLOBAL, IDENTITY, INDIGENOUS, NATIONALIST, RACE, WEST

EVOLUTION

Evolution came from the sense of unrolling something and eventually indicated something being unrolled. It is now standard in two common senses, but in one of these, and in its specialized contrast with *revolution*, this complexity of its history is significant.

Evolve is from fw *evolvere*, L—roll out, unroll, from rw *volvere*, L—to roll. It appeared in English, with **evolution**, in mC17. **Evolution** is from fw *évolution*, F, from *evolutionem*, L, which is recorded in the sense of unrolling a book. Its early uses were mainly physical and mathematical in the root sense, but it was soon applied, metaphorically, both to the divine creation and to the working-out, the developing formation, of Ideas or Ideal Principles. It is clear from the root sense and from these early applications that what is implied is the "unrolling" of something that already exists. God comprehends "the whole evolution of ages" (1667) in one eternal moment; there is an "Evolution of Outward forms" (More, 1647); there is a "whole Systeme of Humane Nature . . . in the evolution whereof the complement and formation of the Humane Nature must consist" (Hale, 1677).

An apparently modern sense is then indicated in biology. **Evolution** took the sense of development from rudimentary to mature organs, and the **theory of evolution**, as argued by Bonnet in 1762, was a description of development from an embryo which already contains, in rudimentary form, all the parts of the mature organism, and where the embryo itself is a development of a preexisting form. The sense of "unrolling" from something that already exists is thus still crucially present. However, in the course of description of various natural processes, **evolution** came to be used as virtually equivalent to *development* (mC18, from *develop*, C17—to unfold, to lay open; C18—to unfold fully, to complete). But it is still difficult to be sure whether any particular use carries the firm sense of something pre-existent or implicit, thus making the **evolution** natural or necessary. In the not particularly common but still standard contemporary use of the **evolution** of an argument or an idea, this sense of a necessary or rational *development* is still usually present.

What then happened in biology was a generalization of the sense of *development* (fully bringing out) from immature to mature forms, and especially the specialized sense of *development* from "lower" to "higher" organisms. From 1C18 and eC19 this sense of a general natural process—a natural HISTORY over and above specific natural processes—was becoming known. It was explicit in Lyell on the evolution of land animals in 1832 and was referred to by Darwin in *The Origin of Species* (sixth edition, 1872) as admitted "at the present day" by "almost all naturalists," "under some form." Herbert Spencer in 1852 defined a general **Theory of Evolution** from lower to higher forms of life and organization.

What Darwin did that was new was to describe some of the processes by which new species developed and to generalize these as *natural selection*. It is ironic that this radically new metaphor, in which NATURE was seen as discarding as well as developing various forms of LIFE, was sustained within a continuing description of the process as **evolution**, with its sense of unrolling what already existed or maturing what was already preformed. Of course the metaphor of Nature *selecting* could be associated with a different sense of inherent design. A process shown in detail as generally material, environmental, and in one sense accidental could be generalized as a process in which *Nature* had purpose or purposes. Nevertheless, as the new understanding of the origins of species spread, **evolution** lost, in biology, its sense of inherent design and became a process of natural historical development. It had happened because it had happened, and would go on happening because it was a natural process. The idea of necessary purpose became restricted to particular interpretations (**creative evolution**, Catholic biology, and so on).

It was in the confusion of debate about **evolution** in this biological sense, and the even greater confusion of analogical applications from natural history to social history, that the contrast between **evolution** and *revolution* came to be made. *Revolution* had now its developed sense of sudden and violent change, as well as its sense of the institution of a new order. **Evolution** in the sense of gradual development could readily be opposed to it, and the metaphors of "growth" and of the ORGANIC had a simple association with this sense. Ironically, as can be seen in the development of Social Darwinism, the generalized natural history provided images for any imaginable kind of social action and change. Ruthless competition or mutual cooperation; slow change in the record of the rocks or sudden change in the appearance of mutations; violent change in the course of altered ENVIRONMENT, or the disappearance of species in ruthless struggle: all could be and were adduced as the "lessons" of nature to be applied or extended to society. To say that social change should be **evolutionary** might mean any or all of these things, from the slow development of new institutions to the wiping-out of former classes (species) and their replacement by higher forms. But in the contrast with *revolution* the earlier sense of **evolution** had primary effect. What was usually meant was the unrolling of something already implicitly formed (like a national *way of life*), or the *development* of something according to its inherent tendencies (like an existing constitution or economic system). (Cf. the conventional modern contrast between *developed* and *underdeveloped* societies, where the assumption of all societies as destined to become URBAN and industrial—not to say capitalist—is taken for granted, as if it were a technical term.) Radical change, which would include rejection of some existing forms or reversal of some existing tendencies, could then, within the metaphor, be described as "unnatural" and, in the contrast with the specialized sense of *revolution,* be associated with sudden VIOLENCE as opposed to steady growth.

In the real history of the last hundred years, in which the **evolution**/*revolution* contrast has become commonplace, the application has to be seen as absurd. It is carefully applied only to planned change, where in practice it is a distinction between a few slow changes controlled by what already exists and more and faster changes intended to alter much of what exists. The distinction is not really one of political process or method but of political affiliation. In "unplanned" change—that is to say the **evolution** of forces and factors already inherent in a social order—there has, after all, been suddenness and violence enough, and the contrast with *revolution* seems merely arbitrary. But then the overlap and confusion between **evolution** as (i) inherent development, (ii) unplanned natural history, and (iii) slow and conditioned change become matters for constant scrutiny.

RECENT DEVELOPMENTS

The final section of this entry, which contrasts **evolution** and *revolution,* may be particularly opaque for any reader born after the fall of the Soviet Empire. It was the Russian Revolution of 1917 that crystallized an argument between those who believed that the socialist development of society could be achieved through parliamentary democracy and those who believed that it required violent revolution and a direct seizure of state power by a proletarian party. While Williams agreed with the Communist argument that the establishment of socialism required fundamental changes in the organization of society, he believed strongly that these had to come about through an ever widening democratic argument: his Long Revolution. He is therefore concerned to reject most forms of the opposition between **evolution** and *revolution* in terms of violence or speed and to insist that the crucial question is a belief in the ability consciously to plan social change. It is the building of this conscious planning into the development of the means of communication that marks the originality of Williams's thought.

The debate that opposes **evolution** to *revolution* has diminished, for now, into history, but the conflict of meanings within the word **evolution** that Williams identifies remains at the center of two vigorous and often vicious debates that in one form or other have been ongoing since Darwin published. His theory of

evolution by natural selection breaks decisively with any notion of the working out of a pre-planned design. It is thus fatal to a notion of a theistic God designing a world into which man would fit. After Darwin, man and world are functions of each other and no designer is required. This explains why the fight with revealed religion is so bitter and so unending. The argument from Design is the most powerful of the traditional arguments for God. Darwin deals it a potentially mortal blow. From the beginning there have been many Christian arguments in favor of accepting the account of creation laid out in the first books of the Bible. And by 1860, a year after the publication of *On the Origin of Species*, these arguments were named *creationism*. In the 1980s, partly in relation to rulings in the US which had refused to allow creationism to be taught in schools, a new term entered the creationist textbooks: *intelligent design*. Relying on admitted gaps in evolutionary accounts, this argument postulated the need for an intelligent designer to fill these gaps. By avoiding the identification of the intelligent designer with God, the authors of these textbooks hoped to avoid the court rulings that the teachings of creationism offended the separation between Church and State fundamental to the US Constitution. Although subsequent court rulings continued to hold that intelligent design was not a scientific theory, the demand that intelligent design be taught in schools as scientific has become part of a constellation of issues that define the Tea Party right in America.

If **evolution** has always had to contend with those who believe in God, it has also continuously had to cope with its appropriation by those who would use it to explain human behavior. Hitler's race theories are only the most objectionable of a whole series of arguments known as social Darwinism, which understood the survival of the fittest as a license to analyze human social life in terms of evolution via constant conflict. The fundamental mistake of all these theories is to ignore the extent to which human social life is a tremendously complicated cultural construct that differs widely from society to society. The notion that we have biologically programmed social behavior ignores this central fact.

Perhaps the most egregious appeal to such biologically programmed social behavior is the deeply controversial field of **evolutionary psychology**, which argues that our brains were biologically formed by the Stone Age and that therefore our social behavior was also biologically fixed at that time. The result is an industry of what Stephen Jay Gould characterized as "Just So Stories," in which some aspect of human behavior is universalized in the present, random confirmation is then taken from some animal behavior, and then an account of that human behavior is mapped onto a presumed Stone Age man. The power of this form of explanation seems littled dented by the fact that the vast majority of philosophers of biology dismiss its claims to scientific status: "Among the successes of this group [evolutionary psychologists] has been to either ignore or caricature their critics, and to concentrate on establishing the paraphernalia of a recognized and reputable scientific programme—specialist journals, conferences, postgraduate degrees, and the like. This appearance of scientific respectability, of what Thomas Kuhn in his classic *The Structure of Scientific Revolutions* described as 'normal science,' is illusory" (John Dupré, *Darwin's Legacy*, 2003, 78).

A parallel and even more influential development has been the interpretation of Darwinism most eloquently articulated in Richard Dawkins's *The Selfish Gene* (1976). Dawkins argues that natural selection operates on genes, not organisms, and while he continuously proclaims that his arguments do not provide explanations of human social life, his metaphors continuously proclaim that the most important level of the description of human life is the genetic: "We are survival machines—robot vehicles blindly programmed to preserve the selfish molecules known as genes." Few explanations of science have been so persuasive to so many, despite the fact that many contemporary biologists dissent from Dawkins's analysis. All the advances in cell and molecular biology since the 1970s suggest that the gene is not the discrete entity that Dawkins proposes and that the process of natural selection is best understood by a multi-level analysis that includes the organism, its wider environments, and its genes.

Both Dawkins's work and **evolutionary psychology** belong within a wider movement—sometimes known as "universal Darwinism"—which aims to detect analogues in other domains for Darwin's account of evolution in biological organisms. This movement has produced an ongoing proliferation of the classifier **"evolutionary"** in the title of a wide range of new sub-disciplines, including, besides **evolutionary psychology: evolutionary aesthetics, evolutionary anthropology, evolutionary computation, evolutionary epistemology, evolutionary ethics, evolutionary linguistics, evolutionary music, evolutionary robotics.** Many of these research agendas have proved to be controversial, depending on which aspects of Darwin's model they adopt and what challenges they present to previous orthodoxies in their domain. Often the controversy seems to hinge on what Williams called the "overlap and confusion" between the different senses of the word **evolution** itself.

A possible cause for the persistent widespread attractiveness of such ideas is that the word **evolution** may still evoke the teleological sense that Williams defines as "inherent development" that has little to do with the very limited claims of scientific evolution concerned with understanding such matters as how a fish's swim bladder developed into lungs or how the shape of the human tongue has been modified to permit the production of vowels.

The *OED* claims that the important figurative sense of **evolution** which transposed the unrolling of a parchment onto the unrolling of all of God's creation becomes rare after C17. Williams's account is more nuanced, as he sees this sense working through C18 biological developments so that it is at least implicit in most of the formulations. Both Williams and the *OED* are at one that Darwin's use of the word contains no trace of this theological meaning. Darwin himself seems not to have been so sure about **evolution** having lost its theological connotations, as he refused to use the term until the sixth edition of *On the Origin of Species*. In the original edition, he does use the verb "**evolve**" and indeed it is the word that ends the book, but, as a verb, **evolve** stresses process rather than conclusion and inherits none of the theological meanings that attach to the early history of the noun **evolution**.

When Darwin does use the word **evolution** in the sixth edition, it is in an additional chapter in which he considers various criticisms of his theory. Darwin may well have felt by then, after a decade of vigorous and voluminous debate, that the word had shrugged off unwelcome theological connotations. However, uses such as the **evolution** of an argument or an idea continue to provide examples in the current language: "the evolution of an idea into a script" or "the evolution of a design into the product" where **evolution** carries the meaning of a complex process that comes to a predetermined end. The word **evolution** thus continues to promise an account of the world that has both ends and purposes, although Darwin's theory of natural selection and its developments in contemporary biology offer no such consolations.

Evolution is deeply entrenched as the simple word that summarizes the history of life on earth. In some ways it is a word whose semantic force makes it very ill-suited to its historical scientific role. It is likely that those who seek in **evolution** a comprehensive explanation of the biological and social universe will continue to be licensed as long as the meaning of **evolution** hints at a development that comes to a definite end.

See ENVIRONMENT, HISTORY, LIFE, NATURE, ORGANIC, VIOLENCE

EXCELLENCE

Excellence is a prominent term in contemporary political discourse related to public services, especially in the context of EDUCATION, where the word has attracted widespread ridicule. Writing about how the notion of a university changed in response to the 1990s restructuring of UK Higher Education, for example, the author of the 1997 critique *The University in Ruins*, Bill Readings, claimed that **excellence** had become a "non-referential unit of value entirely internal to the system" and an "empty notion" (39). This and similar observations suggest that despite appearing to offer a key measure of quality, the terms **excellence** and **excellent** have become effectively meaningless, or at least have undergone a significant process of semantic change. Prominent use of these words in university mission statements, governmental initiatives, and education journals points to an important site of semantic weakening or bleaching, as well as illustrates consequences of the complex functioning of **excellence** as a keyword in discourse about education and other public services.

The *OED* offers the following definition for the core current sense of **excellence**: "The state or fact of excelling; the possession chiefly of good qualities in an eminent or unusual degree; surpassing merit, skill, virtue, worth etc.; dignity, eminence." Etymologically, **excellence**, **excellent**, and **excel** are closely related, all derived from similarly related French models; ultimately the cluster of words in both languages can be traced to Latin verb *excellere*, glossed in the *OED* as "to rise above others, be eminent." In early use (attested from lC14) all three forms reflect this meaning. But the *OED* evidence shows they have diverged over time. The definitions of both the transitive and intransitive senses of the verb **excel** show that the word implies comparison: something can only excel relative to something else, which must therefore be inferior in some way. Earliest senses of the corresponding noun and adjective **excellence** and **excellent** also imply comparison. But the *OED* entries show that, in the case of **excellent**, a significant semantic change has taken place: some kind of bleaching, through which an element of meaning has been lost. As a result, the most common sense of **excellent** has shifted from "better than others" to simply "very good"; the term is still positive, but the implication of comparison has been lost.

The *OED* does not record a corresponding bleached sense for **excellence**. However, the entry in *The New Oxford Dictionary of English* suggests that one has emerged: **excellence** is defined as "the quality of being outstanding or extremely good," with no clear distinction between the unbleached sense (suggested by "outstanding") and a bleached sense (suggested by "extremely good"). In the context of educational discourse, uncertainty between these available meanings has acquired a complex function. The frequency with which **excellence** is used in university mission statements and related material makes an *un*-bleached meaning problematic: self-evidently, not all universities can be better than all others, or have realistic aims to become better than all the others. Despite this, in a sample of twenty-one UK university mission statements, more than half (12) were found to describe themselves in terms of **excellence**. Typical examples are Birkbeck's (University of London) aim to "maintain and develop excellence in research," and the University of Strathclyde's intention "to combine excellence with relevance." Such usage suggests that **excellence** has come to be equated with a (high) standard of performance, rather than performance that is relatively better than others; in other words, the term is being used as a nominalized form of bleached **excellent** rather than as the noun form **excellence** as presently defined in the *OED*. In such use, rather than the adjective **excellent** being used to modify a following noun (as in **excellent teaching**), it has become common to use the noun form with a following prepositional phrase: e.g., **excellence in teaching**. This pattern is regarded as stylistically more formal but is semantically less precise. **Excellent teaching** is specific and implies an overall high standard; **excellence in teaching** is vaguer. While **excellence in teaching** suggests a relationship between a high standard and teaching, it does not specify precisely what that relationship is. In this context, tracking the frequency of use of **excellence** in educational discourse over the past three decades is revealing. Use of the term in educational journals increased dramatically from the 1970s to the 1990s; by contrast, the frequency of **excellent** appears relatively stable.

Choice of preposition following **excellence** affects the word's meaning and implications. **Excellence** occurs with *in* and *of*, e.g., in phrases such as **excellence in teaching** and **the excellence of its research**. Historically, **excellence of** is earlier, and appears to be the more usual construction until relatively recently. In contemporary usage, however, the newer construction **excellence in** appears to be becoming more frequent, while **excellence of** may be in decline, a change signaling complex interaction between the word's syntax and semantics. Characteristically, **excellence of** is preceded by *the*, and carries an implicit comparative sense: if X is recognized for **the excellence of** its performance in a specified area, by implication it is doing better than some others even if those others are not explicitly identified. By contrast, if X is recognized as showing **excellence in** a specified area, there is no implied comparison with others. It is possible that everyone could show **excellence** in the same area. In this respect **excellence in** is aligned to the bleached sense of **excellent**, in which the element of comparison is either greatly reduced or entirely absent.

The significance of what might otherwise seem a nuance is that the semantic difference underpins alternative policy models and aspirations. On one interpretation, it is possible that everyone can achieve **excellence in** a given area (if the measure is set sufficiently abstractly), whereas on the other interpretation, performance in the area requires assessed achievement favoring only a subset. What makes **excellence** and related forms problematic in institutional and public-policy discourse is that there is little or no acknowledgment, in government pronouncements or in the relevant literature, that the word is ambiguous. In the absence of recognition of such semantic complexity, it is inevitable that the comparative sense will be (consciously or unconsciously) exploited, but not directly conveyed, in pervasive use of **excellence** in preference to less ambiguous alternatives. It can be noted that uses of **excellence** have become current in the wider sphere of marketing and consumer culture—as, for instance, logos such as "Lindt Excellence" or "DHL—Excellence. Simply Delivered."

See EDUCATION, PERFORMANCE

EXPERIENCE

The old association between **experience** and *experiment* can seem, in some of the most important modern uses, merely obsolete. **Experience**, in one main sense, was until 1C18 interchangeable with *experiment* (cf. modern French) from the common rw *experiri*, L—to try, to put to the test. **Experience**, from the present participle, became not only a conscious test or trial but a consciousness of what has been tested or tried, and thence a consciousness of an effect or state. From C16 it took on a more general meaning, with more deliberate inclusion of the past (the tried and tested), to indicate knowledge derived from real events as well as from particular observation. *Experiment*, a noun of action, maintained the simple sense of a test or trial. The problem now is to consider the relations between two main senses which have been important since 1C18. These can be summarized as (i) knowledge gathered from past events, whether by conscious observation or by consideration and reflection; and (ii) a particular kind of consciousness, which can in some contexts be distinguished from "reason" or "knowledge." We can give a famous and influential example of each sense.

Burke, in the *Reflections on the Revolution in France* (1790), wrote:

If I might venture to appeal to what is so much out of fashion in Paris,
I mean to experience. . . .

This is a conservative argument against "rash" political innovation, stressing the
need for "slow but well-sustained progress," taking each step as it comes and
watching its effect. We can see how this developed from the sense of experiment
and observation, but what is new is the confident generalization of the "lessons
of experience": particular conclusions as well as particular methods. Someone in
Paris might have replied that the Revolution itself was an "experience," in the sense
of putting a new kind of politics to trial and observation, but for all those older
implications of the word it seems certain that this would have been overborne, at
least in English, by the riper and more gathered sense, then and now, of "lessons" as
against "innovations" or "experiments."

That is **experience** past. We can see **experience** present in T. S. Eliot (*Metaphysical
Poets*, 1921):

a thought to Donne was an experience, it modified his sensibility.

What is implicit here is a distinction between kinds of consciousness; to some
people, it seems, a thought would *not* be an experience, but a (lesser) act of reasoning or OPINION. **Experience**, in this major tendency, is then the fullest, most
open, most active kind of consciousness, and it includes feeling as well as thought.
This sense has been very active in *aesthetic* discussion, following an earlier religious
sense, and it can come to be contrasted, over a wide area, with the kinds of consciousness involved in reasoning and conscious experiment.

It is evident that the grounds for reliance on **experience** past ("lessons") and **experience** present (full and active "awareness") are radically different, yet there is nevertheless a link between them, in some of the kinds of action and consciousness which
they both oppose. This does not have to be the case, but the two distinct senses, from
1C18, have in practice moved together, within a common historical situation.

It is very difficult, in the complexity of the emergence of these senses from
the always latent significances in much earlier uses, to mark definite phases. The

general usefulness of **experience** past is so widely recognized that it is difficult to know who would want to challenge it while it remains a neutral sense, permitting radically different conclusions to be drawn from diversely gathered and interpreted observations. But it is of course just this which the rhetorical use against *experiment* or *innovation* prevents. It is interesting that Blake, at almost the same time as Burke, used **experience** in a much more problematic way: less bland, less confident; indeed a troubled contrast with *innocence*. So far from being an available and positive set of recommendations, it was "bought with the price of all that a man hath" (*Four Zoas*, II, *c*1800). No specific interpretation of **experience** can in practice be assumed to be directive; it is quite possible from **experience** to see a need for *experiment* or *innovation*.

This might be easier to agree than the problem of **experience** present. It is clear that this involves an appeal to the whole consciousness, the whole being, as against reliance on more specialized or more limited states or faculties. As such it is part of that general movement which underlies the development of CULTURE and its directly associated terms. The strength of this appeal to wholeness, against forms of thought which would exclude certain kinds of consciousness as merely "personal," "subjective," or "emotional," is evident. Yet within the form of appeal (as again in CULTURE and ART) the stress on wholeness can become a form of exclusion of other nominated partialities. The recent history of this shift is in aesthetics (understandably so, when we recall the development of aesthetics itself), but the decisive phase was probably in a certain form of religion, and especially Methodism.

The sense develops from **experience** as "being consciously the subject of a state or condition" (*OED*, 4) and especially from the application of this to an "inner," "personal," religious experience. While this was available within many religious forms, it became especially important within Protestantism, and was increasingly relied on in later and more radical Protestant movements. Thus in Methodism there were *experience-meetings*, classes "held for the recital of religious experiences." A description of 1857 records that "there was praying, and exhorting, and telling experiences, and singing . . . sentimental hymns." This is then a notion of *subjective* witness, offered to be shared. What is important about it, for a later more general sense, is that such **experiences** are offered not only as TRUTHS, but as the most AUTHENTIC kind of truths. Within theology, this claim has been the matter of an immense argument. The caution of Jonathan Edwards—"those experiences which are agreeable to the word of God are right" (1758)—is among the more moderate reactions. It is clear that in C20 both the claim and the doubts and objections have moved into a much wider field. At one extreme **experience** (present) is offered as the necessary (immediate and authentic) ground for all (subsequent) reasoning and analysis. At the other extreme, **experience** (once the present participle not of "feeling" but of "trying" or "testing" something) is seen as the product of social conditions or of systems of belief or of fundamental systems of perception, and thus not as material for truths but as evidence of conditions or systems which by definition it cannot itself explain.

This remains a fundamental controversy, and it is not, fortunately, limited to its extreme positions. But much of the controversy is confused, from the beginning, by the complex and often alternative senses of **experience** itself. **Experience** past already includes, at its most serious, those processes of consideration, reflection, and analysis which the most extreme use of **experience** present—an unquestionable authenticity and immediacy—excludes. Similarly, the reduction of **experience** to material always produced from elsewhere depends on an exclusion of kinds of consideration, reflection, and analysis which are not of a consciously separated systematic type. It is then not that such kinds should not be tested, but that in the deepest sense of **experience** all kinds of evidence and its consideration should be tried.

Recent Developments

The Marxist argument, most ably articulated by Louis Althusser, that **experience** is not immediate but mediated by the social formation, retains some force but has lost all currency. The belief in **experience** as the most immediate touchstone for VALUE has gained ground in the last half-century, as the use of the word has increased considerably in frequency. Perhaps the most important developments have come in advertising and marketing, where **customer experience** has become central and where the argument has been advanced that we live in an **experience economy**; just as services replaced goods, so **experiences** are now replacing services as the most important element in advanced economies. These new uses play on the ambiguity in **experience** that allows it to be both individual and collective. In the contemporary **experience economy** every customer is offered a collective good that he or she **experiences** individually. These new uses heavily emphasize both the individual and the moment, as **experience** becomes centrally linked to acquisition.

There is an increasing use of the noun as qualified by proper names, as in **The Jimi Hendrix Experience**, the **Doctor Who Experience**, the **Air New Zealand Experience**, and this usage is in line with the general commodification of

experience, also evident in the offer of **the cruise experience, experience gifts,** and **experience days**. The verb, however, has developed a different set of collocates in which the positive pleasing products we might purchase are replaced by the grimmest forms of suffering: **experiencing homelessness, experiencing trauma,** and **experiencing pain**. This usage distinction is quite consistent: whereas people "have a shopping experience," they do not "have a homelessness experience," and while people "experience trauma," they do not "experience shopping." This distinction in semantics and usage between the noun and the verb seems to distinguish between experiences that we choose and experiences that we suffer.

See AUTHENTIC, CULTURE, OPINION, TRUTH, VALUE

FAIR

Fair is part of the core inherited vocabulary of Germanic, with a history going back to the earliest documentary records of the English language. **Fair** and **fairness** have both also figured prominently in recent political discourse. A widely quoted sentence from British prime minister David Cameron's 2010 Conservative Party conference speech, for example, was:

> Fairness means giving people what they deserve—and what people
> deserve depends on how they behave.

Fair has a very complex semantic history, and remains polysemous in contemporary use. Additionally, its core modern use is rather difficult to define, and has difficult relationships with a number of other important terms in contemporary social and political discourse. These tensions point to an interesting gap in Williams's "vocabulary of culture and society," at least in the context of contemporary discourse.

The *Oxford Dictionary of English* (*ODE*) gives the following definitions of the main contemporary uses of **fair**, based on analysis of corpus data:

(1) Treating people equally without favouritism or discrimination; just or appropriate in the circumstances.

(2) (Of hair or complexion) light; blonde; (of a person) having a light complexion or hair.

(3) Considerable though not outstanding in size or amount; moderately good; (*Australian /NZ informal*) complete, utter.

(4) (Of weather) Fine and dry.

(5) (*archaic*) Beautiful.

If we look at large text databases, the most frequently found collocations today include **fair share, fair amount, fair market, fair value, fair use**. A recent big climb in frequency has been shown by **fair trade**. A decline since C19 is shown by **fair wind, fair young [person], fair lady, fair sex, fair game**. Two collocations that seem to have peaked around the turn of C20 are **fair hearing** and **fair play**.

If we take a much longer-range historical perspective, in Old English the core meaning of **fair** is "beautiful (to behold)," with occasional use with reference to behavior or conduct that is "free from impropriety, according to custom, appropriate, fit." In Middle English, some important semantic complexity enters: a person's appearance, speech, or conduct may be **fair** if it is "benign, kindly, gracious, courteous" (also if it is "beguilingly benign," reflected later particularly by the collocation **fair words**). Alongside the meaning "according to custom, appropriate" we find (as defined by the *Middle English Dictionary*) "accordant with truth, reason, approved practice, or justice; right, proper, sound; equitable, impartial, just" and "morally good and proper," as well as "highly to be approved of; splendid, excellent; fine, good." The meaning "above average; considerable, sizable" also enters in this period.

OED (first edition) defines the core later meaning:

> Of conduct, actions, arguments, methods: Free from bias, fraud, or injustice; equitable, legitimate. Hence of persons: Equitable; not taking undue advantage; disposed to concede every reasonable claim. Of objects: That may be legitimately aimed at; often in *fair game*.

Here we have *equitable*, rather than, as in *ODE*'s formulation, *treating people equally*. This suggests that there is ambiguity here even for lexicographers: the first part of the *ODE* definition, "treating people equally without favouritism or discrimination," would place **fair** in the same semantic category as a core use of *equal* and *equality*; by contrast, the second part of the definition, "just or appropriate in the circumstances," brings us back to the same semantic area as *OED*'s *equitable*.

The semantic classification of the *Historical Thesaurus of the Oxford English Dictionary* (*HTOED*) can be helpful here. **Fair** appears in a total of eighty different *HTOED* categories, reflecting its high degree of polysemy. The relevant uses of **fair** and *equitable* appear together under the category "society/morality/rightness or justice/fair or equitable." In this category, *equal* appears only as an obsolete synonym. *Equitable* and *equity* are difficult concepts, frequently defined by equation with **fair** and **fairness**; definitions of both sets of terms also typically draw in the word group of *just* and *justice*. However, working definitions of what is **fair** and *equitable* frequently invoke the concept of *desert*, precisely as in David Cameron's formulation, "Fairness means giving people what they deserve." Of course in an entirely egalitarian social and political framework, this may still equate with total *equality* of treatment, if all people are taken to be equally deserving, fundamentally. However, a very different construction is also possible, as in the second part of Cameron's sentence, "what people deserve depends on how they behave."

Reactions to this speech by David Cameron in the UK media in 2010 illuminate the ambiguity of the term **fair** as regards questions of culture and society. Some commentators pointedly equated **fairness** with *egalitarianism* and the reduction of *inequality*; others accepted Cameron's hypothesis that **fairness** (also) involves taking into account the earned *desert* of the *hard-working*. Here we see the clearest evidence for a keyword in contemporary political debate. Struggles over the meaning of **fairness** encapsulate key divisions over questions of social justice, equity, and EQUALITY. It is probably no accident, therefore, that the debate has centered on a familiar item of core vocabulary, which is polysemous even in contemporary use and notoriously slippery and difficult to define in its relevant meanings. Everyone feels they know intuitively what it is to be **fair**, and that to be **fair** is a good thing; and such words are attractive verbal territory for politicians. The difficulty with the word and the difficulty of the debate come in determining what is **fair** in the context of a complex modern society. The shifting and conflicting relationships between **fair** (and **fairness**) and other words in this area of social and political discourse point up the importance of **fair** as a keyword in contemporary debate.

See EQUALITY

FAITH

Faith has been in common usage in English from C14 to denote "religious belief." Originally appearing primarily in theological contexts, it came to be used from C18 to name a confidence in any system of belief, religious, or otherwise. **Faith** was frequently used to contrast that which could not be empirically proven over and against belief systems claiming an empirical basis (such as natural philosophy and, from C19, *science, rationalism*, or *skepticism*). In recent years, **faith** has re-emerged as a polarizing term both in the US and in the UK in debates concerning the proper role of RELIGION in relation to government and other social institutions (as in **faith-based initiatives** and **faith schools**).

Faith has historically presented semantic difficulties insofar as it names both (i) what a person believes (a particular belief or creed); and (ii) how she or he believes it (the act of having faithfulness to a belief). In English, this confusion is not present in the term *belief*, which **faith** superseded by the end of C14. **Faith**, from oF *fei*, originally meant "loyalty to a person to whom one is bound by a promise or duty," such as a liege lord or spouse. Thus Chaucer's Parson asserts that "[m]an sholde bere hym to his wyf in feith, in trouthe, and in loue" (*c*1390). In this usage, there was no reference to *belief*, since it essentially meant "fidelity" or "fealty." However, as etymological descendant of Latin *fides*, **faith** began to be used more frequently (particularly in theological language) in C14 to mean "the thing believed, a set of propositions regarded as true." "Which is thi creance and thi feith?" can be answered: " 'I am paien [pagan],' that other seith" (John Gower, *c*1391).

The Protestant Reformation promoted **faith** from a theological handmaiden to the central tenet of its worldview; a corollary of this shift was that **faith** moved from the realm of the PUBLIC to the PRIVATE. In the medieval period, an inward **faith** on its own was seen to be insufficient without benefit of charitable works that could be witnessed by others: "Feith is deed [dead] with outen werkis" (*c*1380). However, **faith** would soon go it alone with the advent of the Reformation and the rise of the doctrine of *sola fide* (Latin for "by faith alone"). This doctrine held that salvation arrived through God's grace, channeled through the **faith** of the believer. "We are justified," Martin Luther writes in his commentary on St. Paul's Epistle to the Galatians, "not by faith furnished with charity, but by faith only and alone" (English translation, 1575). Over the course of C16 and C17, **faith** migrated from the public sphere—the communal, practiced piety of medieval religion—to something contained within an individual's breast.

While in the medieval and early modern periods, the opposite of **faith** was *heresy* or incorrect belief, it also came to be opposed to *reason*. As the opposite of that which can be seen or touched, **faith** is often opposed to empirical evidence from its earliest usages. While **faith** was seen to be superior to reason in early Christian writings (as in Gregory the Great's oft-quoted homily: "faith has no merit where human reason offers proof"), it would come to be disparaged in C19. The conflict between *science* and **faith** took a form still recognizable today in the late Victorian period, where an enlightened "science" was seen to fight a battle against the repressive but slowly receding forces of "traditionary faith." Science came to be synonymous with an understanding of the material world and the validity of sensory observation over and against the immaterial world of belief.

There is an important use of **faith** that does not depend on the Christian tradition and which comes from the Latin phrase *bona fides*, "good faith." This makes a legal presupposition that both sides in an agreement or contract will act honestly or fairly. The opposite of this is "bad faith," *mala fides*. The philosopher Jean-Paul Sartre developed this concept in the 1940s and 1950s to describe someone who was acting dishonestly with themselves by accepting social roles that denied their own fundamental FREEDOM. This use of **bad faith** is a relatively rare example of a philosophical term gaining a wider currency in the language.

In more recent usage, **faith** has become synonymous not just with religious belief, but with irrationalism more generally. **Anti-faith** writings by prominent atheists contend that **faith** is simply belief without evidence, framing such understanding as a radical and potentially dangerous subjectivism. The inevitability of conflict between **faith** and *science* has been countered by writers such as Stephen Jay Gould, who attempt to reconcile **faith** and *science* by suggesting that they constitute "non-overlapping magisteria" or mutually exclusive domains that should not be measured with the same criteria. In *The Selfish Gene*, Richard Dawkins argues that **faith** can "immunize" believers against the feelings of common HUMANITY and lead them to martyrdom (1976). The equation of **faith** with fanaticism is a lC20 usage, increasingly found in eC21, given impetus by global acts of terrorism as well as, in the US, by debates about the validity of EVOLUTION and biblical literalism.

Finally, the term's network of association has broadened in C21 to include conflicts between opposing domains of knowledge in the public sphere. In the US, **faith-based initiatives** have come to be synonymous with charitable, nongovernmental organizations that undertake certain functions previously seen to be the domain of the government and are thus embroiled in debates about the

proper relation of church to government: compare "Congress . . . has swung behind a series of policy changes . . . which allow federal, state and local funds to
flow to faith-based anti-poverty groups" (*Newsweek*, June 1, 1998); and "George
W. Bush's 'faith-based' initiative could be the best, or the worst, new idea of his
presidency. The idea is to put God to work solving social problems" (*Newsday*,
February 1, 2001). In the UK, arguments over the viability of **faith schools** have
become a coded way of arguing about the social and political stakes of multiculturalism: "They have recently joined forces with the Muslims to demand government
funding for separate faith schools against the prevailing trend of multi-faith education" (*Independent*, March 25, 1990); and "In Britain they have also succeeded
in obtaining state funding for faith schools—putting them on a par with children
from Christian and Jewish backgrounds" (*New Internationalist*, May 27, 2002).
Such usages may suggest that the opposition between **faith** and *science* is being
superseded by renewed concerns about the relations of church and STATE in a new
era of FUNDAMENTALISM.

See FUNDAMENTALISM, PRIVATE, PUBLIC, RELIGION, SECULAR, SPIRITUAL, STATE

FAMILY

Family has an especially significant social history. It came into English in 1C14 and
eC15, from fw *familia*, L—household, from rw *famulus*—servant. The associated
adjective **familiar** appears to be somewhat earlier in common use, and its range of
meanings reminds us of the range of meanings which were predominant in **family**
before mC17. There is the direct sense of the Latin *household*, either in the sense
of a group of servants or a group of blood-relations and servants living together in
one house. **Familiar** related to this, in phrases like **familiar angel, familiar devil**,
and the later noun **familiar**, where the sense is of being associated with or serving
someone. There is also the common C15 and C16 phrase **familiar enemy**, to indicate an enemy within one's household, "within the gates," and thence by extension
an enemy within one's own people. But the strongest early senses of **familiar** were
those which are still current in modern English: on terms of friendship or intimate
with someone (cf. "don't be too familiar"); well known, well used to, or habitual (cf.
"familiar in his mouth as household words," *Henry V*). These uses came from the
experience of people living together in a household, in close relations with each
other and well used to each other's ways. They do not, and **familiar** still does not,
relate to the sense of a blood-group.

Family was then extended, from at latest C15, to describe not a household but what was significantly called a *house*, in the sense of a particular lineage or kin-group, ordinarily by descent from a common ancestor. This sense was extended to indicate a people or group of peoples, again with a sense of specific descent from an ancestor; also to a particular religious sense, itself associated with previous social meanings, as in "the Father of our Lord Jesus Christ, of whom the whole family in heaven and earth is named" (Ephesians 3:14–15). **Family** in the Authorized Version of the Bible (1611) was restricted to these wide senses: either a large kin-group, often virtually equivalent to *tribe* (Genesis 10:5; 12:3; Jeremiah 1:15; 31:1; Ezekiel 20:32) or the kin-group of a common father: "and then shall he (a brother) depart from thee, both he and his children with him, and shall return unto his own family, and unto the possession of his fathers shall he return" (Leviticus 25:41; cf. Numbers 36:6). The 1C16 and C17 sect of the **Family of Love** or **Familists** is interesting in that it drew on the sense of a large group, but made this open and voluntary through love.

In none of the pre-mC17 senses, therefore, can we find the distinctive modern sense of a small group confined to immediate blood relations. When this sense of relations between parents and children was required in A.V. Genesis it was rendered by *near kin*. Yet it is clear that between C17 and C19 the sense of the small kin-group, usually living in one house, came to be dominant; so dominant indeed that in C20 there has been an invention of terms to distinguish between this and the surviving subordinate sense of a large kin-group: the distinction between **nuclear family** and **extended family**. It is very difficult to trace this evolution, which has a complicated social history. We can still read from 1631: "his family were himself and his wife and daughters, two mayds and a man," where the sense is clearly that of *household*. This survived in rural use, with living-in farm servants who ate at the same table, until 1C18 and perhaps beyond; the later distinction between **family** and *servants* was in this instance much resented. There was also a long influence from aristocratic use, in the sense of *lineage*, and this remained strong in the characteristic C18 **found a family**. CLASS distinction was expressed as late as C19 (and residually beyond it) in phrases like "a person of no family," where the large kin-group is evidently in question but in the specialized sense of traceable lineage. Expressions like **the family** were still used to C20 to indicate a distinguishable upper-class group: "the family is in residence," where the kin-group sense has clearly been separated from the household sense, since the servants are there in any case (but not "in residence" even if "resident").

The specialization of **family** to the small kin-group in a single house can be related to the rise of what is now called the **bourgeois family**. But this, with its senses of household and PROPERTY, relates more properly, at least until C19, to the older sense. From eC19 (James Mill) we find this definition: "the group which consists of a Father, Mother and Children is called a Family"; yet the fact that the conscious definition is necessary is in itself significant. Several 1C17 and C18 uses of **family** in a small kin-group sense often refer specifically to children: "but duly sent his family and wife" (Pope, *Bathurst*), where the sense of household, however, may still be present. **Family-way**, common since eC18, referred first to the sense of **familiar** but then, through the specific sense of children, to pregnancy. There was thus considerable overlap, between mC17 and 1C18, of these varying senses of lineage, household, large kin-group, and small kin-group.

The dominance of the sense of small kin-group was probably not established before eC19. The now predominant pressure of the word, and the definition of many kinds of feeling in relation to it, came in mC19 and later. This can be represented as the apotheosis of the **bourgeois family**, and the sense of the isolated family as a working economic unit is clearly stressed in the development of CAPITALISM. But it has even stronger links to early capitalist production, and the C19 development represents, in one sense, a distinction between a man's *work* and his **family**: he works to support a **family**; the **family** is supported by his work. It is more probable, in fact, that the small kin-group definition, supported by the development of smaller separate houses and therefore households, relates to the new working class and lower-middle class who were defined by wage-labor: not **family** as lineage or property or as including these, and not **family** as *household* in the older established sense which included servants, but the near kin-group which can define its social relationships, in any positive sense, only in this way. **Family** or **family** and **friends** can represent the only immediately positive attachments in a large-scale and complex wage-earning society. And it is significant that class-feeling, the other major response to the new society, used *brother* and *sister* to express class affiliation, as in trade union membership, though there is also in this a clear religious precedent in certain related religious sects. It is significant also that this use of *brother* and *sister* came to seem artificial or comic in middle-class eyes. **Family**, there, combined the strong sense of immediate and positive blood-group relationships and the strong implicit sense of property.

It is a fascinating and difficult history, which can be only partly traced through the development of the word. But it is a history worth remembering when we hear that "the **family**, as an institution, is breaking up" or that, in times gone by and still hopefully today, "the **family** is the necessary foundation of all order and morality." In these and similar contemporary uses it can be useful to remember the major historical variations, with some of their surviving complexities, and the sense, through these, of radically changing definitions of primary relationships.

Recent Developments

In the past fifty years, **family** has developed further changes both in range of reference and intensity of meaning. The 1960s saw a series of linked ideological attacks on the **family**, including anti-psychiatry, feminism, and Marxism at the service of notions of communal living that would break with the traditional **family**. The efforts to forge alternative forms of communal living were in their own terms failures, often degenerating into cults of which the Manson Family was the most notorious. However, **family** itself, partly because of these experiments, has a much wider range of reference than in the immediate postwar era. CONSERVATIVE attempts to link appeals to **family values** with a reactionary moral agenda have foundered on the reality of a world in which a huge number of marriages end in divorce and in which same-sex MARRIAGE and same-sex parenting are well established. **Family** has re-established itself as a very strong term of approval in recent decades while extending its reference beyond a strict definition of the nuclear **family**.

The idea of the **family** as constituting the sole repository of affective ties that escape dominant economic and social relationships can be found, as much in fiction as in fact, in the widespread use from mC20 of **family** to describe American Mafia organizations. This use may be related to the most important modern development of the term, in which **family** relationships are mapped onto modern CORPORATE structures. Management textbooks such as *Family Ties, Corporate Bonds* (1985) or *Corporate Families: The Next Evolution in Teams* (2008) bear witness to a major attempt to recast economic relations of domination and exploitation in terms of direct affective relationships. This striking trend in modern corporate capitalism is also reflected in the growth of terms such as *mentor, buddy*, and *coach* to recast hierarchical relationships of power into older models of human development.

See CAPITALISM, CLASS, HOME, LOVE, MARRIAGE

FEMINIST

The word **feminism** derives from classical Latin *femina*, woman. It appears in English from mC19 with the meaning, now rare, of feminine, womanly; *OED*'s first example is the definition offered by the 1841 edition of *Webster's Dictionary of the American Language*: "*Feminism*, the qualities of females." A second, medical sense, recorded from 1875, again now rare, concerns the manifestation in a man of female secondary sexual characteristics. The word's current use for advocacy of women's RIGHTS and social-political movements directed toward achieving this follows from the French *féminisme* introduced by the philosopher Charles Fourier, who proposed the extension of the role of woman in society. *OED*'s initial quotation from 1895 is ironical, referring to the humorous portrayal of a woman's "coquettings with the doctrines of 'feminism.'" The term **feminist**, an advocate of **feminism**, is earlier: *OED*'s first example, from 1851, refers to a woman as "among the most moderate of feminist reformers." Alternative forms were **femininism** (1824) and **femininist** (1873); the former was used only with the sense of being feminine, while the latter was synonymous with **feminist** as used today. The history of **womanism** is significant: its initial sense, as for **feminism/femininism**, was that of characteristic womanliness (1824), then that of advocacy of women's rights (1850, equivalent to **feminism**), but then in lC20 claimed by the novelist Alice Walker as a term distinct from dominant white-centered **feminism**, in celebration of black women's lives and of a non-exclusionary universalist commitment to female and male peoples and their cultures.

From the start, **feminism** and **feminist** were controversial words; the socialist writer Rebecca West said she had been unable "to find out precisely what Feminism is": "I only know that people call me a Feminist whenever I express sentiments that differentiate me from a doormat or a prostitute" (1913). The appearance of **feminism** in lC19 came in the context of advances in democracy and demands for social-political rights made by men and women, including for *women's rights* (the compound term is recorded in 1632 in the title of a work on "the lawes resolutions of women's rights," but gains general political and cultural currency in C19). The particular focus was on votes for women, *women's suffragism* (1888). The word *suffragist* (1822) predated *suffragism* but commonly referred to proponents of the extension of the franchise for men, gaining its particular use for advocates of votes for women from lC19. In 1859, a journal supportive of suffrage for women noted that this was the case "for the majority of universal suffragists," recognizing that *suffragist* did not necessarily mean a supporter of votes for women, the specific meaning it would then quickly gain. The complex history sees **feminism** in its different versions accompanying and challenging the various demands for suffrage in Britain and the US and their exclusion or not of women, or of other sections of the population, notably African Americans: the beginnings of **feminism** in C19 US were in women's participation in the anti-slavery movement, though *OED* cites a newspaper referring to "anti-negro-suffragists in Connecticut" (1859). The later term *suffragette* (1906), distinct from *suffragist*, was used specifically for turn-of-the-century militant women activists demanding the vote for women, those involved in *suffragettism* (1913).

"Suffragists, suffragettes, and all the other phases in the crescendo of feminism" (1909), was a newspaper's characteristic summary at the turn of the century regarding the movements for women's political and civil rights and the development—"the crescendo"—of **feminism**. It is conventional to talk of succeeding "waves" of **feminism**, in each of which the word takes on different inflections, different references and uses. If movements for EQUALITY of political rights are seen at the center of a "first wave" in the recent history of Western countries, a "second wave" in the 1960s–1970s saw the word **feminism** become generally current (leaving *suffragettism* a historical term). In the late sixties feminism moves into the mainstream of political and ideological discourse, with both **feminism** and **feminist** used ever more frequently through the next three decades. This accompanied a resurgence of the *women's movement* focused on issues of SEXUALITY and women's rights freely to have ownership of their bodies—"our bodies ourselves," the significant title of the influential work "by and for women themselves" produced and circulated in 1970 by the Boston Women's Health Collective (published commercially 1973). *OED* records use of *women's liberation movement* from 1898, but this is in the context of suffragism, and it is in the last half of C20 that *women's liberation* becomes widely used (along with the colloquial abbreviation *women's lib*); an *OED* quotation from the *New Left Review* looks back to Fourier as "the most ardent . . . advocate of women's liberation and of sexual freedom" (1966). "The personal is political" (1969), the title of a paper by Carol Hanisch, was a key expression of the aim of this **feminism**: so-called personal matters in fact involving relations of power and control to be confronted as fundamental for any liberation of women.

The academic success of **feminism** was marked by the establishment of *women's studies* (1969) in universities and colleges during the 1970s, with *Feminist Studies*, self-described as the "first scholarly journal in women's studies," started in 1972. The particular development of *gender studies* in the 1990s, contemporary with *queer theory*, stressed the fluidity of sex and GENDER identities, these as processes of construction rather than "naturally" grounded, thus calling into question any **feminism** appealing to some given assumption of *woman* and leading to complex theoretical discussions and debates. Symptomatically enough, *USA Today* recently felt the need to provide "A feminist glossary because we didn't all major in gender studies" (March 16, 2017).

The word **post-feminism** (1983) was used to designate reaction against this "second-wave" **feminism**; women coming after and benefiting from the substantial gains it achieved, but taking a distance from its perceived assumptions and constraints, its very language—as in the common disclaimer: "I am not a feminist," a focus here on the individual rather than the collective *women*; what *Time Out N.Y.*, cited by *OED*, was to qualify as "[b]acklash 'do-me' post-feminism" (June 12, 2003, 65/3). *OED*'s first **post-feminism** quotation concerns "women . . . moving beyond doctrine." The 1980s saw **power feminism** urged in opposition to a **victim feminism** regarded as having disempowered women through placing them definingly in a position of oppression (crucial for this argument was Naomi Wolf's *Fire with Fire*, 1993). The word *backlash* indeed was also commonly employed to name the reaction in masculine culture against the previous "second-wave" **feminism**, the reaction indicated in the titles of two significant books of the time: *Backlash: The Undeclared War against Women* (Susan Faludi, 1991); *Who's Afraid of Feminism? Seeing through the Backlash* (Juliet Mitchell and Ann Oakley, 1998).

A "third wave" of **feminism** from 1980s–1990s is taken as having brought renewed attention to social inequalities as regards pay, treatment at work, "the glass ceiling" (1984, used especially for limits on the promotion of women to higher positions), and so on; together with the need to counter failures to recognize the diversity of ethnic background and social condition of women's lives, to reject Western feminism's consideration of *woman* as a universal category, of women as forming a common IDENTITY. Significantly, *OED*'s first quotation for *intersectionality* (1989), as used in sociology to point to the interconnected nature of various social identities, stresses that "[a]ny analysis that does not take intersectionality into account cannot sufficiently address the particular manner in which Black women are subordinated." The intersections of ethnicity, class, gender, sexual orientation and so on came to the fore. *USA Today* recently listed **intersectional feminism** as a recognized compound, referring to a currently significant form of **feminism** (March 16, 2017); this at the center of a "fourth wave" that is characterized by the globalization and forms of activism afforded by the Internet and social media.

Accounts in terms of a succession of waves point to generational shifts in versions of **feminism**. At the same time, they are misleading if the impression given is of sharp breaks rather than overlapping layers of development, with issues carried over; the "waves" are an indication that **feminism** has a varied history, and is also **feminisms**. **Feminism**, the word, is linguistically straightforward; it is the cultural and critical work it has been called upon to do over the last hundred and fifty years or so that marshals the particular senses that accrue to it in any given period. Virginia Woolf in *Three Guineas* (1938) thought **feminist** was a dead word, no longer with any meaning, since for her women had gained the right to earn a living. The subsequent history has shown **feminism** and **feminist** to be nonetheless alive, to be keywords indeed. This can be seen not least in the dismissals and violent rejections they have encountered—from the initial irony directed in 1898 at the woman's "coquettings with the doctrines of 'feminism'" through to anti-abortionists' use of **feminazi** (1989).

See EQUALITY, GENDER, RIGHTS, SEXUALITY

FREEDOM

Freedom is part of the inherited Old English vocabulary. It derives from **free**, and many of its most important uses are in compounds, collocations, phrases, and constructions determined by its relationship with this adjective. From its earliest history it has defined the RIGHTS and PRIVILEGES of a free individual, and the state of having such rights and privileges, in early use especially in contrast with slavery or serfdom, but increasingly seen as liberty from despotic or autocratic control. It is instructive to compare **freedom** with the semantically close *liberty*. *Liberty* is a borrowing from French and in turn from Latin, and is first found in lC14. As a simple uncompounded word, its core meanings overlap almost completely with those of **freedom**. Both words are used to denote both "freedom to act" and "freedom from despotism." This broad synonymy has held true from the early modern period onward.

Both words have singular and plural uses, although in the case of *liberty* these are usually more restricted semantically; compare, e.g., "hard-won freedoms" with "to take liberties." Special countable uses of *liberty* also occur in legal usage, as e.g., with reference to a liberty granted by a sovereign.

In non-countable uses the two words overlap very considerably, although **freedom** is more frequent with reference to specific actions performed without (or only with legally or technically restricted) restraint, as in "freedom of speech," "the freedom of his remarks," "freedom of movement," "the freedom of his brush strokes"; many such uses are clearly nominalizations of expressions with the adjective **free**, especially **free speech**. Similarly, **free from** is the model for **freedom from** (persecution, harm, taxes, etc.). In some cases, questions of alliteration and/or prosody have clearly shaped choices between the two words. Hence *liberation* struggles are typically conducted by **freedom fighters**, probably on account of alliteration and prosody; hence also such collocations as **the fight for freedom, those who are fighting for freedom**, etc.

The relative frequency of the two words, however, has shifted dramatically, and this seems to hold true both for newspapers and for general corpora representing a wide range of different genres. In C16 and C17, in spite of being a relatively recent borrowing, *liberty* outnumbers **freedom** by approximately four to one; in C18 it continues to be more frequent, but by rather less than two to one. In C19 British newspapers, *liberty* remains approximately twice as frequent as **freedom**; in C19 US sources, *liberty* only very slightly outnumbers **freedom**, if at all. This is in contrast to lC20 and eC21 sources, in which **freedom** is typically about three times more frequent than *liberty*, in both British and US sources. Corpus searches indicate no extremely frequent collocations or compound uses that alone can account for this shift (although, e.g., **academic freedom, religious freedom, individual freedom, press freedom, freedom fighter, freedom of speech, freedom of expression** are all very common, as is *civil liberty*).

During the course of its history, *liberty* shows a complex set of relationships with a number of other words ultimately from the same derivational group, which characteristically have connections with aspects of radical politics in their early use. An interesting question is whether any of these associations have contributed to the decreasing frequency of *liberty* relative to **freedom**.

From the early modern period *libertine* (with its derivatives *libertinism* and *libertinage*) is found in English as a borrowing from French and Latin, ultimately showing, like *liberty*, a derivative formation from Latin *liber*, "free." As both noun and adjective the word has important early uses denoting a **free-thinker**, especially in RELIGION, although in later use lack of restraint in moral life, especially with regard to sexual morality, becomes the dominant meaning. In early use, the relationship between the terms *liberty* and *libertinism* is ambiguous: sometimes *liberty* is identified as the aim of *libertines*, sometimes *liberty* is the ideal condition to be protected from the excesses of *libertinism*; the latter seems to have become more dominant over time.

The positive connotations of *liberty* in C18 are reflected by the frequency of *defense of liberty*, which is found only sparingly in the early modern period (when **defense of freedom** is found hardly at all). *Defense of liberty* continues to be more common than **defense of freedom** in C19, although again this situation is reversed in contemporary usage. The range of conflicts in which both phrases have been employed for propaganda purposes is huge. In C20 the Cold War collocation the **Free World** (now frequently, albeit most often tacitly, redefined in the context of the "War on Terror") may be a factor favoring **defense of freedom**, although this must be seen in the context of the general increase in frequency of **freedom** relative to *liberty* over time. The recent past has additionally seen, for example, Operation Iraqi Freedom and Operation Enduring Freedom in Afghanistan.

In lC18 we find a very strong association of *liberty*'s French equivalent *liberté* with the Revolutionary motto *liberté, égalité, fraternité*. *Liberty* also has a prominent use in the US Declaration of Independence ("Life, Liberty and the pursuit of Happiness"), as well as the US Constitution. In C19 (and later) Anglophone discourse, **freedom** has at least the capacity for uses dissociated from the radical associations of *liberty*, however. Arguably these uses occur in the tradition of nationalistic accounts of early English history, in which the **freedom** of the Anglo-Saxon churl is stressed as an inherited fundamental aspect of English society stretching back into the mists of an early Germanic inheritance (following an analysis abandoned by more recent historians).

In C19 both *liberalism* and *libertarianism* take on political meanings starkly opposed to *conservatism*, although a "liberal" position is also eschewed by many on the more radical left. As Williams notes, association with the broader use of the word LIBERAL, and hence connotations of "wishy-washiness" or excessive generosity, probably have a part to play here. The derivational relationship is clearest and strongest in the case of *libertarianism*, although this is also the term that has achieved much less extensive general currency.

In mC20 *liberty* shows a further derivational relationship with *liberation*, and is used in relation to post-colonialism, theology, and women's and gay liberation. However, as noted, those engaged in such *liberation* struggles are typically **freedom fighters**. Further, close stylistic and linguistic analysis of the use of either *liberty* or **freedom** (or, as frequently today, **liberty and freedom**) in different contexts may yield interesting insights into the influences and sympathies of particular individuals or groups.

See DEMOCRACY, LIBERAL, PRIVILEGE, RIGHTS

FUNDAMENTALISM

Fundamentalism is a surprisingly new word which is applied to a wide variety of religions—Islam, Christianity, Judaism, Hinduism—to denote a strict and unquestioning set of beliefs linked to literal readings of sacred texts. So common has it now become that it can be used to describe anyone with a fixed and rigid set of beliefs, as in the recent **market fundamentalism**.

A new word, it has very old origins. It is derived from **fundamental**, which is a Middle English borrowing from French, the French word deriving from a Latin root meaning "bottom." **Fundament** can thus refer both to the base of a building and the lower part of the body, specifically the anus. **Fundamental** also comes to be used as a noun in Early Modern English referring in a concrete sense to such a foundation or base. **Fundamental** as a plural also has an important meaning to refer to basic medicine, foodstuffs, clothes, but also more abstract senses: "the fundamentals of reading, writing, and arithmetic." In its abstract sense, the word refers to the essential or primary part of a system. **Fundamental** does not generally carry particularly positive or negative connotations; it has technical meanings in mathematics, geology, crystallography, biology, and music pertaining to primary parts of relevant systems in each discipline.

Crucially, however, it was the word used in a determined effort fueled by one of the greatest oil fortunes in America to establish a version of Christianity that would repudiate the advances of philology (which had demonstrated that the Gospels were written down some fifty years after Christ's death), geology (which had made the widely accepted biblical date for the formation of the world in 4004 BCE ludicrous), and biology (where the story of Genesis had been replaced by *The Origin of Species*). This comprehensive rupture between RELIGION and science was linked initially to publication of *The Fundamentals: A Testimony to the Truth* (though the word **fundamentalism** is encountered in religious discourse earlier in C19). *The Fundamentals* consisted of twelve volumes on Christian doctrine published from 1910 to 1915 by the Bible Institute of Los Angeles and edited initially by A. C. Dixon, then later by Reuben Archer Torrey (with revised editions in 1917, 1958, and 1990 reflecting the continuing significance of this publication within American Protestant discourse).

Overall, *The Fundamentals* set out to define the essential elements of a system of American Protestant belief. In particular, the contributing authors affirmed the literal TRUTH of the Bible in opposition to empirically verifiable sciences; they also opposed MODERN developments in FAMILY and political life, including modern warfare, in favor of an (often romanticized or idealized) traditional lifestyle.

Fundamentalism has something in common with the Catholic Church's reaction to modernity, but if American Protestants favored the infallibility of the letter over modern knowledge, forty years earlier at the First Vatican Council in 1870 Catholics favored the infallibility of the pope as representative of the INSTITUTION of the church. In Catholic Europe this **fundamentalist** ideology had a name: *integrism*, but it occurs in the *OED* only in reference to Catholic Europe, and it never gained any currency in English despite the fact that Ireland was almost entirely English-speaking by the time of the Council. The Fundamentals were popular enough that H. L. Mencken in the aftermath of the notorious 1925 Scopes trial about the teaching of EVOLUTION in schools wrote:

> Heave an egg out of a Pullman window and you will hit a Fundamentalist almost anywhere in the United States today. They swarm in the country towns, inflamed by their shamans. . . . They are thick in the mean streets behind the gas-works. They are everywhere where learning is too heavy a burden for mortal minds to carry, even the vague, pathetic learning on tap in little red schoolhouses. They march with the Klan, with the Christian Endeavor Society, with the Junior Order of United American Mechanics, . . . with all the rococo bands that poor and unhappy folk organize to bring some light of purpose into their lives. (1926)

Defining the essential, necessary elements of the Christian belief system and tradition was not new: assessment and reassessment of those fundamentals had been ongoing for centuries. However, the words **fundamental** and **fundamentalism** had played no significant part in such assessments until the rise of science and DEMOCRACY on the one hand and the early suffragette movement and flappers on the other. **Fundamentalism** was thus an increasingly influential but seriously contested term during the 1920s. To some, **fundamentalism** signified a positive, secure grounding in tradition (even if that grounding was, in fact, within a romanticized historical tradition rather than a factual one); to others, **fundamentalism** conveyed a narrow-minded rejection of positive developments in the modern world. To this extent, **fundamentalism** is clearly a reaction to modernity and the modern.

From eC20, claims vested in **fundamental** and **fundamentalism** related to a dynamic negotiation of what is essential within a given belief system. In *The Fundamentals*, some articles accepted that contemporary scientific developments, including evolutionary theory, were compatible with the fundamentals of Christianity. However, among other changes to later editions of *The Fundamentals*, such accommodation of evolutionary theory was removed, and opposition to abortion introduced. Various details in what was fundamental to American Protestantism in C20 in this way evolved, reflected in a changing, dominant meaning of **fundamentalism**. As the modern world changed, practices associated with **fundamentalism** reacted, just as the self-conscious adoption of **fundamentalism** had been largely a specific reaction to modernization. **Fundamentalism** in later C20 was increasingly characterized by romantic idealization of an imaginary past that serves as a foundation for rejecting modernity; in this respect **fundamentalism** signifies something different from many earlier examples of religious activist movements. In contemporary use, **fundamentals** is still a widely embraced term, particularly among Baptist or **fundamental** churches worldwide whose belief systems often resemble beliefs stated in revised versions of *The Fundamentals*. Most Protestant churches today, however, have distanced themselves from the term, perhaps more forcefully following increased use of the term **Islamic fundamentalism** in public discourse over the past two decades. Many English speakers might conflate **fundamental** with *evangelical*, but members of such churches tend to highlight the doctrinal differences between fundamental and evangelical churches. Slightly later than the nouns **fundamentalism** and **fundamentalist** (and adjective **fundamentalist**) as applied to Protestant Christianity, **Hindu fundamentalism** appeared as a term applied by non-Indian writers to Hindu nationalist movements in India, showing the potential overlap between **fundamentalism** and NATIONALISM. The terms **Islamic fundamentalism** and **Islamic fundamentalist** first appear in the 1940s and 1920s, respectively. An early use dates to 1937, when the British Minister in Jeddah wrote that King Ibn al-Aziz, the founder of Saudi Arabia, was coming out strong "as a fundamentalist." Significantly, this description was in the context of disapproval of men and women using ideas of progress to mix socially. Use of these expressions is not directly linked to *The Fundamentals*, or any comparable and explicit statement of religious belief; rather, **fundamentalism** was loosely transferred from its application to C20 American Protestantism to evoke some or all of the same associations, including strict religious adherence to literalist interpretation of scriptures and activism against various elements of modernization, particularly sexual FREEDOM for women and acceptance of homosexuality. The total rejection of gay sex by Protestant fundamentalists is in line with the Christian tradition of homophobia, but the possibly even more virulent hatred of homosexuals by Islamic fundamentalists breaks with more tolerant MUSLIM cultural traditions. **Islamic** is now one of the most common collocates for **fundamentalism**. Other religious terms that are generally less common collocates include **religious**, **Christian**, **Islam**, and **Muslim**; the terms **rise** and **spread**; and the terms **terrorism** and **militant**. These patterns of use created an important contrast: unlike the situation with early American fundamentalists, many of whom identified positively with the term, groups labeled **fundamentalist** today generally have the term thrust on them by adversaries.

The expression **anti-fundamentalism** readily emerged in such circumstances, referring to counterattacks against **fundamentalists**. **Anti-fundamentalism** is inevitably often associated with stereotypes of **fundamentalism**, typically as an outside enemy (with the result that fundamentalist can connote "political enemy of the state"). Popularization of **fundamentalist** and **fundamentalism** by US neoconservatives has facilitated a contested and problematic, generalized application of **fundamentalist** to political enemies worldwide, in which these terms may refer either to persecuted minority groups, who may or may not adhere to fundamentalist religious beliefs, or to hegemonic political powers (e.g., the Iranian state). **Fundamentalism** is also used in relation to spheres beyond religion, such that strict adherents to a particular policy or practice can be referred to as **fundamentalists**. *OED* evidence shows that, in the 1970s, **fundamentalist** was also used neutrally or positively for people who identified as traditional in non-religious ways, though that usage seems to have declined.

The variably technical, but sometimes oblique, expression **religious fundamentalism** has now become an accepted term in academic psychology, sociology, and even neuropsychology, with the result that **religious fundamentalism** is viewed in some fields as quantitatively measurable. Psychologists of religion have developed and revised a twelve-item Religious Fundamentalism Scale which rates subjects' responses in terms of the degree of **religious fundamentalism** exhibited. One implication of such research, however, appears to be that **fundamentalism** may be viewed as a specific psychological or social defect consisting of connections between religious attitude and kinds of prejudice—to the exclusion of social, political, economic, and cultural contexts in which it is cultivated, and separated from the wider process of modernization to which the C20 development of the phenomenon is undoubtedly tied.

While **fundamentalism** covers a vast array of different kinds of religious belief, there are striking similarities: a shared belief in a literal TEXT, a desire to return to an imagined perfect past, and a virulent hatred of both female and homosexual desire.

See FAITH, INSTITUTION, MODERN, NATIONALIST, RELIGION, TEXT, TRUTH

GENDER

The word **gender** is not new, but its semantics has only recently become the focus of heated debate both within and outside the academy. It has since its early days been a polysemous word, but new meanings related to social IDENTITY and biological sex render **gender** an important contemporary keyword. Indeed, in contemporary corpora **gender identity** and **biological gender** are two of the most common collocations for **gender**.

Gender is derived from the same French roots as *genre*, marking it as a classificatory word. Early uses of **gender**, from lC14, indicated a class of things or beings as having something in common. The connection to the current use of **gender** is clear; it is still being used as a classificatory word to describe a group that has something in common. In fact, corpus data shows that **gender** is often discussed alongside terms for other human demographic categories: *age, ethnicity, race, religion,* SEXUALITY, *disability*, and *nationality*.

Gender has several senses that are not contentious, mostly related to **grammatical gender**. It is the third sense in the *OED* that displays conflict, as suggested by overlapping subsenses. The first subsense defines **gender** as "males or females viewed as a group" or "the property or fact of belonging to one of these groups." This definition certainly includes biological elements of **gender** (such as chromosomes, hormones, reproductive systems, and genitals) but, as noted in the *OED*, may also include social or cultural elements of **gender** (such as historical or regional gender norms, expectations, or standards). This is the older of the two senses, having been in use since 1474, and was extended from the grammatical definition of **gender** to replace *sex*, as *sex* became strongly associated with sexual intercourse. We can see an example of this from historian Natalie Davis (1975), who states, "Our goal is to understand the significance of the *sexes*, of gender groups in the historical past." Here **gender** is explicitly equated with *sex*. According to the Corpus of Historical American English, one of the most common and oldest collocations is **gender difference** (1892), in uses that may or may not have explicitly distinguished social from biological factors.

The second subsense has only been in use since 1945, and is explicitly, exclusively social and cultural: "The state of being male or female as expressed by social or cultural distinctions and differences, rather than biological ones." When using this sense of **gender**, with an exclusively social and cultural meaning, *sex* generally becomes the preferred term for the biological elements that could be indicated by the older sense of **gender**. However, **biological gender** remains an extremely common collocation, indicating the need to disambiguate biological definitions of **gender** from social and cultural ones. In this case, **biological gender** is often used in contrast to **self-identified gender**, another common collocate.

As is typical of keywords, both subsenses are common in use, and it is often context, broadly defined, that clarifies the meaning. The *American Journal of Psychology* (1950) states that Margaret Mead's *Male and Female* "informs the reader upon 'gender' as well as upon 'sex,' upon masculine and feminine roles as well as upon male and female and their reproductive functions," clearly and explicitly separating the social and cultural definition from a biological definition (in this case, reproductive functions, but not chromosomes or other biological features).

The second subsense is becoming ever more standard. For example, a 2016 article from a British consultancy, the Governance and Social Development Resource Centre, states: "According to the World Development Report (WDR) 2012, gender is defined as socially constructed norms and ideologies which determine the behaviour and actions of men and women." This illustrates the socially governed definition, and that it is widely used in modern sources.

While the social and cultural definition is ever more standard, biological definitions remain extremely important, and dominant in some spheres. For example, **legal gender** is often used interchangeably with *legal sex*, and some form of legally recognized gender or sex exists in most, if not all, countries of the world. Legal gender is generally defined at birth based on an infant's genitals (but usually not other biological features such as chromosomes). When legal gender is not identifiable at birth via an infant's genitals, the term *intersex* may be used (though Germany is the only country that defines *intersex* as a third legal gender). This definition of **legal gender** is related to **trans** and **cisgender** identities; a TRANS identity is often defined as a self-identified gender that differs from the legal gender defined at birth, whereas **cisgender** refers to self-identified gender that is aligned with the legal gender defined at birth.

Legal gender for athletes has also been defined biologically. In 2009, the International Association for Athletics Federations (IAAF) began instituting hormone measures to define **gender**, which specifically disqualified women with high testosterone levels from women's competitions. That 2009 rule was overturned in the Court of Arbitration for Sport in 2015. The IAAF's biological definition differed dramatically from most countries' legal definitions, which tend to be based on genitals rather than hormones.

It is clear, then, that there are multiple, often mutually exclusive or contradictory biological definitions of **gender**. This vagueness in **biological gender** contributes to the contentiousness of **gender**. The terms **experienced gender** and **perceived gender**, as well as **gender identity** and **gender expression**, have been used to negotiate those intrinsic and extrinsic factors.

In both the UK and the US, it is possible to change one's **legal gender**, as identified at birth, via an application procedure. In the UK, biological evidence (such as hormone treatment or sex reassignment surgery) is not required, whereas in US states, specific clinical evidence is mandatory. Some individuals move between **genders** (or along a **gender spectrum**) with no biological or clinical support whatsoever, i.e., without the use of hormones, surgery, or other treatments, and some individuals use some biological treatments but not others. Many define **gender** exclusively in personal, social, or cultural terms rather than biologically or legally; for others, biological features, such as hormones, are crucial to their defined **gender**.

Nations including Bangladesh, India, Nepal, and Pakistan all legally define three **genders**, a recent recognition of a third **gender** that has been discussed in South Asian texts for thousands of years. This third **gender** can cover a range of individuals and **gender identities**; some trans people, for example, choose to identify as the third legal gender, while others do not. Third genders have been defined in many other times and places, including Two-Spirit people in many North American Indian societies from pre-contact time to the present day.

Non-binary definitions are becoming more common, even in the WEST. The National Health Service in the UK provides support for an increasing number of patients who identify as *non-binary*. In contemporary corpora, common collocates of **gender** include **non-binary**, as well as **fluid**, **spectrum**, and **neutral**. This relates to another key term that is still infrequent in most general corpora: **genderqueer**. **Gender** remains a contentious keyword due to vagueness and misunderstandings in its biological definitions as well as ongoing change in its social and cultural definitions.

See IDENTITY, QUEER, SEXUALITY, TRANS

GENETIC

Genetic sometimes presents difficulties because it has two senses: a general meaning, which has become relatively uncommon in English though it is still common, for example, in French, and a specialized meaning, in a particular branch of science, which has become well known. **Genetic** is an adjective from *genesis*, L, *genesis*, Gk—origin, creation, generation. It came into English in eC19, at first with the sense of a reference to origins, as in Carlyle: "genetic Histories" (1831). It still had this main sense of origin in Darwin, where "genetic connection" (1859) referred to a common origin of species. But **genetic** carried also the sense of development, as in "genetic definitions" (1837) where the defined subject was "considered as in the progress to be, as becoming," and this was present again in "the genetic development of the parts of speech" (1860). In 1897 **genetics** was defined in distinction from *telics*, to describe a process of *development* rather than a fully developed or final state. Developments in eC20 biology showed the need for a new word. Bateson in 1905 referred to the "Study of Heredity" and wrote: "no word in common use quite gives this meaning . . . and if it were desirable to coin one, 'Genetics' might do." From this use the now normal scientific description became established: "the physiology of heredity and variation . . . genetics" (*Nature*, 1906). But the older and more general sense of development was still active, as in "genetic psychology" (1909), which we would now more often call *developmental* psychology, without reference to biological **genetics**. Moreover the earliest sense also survived, as in "genetic fallacy" (1934)—the fallacy of explaining or discrediting something by reference to its original causes.

In normal English usage, **genetic** now refers to the facts of heredity and variation, in a biological context (**genetic inheritance, genetic code**, etc.). But in addition to the residual English uses, **genetic** also often appears in translations, especially from French, where the sense is normally of formation and development. Thus **genetic structuralism** (Goldmann) is distinguished from other forms of structuralism by its emphasis on the historical (not biological) formation and development of *structures* (forms of consciousness). It is probable that in this translated use it is often misunderstood, or becomes loosely associated with biological **genetics**.

Recent Developments

Genetic is a neutral description in its general sense, designating the origin (or genesis) of something. It arrived in English in eC19 and is used in this sense by Darwin in the sixth edition of *On the Origin of Species* (1869). The evolution of the adjective **genetic** largely follows on the scientific advances of C20. The nominative **genetics**, designating the study of heredity, first appears in print in 1905. The term describes those entities where a carrier of traits could be inherited or partly inherited. Its recent collocations largely reflect advances in biogenetic medicine and include **genetic defect, genetic mutation, genetic makeup, genetic testing**, and similar combinations.

Most recently, **genetic** has become caught up in a series of debates over the extent to which humans can or should intervene in what were previously assumed to be natural processes. The phrase **genetic modification** may conjure emotionally charged images of Dolly the cloned sheep, Onco-mouse, and Frankenfood. To describe something as **genetic** in the sense of "determined by genes" (*OED*) is to suggest that an outcome may be known on the basis of its origin. As such, the term invokes questions of agency: To what extent do we choose our IDENTITY? To what extent or in what ways is it preordained? How does our somatic past influence not just our present but also our future? How a person uses the word **genetic** may reflect what he or she believes about a variety of issues from health to sexual orientation to mental illness to the nature of human consciousness.

The term **genetic** often figures in the nature versus nurture debate, where it appears as a synonym for "biologically determined." If a disease is described as **genetic**, this may arouse the fear that little can be done to deter its onset. Recent work in genetics suggests a more complicated interplay between genes and their ENVIRONMENT. Geneticists now believe that the relation between environmental factors and genes is fully dialectical. This counters the idea that human characteristics (or indeed human behavior) can be reduced to DNA. This newer theory suggests that, if genes load the gun, the environment pulls the trigger. The result of this research into genetic-environmental interactions has essentially made it impossible to speak about NATURE or nurture in absolute terms. It also means that the adjective **genetic** is no longer synonymous with *predetermined*.

The realms of medicine and agro-business have increasingly used the terms **genetic modification** and **genetically modified organisms** (GMOs). The ability to add genetic traits to organisms raises the problem not only of how we instrumentalize the non-human world, but also of where we imagine the boundaries of the human to be. Genetic procedures have allowed scientists to map genes identified with certain diseases, and they have also made it possible to create genetic hybrids. Concerns over such inter-species transfer, or **genetic pollution**, were voiced in a 2003 issue of a psychiatric journal: "The most talked about risk in [genetic modification] technology is horizontal gene transfer. What if the artificial genes were transferred to another species?" (*Focus* July 69/1). This raises fears about **genetic pollution**, or the undesirable transfer of genes from one organism to another. In addition to the problem of what hybrids may arise, there is concern over what it would mean for humans. In a 2001 apostolic letter, Pope John Paul II described several dangers to the autonomy of the human: "To this list we must add irresponsible practices of genetic engineering, such as the cloning and use of human embryos for research, which are justified by an illegitimate appeal to freedom, to cultural progress, to the advancement of mankind." Worries about **genetic engineering**—the ability to add to the genetic germline rather than just to edit out the damaging parts—are shared among scientists and laypeople.

How one understands the term **genetic**—whether as a determining force or as an opportunity to change one's future—suggests much about what one believes about identity formation. The adjective **genetic** reaches beyond debates about physical bodies and into the metaphysical realm: it is a heuristic for thinking about consciousness and free will. While the promise of genetic research is great, the dangers of it are summed up by Siddhartha Mukherjee in *The Gene: An Intimate History* (2016), which concludes: "Once we start thinking of genes as destiny, manifest, then it is inevitable to begin imagining the human genome as manifest destiny" (492). If the **genetic** is not our destiny, it is a reminder that looking back to our origins is also to look ahead to our future.

See ENVIRONMENT, EVOLUTION, HISTORY, HUMANITY, IDENTITY, NATURE

GLOBAL

In a well-publicized open letter to between one and two billion Facebook users around the world (February 2017), Mark Zuckerberg suggested that "our greatest opportunities are now global" and that "our greatest challenges also need global responses." There are many people, he noted, "left behind by globalization, and movements for withdrawing from global connection." In contrast, Zuckerberg proposed online strategies for "Building Global Community." But running through his newsfeed—which ventured into territory far beyond Marshall McLuhan's early 1960s vision of instantly transferred INFORMATION creating a global village—ran persistent tensions in what **global** means.

Adjectival **global** derives from the noun **globe**. The Latin word *globus* means a spherical shape, and it was the Greek astronomers of the third century BCE who first proposed that the earth was not flat but a sphere, visualized as a fixed sphere within a universe whose other spheres revolve around it in circular motion. This view was acknowledged in both medieval Chistianity and Islam. The heliocentric revolution of Copernicus and Galileo placed this **globe** in orbit around the sun. In the modern period it is the adjective **global** rather than **globe** which creates tensions, for different reasons: foremost, because of its reference to notions of social organization layered onto understanding of the earth as spherical.

The adjective **global** is attested in English from 1637 (W. Prynne, "The worlde beinge plainely Circular, & globall, havinge no angles nor squares") and entered the language from Latin *globus* via English **globe** (the noun appearing nearly 200 years before its related adjective). Signifying shape both as a matter of observation and speculatively by way of cosmology, **globe** accreted meanings including that of a religious or mystical "globe" of fire around someone's head; the human eye or a woman's breast; fireballs and meteors; cannonballs; and electric light bulbs. From mC16, **globe** also meant a spherical model, with a map of the world on it, which can be rotated on a stand; and in its name, Shakespeare's Globe Theatre combined a roughly circular shape with theatre's symbolic capacity to represent all the world on a stage—a naming device transferred later to many newspapers called *The Globe*. Prefiguring later developments, an 1891 citation for **globe** in the *OED* refers to the economic and social interaction entailed by "the commerce of the globe."

Global carries over and has extended the geographical and social meanings of **globe**. The meaning "pertaining to the whole planet" continues, including in new combinations: **global distillation**, a natural process driven by atmospheric circulation; **global orbit; Global Positioning System** (GPS); and **global temperature**. In C20 mathematics, computing, and IT, the word's inclusive meaning, "relating to or encompassing the whole of anything or any group of things," added specialized expressions including **global theorems** and **global commands**, as well as **global emails** (i.e., messages addressed to an entire group of recipients).

Importantly from eC19, however, **global** acquired other non-concrete meanings, conceiving the world as a single, continuous social field, as opposed to separate localities, regions, or even sovereign nations on the C17 Westphalian model. Development of this meaning accounts for a rapid increase in frequency of the term from the 1940s. Such use reflects changing technological, economic, and political conditions and possibilities, and shifts the emphasis made by **global** toward a social rather than physical sphere: in effect, the word changed from describing something found everywhere to something affecting everyone: processes involving interdependent economic, political, or cultural relations "at world level." Description in such contexts is often infused with either aspiration or critique of how things affecting everyone have been addressed, hence the word's highly divergent connotations.

Globalization is attested from around 1930 but far more frequent from the 1980s, and has become the general term for processes involved in, as well as outcomes of, the transformation of local, regional, and national financial practices "at world level" (**global financial markets, global economic order**), along with related changes in social and political organization (**global civil society**) and cultural behavior and values (**global brand**). Various definitions have been advanced in different academic fields, as well as in political programs and policies. But such definitions remain highly general if they are to avoid becoming entangled in complexity and controversy.

When used as a verbal noun to describe a process rather than resulting condition, **globalization** has a temporal aspect that prompts major disagreement. Reference is commonly assumed to continuing projection of Western neoliberal values and policies onto the rest of the world over the last forty years. Even leaving out of account a far longer history of intercultural contact, trade routes, and migration, however, or geographically expansive empires, many characteristics of modern **globalization** are considered by some users of the word to have existed in earlier periods and so to illustrate the same process.

Economically, societies distributed across the globe began to diverge most obviously from similar levels of average prosperity or poverty (for the vast majority, mere subsistence) in eC15. A first stage is conventionally considered a mercantilist period of European maritime power, beginning with the voyages of Columbus, Magellan, and others, and leading to a connected but fundamentally exploitative **global economy** based on fortified trading posts, tariffs, and wars over trade in extracted materials, as well as transported slaves. This pattern changed, according to general economic accounts, in the period beginning with the Industrial Revolution in lC18: a period also disproportionately favorable to Western interests which similarly depended on inventions (in this case, for example, steam power) but which, for successful countries participating in **global markets** and **global competition**, was underpinned by more concentrated colonial power. Developments of this economic system following World War II were again linked to technological advances. In the aftermath of **global conflict** and recognizing **global inequality**, political actors attempted new measures of **global governance**. In one direction, a liberalizing process leading—ironically during a period of decolonization—to a rising number of *transnational* corporations (TNCs) with more WEALTH than many of the decolonized states. At the same time, creation or reform at macro level of *international, world, universal,* or *united* institutions directed toward economic and political engagement during a period of regional Cold War (from the Bretton Woods conference to the United Nations, and its agencies; the OECD reshaping earlier OECC; GATT from 1947; the Universal Declaration of Human Rights, 1948, and subsequent covenants; the IMF, World Bank, WTO, G8, then G7 and G20).

The current period of **globality** extends earlier trends, with its supply chains of cargo jets and container ships, instantaneous communications and electronic financial transactions, increased mobility of capital and labor, and interaction between cultures not only in goods and services but in new forms of cultural hybridization. Conflicting tendencies, however, include the widening gap between the global **North** and global **South**, intensified **anti-globalist** and **anti-globalization** demonstrations such as Seattle or Occupy, retrenchment toward economic and cultural protectionism, heightened hostility toward immigration, and concern over **global questions** including planetary-level problems such as water shortage, food supply, preventable illness, loss of biodiversity, and environmental **global degradation** and **global warming**.

Globalization cannot be defined purely by economics. Many users of the word prioritize political over economic considerations, while others highlight cultural processes including 24/7 **global media**, networking, and a **global public** made possible by the Internet, as well as cultural interaction ranging from styles of clothing through food tastes and sport to choice of language (including **global English**). What **globalization** means, in such varied contexts, appears a matter of conflicting ideological NARRATIVES: no singular meaning commands assent if abstracted from some detailed context of use. When a city such as London is proclaimed (with an unstable hint of oxymoron) to be a **global city**, for example, characteristics are variously implied, including size, transport, and communications hub, presence of an international financial sector, diverse population, and civil pluralism—all combined in some mixture of description, aspiration (or concealed criticism), and effort to attract **global investors**.

In what was reported as a new, politicized agenda for Facebook, Zuckerberg was not suggesting that one social media site could substitute for geopolitical initiatives on the scale of the UN's 17 Global Goals for Sustainable Development (agreed in 2015 by 193 world leaders). That UN initiative also drew on the rallying attraction of **global** in articulating a vision beyond historical experience or present international relations: that there will be, "[i]f these Goals are completed . . . an end to extreme poverty, inequality and climate change by 2030." Yet the multidimensional meanings and implications of **global** and **globalization** expose how far dominant concepts associated with these words are contested, rather than the outcome of a logic of convergent political interests or common HUMANITY—something visions inspired by these words should acknowledge if they are to contribute to **global community**.

See COMMON, COMMUNITY, EUROPEAN, HUMANITY, WEST

HISTORY

In its earliest uses **history** was a narrative account of events. The word came into English from fw *histoire*, F, *historia*, L, from rw *istoria*, Gk, which had the early sense of *inquiry* and a developed sense of the results of inquiry and then an *account* of knowledge. In all these words the sense has ranged from a *story* of events to a NARRATIVE of past events, but the sense of *inquiry* has also often been present (cf. Herodotus: ". . . why they went to war with each other"). In early English use, **history** and *story* (the alternative English form derived ultimately from the same root) were both applied to an account either of imaginary events or of events supposed to be true. The use of **history** for imagined events has persisted, in a diminished form, especially in novels. But from C15 **history** moved towards an account of past real events, and *story* towards a range which includes less formal accounts of past events and accounts of imagined events. **History** in the sense of organized knowledge of the past was from 1C15 a generalized extension from the earlier sense of a specific written account. **Historian, historic**, and **historical** followed mainly this general sense, although with some persistent uses referring to actual writing.

It can be said that this established general sense of **history** has lasted into contemporary English as the predominant meaning. But it is necessary to distinguish an important sense of **history** which is more than, though it includes, organized knowledge of the past. It is not easy either to date or define this, but the source is probably the sense of **history** as human self-development which is evident from eC18 in Vico and in the new kinds of **Universal Histories**. One way of expressing this new sense is to say that past events are seen not as specific **histories** but as a

continuous and connected process. Various systematizations and interpretations
of this continuous and connected process then become **history** in a new general
and eventually abstract sense. Moreover, given the stress on human *self-develop-*
ment, **history** in many of these uses loses its exclusive association with the past
and becomes connected not only to the present but also to the future. In German
there is a verbal distinction which makes this clearer: *Historie* refers mainly to the
past, while *Geschichte* (and the associated *Geschichtsphilosophie*) can refer to a process including past, present, and future. **History** in this controversial modern sense
draws on several kinds of intellectual system: notably on the ENLIGHTENMENT sense
of the progress and development of CIVILIZATION; on the idealist sense, as in Hegel,
of **world-historical** process; and on the political sense, primarily associated with
the French Revolution and later with the socialist movement and especially with
Marxism, of **historical forces**—products of the past which are active in the present and which will shape the future in knowable ways. There is of course controversy between these varying forms of the sense of process, and between all of them
and those who continue to regard **history** as an account, or a series of accounts, of
actual past events, in which no necessary design, or, sometimes alternatively, no
necessary implication for the future, can properly be discerned. **Historicism**, as
it has been used in mC20, has three senses: (i) a relatively neutral definition of a
method of study which relies on the facts of the past and traces precedents of current events; (ii) a deliberate emphasis on variable historical conditions and contexts,
through which all specific events must be interpreted; (iii) a hostile sense, to attack
all forms of interpretation or prediction by "historical necessity" or the discovery of
general "laws of historical development" (cf. Popper). It is not always easy to distinguish this kind of attack on historicism, which rejects ideas of a necessary or even
probable future, from a related attack on the notion of any *future* (in its specialized
sense of a better, a more developed life) which uses the lessons of history, in a quite
generalized sense (**history** as a tale of accidents, unforeseen events, frustration of
conscious purposes), as an argument especially against hope. Though it is not always recognized or acknowledged as such, this latter use of **history** is probably a
specific C20 form of **history** as general process, though now used, in contrast with
the sense of achievement or promise of the earlier and still active versions, to indicate a general pattern of frustration and defeat.

It is then not easy to say which sense of **history** is currently dominant. **Historian**
remains precise, in its earlier meaning. **Historical** relates mainly but not exclusively to this sense of the past, but **historic** is most often used to include a sense

of process or destiny. **History** itself retains its whole range, and still, in different hands, *teaches* or *shows* us most kinds of knowable past and almost every kind of imaginable future.

RECENT DEVELOPMENTS

In the years since Williams wrote, **history** has found its value upgraded and downgraded. To feminist scholars and activists, **history** was so important that it was necessary to claim for women a **herstory** (*OED* first cites 1970), while for others in an American usage, drawing on Henry Ford's "History is . . . more or less bunk" (1916), it has become a put-down: ". . . you go on the streets and talk that trash and you're history!" (*Playboy*, November 1983).

The German ideas of **history** in C19, to which Williams refers, have developed further range and complication in active debates. Beyond the three senses of **historicism** charted by Williams, a fourth sense emerged, developed by the German historian Leopold von Ranke, who asserted that "every epoch is immediate to God, and that its value in no way depends on what may have eventuated from it, but rather in its existence alone, its own unique particularity" (1854). He thus challenged both teleological theories, associated with Hegel and Marx, which see historical progress toward a future goal, and also presentist theories, which challenge past values with those of the historian's time; as Walter Benjamin did when he stated that "historical materialism wishes to hold fast that image of the past which unexpectedly appears to the historical subject in a moment of danger." Jean François Lyotard in *The Postmodern Condition* (1979) provided historical perspective on the "controversial modern sense" to which Williams refers by designating as the "grand narratives" [*grands récits*] of the modern age the interpretive accounts of "progress and development" and class-based "historical forces." From Lyotard's understanding of his postmodern present, these ideas had been superseded. But they came back. Under the impact of major transformations both in **world history** and in the **history of the arts**, Hegel's ideas of world-historical process took on renewed currency. In 1989, the year the Berlin Wall fell and the Soviet Union began to dissolve, political theorist Francis Fukuyama proposed "the end of history": "not just the end of the Cold War, or the passing of a particular period of post-war history, but . . . the end point of mankind's ideological evolution and the universalization of Western liberal democracy as the final form of human government." In contrast to Fukuyama's model of increasing uniformity, the philosopher and critic

Arthur Danto saw "the end of art" (1997) as enhancing diversity: for much of C20 ever more radical abstraction had seemed obligatory for important art, but, after Warhol, necessity no longer ruled future artists. The end of art meant the end of what Hegel had envisioned as the **history** of art.

In the decades since the first publications of Williams's *Keywords*, the writing and study of **history** has taken many various forms, finding new histories, involving new practices. Williams's contribution in this was the development of *cultural materialism*, looking at culture and cultures as material formations to be studied in their modes of production and thought, their social relations, the reality of their historical experience, the texts, objects, art they created. One prominent academic form of cultural materialism after Williams has been **new historicism** which, refusing any overall account of history and historical periods, focused on analysis of power relations grasped through interpretive analysis of the text-events of a period. Another and increasingly evident form is not text-based but that of the "history of things," the study of the material artifacts of a culture and the ways in which societies and individuals produce and relate to things.

See EVOLUTION, NARRATIVE

HOME

The word **home** comes from the Germanic *heim* and had a general sense of a place where a person was raised, one's own COUNTRY or NATIVE land. It has been in use in early English as a place where a person dwells and even in C16 had the meaning of being a place "where one was brought up, with reference to feelings of belonging, comfort, etc. associated with it." Other early meanings that continue to have contemporary resonance are **home** as "a refuge, a sanctuary; a place or region to which one naturally belongs or where one feels at ease," and **home** as "a person's own country or native land." In other words, **home** may describe the most intimate domestic ENVIRONMENT and also the grandest national identification. It follows that it can function either as a term of inclusion or of exclusion.

Since C19, the question of who does or does not have a **home,** in the domestic sense, has been central to British POLITICAL debate and remains so today. Following World War I, Prime Minister Lloyd George's campaign to provide "Homes Fit for Heroes" is credited with leading to the passage of the 1919 Housing Act, which gave local authorities a continuing responsibility for building new **homes** and for housing the **homeless.** The documentary *Cathy Come Home,* broadcast in 1966, which highlighted the life of a **homeless** family, had great public impact and led to the founding of Shelter, a "housing and homeless charity." Both continuing individual aspiration and government programs have sought to achieve **homeownership** over the same period. In 2015, the Conservative Party promised to build a "home-owning democracy," providing "the kind of security that comes with owning your own home."

Over the past century, **home**, defined as the domestic setting, has come to be seen as a center of consumption, as increasing numbers earned sufficient income to acquire **home comforts**, things which according to the *OED* "contribute to physical ease and well-being." Thus, 1908 saw the first Ideal Home Exhibition, which displayed designs of houses, gardens, and later on household gadgets. The first mass-produced goods which catered to these early consumers of **home furnishing** were frequently produced by a system of sweated **home work** (thus, the 1907 *Fabian Tract*, "Home Work and Sweating: The Causes and the Remedies"). Today, **home working** seems a preserve of the privileged, facilitated by the ubiquity of the computer and the Internet, where many organizations and the self-employed will have a **homepage**. Furthermore, many **homeowners** enjoy undertaking their own **home improvements** and are served by retailers, such as Home Depot, the fifth-largest private employer in the US. Indeed, how one decorates one's **home** is often seen as an important form of self-expression.

The **home** as an individual refuge or sanctuary is reflected in the phrase, "the sanctity of the home," which might have both a religious and a SECULAR connotation. The phrase has been adopted by the US courts in interpreting the Fourth Amendment as meaning a place where police cannot enter without a warrant. In Europe, the idea of **home** as a sanctuary has been enshrined in Article 8 of the European Convention on Human Rights, which identifies the right to RESPECT for family life, **home**, and correspondence. According to the UK independent human rights organization Liberty: "Right to respect for the home includes a right not to have one's home life interfered with, including by unlawful surveillance, unlawful entry, arbitrary evictions etc."

Home has also been identified in the wider sense as "a person's own country or native land" and "the country of one's ancestors," as in the compound noun **homeland**. Thus, opponents of recent foreign wars have campaigned to "bring the troops home." At the same time, **home** is often seen as the territory that needs defending. Following the 9/11 attacks in the US, the government created the Department of Homeland Security. On a more local level, this same sense of **home** as representing an inviolate territory is embodied in the word **homie** (also **homeboy**), meaning "a person from one's home town or neighborhood; a member of one's peer group or gang," seen in the lyrics of Ludacris's song "Call Up the Homies."

In the UK, the Home Secretary is responsible not just for domestic prisons and policing, but also for defending the nation's borders from immigrants and refugees who might leave both their own **homes** and their **homelands** to travel to the UK. As an example, in October 2013, the Home Secretary sent vans across London carrying posters which read: "In the UK illegally? Go home or face arrest." Those who needed help in repatriating themselves were given a phone number or encouraged to text "HOME." The idea that illegal migrants should go **home** underscores the fact that the word **home** carries multiple meanings, which include both the place where one lives but also one's own country of origin. Ironically, for the illegal immigrants, who have settled in the UK, the two might be continents apart.

There is a final meaning of **home** which adds in large measure to the word's contemporary resonance. That is **home** as "a residential institution providing care, rest, refuge, accommodation or treatment," a meaning which first became current in eC19. Ironically, the use of **home** in this sense began as a place for those who had no home, in the domestic sense, such as an early **Sailors' Home** and later **children's homes**. But it now also includes **homes** for those who can no longer stay at home because they lack **home carers**, such as the chronically ill and the elderly (who make up 85% of the residents of such **homes**). Many of those who go to **homes** do so because of the decision of others, social workers or family members. Far from being places of refuge or even of domesticity, they are often seen as the opposite. People speak of the anguish of putting their parents in a **home** or of handing them over to strangers. **Homes** in the sense of residential INSTITUTIONS have been the location of widespread cruelty, exploitation, and criminality. Perhaps most notoriously, the Kincora Boy's Home in Northern Ireland was the scene of sexual abuse of its residents and then an establishment cover-up over thirty years. The evidence of Kincora, and there are many others, suggests that not all **homes** have experienced an improvement since C19 when Oliver Twist was punished because he asked for more. Perhaps with less hypocrisy than the present, Oliver Twist was living in a work*house* rather than a **home**.

See COUNTRY, ENVIRONMENT, FAMILY, INSTITUTION, NATIVE

HUMANITY

Humanity belongs to a complex group of words, including **human, humane, humanism, humanist, humanitarian**, which represent, in some or all of their senses, particular specializations of a root word for *man* (*homo, hominis*, L—man, of a man; *humanus*, L—of or belonging to men).

It is necessary first to understand the distinction between **human** and **humane**, which only became settled in its modern form from eC18. Before this **humane** was the normal spelling for the main range of meanings which can be summarized as the characteristic or distinct elements of *men*, in the general sense (cf. *man*) of the **human** species. (All men are **human**, or in the earlier spelling **humane**, but all **humans** are either *men* [in the specialized male sense] or *women* or *children*.) Early uses of **humane** referred to **human nature, human language, human reason**, and so on, but there was also from eC16 a use of **humane** to mean kind, gentle, courteous, sympathetic. After eC18 the old spelling was specialized to the now distinct word **humane**, in this latter range of senses, while **human** became standard for the most general uses.

Humanity has a different but related development. First used in 1C14, from fw *humanité*, F, it had an initial sense much closer to the specialized **humane** than to the general **human**. In medieval use it appears synonymous with courtesy and politeness, and this must be related to, though it is not identical with, the development of *umanità*, It, and *humanité*, F, from *humanitas*, L, which had contained a strong sense of *civility*. *Humanitas* had also an important specific sense of mental cultivation and a LIBERAL EDUCATION; it thus relates directly to the modern complex of *cultivation*, CULTURE, and CIVILIZATION. From eC16, in English, the development is complex. The sense of courtesy and politeness is extended to kindness and generosity: "Humanitie . . . is a generall name to those vertues, in whome semeth to be a mutuall concorde and love, in the nature of man" (Elyot, 1531). But there is also, from 1C15, a use of **humanity** in distinction from *divinity*. This rested (cf. Panofsky) on the medieval substitution of a contrast between limited **humanity** and absolute *divinity* for the older classical contrast between **humanity** and that which was less than *human*, whether ANIMAL or (significantly) *barbaric*. From C16 there is then both controversy and complexity in the term, over a range from cultivated achievement to natural limitation. It was from this sense of some players as "neither having th' accent of Christians, nor the gait of Christian, pagan, nor man" that Shakespeare's Hamlet

> thought some of Natures Journey-men had made men, and not made them well, they imitated Humanity so abhominably. (*Hamlet*)

But cf. "I would change my Humanity with a Baboone" (*Othello*).

Yet the use of **humanity** to indicate, neutrally, a set of human characteristics or attributes is not really common, in its most abstract sense, before C18, though thereafter it is very common indeed. There was the persistent sense ranging from courtesy to kindness, and there was also the sense, developing from *umanità* and *humanitas*, of a particular kind of learning. There were C15 and C16 uses of **humanity** as a kind of learning distinct from divinity, and Bacon defined "three knowledges, Divine Philosophy, Natural Philosophy and Humane Philosophy, or Humanitie" (*Advancement of Learning*, II, v; 1605). Yet in academic use **Humanity** became equivalent to what we now call *classics*, and especially Latin (there are still residual uses in this sense). From C18 a French form, **the humanities** (*les humanités*) became steadily more common in academic and related usage, eventually adding modern literature and philosophy to the *classics*. This usage has remained normal in American English, as distinct from the more common English grouping of THE ARTS.

Parts of this range are reflected in the development of **humanist** and eventually **humanism**. **Humanist** was probably taken directly from *umanista*, It, which from eC16 had been a significant Renaissance word. It had 1C16 senses equivalent both to *classicist* and to the student of **human** as distinct from divine matters. This is a real complexity, related on the one hand to surviving distinctions between "pagan" and "Christian" learning, and on the other hand to distinctions between the "learned" (defined as in classical languages) and others. There is also an ultimate relation to the double quality of the Renaissance: the "rebirth" of classical learning; the new kinds of interest in *man* and in **human** activities. It is not surprising, given this complex, to find an eC17 use of **humanist** (Moryson, 1617) to describe someone interested in state affairs and history. The use of **Humanist** to describe one of the group of scholars prominent in the Renaissance and the Revival of Learning seems to come later in C17, but has since been common.

Humanism, on the other hand, was probably taken direct from *Humanismus*, a 1C18 German formation which depended on the developed abstract sense of **humanity**. What was picked out from a complex argument, which belongs, essentially, with the contemporary development of CULTURE and CIVILIZATION, was the attitude to RELIGION, and **humanism** in this sense (as a positive word preferred to the negative *atheism*) has become common. But a broader sense of **humanism**, related to post-ENLIGHTENMENT ideas of HISTORY as human self-development and self-perfection, also became established in C19, and this overlapped with a new use of **humanism** to represent the developed sense of **humanist** and **the humanities**: a particular kind of learning associated with particular attitudes to CULTURE and **human** development or perfection.

Humanitarian appeared first, in eC19, in the context of arguments about religion: it described the position from which Christ was affirmed as a man and not a god. Moore (*Diary*, 1819) noted an acquaintance as "more shocked as a grammarian at the word than as a divine at the sect." The word took this particular form by analogy with *unitarian* and *trinitarian*. But this was soon left behind. By association with the developmental sense of **humanism**, but even more with new kinds of action and attitude belonging to the now specialized sense of **humane, humanitarian** became established from mC19 in the sense of a deliberately general exercise or consideration of *welfare*. (There is one special and ironic sense in **humane killer**, eC20.) It is interesting that through much of C19 the use of **humanitarian** was hostile or contemptuous (as in mC20 *do-gooder*). But it is now one of the least contentious of words. It was probably its conscious social generalization of what had been seen as local and individual acts and attitudes which attracted hostility (cf. *welfare* in C20).

It is necessary to add a final note on **human** in mC20 usage. It is of course now standard in general and abstract senses. It is also commonly used to indicate warmth and congeniality ("a very **human** person"). But there is also a significant use to indicate what might be called condoned fallibility ("human error," "natural human error") and this is extended, in some uses, to indicate something more than this relatively neutral observation. "He had a human side to him after all" need not mean only that some respected man was fallible; it can mean also that he was confused or, in some uses, that he committed various acts of meanness, deceit, or even crime. (Cf. "Jane [Austen] was very human, too—bitchy, even cruel and a bit crude sometimes"—*TV Times*, November 15–21, 1975.) The sense relates, obviously, to a traditional sense that it is **human** not only to err but to sin. But what is interesting about the contemporary use, especially in fashionable late bourgeois culture, is that "sin" has been transvalued so that acts which would formerly have been described in this way as proof of the faults of **humanity** are now adduced, with a sense of approval that is not always either wry or covert, as proof of being **human** (and *likeable* is usually not far away).

Recent Developments

The question "What does it mean to be **human**?" has become inescapable due to advances in fields as diverse as artificial intelligence, microbiology, neuroscience, and animal studies that have destabilized previous understandings of **humanity**. While the relative frequencies of **human** and **humanity** have remained fairly constant since eC19, **non-human** (first attested in 1839, according to the *OED*) seems to have increased substantially in use in mC20 and again in lC20. This trend points to a growing interest in delineating the boundaries of **humanity**, that is, in distinguishing **humans** from machines and **non-human** ANIMALS and organisms. In her recent book *10% Human* (2015), biologist Alanna Collen discusses how **humans** consist of more colonies of microbes than **human** cells: "You are just 10% human. For every one of the cells that make up the vessel that you call your body, there are nine imposter cells hitching a ride." Such scientific research has revealed the difficulty in differentiating between the **human** and the **non-human**.

Important C20 coinages first appearing in the third edition of the *OED* include **post-human** and **post-humanism**. The noun and adjective **post-human** describe "a hypothetical species that might evolve from human beings, as by means of genetic or bionic augmentation." **Post-humanism** is used in two different senses: it can denote (i) a critique of the tenets of **humanism** and the idea of the autonomous, rational **human** subject, and (ii) "the idea that humanity can be transformed, transcended, or eliminated either by technological advances or the evolutionary process." No longer limited to science fiction, developments in robotics and artificial intelligence have made it possible to think of a **post-human** future in which **humans** will merge with software and machines in order to overcome biological limitations. Optimism about the potential of TECHNOLOGY to improve **human** LIFE has been matched with skepticism and fear that it could threaten the future of **humanity**, as Stephen Hawking warned: "The rise of powerful AI will either be the best or the worst thing ever to happen to humanity. We do not yet know which."

See ANIMAL, CIVILIZATION, CULTURE, HISTORY, LIFE, TECHNOLOGY

IDENTITY

Identity is a word that features in an unusually wide range of discourses from logic to politics. Originally a technical term in theology and philosophy, it became a favorite of mathematicians and policemen before achieving a central role in psychoanalysis in the postwar United States. In the early 1970s, **identity** migrated into the POLITICAL arena, where the phrase **identity politics** has become central to both political and ideological debate in the past four decades.

Identity is multiply derived from French and Latin. Its underlying root is the Latin *idem*, the same, and its first appearance is recorded in the *OED* in 1545 in the context of theological debates about transubstantiation. Already by 1570 it is used in a translation of Euclid and will remain a key term in mathematics developing a series of uses in C19 in logic and algebra. More centrally, it becomes an important word in the empirical philosophy of John Locke at the end of C17, where it is used in place of religious terms which are not susceptible of empirical verification, such as SOUL: "The Identity of the same Man consists . . . in nothing but a participation of the same continued Life, by constantly fleeting Particles of Matter, in succession, vitally united to the same organized Body. . . . consciousness always accompanies thinking . . . in this alone consists *personal Identity*, i.e. the sameness of a rational Being" (1690). David Hume famously dissented from this overarching view of **identity**, discerning in the self merely a succession of experiences. It was in an attempt to refute Hume that Thomas Reid best articulates what remains one important current meaning: "My personal identity, therefore, implies the continued existence of that indivisible thing which I call *myself*. Whatever this *self* may be, it is something which thinks, and deliberates, and resolves, and acts, and suffers. I am not thought, I am not action, I am not feeling; I am something that thinks, and acts, and suffers. My thoughts, and actions, and feelings, change every moment—they have no continued, but a successive existence; but that *self* or *I* to which they belong, is permanent, and has the same relation to all the succeeding thoughts, actions, and feelings, which I call mine" (*Essays on the Intellectual Powers of Man*, 1785).

From the end of C19 and in the context both of modern policing and the ever greater reproducibility of photographs, there are a significant number of compounds that indicate the importance of the documentation of **identity** in modern states: **identity card, identity certificate, identity document, identity papers, identity check**. More recently, and increasingly with reference to digital and not analog **identities,** we have **identity theft**. The most important and widespread of **identity** documents is the passport, the use of which is generalized by the end of World War I. From a bureaucratic perspective, personal identity thus takes a national form.

It is just after the end of World War I that Freud turns his attention to the relation between the individual and the social in *Group Psychology and the Analysis of the Ego* (1921). Freud does not use the word **identity** (*Identität*) to describe a state, but the word **identification** (*Identifizierung*) to describe a process. However, the state of identity is the crucial focus for the Ego Psychology school which becomes dominant in the US in the decades after World War II. Erik Erikson, the most prominent proponent of Ego Psychology, claims, "The study of identity . . . becomes as strategic in our time as the study of sexuality was in Freud's." Erikson argues that "[p]sychosocial identity develops out of a gradual integration of all identifications. . . . [H]ere, if anywhere, the whole has a different character from the sum of its parts." Erikson ranges very widely in his elaboration of the different elements which are integrated into a mature **identity,** using all of the following phrases: **cultural identity, ethnic identity, racial identity, religious identity, sexual identity, tribal identity**. It is an indication of the very increased importance of **identity** in contemporary discourse that most of these phrases seem very familiar, although many of them still do not yet have entries in the *OED*. Yet for all these inflections, the core meaning of **identity** for Erikson remained in the tradition of Locke: "the ability to experience one's self as something that has continuity and sameness."

For Erikson, the notion of **identity** as the integration of heterogeneous elements into a unity was not limited to individuals. There was much debate in the postwar era about finding a word that could function as a non-political category for defining a people, given that race had been irredeemably tarnished by Nazi theory. In *Childhood and Society* (1950), Erikson opted for "national identities" as his preferred term. An indication of the fertility of Erikson's notion of **identity** and particularly of his signature concept of **identity crisis** can be found in Edward Said's use of the term in 1969 to help characterize the then current moment in "Palestinian experience": "That is why the present identity crisis is not minimal, but a matter of profound moment" (*The Politics of Dispossession*, 1994, 15).

In the 1970s, **identity** emerged as a crucial POLITICAL term in the phrase **identity politics**. Its most immediate meaning was an opposition to class politics and reflected struggles both in the Black Power and women's movements to refuse to subordinate questions of RACE and GENDER to traditional definitions of political struggle in terms of class. However, **identity** was more than just a counter to CLASS; it was an appeal to a different kind of politics in which questions of subjectivity and consciousness were central. **Identity** here is multiply ambiguous: it is what you can't help being, but also what you choose to become. As such, it hovers between a desire to choose a different **identity** and a desire to reject what for Erikson is a struggle and for Locke a simple evidence: the dominant notion of **identity** itself. Particularly in recent debates about **gender identity**, one can discern not simply the assertion of new **identities**, but a further desire to move beyond **identity** altogether.

This questioning of **identity** itself has also arisen as the recognition of **identities** has multiplied in recent decades. One reaction has been the coining of the word *intersectionality*: "The term intersectionality references the critical insight that race, class, gender, sexuality, ethnicity, nation, ability, and age operate not as unitary, mutually exclusive entities, but rather as reciprocally constructing phenomena" (*Annual Review of Sociology*, 2015). **Identity politics** opened up in the heart of **identity** a vision of difference and, for many, that vision needs to understand **identity** as a perpetually shifting construction as individual and world interact.

See CLASS, CULTURE, DIVERSITY, GENDER, POLITICAL, RACE, RELIGION, SEXUALITY, SOUL

IMAGE

The history of the word **image** is more than rich. It was borrowed into English in C13 from Anglo-Norman French, which in turn borrowed the word from Latin *imago* (which is ultimately from the same base as *to imitate*). From eC13 there is the emphasis on artificiality, there have never been natural **images**. Also from very early the notion of likenesses: at first material copies of the external world, but then also mental representations. It becomes important both in astronomy and physics, and in the complex grammar and rhetoric of the High Middle Ages. Interestingly, it also comes to name phenomena that emphasize the limits of consciousness: the death mask of an ancestor, a reflection in a mirror, a phantom, a hallucination.

This richness does not trouble the simple semantic core of the word, "an artificial imitation or representation of something" (*OED*). Complications arise not from the meaning of the word but from the exponential growth in the production of **images**. This multiplication takes place even though **images** of any kind are explicitly outlawed by the second commandment:

> Thou shalt not make unto thee any graven image, or any likeness of *any thing* that *is* in heaven above, or that *is* in the earth beneath, or that *is* in the water under the earth. Thou shalt not bow down thyself to them, nor serve them: for I the LORD thy God *am* a jealous God, visiting the iniquity of the fathers upon the children unto the third and fourth *generation* of them that hate me; And shewing mercy unto thousands of them that love me, and keep my commandments.

Despite this clear interdiction, supported by Plato's analysis that the **image** is necessarily erroneous, the WEST has largely gloried in its **images** in a fashion that the Islamic tradition, more faithful to the second commandment, has not.

In a simplified history we can imagine the medieval peasant with only two **images**: the king's head on the coin and the Lord's body on the cross. As **images** accumulated in the Middle Ages, they were almost all in public buildings: stained glass windows, altar pieces, frescoes, crosses. The Renaissance and the development of a bourgeois class encouraged **images** to migrate onto easels and canvases and into private homes. But until C19, the **image** is predominantly the possession of the rich, the visible sign of surplus.

However, printing had from C16 brought **images** to a more popular audience with almanacs and woodcuts. This audience becomes dominant when a new regime of the **image** is inaugurated by the photograph and above all its use in the popular press of lC19. The new TECHNOLOGY of cinema both confirms and develops this new regime of the **image**. The **images** on the walls of medieval churches and the paintings in private homes and municipal galleries were permanent. These new **images** are transient, the film moving at 24 frames a second, today's newspaper tomorrow's trash. When G. K. Chesterton uses the new meaning of **image** that this world requires, he applies it paradoxically to the past: "When courtiers sang the praises of a King they attributed to him things that were entirely improbable. . . . Between the King and his public image there was really no relation" (1908). The notion of a **public image** requires the public space opened up by newspapers and newsreels, and a **public image** further opens up the possibility that the **image** is mutable, that it is possible for one's **image** to change, possibly under the pressure of events, even more certainly by the spending of money. Thus, the worlds of advertising and PR are born and tower over the first half of C20 from Bernays and Madison Avenue to Goebbels and the Third Reich. This new dominance of the **image**, next amplified by television, is understood almost entirely negatively by Anglo-Saxon academics: the **image** is a "pseudo event" for the conservative American historian Daniel J. Boorstin; "a jargon term of advertising and public relations" for the Welsh socialist thinker Raymond Williams. French reactions were even more extreme: the Situationists claimed that the **image** produced a society of the spectacle which "is not a collection of images; it is a social relation between people that is mediated by images." There are, however, more optimistic views. André Bazin in his "Ontology of the Photographic Image" saw the new regime of the **image** as offering a new RE-ALISM of social transformation, and Marshall McLuhan thought television would produce a GLOBAL village.

For some, this new regime of the mutable **image** is liberation, and Andy Warhol can be taken as both figurehead and spokesman: "Isn't life a series of images that change as they repeat themselves?" Warhol's use of **image** here draws both on the old sense of a fixed REPRESENTATION and the new sense of the **image** as a mutable reputation. This semantic stretch built into **image** makes it such a keyword in the new digital era, where cable television has been supplemented by the Internet and the smartphone to make the **image** even more ubiquitous than in the eras of broadcast television and film. It has also generated recent developments of law where the compound **image rights** recognizes a new form of PROPERTY related to the ownership of images. What is significant about this new form of property is that it is only available to the famous. You need both a representation and a reputation to claim image rights.

Digital TECHNOLOGY provides a new material basis for the **image**, but it is the new forms of distribution that really modify its political effects. To take two striking examples, it is difficult to imagine the new conservative right in America without the cable channels which linked evangelical churches in the 1980s, or contemporary jihadi movements without martyrdom videos on the Internet.

See ART, ARTIFICIAL, BRAND, MEDIA, REALISM, REPRESENTATION, TECHNOLOGY

IMPERIALISM

Imperialism developed as a word during the second half of C19. **Imperialist** is much older, from eC17, but until 1C19 it meant the adherent of an emperor or of an imperial form of government. **Imperial** itself, in the same older sense, was in English from C14; fw *imperialis*, L, rw *imperium*, L—command or supreme power.

Imperialism, and **imperialist** in its modern sense, developed primarily in English, especially after 1870. Its meaning was always in some dispute, as different justifications and glosses were given to a system of organized colonial trade and organized colonial rule. The argument within England was sharply altered by the evident emergence of rival imperialisms. There were arguments for and against the military control of colonies to keep them within a single economic, usually protectionist system. There was also a sustained political campaign to equate imperialism with modern CIVILIZATION and a "civilizing mission."

Imperialism acquired a new specific connotation in eC20, in the work of a number of writers—Kautsky, Bauer, Hobson, Hilferding, Lenin—who in varying ways related the phenomenon of MODERN imperialism to a particular stage of development of CAPITALIST economy. There is an immense continuing literature on this subject. Its main effect on the use of the word has been an evident uncertainty, and at times ambiguity, between emphases on a POLITICAL system and on an economic system. If **imperialism**, as normally defined in 1C19 England, is primarily a political system in which colonies are governed from an imperial center, for economic but also for other reasons held to be important, then the subsequent grant of independence or self-government to these colonies can be described, as indeed it widely has been, as "the end of imperialism." On the other hand, if **imperialism** is understood primarily as an economic system of external investment and the penetration and control of markets and sources of raw materials, political changes in the status of colonies or former colonies will not greatly affect description of the continuing economic system as **imperialist**. In current political argument the ambiguity is often confusing. This is especially the case with "American imperialism," where the primarily political reference is less relevant, especially if it carries the C19 sense of direct government from an imperial center, but where the primarily economic reference, with implications of consequent indirect or manipulated political and military control, is still exact. **Neo-imperialism** and especially *neo-colonialism* have been widely used, from mC20, to describe this latter type of imperialism. At the same time, a variation of the older sense has been revived in counter-descriptions of "Soviet imperialism," and, in the Chinese version, "*social imperialism*" to describe either the political or the economic nature of the relations of the USSR with its "satellites" (cf. "the Soviet Empire"). Thus the same powerful word, now used almost universally in a negative sense, is employed to indicate radically different and consciously opposed political and economic systems. But as in the case of DE-MOCRACY, which is used in a positive sense to describe, from particular positions, radically different and consciously opposed political systems, **imperialism**, like any word which refers to fundamental social and political conflicts, cannot be reduced, semantically, to a single proper meaning. Its important historical and contemporary variations of meaning point to real processes which have to be studied in their own terms.

RECENT DEVELOPMENTS

In lC19, **imperialism** came to describe the interrelated systems of political and economic expansion undertaken by Western colonial powers in Asia, Africa, and the Americas. Williams outlines the tension between these two systems, noting that the usage has consistently negative connotations even when describing antithetical forms of government. Following the US invasion of Iraq and the subsequent "War on Terror," the term has seen a resurgence in describing Western engagement in the Middle East. The phrases **American imperialism** and **British imperialism** remain frequent collocates, though they now more regularly denote the indirect effects of national trade and monetary policy, rather than the effects of direct political intervention (though that sense remains active). **Imperialism** can also describe the actions of a majority against an internal minority: for example, Frantz Fanon's analysis of French imperialism in Algeria was applied by Bobby Seale and Huey Newton to discuss the American state's imperialist, or colonialist, actions in American black communities.

Alongside these political and economic uses, frequent reference is made to **cultural imperialism**—the imposition of one nation's values on another through the ideological deployment of religion, education, popular culture, or art. Historically, it has been practiced by Greek, Roman, Chinese, and Mongol empires, among others; today **cultural imperialism** usually refers to the export of Western values (especially US values) through entertainment, social media, advertising, or corporate practices. While the age of colonial power has largely waned, these exports manifest a continuity with earlier political practices; what had previously been an overt land grab morphed into a grab for consumer consciousness and market share. In addition to the well-known critiques of cultural imperialism by literary scholars such as Edward Said and Gayatri Spivak, sociologists such as Krishan Kumar have more recently focused on the effects of **banal imperialism**, how the daily lives of citizens are impacted by the continuous press of national signifiers: on coins, in advertising, and in daily rituals. This model emphasizes **imperialism** as a voluntary (sometimes unconscious) embrace of the dominant culture, rather than forced acculturation.

The related concept of **linguistic imperialism** is similarly associated with the legacy of C19 colonialism and particularly the GLOBAL expansion of English. Differences among the prestige of competing languages come to stand in for power differentials among countries or among different ethnic groups within a single country or region. Nationalist groups as well as sociolinguists continue to debate the usefulness of European vernaculars in former colonial states for the purposes of administration and national unity. In these ways, C19 **imperialism** has not become obsolete with the lessening of direct colonial rule; rather, the term's semantic reach has broadened through expansion into contiguous spheres.

See CULTURE, GLOBAL, INDIGENOUS, NATIVE, WEST

INDEPENDENT

The adjective **independent** as well as the related noun **independence** and adverb **independently** are important terms because of the significant claim they convey in fields including politics, law, and finance. They are also important words in wider social debates concerning individuality and individualism, the nature of relationships and affiliation to social groups, beliefs and values of different kinds, and orientation toward social norms. The difficulty created by **independent**, however, is that the word's meanings are strongly affected by its contexts of use, and crucially altered by the referent being described. The result is that **independent** can be applied to either inanimate or animate entities, and can be exploited to suggest positive or negative qualities not inherent in its core meaning.

The *OED* entry for **independent** suggests that the word was formed in English from an established adjective **dependent** in mC16; the related noun and adverb forms appear a little later. In earliest attestations, **independent** is used to describe abstract entities such as causes, power, or faith, which are "[n]ot depending on something else for its existence, validity, efficiency, operation, or some other attribute; not contingent on or conditioned by anything else." This neutral sense remains frequent, for example in one of the word's most common collocations as a modifier in British and US English, **independent variable(s)**, a phrase particularly associated with technical registers. For this use, an intriguing example can be found of how technical use diffuses into wider contexts, picking up on other, more recent meanings of **independent** as it does so, in the title of a psychology book, *Woman: Dependent or Independent Variable?* (1975).

OED quotations for the neutral sense of **independent** show that when the word is first found in English it is applied to groups, states, and nations with a narrower but still neutral meaning: "Not depending upon the authority of another, not in a position of subordination or subjection; . . . self-governing, autonomous, free." This more specific meaning continues into current use, and accounts for the large number of recent attestations in political writing, often with reference to ideologically charged notions that are not necessarily geographical (as had been typical of earlier uses): an **independent Jewish nation** or **independent Arab states**. From the US Declaration of Independence in 1776, **independence** has been a much desired political goal. For much of C20 this focused on the struggle of colonial nations to emancipate themselves from their imperial masters. In C21 many struggles for **independence** have involved the breakup of established nation-states, as for example the movements for **independence** in both Scotland and Catalonia. The United Kingdom Independence Party uses **independence** to mean secession from the European Union.

By lC17 **independent**, however, had also begun to be used with narrower scope to refer to individuals. Several related strands of meaning developed. Initially, **independent** in this C17 development referred to material needs, especially financial status: an **independent gentleman**, or person of **independent means**, was financially self-sufficient and in this respect not reliant on others. This material-support sense continues into current use, although it is now clearest when specified by a modifier such as **financially** or **economically**. Either individuals or households (or larger groups) can be described in this way.

A second sense, more limited to individuals, also emerged in parallel, in phrases like **independent minded** and having an **independent spirit**. This meaning relates to opinions and attitude, rather than physical or material needs. The *OED* gives the definition "Not depending on others for the formation of opinions or guidance of conduct; not influenced or biased by the opinions of others; thinking or acting, or disposed to think or act, for oneself." Entries for this sense in modern, synchronic dictionaries show "confidence" as a defining feature of this meaning. Such **independence** is also often presented as gradable, and a value to aspire to, with self-help books and Internet sites full of advice on how to become **more independent**, particularly in relationships: for example, Oprah Winfrey's website asks in one of its articles, "Is Independence the Key to Happiness?"

In many cases, **emotional** and **financial independence** are not clearly distinguished from one another in discussions of personal circumstances and relationships, or they are seen as closely connected. Much of the guidance and self-help discourse concerned with **independence** is addressed to women. Evidence from large corpora provides evidence for this: in both British and US English, the phrase **independent woman** tends to be much more frequent than **independent man**, though only since the 1980s. The shift in relative frequency is most marked in US English. **Independent man** tended to be more frequent in earlier periods, though generally referring in those earlier uses to financial status.

In the complex contemporary terrain of **independence**, too much as well as too little of the quality can be perceived as a problem. Tabloid publications regularly warn women against becoming **too independent**, since potential partners may find this characteristic threatening and it can prevent women from being "wife material." The idea that **independence** can be an inappropriate quality for women is not new in itself: in Jane Austen's *Mansfield Park* (1814), Sir Thomas complains to Fanny about "that independence of spirit, which prevails so much in modern days, even in young women, and which in young women is offensive and disgusting beyond all common offence." Yet being **fiercely independent** is not exclusively associated with women; it is also a perceived characteristic of young people, as well as others who need to assert their independence because they lack power of some kind. Widening application of **independent** and **independence** in these contexts strengthens a related, more positive sense that increases in use from the 1980s referring to physical abilities rather than an emotional state, particularly associated with the elderly: being able to **live independently** means staying in one's own home, perhaps with family or professional support, rather than moving to sheltered accommodation or into a care home. (In earlier periods, **independent living** would have meant having money.)

In politics a distinct use of **independence** is found: an **independent candidate** has no affiliation to an organized political party. Such **independence** includes— in some perspectives, requires—financial separateness, while also implying **independent-mindedness**: independent candidates should be free to make their own decisions without reference to a party line. **Political independence** may, however, also be a feature of parties and political objectives, and different nuances in the term may become entangled.

The interlocking political meanings of free opinion and agency can shade into a meaning of "non-governmental," not government-controlled, in contexts where **independent** is applied to organizations. The phrase **independent schools** (denoting fee-paying schools in the UK and US) exploits positive connotations available with this kind of use, since the phrase avoids the elitism of *private* (or *public*) school and at the same time implies a certain kind of FREEDOM and free thinking (compare recent use of *free school*, denoting in the UK a type of state-funded school outside the control of local authorities).

A particular cultural sense developed in the American film industry, because its beginnings were closely tied to a monopoly on distribution. From 1908 films produced outside this monopoly were called **independents**. This use gained importance in the late 1960s as **economic independence** was linked to a particular cultural stance. The Sundance Film Festival was founded in 1978 to celebrate and support **independent films**. Often shortened to **indie**, the term is also used in the music industry to contrast with the big four record labels: Universal, Sony, Warner, and EMI.

Facts or results that are **independently verified** are in most modern social systems considered more trustworthy and secure than those which are government-produced or commercially sponsored. In a promotional culture, verification is often taken to require separation between those making a claim and those providing the evidence for it. Emphasis on the idea that **independence** allows honest opinion and judgment is accordingly often accentuated in references to NGOs, think tanks, and consumer research (even where the research in question may have been specifically commissioned), by use of phrases such as **independent body** or **independent inquiry**. The separateness signified by claimed **independence** in these contexts implies impartiality and lack of bias, and is used to support the AUTHORITY or LEGITIMACY of findings even where there may be little consensus on what the criteria of **independence** should be or how such independence can be demonstrated.

See FREEDOM, OPINION

INDIGENOUS

The origin and derivation of the adjective **indigenous** show little ambiguity or range, but the usage of the word as a less objectionable alternative to NATIVE charts an important political-semantic terrain today. In fact, **indigene** was used, both as adjective and noun, in English in C17 and C18, as a synonym of *native*, though it is now obsolete. Coming from the Latin *indigenus*, which meant anyone "born in a country, native," **indigenous**, in its mainstream use, has gradually narrowed to signify only current representatives of select pre-colonial groups with distinct lifestyles.

This reduction in scope of the original use of the term, as well as its technical application, which has taken on a specialized character after lC20, fulfills the need for a politically correct label for the "aboriginal" inhabitants of a specific (often third-world) area, once "native" became unacceptable. There is, thus, continuity in change here. In the early recorded uses from mC17 onward, **indigenous** referred more generally to "born or produced naturally in a land or region: native or belonging naturally to (the soil, region, etc.)," but even at that time it was "used primarily of aboriginal inhabitants or natural products." The earliest recorded use in 1646 is instructive because it so clearly defines **indigenous** as the proper (most LEGITIMATE) native: "Although . . . there bee . . . swarmes of Negroes serving under the Spaniard, yet were they all transported from Africa . . . and are not indigenous or proper natives of America."

There is, however, a productive tension between the crucial gains achieved by the international **indigenous** peoples' movement over the past fifty years and this general usage. This UN-facilitated movement is aspirational as well as POLITICAL, describing **indigenous peoples** in terms of their distinct lifestyles and marginalization—both externally through European colonialism and internally by more localized conquests—who seek the preservation and transmission of their identities, cultures, and territories. Thus, individuals self-identify as **indigenous** but require group acceptance through a shared consciousness.

The link between the more specialized and selective current meaning with the more general past use of **indigenous** is its meticulous relationship as the

(EUROPEAN) Other, though "indigenous peoples" is also a political construct that, in theory at least, can also refer to a small number of distinct marginalized groups living in the European continent, and it is deliberately less pejorative than its now discredited near-synonym, *native*. A parallel, though much less frequent meaning relates to "innateness," and this is without any pejorative comparison at all, as in "Joy and hope are emotions indigenous to the human mind" (*a*1864; compare similar use of *native* in, for instance, "native intelligence").

Hence, **indigenization**, an addition to English in mC20, seeks to describe a process in which there is "an increased use of indigenous people in government, employment etc." as an end result of "adaptation or subjection to the influence or dominance of the indigenous inhabitants of a country." A good example of the complicated processes at work is in the 1954 example, "Making the Church really indigenous with greater indigenization of leadership as well as support." This captures the substance of the term's meaning while clarifying that this salutary agenda involves a complicated pattern of manipulation, for those instrumental in this "making" remain outside it.

The range of contemporary uses of this term mirrors the current geopolitics of selective inclusivity. Peoples of the world are now divided into two categories: the **indigenous** and everyone else. What appears on the surface to be a scrupulous acknowledgment of radical difference has also become a debilitating homogenization that lumps together (South Asian) Adivasis [literally original/beginning dweller/inhabitant] with Australian Aborigines and the Kalaallit of Greenland, for instance. While this may lead to mobilization and sharing in common causes at the political level, it effaces and distorts differences that are as stark as those that obtain between "indigenous" and "non-indigenous" peoples.

The UN Declaration on the Rights of Indigenous Peoples, adopted in 2007 after twenty-five years of negotiation, contains no definition or even description of who is or is not **indigenous**, and, tellingly, its preamble only refers to common or shared characteristics indirectly, as in "indigenous peoples have suffered from historic injustices as a result of, inter alia, their colonization and dispossession of their lands, territories and resources, thus preventing them from exercising, in particular, their right to development in accordance with their own needs and interests." Two crucial distinctions emerge in this now dominant discourse on **indigenous**, which are not foregrounded in relation to other groups.

First is the recognition of their collective, over and above their individual, rights—"indigenous peoples possess collective rights which are indispensable for their existence, well-being and integral development as peoples." This recognition lacks adequate weight because there is no specifying of these RIGHTS and because the crucial preambular paragraph emphasizing that "indigenous peoples have the right freely to determine their relationships with States in a spirit of coexistence, mutual benefit and full respect" was deleted from the final version. As Charmaine White Face, an Oglala Tetuwan woman who served as official spokesperson for the Sioux National Treaty Council, states, "Without the approval or consensus of Indigenous Peoples and Nations, the [UN] General Assembly deleted one of the most basic reasons for the need for the Declaration in the first place: Indigenous Peoples' right to coexist with others."

The reason for this back-peddling is clearest in relation to transnational land issues because collective rights, if taken seriously, would destabilize the very notions of state sovereignty and territorial integrity, paradoxically more stringently enforced via "globalization" than before. Second and even more contentious is their right to reparation for past injustice and worse. Article 28 states, "Indigenous peoples have the right to redress, by means that can include restitution or, when this is not possible, just, fair and equitable compensation." However, here too, states' obligation to comply has been carefully omitted, unlike in other similar Articles in the Declaration.

Indigenous carries with it two potentially contradictory layers of meaning, even in its politically correct current usage. The more visible of the two, emphasized in the discourse of the United Nations, relates to the **indigenous** peoples' radical distinctiveness and uniquely ORGANIC links to land and tradition, literally positing an unchanging, even primordialist, worldview. In this sense, **indigenous** is invariably coupled with *tribal*. This is strikingly evident in the International Labour Organization's 1989 Indigenous and Tribal Peoples Convention, where the two groups are combined together and referred to collectively as "these peoples" on forty-three occasions in the forty-four articles of the Convention. This Convention makes no reference at all to change and transformation within **indigenous** communities over time.

The other parallel meaning homogenizes all **indigenous** peoples into one portmanteau, where the explicit argument is that their simplicity and direct organic links to NATURE represent a unifying principle overriding (huge) cultural, religious, linguistic, geographical, and other differences. This formula of (a) radical-difference-from-us who are fundamentally individualist even when collective, combined with (b) they-are-all-the-same because they are undifferentiated both within their group and among all such groups, reflects the great difficulty of engaging productively and equally with a fundamentally different worldview, while recognizing that this worldview is itself internally differentiated, without descending into unexamined racism appearing as benevolence. While the dynamic nature of **indigenous** cultures, as well as their vast DIVERSITY and plurality, is recognized in principle, in practice the term **indigenous** works against this understanding, not least in part due to misplaced "political correctness" that fetishizes cultural relativism.

The term **indigenous** is crucial both as an (anti-evolutionary) concept and (partial) description, which understands and advocates for recognizing the limits of "development" as an unquestioned good by focusing on groups that remain largely outside this paradigm. It is, thus, mainly positive in its current range of meanings, unlike *native* and *tribal*, for instance, but it too has become a counter- (or alternative) development buzzword, like SUSTAINABILITY, which reproduces the very incompatibilities and unexamined homogeneity that it seeks to question.

See COUNTRY, NATIVE

INFORMATION

Among other uses, **information** refers to rapid social transformation associated with digital technologies and global communications (especially in lC20 compounds such as **information superhighway**, **information age**, and **information revolution**). Yet because of **information**'s range of technical and general senses, in many circumstances it remains unclear exactly what **information** is. What **information** means, accordingly, is both a practical problem (for example in assessing who the rightful owners, controllers, or appropriate recipients are for whatever is called **information**) and also a wider social question: what kind of economic, regulatory, or cultural **information regime** will allow societies to secure appropriate ACCESS to **information** as an essential quality of civil society and DEMOCRACY, regardless of whether they are, in recent "digital divide" thinking, **information-rich** or **information-poor**?

The noun **information** (which for much of its history in English is found as both a count noun—plural **informations**—and as an abstract noun) comes into English from a classical Latin root *informatio*, meaning "formation (of an idea); conception"; it was borrowed into English in lC17, partly via French. In post-classical Latin the word had several meanings, including "teaching, instruction, . . . creation, arrangement"; as well as, in philosophy, "infusion with [or crystallisation into] form."

These senses persisted in English. But they mutated, influenced by changing use of the verb **inform** (Latin: *informare*) as well as by different meanings of *form* itself, including the new relationship in English between *form* and *idea* in translated understandings of Plato and Aristotle.

The now rare or obsolete *OED* sense ("the giving of form or essential character to something; the action of imbuing with a particular quality; animation, esp. of the body by the soul") imported into Christianity a Classical understanding of conception or arrangement as manifestation of a conceptually prior or divine origin. Another *OED* sense, described as chiefly associated with the Christian Church, retains this emphasis: "divine influence or direction; inspiration, esp. through the Holy Spirit." In concurrent senses, however, **information** did not pass from divine AUTHORITY into human beings but was presented by human beings in petitions to SECULAR, legal authority. A further sense traces **information** from its now obsolete meaning of "public denunciation or accusation," through legal "laying a charge," to use for complaints that form the basis of a CIVIL claim (legal variants which link **information** with *intelligence* and with modern **informer**).

The main modern senses of **information** combine the process of informing with a product that results from such a process. Focus is typically on person-to-person human interaction, rather than on invoking divine or secular authority. But the major extensions of meaning that make **information** a contemporary keyword involve more recent specialization during C20, first in technical fields then widening and overlapping in general use.

As evoked in **information theory**, **information** is attested in *OED* with a 1948 quotation from C. E. Shannon & W. Weaver's *Mathematical Theory of Communication*: "The word *information*, in this theory, is used in a special sense that must not be confused with its ordinary usage. . . . In fact, two messages, one of which is heavily loaded with meaning and the other of which is pure nonsense, can be exactly equivalent, from the present viewpoint, as regards information." **Information** in this sense is defined in statistical probabilities of occurrence of symbols, and is measured in *bits*: a minimal unit based on binary choice. Amounts of information are calculable, including how many exabytes of information might exist in the world; and efficiency in the transmission of information along a channel, such as a fiber-optic cable, can be assessed. This emergent **information technology** meaning presents **information** as something abstracted from any human practice of "informing" or "being informed." Instead, **information** is a characteristic of any arrangement of signs that can be stored, viewed as a message, and transmitted in signal form; so it can—and increasingly does—pass between inanimate devices as much as between animate beings, as well as through combinations of the two.

In C20 **bio-informatics, information** reactivated the word's earlier meanings of *formation* and ultimately *form*, without necessary human creation. Instead the reference historically is more to what was considered, in C19 biology, to pass along bodily nerve fibers as a kind of relay before being represented in the brain and entertained by the mind. In modern genetics, DNA is also a kind of **information**, a kind that can be discovered but need not be perceived by humans. Such **information** could be considered communicated to human beings only in a framework of religious or Neo-Platonist thinking, an implication that pulls meanings of **information** away from human interaction back toward earlier senses of embodiment or crystallization of immanent form, and prompts intense debate between religious and secular positions.

During C20, **information** also became a significant term in economics, especially when combined in the expression **information asymmetry**. In this use, **information** provides a measure of relative power conferred by unequal awareness among parties to an economic transaction, with the significance that, in order to satisfy conditions of a theoretically ideal market, **information flow** should be abundant, ubiquitous, and freely distributed. Anything less—for instance where a monopoly exists—involves a damaging transaction cost and restricts availability, compromising efficiency. At the same time, **information** has to be gathered and presented; so **information services** require incentivization if production levels are to be assured, hence an emphasis on **information value** and the emergence of a field of **information economics**.

In these varied meanings, **information** makes available new contrasts with other important and problematic words competing for an area of conceptual space in English, including: COMMUNICATION (**information** accentuates what is notified, rather than how something is notified); *idea* (**information** accentuates content nuggets, rather than concepts or argument); *knowledge* (**information** accentuates incremental acquisition, rather than epistemological status); *data* (**information** accentuates processing—*datamining*—toward useful content extracted from raw material); *intelligence* and *news* (**information** places less emphasis on novelty); **misinformation** (**information** implies assumed accuracy); and OPINION (**information** implicates objective rather than subjective value).

Perhaps less obviously, **information** now also contrasts with MEDIA. Since the 1970s, Marshall McLuhan's "information age of the wired planet" has undergone separation of "message" from "medium," such that medium is now only rarely claimed to be the message. Rather, *medium* signifies mere carrier: cheap and convergent platforms for content that is easily transferred, edited and mixed, copied, and disseminated. Prioritized instead is **information** as underlying resource or asset which, by being intangible, can in principle be made freely available to everyone irrespective of technicalities associated with media, or alternatively may be selectively distributed and accessed, accumulating economic value and conferring advantage if made subject to incentive and monopoly.

Alternatives here are a crucial watershed in relation to the claimed **information explosion** that precipitated influential verbal combinations of **information** with other words including **storage, retrieval, processing, flow, architecture, science**, and **economy**, as well as more distinct **informatics** and **infosphere**. Enthusiasm for social changes facilitated by **information technology** tends in this vocabulary toward verbal intoxication: e.g., in widespread use of Internet-activist Stewart Brand's aphorism "Information wants to be free" (convenient truncation of his published statement "Information wants to be free. Information also wants to be expensive . . ."); or use of the popular slogan, "**too much information**" (TMI) as excited alternative to more formal **information overload**; or figurative application in nontechnical contexts of the claim in physics that "information cannot travel faster than the speed of light."

Given the complexity of present challenges, **information** also attracts ambivalent overtones and associations: **commercially sensitive information, classified information, freedom of information**, and looming **information warfare**. Implications of each of these expressions depend on political context and viewpoint, and inevitably intersect with general political concepts including notions of VALUE, the public interest, and competing notions of FREEDOM.

Highly varied contemporary use of **information** gives expression to important tensions in how we understand what information is and how it should be used. Emergence during C20 of perhaps the widest sense of **information**—"any kind of input or event that affects the state of a dynamic organism or system"—has clouded a historically largely settled relation, implied by communication-related uses of the word, between transmission of content and human relevance or significance. Confusion between the narrower and wider senses potentially disconnects encounters with **information** from active questioning of source and authority, as well as from questions of significance and use. As burgeoning use of **information** in preference to related terms encroaches on the word's surrounding lexical field, questions arise as to how everything from the human genome to celebrity gossip can so readily be referred to as **information**.

See ACCESS, COMMUNICATION, MEDIA, OPINION, TECHNOLOGY

INSTITUTION

Institution is one of several examples (cf. CULTURE, *society*, EDUCATION) of a noun of action or process which became, at a certain stage, a general and abstract noun describing something apparently objective and systematic; in fact, in the modern sense, an **institution**. It has been used in English since C14, from fw *institution*, oF, *institutionem*, L, from rw *statuere*, L—establish, found, appoint. In its earliest uses it had the strong sense of an act of origin—something **instituted** at a particular point in time—but by mC16 there was a developing general sense of practices established in certain ways, and this can be read in a virtually modern sense: "in one tonge, in lyke maners, institucions and lawes" (Ralph Robinson's translation of More's *Utopia*, 1551); "many good institutions, Lawes, maners, the art of government" (Ashley, 1594). But there was still, in context, a strong sense of custom, as in the surviving sense of "one of the institutions of the place." It is not easy to date the emergence of a fully abstract sense; it appears linked, throughout, with the related abstraction of *society*. By mC18 an abstract sense is quite evident, and examples multiply in C19 and C20. At the same time, from mC18, **institution** and, later, **institute** (which had carried the same general sense as **institution** from C16) began to be used in the titles of specific organizations or types of organization: "Charitable Institutions" (1764) and several titles from 1C18; **Mechanics' Institutes, Royal Institute of British Architects**, and comparable organizations from eC19, here probably imitated from the *Institut National*, created in France in 1795 in consciously modern terminology. **Institute** has since been widely used for professional, educational, and research organizations; **institution** for charitable and benevolent organizations. Meanwhile the general sense of a form of social organization, specific or abstract, was confirmed in mC19 development of **institutional** and **institutionalize**. In C20 **institution** has become the normal term for any organized element of a society.

Recent Developments

Over the past half-century, **institution** has remained somewhat of an **"institution"** in the English language in the modern colloquial sense to which Williams alludes in his entry. The first edition of the *OED* defines this colloquial sense of **institution** as "Something having the fixity or importance of a social institution; a well-established or familiar practice or object." Perhaps due to the word's association with that which is established or permanent, **institutions** have often been considered "natural" and unchanging. Research in the social sciences, however, has tended to show that **institutions**, such as the **institution** of MARRIAGE, the **institution** of the FAMILY, and **religious** and **educational institutions**, are social constructions shaped by the customs and values of people in a society.

Since lC20, fields such as **institutional economics** and comparative politics have distinguished between **formal** and **informal institutions**, but there is often little consensus on precise definitions of the terms. **Formal institutions** include those that enforce laws or social rules (e.g., governments, religious organizations), and **informal institutions** typically refer to uncodified cultural practices or traditions. This distinction is complicated because both **formal** and **informal institutions** can be abstract or concrete entities, and both types of **institutions**, not only **formal institutions**, regulate social behavior. The sense of **institution** as constraining and determining behavior reaches its peak in the work of Erving Goffman on **total institutions** (1957) and colors an important use of the term **institutionalization**, which describes the adverse social and the psychological effects on individuals who reside in large-scale institutions such as mental hospitals or prisons. However, **institutionalization** can also be used in the positive sense of setting in place new forms of social and educational provision: "This order is brought about by the systematization, or institutionalization, of social activities so that certain persons have certain roles in them and so that the activities have certain functions in the general social life" (Evans Pritchard, 1951).

See CULTURE, EDUCATION, FAMILY, MARRIAGE

KARMA

The word **karma** derives from the Sanskrit *karma*, meaning both "action" and "fate." **Karma** has a rich history in Buddhist, Jain, and Hindu philosophy and theology, and the word entered English first through the theosophical movement at the end of C19 and then massively in the 1960s through an ever greater interest in Buddhism and also other strands of Indian theology. After a slight falling off in the late 1970s, it has increased its frequency in contemporary English. It would seem to represent an alternative to Western non-Christian notions of fate or destiny as imposed from external forces. Instead, it proffers a notion of a future determined by an individual's past actions. A significant text of this new meaning is John Lennon's song "Instant Karma!" (1970). This new Western meaning of **karma** is generally detached from notions of previous lives to focus on the accumulations of actions in a particular individual life.

The (Buddhist) theory of **karma**, which holds that conscious beings (i.e., humans) determine their future destinies through the merit or quality of their actions (both active and passive), is still the underlying assumption when the word is used by cultural believers in the Indian subcontinent. In turn, this one sense that suggests that a person's destiny is always already predetermined by the work or actions of previous births led to the popular understanding and use of the word in a negative or passive sense of resignation, where a speaker sighs over a fate that cannot be controlled. Hence, in South Asia one typically says, "What can I do? This must be [or is] my karma."

From the original sense of action or deed, **karma** came to mean the sum totality of an individual's actions in a particular life or state of existence, moving from the individual to the whole in which good and bad acts are weighed against each other. From this composite public understanding in South Asia, the term continues to mark a belief in both rebirth and the causal connection between successive births or forms of existence. In this popular sense, **karma** now represents the consequence or *result* of karma, not (only) karma (or the action/deed) itself, which is an important broadening of its meaning. Hence, in contemporary Buddhist and Jainist popular discourse, **karma** is both the act *and* its consequence, a uniquely complex epistemological concept, which, nonetheless, seems to sit easily in ordinary usage across the range of Indian languages.

The Sanskrit *karma* was derived from the general verb *kr*, which meant "to do, to make." Early usage in the Vedic texts referred mainly to rituals, and **karma** was a ritualistic act or rite. People who performed these designated acts were assured of rebirth in a heaven, with the governing metaphor being that of harvesting. This early Brahminic understanding was first contested by the Jains, who defined **karma** as matter and the result of overt action, whereas the Buddhist theory of **karma** focuses exclusively on intention [*cetanaa*] since for the Buddha the ETHICAL or moral value of an act depends entirely on the intention behind it.

Thus, in this sense, contemporary mainstream "Western" use has reduced out much of the philosophical complexity inherent in the concept of **karma**, restricting its meanings, except for believers in Indian religions, to the result of individual actions in future events. This usage is only *one* of the current meanings of the word in the Indian subcontinent, though it has become the *only* sense in which the word is used, broadly speaking, in the rest of the world. In addition, whereas there is hardly ever a positive use of the term among, say, Theravada Buddhists, in the global North the term is also used optimistically, often with adjectival embellishment, such as in **good karma**.

This usage of **karma** in English has increased dramatically since the 1950s, demonstrating that it is one of the key "Indian" borrowings of the latter half of C20. In fact, frequency data show that **karma** has overtaken the use of the much more general term *fate*, which has seen a drastic decline that mirrors the rise of **karma** in popular discourse. Even the more formal term *destiny* ranks well below **karma**. The adjectives **good** and **bad** employed to modify and explain **karma** have become very popular since the last two decades of C20. **Bad karma** is still more frequently used than **good karma**, but the positive sense seems to be on the increase.

Karma in popular English usage is then a consequence of the generalized cultural revolution of the 1960s principally located in the US and in a generalized interest in Eastern religions, particularly Buddhism. This shift from the formal philosophical use of the term, as in "The individual's choice of a future earthly body is limited however by what is known as the 'Law of Karma'" (1962), to the demotic, such as "This is a bad Karma contest" (1969), exemplifies this drastic change. **Karma** became a symptomatic "hippie" word, but significantly survived the demise of the hippie movement to enter the mainstream of Western thought. Citations like "John Sebastian's recording career has been plagued with an unusually bad karma" (*Rolling Stone*, 1971) clearly demonstrate how the concept has undergone drastic simplification while continuing to mark a distinction from notions of *destiny* and *fate*.

Thus, **karma** in current Western English usage has been unmoored from its religious and cultural bearings in rebirth to focus on Buddhist conceptions of the accumulated effect of actions. In the Indian subcontinent it is still tied to its religious roots and has become a synonym for rebirth, or at least the tacit acceptance of the logic of causality affecting a person's chain of lives. It can thus be used lightly in casual conversation without any hint of disrespect or deprecation, though it makes no claim to depth or sophistication.

It is worth noting that the *OED*'s entry for **karma** relates it to the complicated Indian belief systems from which it originates without separating out the distinctive new Western sense of the last fifty years (the entry has not yet been fully updated). This sense seems strongly correlated with the phrase "what goes around comes around." Unrecorded before the 1970s, this phrase has greatly increased in frequency in the last forty years, occurring across a variety of song lyrics and popular self-help and religious books. It is difficult to know how at this stage to evaluate this new Western sense of **karma**. While it has undoubtedly outlasted its particular origins in the hippie moment of the 1960s, whether it signals a major change in notions of fate and RESPONSIBILITY in the WEST or is to be classed as merely a weak cultural borrowing from the East is impossible to determine in the second decade of C21.

The differentiated use of **karma** in English today represents the strong DIVERSITY of its users from different parts of the world, while bearing witness to a significant shift in Western conceptions of fate and responsibility. As a borrowing from Sanskrit, its semantic range is tied to geographic and ideological variation, and is an instructive example of the impossibility of fixing a single meaning of a word, as well as the danger of trying to limit English semantics to its traditional homelands.

See ETHICAL, RELIGION, RESPONSIBILITY, SPIRITUAL, WEST

LANGUAGE

Language has been one of the key elements in almost all the NATIONALIST movements of the last two centuries, and it was also the single most important concept in C20 philosophy. Its use in politics and philosophy depends on two very different senses. When the Gaelic revival promoted the use of Irish as a **language** at the end of C19, they were referring to a particular organization of sounds that constituted an individual **language** and the COMMUNITY who spoke it. When Wittgenstein and Derrida talked about **language,** they were talking about the universal faculty of speech or writing without reference to a specific **language community**. In Modern English we have one word for both these senses, while most of the Romance languages have two. Thus, in French *langue* refers to an individual language and *langage* to the general faculty. The French word *langue* also refers to the tongue, the physical organ that is crucial for articulate speech. The English word *tongue* is derived from Anglo-Saxon and the form is general to a host of Germanic languages. In Early Modern English *tongue* referred to the physical organ and, by a metonymy similar to that operating in French, to individual languages as well. Those meanings are no longer current and are almost all archaic, although there are phrases such as "speaking in tongues" or "gift of tongues" where it persists, and one might hazard that most speakers of current English would understand a reference to "the Latin tongue" or "the German tongue." The overlapping senses in English can be found in medieval French, where both *langue* and *langage* are used variously to refer to a particular language and to the general faculty before the senses were allocated as they are in modern French. Both French words are derived from the Latin *lingua* that has meanings stretching from the physical organ to the general faculty and where an extension also occurs from the meaning "individual language" to a particular people (speaking a particular language).

Language as defining a people figured crucially in a highly diverse set of debates at the beginning of C20, debates that stretch from Nazi ideology to Saussurean linguistics. Saussure used the distinction between *langue* and *langage* in French to focus his argument that linguistics was not concerned with the very diverse facts of language (*langage*), but with the very specific set of differences that constituted a specific language (*langue*). Saussurean linguistics (and its Chomskyan successor) assert that the *langue* is defined by its systematic differences and it is these shared systematic differences that constitute a speech community. This equation between a **language** and a *community* is written deep into the etymological history of both Romance and Germanic languages and surfaces in very different forms in ideological nationalism and scientific linguistics. Both can trace important origins in Johann Gottfried Herder's *Treatise on the Origin of Language* (1772) that argued strongly for an identification of **language** and people.

However, one could argue that this deep-seated assumption is fundamentally incorrect. For there is another sense of **language** which ranges from the accusation that someone is using **bad language** to the description of a sentence as *dialect* which presupposes different speech communities within a speech community. The famous joke about how to distinguish a **language** from a *dialect*—"A language is a dialect with an army and a navy"—makes the very serious point that speech communities are formed and reformed in ways that are not directly related to **language** but to a wide variety of factors that include politics, education, and technological development. *Dialects* are usually defined in relation to regions and are held to be regional forms of the given national language. But by defining **language** with relation to *nation*, we make clear how intimately language is linked to politics. While it may be easy in practice to define the moment at which a dialect becomes a language, it is very difficult to make this distinction in theory. The moment at which two versions of a language become mutually incomprehensible, and thus two different languages, cannot be fully described in linguistic terms. Linguistics uses the notion of a **standard language**, but how much variation is possible within a standard language (for example between dialects spoken in regions geographically remote from one another) is a question that is seldom posed within the academic discipline. However, an answer to that question would be essential to make clear distinctions between a language and its dialects. This question is not merely theoretical. In particular it can be argued that at the level of meaning there is never a unified speech community but a set of competing dialects defined by CLASS, GENDER, RACE, and age, among other differences. Indeed, Williams's *Keywords*, as his introduction makes clear, is based on that sense of **language** which is being used in the common phrase about other speakers of English that "they are speaking a different language." This locution assumes that a language is made up of several languages. Indeed *Keywords* itself could be considered as the semantics for a language divided among a variety of speech communities. It is here that the sense of **language** that refers to a unified speech community runs up against a sense of **language** that refers to the divisions among language users, whether that be in terms of vocabulary, style, idiolect, or dialect.

The crucial difficulty of how to move from a particular language to the group of people who speak it and the very important ideological stakes in this move can be seen by comparing the definition from the second edition of the *OED*, "The whole body of words and of methods of combination of words used by a nation, people or race, a 'tongue,'" to the third edition, "The system of spoken or written communication used by a particular country, people, community, etc." There can be little doubt that the change from *nation* to COUNTRY and from *race* to *community* was motivated by a desire to distance the dictionary from Nazi theories of nation and race which accorded an extraordinary importance to language. However, what remains unchanged is the fundamental sense of the defining role that language plays in constituting a unified social collectivity.

Another, and arguably more radical change in the third edition of the *OED* is the definition of **animal language**. The second edition spots a transferred meaning: "applied to the inarticulate sounds used by the lower animals, birds etc." But the third edition does not consider the meaning transferred, has it as the second of the primary senses, and defines it as: "The vocal sounds by which mammals and birds communicate." For much of the Western tradition and certainly for all modern linguistics, one of the defining differences between humans and other ANIMALS is that humans have **language** but animals do not. The third edition of the *OED* seems to have abandoned the Western tradition and in doing so it is reacting not only to the developments in ethology which have meant that we now understand far better than we did fifty years ago the complexity of animal systems of COMMUNICATIONS, but also to a widespread ECOLOGICAL movement which refuses to accept the sharp distinction between humans and animals that is such a feature of Western thought.

See COMMUNICATION, COMMUNITY, COUNTRY, MEDIA, NATIONALIST

LEGITIMATE

Some English speakers consider the adjectives *legal* and **legitimate** to be synonymous. In this, their intuition is supported by insistence on some English usage websites that the two are necessarily equivalent. A number of controversial recent political events, by contrast, have been defended precisely in terms of semantic shading between the two words. Some events have been justified as "legitimate but not legal": the Palestinian intifada, by its supporters; the 1999 NATO bombing of Kosovo, as assessed by Kofi Annan; the Iraq War, as described retrospectively by General Wesley Clark; or—more currently—targeted killing by drones. Other events and practices are condemned for being "legal but not legitimate," in a microcosm form of **legitimation crisis**: acts by the official Syrian government against its own population; tax avoidance schemes contrived by multinational companies. When *legal* and **legitimate** are paired by *and* and *or*, their juxtaposition suggests contrast of meaning rather than equivalence. This effect extends even into overtly legal settings. When the phrase **enforceable legitimate expectation** is used in formulating a claim in judicial review, for example, a sense of legal entitlement is conveyed by context and by the word "enforceable." Yet **legitimate** itself in this context does not mean mandated by law; rather it functions as a term of art within the field of law, to be established (or not) in wider terms such as fairness.

Some of the modern meanings conveyed by **legitimate** are carried over into English from the word's Latin antecedent. The English adjective **legitimate**, along with related verb **legitimate** (also modern **legitimize**, and derived **legitimation** and **delegitimation**), comes into the language in lC15 from medieval Latin *lēgitimātus*, the past participle of *lēgitimāre* "to declare to be lawful" and "to cause to be regarded as lawful offspring" (from Classical Latin *lēgitimus*, lawful and < *lēg-*, *lēx*, law). With other words derived from Latin *lex*, **legitimate** forms part of a semantic cluster around the Norse word *law* ("laid down") and Old English *riht*, both of which continue into present use but with nuances between "law," "leg-" and "rights" traditions. From earliest use, however, **legitimate** gave rise to particular complexity, in that the status it confers must have been endorsed by some AUTHORITY. Yet while according to the *OED* **legitimate** displaced an older adjective that did not require such agency (**legitime**), **legitimate** itself shows little trace of its participial, passive sense of a status actively declared rather than simply inherent.

Lack of clarity regarding exactly who or what validates something that is **legitimate** continues to contribute to the word's uncertainty, not only in general discussion but in more technical fields. In social theory, for example (from Weber through Habermas into current sociology), the agency at work in **legitimation** and loss of **legitimacy** of individuals, organizations, new nations, and post-revolutionary societies is conceived as a matter of collective construction of social reality, expressed as orientation toward norms, values, and beliefs that individuals presume are widely shared, whether or not they personally share them.

Complexity and resulting tension have arisen partly because, over three centuries, **legitimate** introduced into English a number of figurative extensions. Five broad and interwoven strands can be traced.

(1) One of the earliest senses recorded by the *OED*, from lC15, is historically the most salient sense: "Of a child: having the status of one born to parents lawfully married to each other, entitled in law to full filial rights; of a parent: lawfully married to the other parent of a child; of status, descent, etc.: of or through such parents or children." This meaning was enforced by changing legal measures with life-altering consequences in different periods, and remains alive and controversial in many parts of the English-using world depending on prevailing FAMILY structures and cultural conventions.

(2) From C16, however, a (now rare) extension from approved parentage widened **legitimate** in such a way that it could refer to objects, products, and processes other than children, including words, books as productions of an author, even medicines (as in the *OED* example: "By the Taste . . . we . . . distinguish the true legitimate [medicines] from the adulterate," 1634). In this sense, **legitimate** means "genuine, real, or authentic" in contrast with "spurious" or "counterfeit" (as well as, more weakly, "regular" or "standard," as contrasted with "idiosyncratic" or "wayward").

(3) Also building on the schema of proper descent, a narrower political sense emerged in mC17 in the constitutional sphere: "justified or validated by the strict principle of hereditary right," within a wider system of lineal succession that combines authenticity by origin with stratification of entitlement and authority. By the time this sense became more dominant, however, in a political culture colored both by industrialization and by the French and American Revolutions, there is already sometimes skepticism in its use, as in this *OED* quotation from the *Saturday Review* (1860): "It is not in irony, but in sober earnest, that we express our belief that any throne is, in

practice, called *legitimate* which has not had the consent of the nation to its establishment or existence."

(4) It is a confusing feature of the history of **legitimate** that this constitutional sense, now familiar across the globe in combinations such as **legitimate government** while symbolically still connected with biological descent in its echoes of **legitimate succession**, should appear long after another, wider sense to which this sense appears closely tied: that of "Conforming to the law or to rules; sanctioned or authorized by law or right principles; lawful; proper" (the sense that makes possible the popular modern equation of *legal* with **legitimate**). This meaning goes right back to the word's earliest history in English, and is (by a small margin) the earliest recorded by *OED*, dating back to mC15. In this meaning, "conforming to the law or to rules; sanctioned or authorized by law or right principles," something is **legitimate** if it is legally permissible ("accordant with law or with established legal forms and requirements"). This sense, which relies both on law and more generally on foundations in morality and reasonable behavior, is clear in Macaulay: "[W]hat would, under ordinary circumstances, be justly condemned as persecution, may fall within the bounds of legitimate self-defence" (*The History of England*, v. 1, 1856).

(5) In yet another direction, **legitimate** is attested from lC18 with the meaning "Sanctioned by the laws of reasoning; logically admissible or inferable." J. S. Mill refers to "legitimate logical processes" (*Dissertations and Discussions*, 1859). This is the sense appealed to in talk of **legitimate** steps in a calculation as opposed to fallacious ones, and **legitimate** inferences in conversation, in contrast with strained or unreasonable interpretations. Despite the association of **legitimate** with degree of recognition afforded to offspring, as well as with constitution and tradition, at this point **legitimacy** is absorbed into ENLIGHTENMENT vocabulary as an ordering of things by reason. Through this striking semantic extension an order guaranteed by physical descent morphs into one validated by continuity of mental operations.

These five still evolving strands in the meaning of **legitimacy** can appear distinct from one another in given situations. They are linked, however, by important complications to which the word gives rise. One major complication stems from persistence of the word's participial force, with its implication that no clear basis for legitimacy exists unless specified. Acknowledging something as **legitimate** on alternative implicit grounds of origin, constitutional standing, law-abiding character, consensual norm, or correct reasoning, accordingly reflects tacit intellectual and political choices. Without specification, on the other hand, **legitimacy** fades into rhetorical appeal to a hall of mirrors of perceptions attributed by others that conjure up some form of quasi-legal endorsement. A second major complication affects not only **legitimate** but a whole cluster of judgment words in English, including FAIR, *valid*, and *reasonable*. Each can be used normatively rather than descriptively to justify or query social obligations and desirable courses of action. But each use requires either an assumption that the assessment put forward expresses subjective viewpoint (even self-interest), or alternatively that the judgment rests on consensual perceptions deemed "objective." In the face of such divergent alternatives, **legitimacy** judgments are very much open to question. As regards an often claimed need for political or legal allowance to be made for "legitimate advertising practices" or "legitimate professional procedures" in banking and finance, for example, it is uncertain what standard the **legitimacy** of such practices derives from. It is also unclear whose point of view such **legitimacy** represents: that of advertisers and bankers themselves; that of a regulatory framework believed to command public trust; that of accepted OPINION, however gathered; or that aligned with some wider but unspecified—and likely to be contested—concept of the PUBLIC interest.

See AUTHENTIC, FAIR

LIBERAL

Liberal has, at first sight, so clear a POLITICAL meaning that some of its further associations are puzzling. Yet the political meaning is comparatively modern, and much of the interesting history of the word is earlier.

It began in a specific social distinction, to refer to a class of free men as distinct from others who were not free. It came into English in C14, from fw *liberal*, oF, *liberalis*, L, rw *liber*, L—free man. In its use in **liberal arts**—"artis liberalis" (1375)—it was predominantly a class term: the skills and pursuits appropriate, as we should now say, to men of independent means and assured social position, as distinct from other skills and pursuits (cf. *mechanical*) appropriate to a lower class. But there was a significant development of a further sense, in which the pursuits had their own independence: "Liberal Sciencis . . . fre scyencis, as gramer, arte, fisike, astronomye, and otheris" (1422). Yet as with any term which distinguishes some free men from others, a tension remained. The cultivated ideal of the **liberal arts** was matched by the sense of **liberal** as generous ("in giffynge liberal," 1387), but at the same time this was flanked by the negative sense of "unrestrained." **Liberty**, though having an early general sense of FREEDOM, had a strong sense from C15 of formal permission or PRIVILEGE; this survives in the naval phrase **liberty boat** and, though often not noticed as such, in the conservative phrase **liberties of the subject**, where **liberty** has no modern sense but the old sense of certain RIGHTS granted within an unquestionable subjection to a particular sovereignty. The other word for such a formal right was *license*, and the play of feeling, towards the sense of "unrestrained," can be clearly seen in the development, from C16, of *licentious*. **Liberal**, as well as being widely used in the stock phrase *lyberal arbytre* (C15)—free will—was close to *licentious* in such uses as Shakespeare's

> Who hath indeed most like a liberall villaine
> Confest the vile encounters they have had.
> (*Much Ado About Nothing*, IV, i)

A weaker but related form of this sense is clear in the development, from 1C18, of the sense of "not rigorous," which could be taken either as "not harsh" or as "not disciplined."

The affirmation of **liberal**, in a social context quite different from that of a special class of free men, came mainly in 1C18 and eC19, following the strong general sense of **Liberty** from mC17. It was used in the sense of "open-minded," and thence of "unorthodox," from 1C18: "liberal opinions" (Gibbon, 1781). The adjective is very clear in a political sense in an example from 1801: "the extinction of every vestige of freedom, and of every liberal idea with which they are associated." This led to the formation of the noun as a political term, proudly and even defiantly announced in the periodical title, *The Liberal* (1822). But, as often since, this term for an unorthodox political opinion was given, by its enemies, a foreign flavor. There was talk of the "Ultras" and "Liberals" of Paris in 1820, and some early uses were in a foreign form: *Liberales* (Southey, 1816); *Liberaux* (Scott, 1826). The term was applied in this sense as a nickname to advanced Whigs and Radicals by their opponents; it was then consciously adopted and within a generation was powerful and in its turn orthodox. **Liberality**, which since C14 had carried the sense of generosity, and later of open-mindedness, was joined by political **Liberalism** from eC19. **Libertarian** in 1C18 indicated a believer in free will as against *determinism*, but from 1C19 acquired social and political senses, sometimes close to **liberal**. It is especially common in mC20 in *libertarian socialism*, which is not **liberalism** but a form of SOCIALISM opposed to centralized and bureaucratic controls.

In the established party-political sense, **Liberal** is now clear enough. But **liberal** as a term of political discourse is complex. It has been under regular and heavy attack from CONSERVATIVE positions, where the senses of lack of restraint and lack of discipline have been brought to bear, and also the sense of a (weak and sentimental) generosity. The sense of a lack of rigor has also been drawn on in intellectual disputes. Against this kind of attack, **liberal** has often been a group term for progressive or radical opinions, and is still clear in this sense, notably in the US. But **liberal** as a pejorative term has also been widely used by socialists and especially Marxists. This use shares the conservative sense of lack of rigor and of weak and sentimental beliefs. Thus far it is interpreted by **liberals** as a familiar complaint, and there is a special edge in their reply to socialists, that they are concerned with political freedom and that socialists are not. But this masks the most serious sense of the socialist use, which is the historically accurate observation that **liberalism** is a doctrine based on *individualist* theories of man and society and is thus in fundamental conflict not only with SOCIALIST but with most strictly *social* theories. The further observation, that **liberalism** is the highest form of thought developed within bourgeois society and in terms of CAPITALISM, is also relevant, for when **liberal** is not being used as a loose swear-word, it is to this mixture of liberating and limiting ideas that it is intended to refer. **Liberalism** is then a doctrine of certain necessary kinds of freedom but also, and essentially, a doctrine of possessive individualism.

Recent Developments

The current *OED* entry (3d ed., 2010) usefully names the term's immense ambiguity: **liberal** refers "to various political parties, usually occupying a position somewhere between socialism and conservatism." In the recent decades of **neoliberalism** it has seemed to many far closer to the CONSERVATIVE end of this middle space. This current sense is illustrated in the *Economist* lead editorial on the 2017 UK general election (June 3, 2017, p. 13), which laments the absence of any serious **liberal** alternative between Labour and Conservative. The desired but absent positives all invoke the root idea of FREEDOM, citing "free market," "free movement of people," and "personal freedom." These correspond to *OED* senses that include

"Favouring or characterized by unrestricted trade" and "Supporting or advocating individual rights, civil liberties, and political and social reform tending towards individual freedom or democracy with little state intervention." However, the *OED* offers also a conflicting sense: "favouring social reform and a degree of state intervention in matters of economics and social justice; left-wing." This entry warns that it is "not to be confused with the political use" just cited, but this seems a hopeless warning. The word is used in contradictory ways. As the *OED* adds, **liberal** is "often used by the political right (esp. in the United States) almost synonymously with *communist* or *socialist*." These negative usages also invoke the root idea of freedom, as in irreligious free-thinking and wasteful free-spending. The dilemmas of individualism, with which Williams concluded his discussion of **liberal**, remain live. The *Economist* mocks Labour leader Corbyn for calling Fidel Castro "a champion of social justice," because Castro has "locked up opponents and muzzled the press." To the magazine's liberalism, freedom of speech is preeminent. Yet Cuban babies are much less likely to die in their first year than are American newborns, despite the US being far more prosperous. The freedom to live may override other freedoms. The **liberal world order** identified with US global hegemony has sought to "elevate universal principles of individual rights and common humanity," according to a recent Brookings Institution paper, but it also has cost many lives among the peoples it has aimed to help.

See ART, CAPITALISM, CONSERVATIVE, FREEDOM, POLITICAL, PRIVILEGE, RIGHTS, SOCIALIST

LIFE

Nearly every era decries the anthropomorphizing definition of **life** assumed by previous periods. Definitions of **life** are often concerned with defining what is human: some historical periods assume a wider, others a narrower, scope for the term. In recent decades, debate over when human life begins, what RIGHTS inhere in it, and how it might end have seen **life** become a polarizing term in the public sphere.

According to the *OED*, the primary meaning of **life** is "animate existence." Its medieval usage, however, was quite broad, encompassing a variety of material and immaterial meanings. It referred to the "vital spirit" that animated earthly bodies, as distinguished from the natural and the animate spirit often thought to reside in the heart as opposed to the brain. By extension, the word also referred to the material body as a whole. In medical and scientific treatises, *lif* could also refer to the material custom that shaped a body, diet, or a regime. In this sense, the term designated nurture rather than NATURE. But Middle English *lif* could also refer to purely SPIRITUAL, immaterial aspects of life, when it was used to translate L *anima*, "soul, breath." Moreover, as the usual translation for L *vita* and oF *vie*, "lif" designated, of a saint's life, a moral example that provided a pattern for spiritual existence. When the drunken Miller of Chaucer's *Canterbury Tales* announces that he will "telle a legende and a lyf / bothe of a carpenter and of his wyf," (3141–2), he prepares us for a hagiographic satire that revolves around not a holy exemplar but around an adulterous wife, wily clerics, and a hard-done-to peasant. Medieval *lif* was simultaneously a thing (sustenance; a body or essence), a disciplinary practice, a mode of life, and a spiritual model. Its meanings fell along a finely graded continuum that ran from the utterly physical to the transcendent, including most points in between.

The broad and continuous nature of these meanings is reflected in medieval beliefs about what qualifies as "animate," a definition that differs markedly from modern ones. In current usage, the *OED* defines **life** primarily as "human or animal existence, cf. soul." This definition restricts it to these categories of being. In medieval scholastic philosophy, by contrast, lively existence and, indeed, SOUL were shared among many ontological categories. Following Aristotle, medieval NATURE was defined as anything that possessed self-motion. For example, rocks were thought to fall to the ground not on account of the law of gravity but because they followed their natural inclination to return "home" to their rightful place in the earth. In this way objects that moderns recognize as inanimate possessed quasi-animate powers of motion. Plants were thought to have souls in the sense that their motion was directed toward a particular end. The human soul contained within it vegetative and animal souls, in addition to the uniquely rational human one. **Life** was therefore a much broader category than we recognize today.

The definition of **life** narrowed considerably in the early modern period, when the word began to be restricted not just to those things that exhibited motion, but also to that immaterial *nous* that supplemented, rather than inhered in, matter. What had been an inner principle of growth and change was now outsourced: imagined as an exterior force that supplied the links between otherwise unrelated parts. The scientific innovations of Gassendi and Descartes led to the mind-body dualism that tightened the circle of **life** to include only intentionally conscious existence, leaving plant and ANIMAL alongside the inanimate rock in the shadows. A corollary of the mechanical philosophy saw the human as *res* *cogitans* (the thinking thing), while the rest of the world was lumped together into *res extensa* (the extended thing or corporeal substance). This definition famously led to animals being excluded from the charmed circle of **life** by Descartes, who concluded that since animals lacked consciousness and could suffer no pain or pleasure, they were, in effect, only machines or automata. What made this belief about animals possible was a new belief in the identity of soul and rational mind— an identity that excluded mere **life**.

In C19, discussions of **life** shifted away from the early modern emphasis on **life** as soul or consciousness. Darwin equated **life** with GENETIC adaptation, and in particular with reproduction rather than observable sentience or vitality. The scientific drive to redefine **life** as a physiological process that could be broken down into its respective parts—**life** as behavior rather than essence or soul—was the result of a long process that existed dialectically with an opposing conception of **life** that, following Spinoza, saw the world as a singular living being, disposed to isomorphism and homology in all its aspects. The effect is what the historian of evolutionary biology Robert J. Richards has called a "romantic conception of life," tracing in the writings of Goethe, Schiller, and others an ideal that sought a holistic, cooperative conception of **life** without Aristotelian teleologies. This tension between the monist celebration of **life** and a particulate science is reflected in Mary Shelley's *Frankenstein*, for instance, a work that long before Darwin had already raised the question of what our moral obligations are to living creatures, especially creatures to whom we have given **life**. Shelley's *Frankenstein* also raised the specter of biohorror, the risks and consequences of **life** gone bad.

These poles continued to shape scientific definitions of **life** in subtle ways, for example in remediated form in attempts to define **life** in genetic terms in the work of physicists and molecular biologists such as Erwin Schrödinger, Freeman Dyson, and others. Their attempts to define what **life** is can be (no doubt simplistically) boiled down to the question: Is **life** guaranteed by relentless replication of the "selfish gene" (in Richard Dawkins's phrase) or by the cooperative homeostasis necessary for maintenance of the genome as a whole (Dyson's view)? Behind this question we can dimly perceive C19 terms: Is biological **life** holistic and communal (Spinozist) or ruggedly individualist (Darwinian)? What is significant is that whatever answer is chosen, both of these interpretations of **life** in terms of genetics are modelled on identifiable human behaviors. Whether we understand genes as essentially selfish or essentially cooperative, in both cases we understand them in terms of human agency.

Our contemporary understandings of **life** have been largely shaped by this disjunctive linguistic and philosophical inheritance. The particularly C19 tensions between biological and theological definitions outlined earlier subtend current public debates and educational policy regarding topics including EVOLUTION, abortion, capital punishment, euthanasia, and end-of-life care, since most of these debates center around how far certain rights can be said to inhere in **life** itself. Such ongoing mobilizations of **life** suggest that, as we consider the contemporary ethical and political implications of scientific innovation, it remains useful to look back to earlier moments where the line between the human and the natural was imagined in ways that continue to influence how we now understand what it means to be human.

See ANIMAL, EVOLUTION, GENETIC, HUMANITY, NATURE, RIGHTS, SOUL

LITERATURE

Literature is a difficult word, in part because its conventional contemporary meaning appears, at first sight, so simple. There is no apparent difficulty in phrases like **English literature** or **contemporary literature**, until we find occasion to ask whether all books and writing are **literature** (and if they are not, which kinds are excluded and by what criteria) or until, to take a significant example, we come across a distinction between **literature** and *drama* on the grounds, apparently, that drama is a form primarily written for spoken performance (though often also to be read). It is not easy to understand what is at stake in these often confused distinctions until we look at the history of the word.

Literature came into English, from C14, in the sense of polite learning through reading. Its fw, *littérature*, F, *litteratura*, L, had the same general sense. The rw is *littera*, L—letter (of the alphabet). Thus a man of **literature**, or of *letters*, meant what we would now describe as a man of wide reading. Thus: "hes nocht sufficient literatur to undirstand the scripture" (1581); "learned in all literature and erudition, divine and humane" (Bacon, 1605). It can be seen from the Bacon example that the noun of condition—being well-read—is at times close to the objective noun—the books in which a man is well-read. But the main sense can be seen from the normal adjective, which was **literate**, from C15, rather than **literary**, which appeared first in C17 as a simple alternative to **literate** and only acquired its more general meaning in C18, though cf. Cave's Latin title *Historia Literaria*, 1688. As late as Johnson's *Life of Milton*, the earlier usage was still normal: "he had probably more than common literature, as his son addresses him in one of his most elaborate Latin poems" (1780).

Literature, that is to say, corresponded mainly to the modern meanings of **literacy**, which, probably because the older meaning had then gone, was a new word from 1C19. It meant both an ability to read and a condition of being well-read. This can be confirmed from the negatives. **Illiterate** usually meant poorly-read or ill-educated: "Judgis illitturate" (1586); "my illeterate and rude stile" (1597); and as late as Chesterfield (1748): "the word *illiterate*, in its common acceptance, means a man who is ignorant of those two languages" (Greek and Latin). Even more clearly there was the now obsolete **illiterature**, from 1C16: "the cause . . . ignorance . . . and . . . illiterature" (1592). By contrast, from eC17, the **literati** were the highly-educated.

But the general sense of "polite learning," firmly attached to the idea of printed books, was laying the basis for the later specialization. Colet, in C16, distinguished between **literature** and what he called **blotterature**; here the sense of inability to write clear letters is extended to a kind of book which was below the standards of polite learning. But the first certain signs of a general change in meaning are from C18. **Literary** was extended beyond its equivalence to **literate**; probably first in the general sense of well-read but from mC18 to refer to the practice and profession of writing: "literary merit" (Goldsmith, 1759); "literary reputation" (Johnson, 1773). This appears to be closely connected with the heightened self-consciousness of the profession of authorship, in the period of transition from patronage to the book-selling market. Where Johnson had used **literature** in the sense of being highly literate in his *Life of Milton*, in his *Life of Cowley* he wrote, in the newly objective sense: "an author whose pregnancy of imagination and elegance of language have deservedly set him high in the ranks of literature." (His *Dictionary* definition was "learning, skill in letters.") Yet **literature** and **literary**, in these new senses, still referred to the whole body of books and writing; or if distinction was made it was in terms of falling below the level of polite learning rather than of particular kinds of writing. A philosopher such as Hume quite naturally described his "Love of literary Fame" as his "ruling passion." All works within the orbit of polite learning came to be described as **literature** and all such interests and practices as **literary**. Thus Hazlitt, in "Of Persons One Would Wish to Have Seen" (*Winterslow*, II), reports: "Ayrton said, 'I suppose the two first persons you would choose to see would be the two greatest names in English literature, Sir Isaac Newton and Mr Locke'" (*c*1825).

That now common phrase, **English literature**, is itself part of a crucial development. The idea of a *Nationallitteratur* developed in Germany from the 1770s, and
the following can be recorded: *Über die neuere deutsche Litteratur* (Herder, 1767);
Les Siècles de littérature française (1772); *Storia della letteratura italiana* (1772).
English literature appears to have followed these, though it is implicit in Johnson.
The sense of "a nation" having "a literature" is a crucial social and cultural, probably
also political, development.

What has then to be traced is the attempted and often successful specialization of **literature** to certain kinds of writing. This is difficult just because it is in-
complete; a **literary editor** or a **literary supplement** still deals generally with all
kinds of books. But there has been a specialization to a sense which is sometimes
emphasized (because of the remaining uncertainty) in phrases like **creative literature** and **imaginative literature** (cf. CREATIVE and *imaginative* as descriptions of
kinds of writing; cf. also *fiction*). In relation to the past, **literature** is still a relatively
general word: Carlyle and Ruskin, for example, who did not write novels or poems
or plays, belong to **English literature**. But there has been a steady distinction and
separation of other kinds of writing—philosophy, essays, history, and so on—which
may or may not possess **literary merit** or be of **literary interest** (meaning that "in
addition to" their intrinsic interest as philosophy or history or whatever they are
"well written") but which are not now normally described as **literature**, which may
be understood as well-written books but which is even more clearly understood as
well-written books of an *imaginative* or *creative* kind. The teaching of English, especially in universities, is understood as the teaching of **literature**, meaning mainly
poems and plays and novels; other kinds of "serious" writing are described as *general* or *discursive*. Or there is **literary criticism**—judgment of how a (*creative* or
imaginative) work is written—as distinct, often, from discussion of "ideas" or "history" or "general subject-matter." At the same time many, even most poems and
plays and novels are not seen as **literature**; they fall below its level, in a sense related
to the old distinction of *polite learning*; they are not "substantial" or "important"
enough to be called **works of literature**. A new category of **popular literature** or
the **sub-literary** has then to be instituted, to describe works which may be *fiction*
but which are not *imaginative* or *creative*, which are therefore devoid of *aesthetic*
interest, and which are not ART.

Clearly the major shift represented by the modern complex of **literature**,
art, aesthetic, creative, and *imaginative* is a matter of social and cultural history.
Literature itself must be seen as a late medieval and Renaissance isolation of

the skills of reading and of the qualities of the book; this was much emphasized by the development of printing. But the sense of *learning* was still inherent, and there were also the active arts of *grammar* and *rhetoric*. Steadily, with the predominance of print, *writing* and *books* became virtually synonymous; hence the subsequent confusion about *drama*, which was writing for speech (but then Shakespeare is obviously **literature**, though with the TEXT proving this). Then **literature** was specialized towards *imaginative writing*, within the basic assumptions of Romanticism. It is interesting to see what word did service for this before the specialization. It was, primarily, *poetry*, defined in 1586 as "the arte of making: which word as it hath alwaies beene especially used of the best of our English Poets, to expresse the very faculty of speaking or wryting Poetically" (note the inclusion of *speaking*). Sidney wrote in 1581: "verse being but an ornament and no cause to Poetry: sith there have been many most excellent Poets, that never versified." The specialization of *poetry* to metrical composition is evident from mC17, though this was still contested by Wordsworth: "I here use the word 'Poetry' (though against my own judgment) as opposed to the word 'Prose', and synonymous with metrical composition" (1800). It is probable that this specialization of *poetry* to verse, together with the increasing importance of prose forms such as the *novel*, made **literature** the most available general word. It had behind it the Renaissance sense of *litterae humanae*, mainly then for SECULAR as distinct from religious writing, and a generalizing use of *letters* had followed from this. *Belles lettres* was developed in French from mC17; it was to narrow when *literature* was eventually established. *Poetry* had been the high skills of writing and speaking in the special context of high imagination; the word could be moved in either direction. **Literature**, in its C19 sense, repeated this, though excluding speaking. But it is then problematic, not only because of the further specialization to *imaginative* and *creative* subject-matter (as distinct from *imaginative* and *creative* writing) but also because of the new importance of many forms of writing for speech (*broadcasting* as well as *drama*) which the specialization to books seemed by definition to exclude.

Significantly in recent years **literature** and **literary**, though they still have effective currency in post-C18 senses, have been increasingly challenged, on what is conventionally their own ground, by concepts of *writing* and COMMUNICATION which seek to recover the most active and general senses which the extreme specialization had seemed to exclude. Moreover, in relation to this reaction, **literary** has acquired two unfavorable senses, as belonging to the printed book or to past literature rather than to active contemporary writing and speech; or as (unreliable) evidence from books rather than "factual inquiry." This latter sense touches the whole difficult complex of the relations between *literature* (poetry, *fiction, imaginative* writing) and *real* or actual experience. Also, of course, *literary* has been a term of disparagement in discussion of certain other arts, notably painting and music, where the work in its own medium is seen as insufficiently autonomous, and as dependent on "external" meanings of a "literary" kind. This sense is also found in discussion of film. Meanwhile **literacy** and **illiteracy** have become key social concepts, in a much wider perspective than in the pre-C19 sense. **Illiteracy** was extended, from C18, to indicate general inability to read and write, and **literacy**, from 1C19, was a new word invented to express the achievement and possession of what were increasingly seen as general and necessary skills.

Recent Developments

Williams shows that **literature** came to replace *poetry* as the most general term for a certain kind of culturally valued writing. Almost as soon as this sense began to prevail, it acquired a familiarizing diminutive, **lit**, first cited in *OED* from Victorian novelists Elizabeth Gaskell and George Eliot and now common in usages such as **kiddie lit** and **chick lit**. More recently, the process Williams charted in which **literature** became the most valued term for writing has been reversed in practices that the print record does not easily register. By the start of C21, many large bookshops demonstrated a newly restrictive specialization in how they categorized their holdings. A large section titled "**literature**" coexists with sections titled "Shakespeare," "drama," "poetry," "essays," "classics" (all of which the literary world would consider **literature**), as well as sections containing prose fiction designated "romance," "crime," "horror," "fantasy," "science fiction," and yet others. The section **literature** contains exclusively "**literary fiction**," "quality" novels in contrast to the "genre" fiction of the other listings. (Much the same structure can be found at Amazon.com: The category "Literature and Fiction" contains a subcategory "Literary," which when clicked yields "literary fiction.") At the same time, the cultural prestige attributed to imagination, so important to Williams's account of the new meaning of **literature**, has diminished. Even in the Romantic period, so crucial for forming the new meaning, the radical critic William Hazlitt worried over the powers of imagination in terms that foreshadow recent concerns with APPROPRIATION and PRIVILEGE. In our time Hazlitt's heretical charge against Shakespeare

(1817) takes on new life: his work "naturally falls in with the language of power" because the imagination is "an exaggerating and exclusive faculty" which "takes from one thing to add to another." Over the last several decades, scandals have repeatedly dogged works believed to be written by members of various IDENTITY groups— for instance, racial and ethnic minorities, indigenous peoples, survivors of Nazi extermination attempts, substance abusers—that have then proved to be written by authors who had not had these particular experiences. As the novel absorbed the category **literature**, a new term became necessary to value kinds of prose that seemed to be excluded: *creative nonfiction*. C18 writers like the historian Edward Gibbon, the philosopher David Hume, and the critic Samuel Johnson were understood to have produced **literature**. However, the new category of *creative nonfiction*, which was originally defined by choice diction, fine sentences, and nuanced characterization, has become especially linked with the burgeoning popularity of *memoir*, emphasizing the accurate representation of experience, while forbidding the construction of plot, the invention of action which for Aristotle defined the craft of the maker and in Romantic theory allowed the autonomy of art as a world of its own, necessary to the new definition of literature. Imagination now yields to perceived AUTHENTICITY.

See   ART,   AUTHENTIC,   COMMUNICATION,   CREATIVE,   IMAGE,   NARRATIVE, NATIONALIST, TEXT

LOVE

Love means an EMOTION possessed, shared, or felt, and the act of any of these, yet clusters of meaning connected to political, social, and economic change have emerged around both its verb and noun forms in the last century that complicate its contemporary usage. **Love**'s increasingly widening meaning, along with its curious ability to maintain emotional gravity, situates it as a complex keyword.

Love's transitive verb meaning "to entertain a great affection, fondness, or regard for (a person)" emerged in early Old English (OE), with related transitive and intransitive meanings referring to strong liking and devotion appearing in Old and Middle English. What we might today call **romantic love** also emerged in OE, though it should be noted that this sense has a complicated history connected to courtly love conventions (centered in the unattainability of **love**, or with the object of **love** as a distant but desirable ideal) and is therefore in some ways a more modern development than its *OED* dating might suggest. **Loving** an object or concept also dates to OE and has remained constant, particularly in biblical contexts, as in the 1535 Coverdale Bible translation "he that loueth money, wil neuer be satisfied with money," but also in regard to material practices or political or ethical beliefs, as in *The Chronicle of Robert of Gloucester* ("Game of houndes he louede inou, & of wilde best" *c*1325) or Thomas Hoccleve's poetry ("Lordes, if ye your estat and honour Louen . . ." *a*1450). The noun form follows a similar trajectory, appearing in OE denoting a sense of affection and an abstract quality. Religious (as signifying God's **love** or the **love** due to Him as an act of FAITH), romantic, and sexual meanings (ranging from lust and desire to the act of sexual intercourse itself) surfaced in OE. The verb and noun forms of **love** have gained only a few additional meanings since the medieval period, with the most recent having to do with **love** designated with a capital "L" as it might appear in literary or mythological contexts (signifying, for example, Aphrodite or Cupid), emerging in C18.

These definitions and their histories ignore the variety of associations that have developed around **love** over time, such as the connection between **love** and MARRIAGE or **love** and familial duty, or the **love** of country or success, and the ways these associations have been deployed for political or social purposes. This is usefully illustrated by looking at a particular cultural moment from mC20, the countercultural movement of the 1960s, and its influence on **love** as it is used today. Barry Miles, in *London Calling: A Countercultural History of London since 1945* (2010), found "love and sexual experimentation as more worthy of their attention than entering the rat race." Much of the hippie philosophy and focus on **love** can be traced, as a 1967 *Time* magazine article argues, to a variety of historical figures (including Jesus, Hillel, Buddha, Thoreau, Gandhi, and Francis of Assisi). **Love** as an idea was central to the hippies, but so, too, was the word itself. It appeared as both a noun and verb in many texts of the 1960s, as can especially be seen in the popular music of the time (for example the Beatles' influential hit "All You Need Is Love"). **Free love**—with **love** referring to both romantic attachment and sex—was a mainstay of hippie culture, with political ramifications, framed in the phrase, "make love not war." Though **free love** has a long history, with links to anti-marriage thinkers like William Blake and utopian movements like those found in Europe and the United States in C19, the phrase was a product of mC20 and became a slogan of the anti–Vietnam War movement. It has since been adopted in other protest contexts or as a response to terrorist attacks, as can be seen in the use of #makelovenotwar on Twitter in response to the 2016 attacks in Brussels. **Love** transformed in the 1960s into a word of political resistance (against CAPITALISM, against war) and social change. In contrast, in South Asia, the compound **love marriage** is still widely used to distinguish instances where people choose their own partners, as opposed to arranged marriages where their families do so, and the phrase is positive or negative, depending on the worldview of the speaker.

The use of **love** in the 1960s could be considered a catalyst for other political uses, as in the case of the recent push for legalizing gay marriage in the United States. Between Frank Sinatra crooning, "Love and marriage, love and marriage [. . .] This I tell ya, brother, you can't have one without the other" in the 1950s and the song reappearing in the nineties sitcom *Married . . . with Children*, it is no surprise that the term became central to the gay marriage movement. According to the Freedom to Marry campaign, the potential within the term **love** for political change was noted in 1983 by "godfather" of the marriage movement Evan Wolfson, who argued that by "claiming the resonant vocabulary of marriage (love, commitment, connectedness, and freedom), same-sex couples could transform the country's understanding of who gay people were" and ultimately enact legal change that would reflect this new understanding. President Obama used the language of **love**, saying "all people should be treated equally, regardless of who they are or who they love" and tweeted using the hashtag #lovewins. This hashtag, featuring **love**, was used 6.2 million times in the first six hours after the Court's ruling on same-sex marriage—rather than a hashtag featuring marriage, or EQUALITY, or even FREEDOM, though all three terms are undoubtedly central to the movement. It is worth noting that the term **love** was also central to those against legalizing gay marriage; in many cases **love** for or of God was evoked as the reason to oppose it. One Christian blog claims, "If [it] is true [that] homosexual behavior is dishonoring [. . .] then the loving thing to do is to stay away from it. To encourage others to indulge in sin is to encourage them to reject God's blessings on their lives. It is the opposite of love."

The 1960s influence on contemporary uses of the term **love** is not limited to the political or social sphere. **Love** was a keyword of the sixties in some ways because of popular culture products, and the term's commercial success in those contexts helps explain its increased presence in advertising today. A 2009 *New York Times* article declares, "Love is selling cars ('Love. It's what makes a Subaru, a Subaru'), LensCrafters eyeglasses ('See what you love, love what you see') and Payless shoes ('I ♥ shoes'), not to mention long-running campaigns for McDonald's ('I'm lovin' it') and Olay ('Love the skin you're in')." **Love** as something with market value is not new, especially when considering the noun form as referring to a sexual act or desire or the verb form as enacting that desire, but in these advertising contexts it is not (necessarily) sex for sale, but rather these companies' products in the name of **love** or, sometimes, **love** itself. **Love** has also gained a conceptual and pictorial icon **♥**; it, too, has been adopted in love-marketing, as in the famous "I ♥ New York" campaign from the 1970s. With **love** in surplus in television commercials and radio and magazine advertisements, it is as common to hear something like "I love Taco Bell" as it is to hear "I love you." To **love** a thing, object, or concept is an old idea, but to **love** so many things, so many products—that seems a lC20 and eC21 CAPITALIST phenomenon. Yet even as **love** is broadened politically, socially, or economically, it retains its emotional, sexual, or philosophical weight. A Google search for the phrase "saying I love you" yields 179,000,000 results; few, if any, have to do with Taco Bell. Perhaps the term's relative linguistic stability lends it the capacity to expand and take on contemporary cultural concerns, even as it retains, from the earliest days of the English language, its basic, emotional meaning.

See EMOTION, EQUALITY, FREEDOM, MARRIAGE, RESPECT, SEXUALITY

MARKET

Market is one of a cluster of words (including ENTERPRISE, VALUE, PROPERTY, and *competition*) which define the economic and social relations of most contemporary societies. Together, such words highlight a trading emphasis for the word *commerce*, rather than its more recent "interaction meaning"; and the pervasiveness of market transactions and relationships in many modern countries makes them kinds of **market societies**. Such societies typically express a political philosophy of **market capitalism** or **market liberalism**, tying **market** not only to changing meanings of LIBERAL and *liberty* but also to the varied meanings of other common but complex words, including *choice* and *trust*. **Market** is in this way part of a configuration of socially defining words whose meanings have altered in range, implication, and connotation in step with transformations of social practices and relations.

Market comes into English (and in varying forms into a number of other European languages) from post-classical Latin *mercatum* and is not attested before C12, having been preceded in Anglo Saxon by *céap* (Middle English *chep* and *chepe*), a place and time for buying and selling cattle. The word's range of modern senses develops in overlapping processes of generalization and specialization, as well as through figurative extension.

Historically and prototypically, from its earliest occurrence in C12, **market** carries over from Latin the meaning of "a place at which trade is conducted," especially "a meeting or gathering together of people for the purchase and sale of provisions or livestock, publicly displayed, at a fixed time and place; the occasion or time of this." Related **market square, marketplace**, and **market town** continue to be used; and the C20 coinage **flea market** describes a street market containing miscellaneous, often secondhand goods. This spatial sense is extended in contemporary, ambiguously spatial and laudatory **supermarket** and **hypermarket**. But **market** in this sense of physical location had perhaps its greatest importance during a period in which the economic relations associated with places for buying and selling were tightly controlled by Norman conquerors and later settlers, as part of wider systems of ownership and obligation in late feudalism and the shift into early capitalism.

Market as a trading place extended in geographic scale with the historical growth of actual markets, linked (and accelerated during C18 and eC19 as a consequence of the Industrial Revolution) with changing means of transport, patterns of financing, industrialization of production, extended supply chains, and expanded areas for distribution. Increasingly, **market** refers to centralized markets in a **market town**, then more **regional** and **national markets** (often for specialized goods and services), then **foreign markets** and larger trade blocs such as the EUROPEAN **market** and GLOBAL **markets**, regulated in new ways by international trade organizations such as WTO (World Trade Organization).

From C15, **market** also denoted particular arenas of commercial activity, or classes of commodity taking over from "horse fairs" and "goose fairs" when used with a qualifier, as in **corn market, poultry market**, then later **import/export market**. Extension of this meaning allows modern **education market** (foreshadowed in Hazlitt's **market of learning**, 1820), **healthcare market**, and other newly designated markets in which forms of organization and systems of value are modelled on the basis of exchange value. Independently of these politically contentious applications, **market** gradually encompasses not only retail sales of prototypically physical goods but Internet sales and intangibles (hence **stock market** and **futures market**), widening into what Justice Oliver Wendell Holmes Jr., building on Mill and earlier Milton, called a "marketplace of ideas." More abstractly again, in cultural theory writers such as Pierre Bourdieu have recently applied a notion of **market relations** across a far wider range of symbolic fields, linked to different modalities of capital.

Widening in what **market** can refer to is accompanied by a different process of abstraction: away from real or virtual occasions for selling toward the action or BUSINESS of buying and selling. Hence, **market** as "a commercial transaction" is reflected in expressions such as "take to market" and "be first to market," whether used of a farmer leading sheep along a track or a car manufacturer launching a new model at a trade show. This transaction sense paved the way for **market** as mechanism or process, as traced by Karl Polanyi as a **market economy** in *The Great Transformation* (1944). The more theoretical use is effectively that of the operation of supply and demand as **market forces**, attested from 1942 but part of a cluster reported much earlier in C20. Analysis of this process meaning of **market** had been central to work by political philosophers for at least two centuries, most influentially in Adam Smith's investigation in *The Wealth of Nations* (1776). **Market**, in this sense, has remained central to traditions of economic theory, across varied models and critical positions, from lC18 to the present.

One implication of a gradually lessened emphasis in **market** on varied social practice than on generalized principles of operation has been normative claims to efficiency. If something sells in a relevant market it may be judged to have succeeded, on the grounds that accumulated subjectively rational decisions reflect Smith's objective "invisible hand." From such confidence in **market testing** follows an increased appeal, in policy thinking, associated with **market solutions**. Yet once **market** combines favorably with "laissez-faire" and "free," as in the compound **free market** (attested from mC17), tension increases regarding the degree and kinds of market regulation required to balance a competitive yet fair society: encouragement of markets and entrepreneurs opens up avenues for trade and assists innovation; yet distortion of markets (for instance, by monopolies and cartels) must be restrained by measures that depend on changing conceptualizations conveyed by other words in the same, difficult semantic cluster as **market**: in this case *competition,* FREEDOM, FAIR, and *trust.*

Almost from its earliest uses, **market** has also conveyed personified meanings denoting participants attending a market, people now usually described as traders or merchants and as customers or CONSUMERS. A **target market** of such customers can be identified by means of a **market survey** (attested 1914), and addressed by **market segmentation** and other techniques developed more recently in the field of **marketing** (both as a neutrally described activity, from C16, and from lC19 either favorably or pejoratively to describe strategic practices of sales promotion). Merchants or vendors themselves are **market traders** (whether in a street market or stock market), and **marketers** or **marketeers**; when viewed as a collective agency, they may be referred to as **the market** or **the markets**: an aggregated force serving either as metonym for actual people engaged in financial speculation, but with human skills, appetites, and fears, or as a depersonalized, abstract power beyond the individual human actors, impelling a market assumed to follow economic laws (and which, according to former UK prime minister Margaret Thatcher, could not be bucked). **The market**, with definite article, becomes in such circumstances a hardened abstraction, sometimes critiqued as part of wider **market fundamentalism**.

In the context of recent global economic and political upheavals, **market** is an especially contested term. But the word's polysemy and figurative application complicate the discussion and assessment of political directions and proposals. What boundaries exist, for example, as regards which social practices may be legitimately commodified and treated as markets? A market in slaves or daughters eligible for marriage, both widely reported as *OED* examples of **market**? A market in healthcare, education, or weapons; or in body parts, human stem cells, and biotech inventions? And what kinds of agency are at work in the different kinds of **market**: the "invisible hand" of aggregated but individually self-interest-maximizing decisions attributed to *homo economicus*, or more volatile social agents with—unless regulated—often little accountability as regards market outcomes?

See BUSINESS, CAPITALISM, CONSUMER, ENTERPRISE, FAIR, FREEDOM, GLOBAL, LIBERAL, PROPERTY, VALUE

MARRIAGE

Marriage was borrowed into English from French in C14, as was the related verb **marry**. It denotes both the state of matrimony and the action of getting married, although *wedding* usually denotes the associated festivities. (*Wedding* and *wedlock* are among the words in Old English and Middle English denoting the state of matrimony and the action of getting married, largely replaced in modern English by **marriage**.)

In contemporary culture there is dispute about which relationships the word **marriage** is applied to, especially as regards relationships between people of the same sex. Its most frequent collocates in general American and British corpora tend to be **gay** and **same-sex**, followed by **arranged, civil, happy, traditional**, and **interracial**. These qualified uses neatly identify the main areas of contemporary debate. The very high frequency of **gay** and **same-sex marriage** partly results from hesitation to use **marriage** unmodified by *gay* or *same-sex* to denote same-sex relationships. (Significantly, in verbal constructions the contested area of meaning is less easily flagged: two people of the same sex may be described as celebrating their **gay marriage** with a *gay wedding*, but not as being "gaily married.") The verbs of which **marriage** tends most frequently to be the object are **ban, recognize, legalize, arrange, define**, and **oppose** (ahead of **propose** or **celebrate**).

Traditional marriage is often regarded as easily defined, but the range of denotation of **marriage** has always been very broad, and it is difficult to frame a definition that covers all uses. In historical British usage, most uses refer to marriages legitimized (post-Reformation) by the Church of England, since this has been the societal norm. However, **marriage** has also denoted unions within a huge variety of different religious and cultural traditions, whether those tolerated within religious minorities within Britain, or marriages in other parts of the world: such uses are not typically marked as problematic or only applying in a limited or metaphorical sense. Formulations such as "so-called marriage" are typically found only where questions of LEGITIMACY within a particular religious or legal context are at stake, although the frequency of the collocation **mixed marriage** reflects debate about marriages between people of different races or (typically in earlier use) between people from different religious or cultural traditions. In the US, multiple different local traditions have long applied. One particularly fiercely contested question in C19 concerned the legitimacy of polygamous marriages.

The historically oriented definition of the core *matrimony* sense of **marriage** in the *OED* is "The condition of being a husband or wife; the relation between persons married to each other; matrimony," followed by a note, "The term is now sometimes used with reference to long-term relationships between partners of the same sex." This is from a revised *OED* entry published in 2000, but the main definition has changed little from the corresponding fascicle of the first edition, from 1905: "The condition of being a husband or wife; the relation between married persons; spousehood, matrimony." The 1905 definition of the corresponding (transitive) use of **marry** is "To join in wedlock or matrimony; to join for life as husband and wife; to constitute as man and wife according to the laws and customs of a nation." A significant difference in the (considerably restructured) revised *OED* entry is that the union is no longer specified as being "for life," reflecting social and legal changes with regard to divorce. However, perhaps what is most interesting about the 1905 definitions is how inclusive they are: looked at from a philological perspective in 1905, the meanings of **marriage** and **marry** were necessarily broad, reflecting the fact that in different nations different laws and customs were found, and the words could be found in unmarked contextual use referring to any of them. No mention is made of procreation, often invoked in contemporary formulations of **traditional marriage**, although in Western traditions there has only very rarely been a requirement that children be conceived, although the consummation of marriage by sexual intercourse has often been required.

This long tradition informs current changes. Since the word **marriage** has long denoted legitimized unions from a wide variety of traditions and jurisdictions, when e.g., same-sex marriage is today legitimized in an increasing number of jurisdictions, this reinforces the tendency to use **marriage** in relation to such unions elsewhere.

However, another major factor has come to prominence recently. The revised *OED* entry comments concerning **be married**: "Now also sometimes used of couples who are not legally married but whose relationship is recognized as long-term." Here the semantic development results directly from change in society. The formal marriage ceremony has become less important for many people. Additionally, some people (often people of the same sex in jurisdictions where they are not permitted to marry) will have a celebration marking their union in many respects identical to a wedding but not resulting in a legally recognized marriage. In the UK many couples of the same sex now mark the beginning of a legally recognized *civil partnership* in this way.

Both of these seemingly contradictory factors are probably working in the same direction: the meaning of **marriage** broadens further as a wider range of unions are legitimized in different places, and simultaneously the less obligatory nature of a legal marriage ceremony for what many regard as a **marriage** leads to still further semantic broadening, even if this results in a mismatch with what is legally recognized as a **marriage**.

There is probably a further mechanism in the semantic broadening of **marriage** and related words. **Marriage** denotes both the state of matrimony and the action of getting married, and the two meanings are not easily separated conceptually. The same applies to **marry**, and although it is not cognate, *wedding* forms part of the same tight semantic field. A *wedding* marks a **marriage**, when two people **get married**, which leads to a **marriage**, in which two people **are married**. Where such close semantic relationships exist, broadening in one area is typically reflected by broadening in the others. Hence, if a speaker is happy with use of the word **marriage** to describe the relationship between two people, it is conceptually a very short step to say that they *are married*, hence that at some point they *got married*, and a party that marked this was their *wedding*, marking their **marriage**. In different social circumstances precisely the same semantic links could work in the opposite direction (this union is not a **marriage**, hence . . .), but where a social trend exists for a more liberal interpretation of one of these terms, the close semantic links lead very readily to broadening in the others as well.

It should be noted that **marry** and **marriage** very rapidly acquire figurative uses in which the emphasis is simply on the merging or blending of two elements. This figurative meaning increasingly informed early modern conceptions of **marriage**, particularly through the growth of the novel. Paradoxically the legal definition of **marriage** in this period developed arguments for the total subordination of the wife to her husband in the doctrine of *coverture* that rendered the wife a possession of the husband. Much of the struggle for women's rights in the past 200 years has focused on the dismantling of *coverture*. The first steps came in the US in 1839, beginning with a series of statutes that allowed women to retain ownership of their property after marriage. Britain followed suit with similar acts in 1870 and 1882. The final stage was ushered in by the European Parliament's call in 1986 for marital rape to be criminalized.

See FAMILY, LOVE, SEXUALITY

MEDIA

Medium, from *medium*, L—middle, has been in regular use in English from 1C16, and from at latest eC17 has had the sense of an intervening or intermediate agency or substance. Thus Burton (1621): "To the Sight three things are required, the Object, the Organ, and the Medium"; Bacon (1605): "expressed by the Medium of Wordes." There was then a conventional C18 use in relation to newspapers: "through the medium of your curious publication" (1795), and this was developed through C19 to such uses as "considering your Journal one of the best possible mediums for such a scheme" (1880). Within this general use, the description of a newspaper as a **medium** for advertising became common in eC20. The mC20 development of **media** (which had been available as a general plural from mC19) was probably mainly in this context. **Media** became widely used when broadcasting as well as the press had become important in COMMUNICATIONS; it was then the necessary general word. **Mass media, media people, media agencies, media studies** followed.

There has probably been a convergence of three senses: (i) the old general sense of an intervening or intermediate agency or substance; (ii) the conscious technical sense, as in the distinction between print and sound and vision as **media**; (iii) the specialized capitalist sense, in which a newspaper or broadcasting service—something that already exists or can be planned—is seen as a medium for something else, such as advertising. It is interesting that sense (i) depended on particular physical or philosophical ideas, where there had to be a substance intermediate between a sense or a thought and its operation or expression. In most modern science and philosophy, and especially in thinking about language, this idea of a **medium** has been dispensed with; thus language is not a **medium** but a primary practice, and writing (for print) and speaking or acting (for broadcasting) would also be practices. It is then controversial whether print and broadcasting, as in the technical sense (ii), are **media** or, more strictly, material *forms* and sign systems. It is probably here that specific social ideas, in which writing and broadcasting are seen as determined by other ends—from the relatively neutral "INFORMATION" to the highly specific "advertising" and "propaganda"—confirm the received sense but then confuse any modern sense of COMMUNICATION. The technical sense of **medium**, as something with its own specific and *determining* properties (in one version taking absolute priority over anything actually said or written or shown), has in practice been compatible with a social sense of **media** in which the practices and institutions are seen as agencies for quite other than their primary purposes.

It might be added that in its rapid popularization since the 1950s **media** has come often to be used as a singular (cf. *phenomena*).

Recent Developments

The meaning of **media** has widened and thus the relative frequency of the word has continued to rise. The two major forms of **mass media** to which Williams refers in his entry—**print media** (newspapers, magazines) and broadcasting (radio, television)—might now be labeled **old media**, which the *OED* defines as "Established or traditional means of mass communication considered collectively, esp. contrasted with newer means; *spec.* media which are not interactive or do not involve the Internet." The contrastive term **new media** is much more commonly used but also more difficult to define, as TECHNOLOGY and new media COMMUNICATIONS continuously change. According to the home page of the New Media Institute in New York City, general characteristics of **new media** include accessibility on digital devices and interactivity. **Social media**, for example, have fostered interaction between users and encouraged the creation of user-generated content. The advent of **social media** platforms such as Facebook, Twitter, and Instagram has marked a shift in the role of **media** CONSUMERS from passive to active, participatory users.

The contemporary difficulty in defining **media** relates to the word's status as a collective noun that can take either a singular or a plural verb. When used as a singular collective noun, **media**, but particularly **the media**, suggests a monolithic entity rather than a variety of different individuals, agencies, communication technologies, and sources of information and advertising. Its use as a singular collective noun has made **the media** an easy target for criticism in eC21, and, as a result, **media** and collocations such as **social media** frequently carry negative connotations. Recently, **the media** has come to be associated with anything that is misleading or unreliable, due in part to the influence of US President Donald Trump, who called **the media** "the enemy of the American people" and on May 28, 2017, tweeted that leaks coming out of the White House were "fabricated lies made up by the #FakeNews media." Although Trump invokes **the media** as the enemy, he expresses hate primarily toward the liberal **mainstream media**, thus distinguishing his preferred news sources (Breitbart, Fox News, etc.).

See CELEBRITY, COMMUNICATION, IMAGE, TECHNOLOGY

MODERN

Modern came into English from fw *moderne*, F, *modernus*, lL, from rw *modo*, L—just now. Its earliest English senses were nearer our *contemporary*, in the sense of something existing now, just now. (*Contemporary*, or the equivalent—till mC19—*co-temporary*, was mainly used, as it is still often used, to mean "of the same period," including periods in the past, rather than "of our own immediate time.") A conventional contrast between *ancient* and **modern** was established before the

Renaissance; a middle or medieval period began to be defined from C15. **Modern** in this comparative and historical sense was common from 1C16. **Modernism**, **modernist**, and **modernity** followed, in C17 and C18; the majority of pre-C19 uses were unfavorable, when the context was comparative. **Modernize**, from C18, had initial special reference to buildings (Walpole, 1748: "the rest of the house is all modernized"); spelling (Fielding, 1752: "I have taken the liberty to modernize the language"); and fashions in dress and behavior (Richardson, 1753: "He scruples not to modernize a little"). We can see from these examples that there was still a clear sense of a kind of alteration that needed to be justified.

The unfavorable sense of **modern** and its associates has persisted, but through C19 and very markedly in C20 there was a strong movement the other way, until **modern** became virtually equivalent to *improved* or satisfactory or efficient. **Modernism** and **modernist** have become more specialized, to particular tendencies, notably to the experimental art and writing of *c*1890—*c*1940, which allows a subsequent distinction between the **modernist** and the (newly) **modern**. **Modernize**, which had become general by mC19 (cf. Thackeray, 1860: "gunpowder and printing tended to modernize the world"), and **modernization** (which in C18 had been used mainly of buildings and spelling) have become increasingly common in C20 argument. In relation to INSTITUTIONS or industry they are normally used to indicate something unquestionably favorable or desirable. As catchwords of particular kinds of change the terms need scrutiny. It is often possible to distinguish **modernizing** and **modernization** from **modern**, if only because (as in many such actual programs) the former terms imply some local alteration or improvement of what is still, basically, an old institution or system. Thus a **modernized democracy** would not necessarily be the same as a **modern democracy**.

Recent Developments

While **modern** has declined in frequency in the last half-century, **modernity, modernize,** and **modernism** have markedly increased. All these terms have multiple meanings and can generate substantial ambiguities because **modern** contrasts the *present* to *past*, yet the content of that contrast varies. Thus, **modernity** can mean the period since the Middle Ages, the period since the Industrial Revolution, or the period since the beginning of C20. **Modernism** can be defined, as Williams does, as a fixed literary period from 1890 to 1940. However, there is a use of **modernism** in which the relation of present to past is still active; this use distinguishes writing which is aware of itself as a medium from a past LITERATURE that took for granted its dominant status as a medium. **Modernize** is perhaps the most difficult term of the three. It attracts so many contrasts that it is impossible to enumerate a closed number of senses: everything depends on context and use. It was a key word (particularly in the self-ascription of **modernizer**) in Tony Blair and New Labour's political project. The content, in that context, was to contrast an old style socialist party and a new Third Way politics in which the political goal of equality had been abandoned. It says something about the protean semantics of **modern** that this POLITICAL sense of **modernize** and **modernizer**, so dominant in the last decade of C20 and the first decade of C21 in British English, is now effectively archaic.

The specific contrast between past and present that **modern** promises implies both a NARRATIVE and a teleology. Both are contested by the notion of the **postmodern**, which contrasts a past that believes in narratives and endings to a present that has abandoned all such certainties. **Postmodernism**, which dates most importantly to a short 1979 text by Jean-François Lyotard, has attracted numerous other definitions ranging from specific styles in architecture to a radical RELATIVISM in epistemology. However, the most precise definition of **postmodern** is the claim to have moved beyond the implied relation between present and past embodied in the word **modern**.

MUSLIM

The word **Muslim** was used in English in eC17 as a borrowing from Arabic which refers to a person who submits to the will of God. **Muslim** is, as *OED* notes, the "active participle of *aslama* to submit oneself to the will of God, of which the noun of action is *islām*."

While the denotation of the word **Muslim** has remained fairly constant in English both as a noun and adjective since it came into English in eC17, its connotations have been transformed in the past twenty-five years to make it a strong marker of cultural difference, in which **Muslim** becomes the definition of political and ideological otherness, in relation to a norm which is identified as, variously, *Western, Judaeo-Christian, secular,* or *white*. This extreme prejudice is both a response to and a cause of contemporary geopolitics. At the same time, the trajectory of the Islamic Empire from its unchecked rise from C7 up to its catastrophic confrontations with the British in India and the French in Egypt in C18, also provides an important geohistorical dimension to the provenance of the term. Yet, while this process of

making **Muslim** the very definition of the political and cultural other is largely negative, **Muslim** has also acquired greater validation as a self-ascription of IDENTITY
(and ideology) by adherents the world over, thereby marking a rallying call and a
sense of pride or even superiority. It is precisely this tension between users of the
word on both sides of the divide that constitutes its heightened duality. However,
as English speakers are predominantly non-Muslim, the overall timbre of the term
and its collocates and compounds resonate with the harsh ring of negativity. The
clearest articulation of this position comes from Fox News's Brian Kilmeade, who
said and defended in 2010: "Not all Muslims are terrorists, but all terrorists are
Muslims."

For some Muslims, a key problem with the use of **Muslim** as an identification
is that it seems to leave no space for them to call themselves Muslim in terms of
cultural values and heritage without expressing religious commitment to Islam.
The most widely known example is Salman Rushdie, who wrote *The Satanic Verses*
(1988) as a Muslim who did not believe in God. The novel and its author were
condemned by the Iranian theocracy. More recently, best-selling author Khaled
Hosseini has publicly identified as a **secular Muslim**. Another best-selling author,
and journalist, Ali Rizvi has proclaimed himself, alternately, an **atheist Muslim**, or
an **atheist ex-Muslim**.

In English the main meaning of the noun **Muslim** since eC17 has been "a follower of the religion of Islam" in any of its various sects or forms. Disputes over the
meaning of the word arise mainly in the adjectival form because here **Muslim** has
a much broader usage, including not merely the religion but also its followers and
their diverse cultural practices, which may differ by sect and region. In 1812 Byron
thus writes, "The pilgrim . . . gaz'd around on Moslem luxury."

In contemporary usage, however, there is also an ambiguity in some instances
where **Muslim** denotes both a RELIGION and an ethnic group. This mistaken conflation of religion with ethnic identity is a result of the discrediting and unten-
ability of older notions of RACE and is a rare instance where the adjectival form
has influenced and reshaped the nominal form of the term. The key point is that
Muslim as both noun and adjective has acquired new connotations in the last
few decades, most of which are negative and relate to the geopolitical polariza-
tion, described by American political scientist Samuel Huntington as the "clash of
civilizations."

A typical formulation of this new ideological formation can be found in a quotation from a journal of the Southern Baptist Theological seminary: "A person can

have any religious identity and be an American. In much of the Muslim world, the opposite is true. Islam is part of their ethnic identity."

The term has developed compounds such as **Black Muslim**, which has a special historical provenance in the US in the 1960s, and **Muslim Brother,** the usual term for members of the Muslim Brotherhood. **Muslim Brotherhood** (Arabic *iḵwān al-muslimīn*) is a movement founded in Egypt in 1928, committed to establishing a nation based on Islamic principles.

The contemporary relationship between **Muslim** and *Islam* is also important because there is both a divergence and a coming together visible here. On the one hand, the older meaning of **Muslims** as followers of *Islam* is unchanged, where *Islam* is the religion and **Muslims** are people who believe and adhere to this religion. However, there is also a growing strand of usage where *Islam* is used instead of **Muslim**, as when *Islamic fundamentalist* replaces *Muslim fundamentalist,* implying that the religion is itself responsible for what is seen as inappropriate, excessive, mindless, and archaic values that necessarily lead to VIOLENCE and TERROR. These developments connect to Saudi Arabian funding of the ultra-conservative Wahhabist version of Islam: "The US State Department has estimated that over the past four decades Riyadh has invested more than $10bn (£6bn) into charitable foundations in an attempt to replace mainstream Sunni Islam with the harsh intolerance of its Wahhabism" (*Telegraph*, May 19, 2017). While many non-Muslims tend to blur together different strands, such as the Shia and Sunni sects of Islam, some Muslims (here used to describe diverse "ethnic" and/or national communities) appear to want to exclude opposing groups from any legitimacy to claim the very title "**Muslim**." The most extreme instance is the Pakistani Constitutional Amendment and 1984 Ordinance that prevent the Ahmedi sect from describing themselves as **Muslim** or "posing as Muslims." Thus, to add to the complexity of the term, there seems to be in the current fraught context a homogenization from outside matched by an increasing contestation within its fold.

So strong are the current negative associations with **Muslim** that a Canadian-based group of Muslims seeking to engage with anti-Muslim sentiment must call themselves "Muslims Against Terrorism." The EU guidelines for reporting on terrorism demonstrates sensitivity to this problem, while recognizing its ubiquity, when it states: "European governments should shun the phrase 'Islamic terrorism' in favour of 'terrorists who abusively invoke Islam.'" A further development of this overwhelmingly negative association leads to the disappearance of the term **Muslim** (or *Islamic*) as if it were implied by the second term in the compound. Other terrorism has to be qualified as *Hindu fundamentalist terrorism,* or *Irish republican terrorism,* for example, whereas terrorism, per se, today, it goes without saying, is Islamic or Muslim. This widespread prejudice, which compounds the already complex contentiousness of the term, prompts Robert Fisk to write in 2016, "If Muslims attack us, they are terrorists. If non-Muslims attack us, they are shooters. If Muslims attack other Muslims, they are attackers" (*Independent,* July 24).

See IDENTITY, RELIGION

NARRATIVE

Narrative has seen a sharp rise in frequency over the last twenty years, especially in such phrases as "change the narrative" and "take control of the narrative," which have become unavoidable in political commentary. This surge in usage followed a period in which **narrative** was identified as an important element across a wide range of human activities and central to ART and entertainment. Studies on **narrative** have developed in both the humanities and social sciences. More recently, it has become a topic for neuroscience. It is, unusually, a word that has migrated from specialist academic uses into general discourse.

Narrative derives from medieval Latin through the French adjective *narratif* and comes into English in C16 as a legal term for a document stating the facts of the case. By 1571 we find the sense of "an account of a series of events, facts, etc. given in order and with the establishing of connections between them." Two centuries pass before the specific literary critical meaning appears, which distinguishes **narrative** from *dialogue*. Although we find **narrative** in both poetry and drama, it is significantly in relation to the novel that the category first finds definition and much of its development into C20. For the most important contemporary meaning of **narrative** we have to go back to the French and to the fact that **narrative** was chosen as the translation for the French word *récit*. French, like English, has a number of words for the recounting of events: *story, plot,* **narrative** in English; *histoire, narration, récit* in French. *Récit* took on a specialized literary use to describe short novels in which the narrator was particularly prominent. This sense of **narrative** as self-consciously aware of its own functioning made *récit* appropriate for analyses attempting to make that functioning more and more explicit. That work in the 1960s (associated with names like Barthes, Greimas, Genette, Todorov, and Eco) took much of its inspiration from Russian formalist work of the 1920s. In particular, Propp and Shklovsky's distinction between *fabula* and *syuzhet* proved particularly important: *fabula* is the chronological sequence of events that a story reveals, and *syuzhet* is the specific way those events are organized in the story. This distinction makes explicit that any complicated sequence of events can have an almost infinite number of **narrative** realizations. In lC20 this understanding of **narrative** as a series of possible permutations and choices and a sophisticated understanding of the various ways in which the narrator relates to both **narrative** and audience spread across the disciplines. It first became widely used in psychology and medicine where, to use Daniel Dennett's formulation, the self is often understood as a center of narrative gravity. **Narrative** analysis also became an important tool in sociology when statistical methods failed to reveal complex social relationships.

The most influential use of **narrative** is by the philosopher Jean François Lyotard in *The Postmodern Condition* (1979, English translation 1984). Lyotard argued that our postmodern age was characterized by an incredulity toward **metanarratives**. In particular, he argued that the **Grand Narratives** (*grands récits*) of the Enlightenment (in which history is the march of progress) and of Marxism (in which history moves toward the inevitable triumph of socialism) no longer commanded assent. Instead, postmoderns find only multiple, competing narratives, none of which could organize the others. This argument suffers from itself being a **grand narrative** of the supersession of grand narratives. More significantly, its account of multiply competing narratives lacks any attention to practices or institutions and the multiple ways in which narratives are tested, compared, and judged. However, its ultra-relativist vision of a world of **narratives** in which no account could claim superiority to any other became everyday currency. By the 1990s, in close correlation with the coinage *spin-doctor,* **narrative** became a term used widely in political commentary. It appears at the same time as twenty-four-hour news channels introduced the rolling coverage that made politics a continuous story.

In this new MEDIA ecology, notions of "changing the **narrative**" and "controlling the **narrative**" became crucial. These uses of **narrative** are extremely ambiguous.

They convey the valuable notion that there is more than one way to articulate an understanding of particular events or arguments. Even more valuably, they can call attention to **narrator** and audience and ask who is speaking to whom. Viewed from this perspective, they would demonstrate the long-term gain in knowledge accomplished by Russian formalists in the 1920s and the French structuralists in the 1960s. On the other hand, they may simply provide a cynical and genuinely terrifying postmodern RELATIVISM in which all that is required to "control the **narrative**" is to spend millions of dollars on television advertisements that are designed to lie.

See ART, HISTORY, LITERATURE, MEDIA, TEXT, THEORY

NATIONALIST

Nation (from fw *nation*, F, *nationem*, L—breed, race) has been in common use in English from 1C13, originally with a primary sense of a racial group rather than a politically organized grouping. Since there is obvious overlap between these senses, it is not easy to date the emergence of the predominant modern sense of a political formation. Indeed, the overlap has continued, in relation to such formations, and has led on the one hand to particularizing definitions of the **nation-state,** and on the other hand to very complex arguments in the context of **nationalist** and **nationalism.** Clear POLITICAL uses were evident from C16 and were common from 1C17, though *realm, kingdom*, and COUNTRY remained more common until 1C18. There was from eC17 a use of **the nation** to mean the whole people of a country, often in contrast, as still in political argument, with some group within it. The adjective **national** (as now in **national interest**) was used in this persuasive unitary sense from C17. The derived noun **national**, which is clearly political, is more recent and still alternates with the older *subject*. **Nationality**, which had been used in a broad sense from 1C17, acquired its modern political sense in 1C18 and eC19.

Nationalist appeared in eC18 and **nationalism** in eC19. Each became common from mC19. The persistent overlap between grouping and political formation has been important, since claims to be a **nation**, and to have **national** RIGHTS, often envisaged the formation of a **nation** in the political sense, even against the will of an existing political **nation** which included and claimed the loyalty of this grouping. It could be and is still often said, by opponents of **nationalism**, that the basis of the group's claims is *racial*. (RACE, of uncertain origin, had been used in the sense of a common stock from C16. *Racial* is a C19 formation. In most C19 uses *racial* was positive and favorable, but discriminating and arbitrary theories of *race* were becoming more explicit in the same period, generalizing **national** distinctions to supposedly radical *scientific* differences. *Racial* was eventually affected by criticism of these kinds of thinking, and acquired both specific and loose negative senses. *Racialism* is a C20 formation to characterize, and usually to criticize, these explicit distinctions and discriminations.) It was also said that the claims were "selfish," as being against the interests of **the nation** (the existing large political group). In practice, given the extent of conquest and domination, **nationalist** movements have been as often based on an existing but subordinate political grouping as upon a group distinguished by a specific language or by a supposed *racial* community. **Nationalism** has been a political movement in subjected countries which include several "races" and languages (as India) as well as in subjected countries or provinces or *regions* where the distinction is a specific language or religion or supposed *racial* origin. Indeed in **nationalism** and **nationalist** there is an applied complexity comparable with that of NATIVE. But this is often masked by separating **national feeling** (good) from **nationalist feeling** (bad if it is another's country, making claims against one's own), or by separating **national interest** (good) from **nationalism** (the asserted national interest of another group). The complexity has been increased by the usually separable distinction between **nationalism** (selfish pursuit of a nation's interests as against others) and **internationalism** (cooperation between nations). But **internationalism**, which refers to relations between **nation-states**, is not the opposite of **nationalism** in the context of a subordinate political group seeking its own distinct identity; it is only the opposite of selfish and competitive policies between existing political nations.

Nationalize and **nationalization** were eC19 introductions to express the processes of making a nation or making something distinctively national. The modern economic sense emerged in mC19 and was not common before 1C19, at first mainly in the context of the proposed **nationalization** of land. In the course of political controversy each word has acquired specific tones, so that it may be said without apparent difficulty that it either is or is not in the **national interest** to **nationalize**.

RECENT DEVELOPMENTS

White nationalist, a phrase that barely figures in English before 1990, shows a practically vertical movement on frequency charts in the past thirty years. It bears witness to the continued entanglement of **nationalist** within the complex and confused imbrications of **nation** and RACE. Williams's own entry charts the philology and the politics very accurately, but his optimism that India can offer an example of different religions and races linked together in a common national project looks outdated when a **Hindu nationalist,** Narendra Modi, now bestrides the Indian stage. However, the linking of the anti-colonial struggle with **nationalism** continues to inform many uses of **nationalist.** For example, in Kenya, Tanzania, Ghana, and Nigeria, **nationalism** shows uniquely strong collocations with "independence," "struggle," and "patriot."

Nonetheless, since Williams wrote, many national liberation struggles have degenerated into narrow nationalisms, and within Europe, right-wing parties have burgeoned, like the UK Independence Party, which mimic the language of anti-colonial struggle at the service of a politics that mixes racism and opposition to the European Union in different national cocktails. In American and British English, this is reflected in collocations with **nationalism** including **xenophobic, racist, jingoistic,** and **chauvinistic nationalism**—collocations that barely register in English usage in the rest of the world. The extent to which this new **nationalism** links an opposition to supranational economic agreements with anti-immigrant policies is signaled in the US by the increasing use of **economic nationalism**—a term resurrected from protectionist discourse of the 1930s.

See COUNTRY, GLOBAL, LITERATURE, NATIVE, RACE, STATE

NATIVE

Native comes into English from the post-classical Latin *nativus* referring to "a person born in bondage or a person born in a specified place." As an adjective, **native** is slightly later in origin, reaching English via Middle French *natif* and once again drawing on the Latin *nativus*, although in the adjectival form the sense of belonging through origin or birth has added to it the sense of occurring naturally that is present in the Latin root word.

The primary sense of relating to "lower birth" (originally within a feudal system) was displaced gradually, along with the feudal system itself, to foreground the meaning as born in a particular place. The word's meaning then bifurcated, for whereas in Britain the notion of **native** began to lose its pejorative origins and indeed to take its place in the ideology of Britain as a political entity composed of free-born men, its use in the ever burgeoning colonies was increasingly accompanied by a new pejorative implication that suggested political and racial inferiority. William Empson's classic analysis of the complex structure of the word's meanings is that these two uses of **native** came into competition as the empire builders brought their vocabulary home: since the new pejorative implications could not be attached to native-born Englishmen, **native** itself took on as its new head meaning a non-EUROPEAN member of the Empire. This new head meaning brought with it the implications of political and racial inferiority, and thus in a single word developed an elaborate ideology of IMPERIALISM in which non-European peoples were innately politically and culturally inferior and thus in need of imperial tutelage. This meaning has become increasingly offensive over the past 150 years, so that the frequency of the word itself has decreased dramatically since mC19. Interestingly, it does survive in the formulation "the natives are getting restless," where the context is not a threat to imperial rule overseas but of objections to authoritarianism at home. In this usage the offensive meanings of the word are mobilized to challenge the assumptions of the legitimacy of domestic AUTHORITY.

The use of **native** to describe a person born in a specified place, region, or COUNTRY is more common in South Asian varieties of English than elsewhere, especially in the compound **native place**, though describing persons as being **natives of** countries, cities, and villages has continued in Anglo-American English from eC16 up to the present. Hence, it is clear that **native** is a word that demonstrates both continuity and change, where certain older meanings have become taboo, or are looked upon with suspicion, whereas other uses appear on the surface to have changed little in 400 years.

It is precisely in this double sense of being "natural" (in the sense of unschooled, innocent, simple, naive) and being quintessentially "non-European" (the "inferior Other" of Europe that allows Europe itself to appear essentially homogeneous) that constitutes the unexamined racism of the term, even in its more technical uses, although there are positive uses such as **native son** and **native wit** where the sense of natural is not accompanied by the meaning of the non-European. The racism of the conjunction of these two elements can be clearly seen in many compounds that **native** has generated from lC19 onward, including **native-built, native-made, native-owned, native-produced**, where fairly straightforward sounding descriptions tend to diminish what is being described because of the denial of universality, disciplinary expertise, technical skill, and so on.

Take, for example, **native-trained** where there is a "damning with faint praise," as in the reference to a "native-trained philosopher activist" in 1986, which clearly subordinates this person to any *foreign-trained* counterpart and also separates him/ her from an *academically-trained* philosopher. **Native** here negatively qualifies the training received, implying an inferiority due to an undeniable lack of formal rigor.

This unexamined negative judgment can also be seen in the adverbial use of **native-fashion** which tends to describe a peculiarity or at least unusual form of behavior or dress. For instance, *The Times* notes in 1997 that "[he had] a habit of holding his cigarette turned into his palm between his middle finger and thumb, native-fashion." What these examples demonstrate is that the term **native** has not yet quite freed itself from the patronizing and/or offensive nature of its origins, even seventy-five years after the demise of overt colonialist racism.

This is true even in technical thinking. The ambiguity, even contradiction, outlined by Empson is most clearly seen in the noun phrase **native speaker**, which was rare in lC19 and eC20 English. It became a widely popular term in the 1980s, increasing considerably in frequency, with the rise of the linguistic movement promoting "other Englishes" and remains a concept in popular use even today. While in theory at least it refers to the group of first-language users of any specific language or dialect, in reality the term is most often used to differentiate **native speakers** of so-called European languages from those who are not, especially in the case where distinct varieties of a European language are involved.

Thus, while it is now acknowledged that LEGITIMATE and fully functional varieties of English are in use in India, Singapore, and Hong Kong, for instance, **native speakers** of English are still often seen as the British and Americans. David Graddol provides a symptomatic example in 1999 when he writes, "The decline of the native speaker in numerical terms is likely to be associated with changing ideas about the centrality of the native speaker to norms of usage. [. . .] Large numbers of people will learn English as a foreign language in the 21st century and they will need teachers, dictionaries and grammar books. But will they continue to look towards the native speaker for authoritative norms of usage?" (67–8). If one considers the **native speakers** of all the established varieties of English, there will be, in future generations at least, a huge increase in numbers, and this increase is already evident. However, here, in a reversal of Empson's explanation of the **native** as non-European "Other," *the* **native (speaker)** is always from the "first world" (the metaphorical Europe) who, in turn, it appears will always have the authority *qua* **native** (in the sense of original, legitimate, naturally prior) to judge and validate, not least through standardized language tests. Thus, the privileged first world intellectual native continues to tower over the simple-minded native of the former colonies. Yet, at the same time, the theoretical importance of this concept has diminished significantly, and today many linguists refer to the "myth of the native speaker" rather than accepting such assumptions for languages in general.

Today, the most common collocates of **native** include **digitally native,** referring to young people who have grown up using digital media. Alongside this is an increase in usages such as **native advertising** (advertising that is integrated into digital media content) and **native app** (a mobile app that is designed for, "native to," a specific platform). In these, the predominant sense is of belonging, of being at home, of integration, thus echoing a positive older meaning of the word. On the other hand, **Nativism,** invariably identified negatively, is a term used more widely alongside *populism* and *nationalism* to indicate a racist, or at least NATIONALIST, isolationism and protectionism.

See COUNTRY, EUROPEAN, IMPERIALISM, INDIGENOUS

NATURE

Nature is perhaps the most complex word in the language. It is relatively easy to distinguish three areas of meaning: (i) the essential quality and character *of* something; (ii) the inherent force which directs either the world or human beings or both; (iii) the material world itself, taken as including or not including human beings. Yet it is evident that within (ii) and (iii), though the area of reference is broadly clear, precise meanings are variable and at times even opposed. The historical development of the word through these three senses is important, but it is also significant that all three senses, and the main variations and alternatives within the two most difficult of them, are still active and widespread in contemporary usage.

Nature comes from fw *nature*, oF, and *natura*, L, from a root in the past participle of *nasci*, L—to be born (from which also derive *nation, native, innate,* etc.). Its earliest sense, as in oF and L, was (i), the essential character and quality *of* something. **Nature** is thus one of several important words, including *culture*, which began as descriptions of a quality or process, immediately defined by a specific reference, but later became independent nouns. The relevant L phrase for the developed meanings is *natura rerum*—the nature of things, which already in some L uses was shortened to *natura*—the constitution of the world. In English sense (i) is from C13, sense (ii) from C14, sense (iii) from C17, though there was an essential continuity and in senses (ii) and (iii) considerable overlap from C16. It is usually not difficult to distinguish (i) from (ii) and (iii); indeed it is often habitual and in effect not noticed in reading.

> In a state of *rude* nature there is no such thing as a people. . . . The idea of a people . . . is wholly artificial; and made, like all other legal fictions, by common agreement. What the particular nature of that agreement was, is collected from the form into which the particular society has been cast.

Here, in Burke, there is a problem about the first use of **nature** but no problem—indeed it hardly seems the same word—about the second (sense [i]) use. Nevertheless, the connection and distinction between senses (i), (ii), and (iii) have sometimes to be made very conscious. The common phrase **human nature**, for example, which is often crucial in important kinds of argument, can contain, without clearly demonstrating it, any of the three main senses and indeed the main variations and alternatives. There is a relatively neutral use in sense (i): that it is an essential quality and characteristic of human beings to do something (though the something that is specified may of course be controversial). But in many uses the descriptive (and hence verifiable or falsifiable) character of sense (i) is less prominent than the very different kind of statement which depends on sense (ii); the directing inherent force, or one of the variants of sense (iii); a fixed property of the material world, in this case "natural man."

What has also to be noticed in the relation between sense (i) and senses (ii) and (iii) is, more generally, that sense (i), by definition, is a specific singular—the **nature** of something, whereas senses (ii) and (iii), in almost all their uses, are abstract singulars—the **nature of** all things having become singular **nature** or **Nature**. The abstract singular is of course now conventional, but it has a precise history. Sense (ii) developed from sense (i), and became abstract, because what was being sought was a single universal "essential quality or character." This is structurally and historically cognate with the emergence of *God* from *a god* or *the gods*. Abstract **Nature**, the essential inherent force, was thus formed by the assumption of a single prime cause, even when it was counterposed, in controversy, to the more explicitly abstract singular cause or force *God*. This has its effect as far as sense (iii), when reference to the whole material world, and therefore to a multiplicity of things and creatures, can carry an assumption of something common to all of them: either

(a) the bare fact of their existence, which is neutral, or, at least as commonly, (b) the generalization of a common quality which is drawn upon for statements of the type, usually explicitly sense (iii), "**Nature** shows us that . . ." This reduction of a multiplicity to a singularity, by the structure and history of the critical word, is then, curiously, compatible either with the assertion of a common quality, which the singular sense suits, or with the general or specific demonstration of differences, including the implicit or explicit denial of a common effective quality, which the singular form yet often manages to contain.

Any full history of the uses of **nature** would be a history of a large part of human thought. (For an important outline, see Lovejoy.) But it is possible to indicate some of the critical uses and changes. There is, first, the very early and surprisingly persistent personification of singular **Nature**: Nature the goddess, "nature herself." This singular personification is critically different from what are now called "nature gods" or "nature spirits": mythical personifications of particular natural forces. "Nature herself" is at one extreme a literal goddess, a universal directing power, and at another extreme (very difficult to distinguish from some non-religious singular uses) an amorphous but still all-powerful creative and shaping force. The associated "Mother Nature" is at this end of the religious and mythical spectrum. There is then great complexity when this kind of singular religious or mythical abstraction has to coexist, as it were, with another singular all-powerful force, namely a monotheistic God. It was orthodox in medieval European belief to use both singular absolutes but to define God as primary and Nature as his minister or deputy. But there was a recurrent tendency to see Nature in another way, as an absolute monarch. It is obviously difficult to separate this from the goddess or the minister, but the concept was especially used to express a sense of fatalism rather than of providence. The emphasis was on the power of natural forces, and on the apparently arbitrary or capricious occasional exercise of these powers, with inevitable, often destructive effects on men.

As might be expected, in matters of such fundamental difficulty, the concept of **nature** was usually in practice much wider and more various than any of the specific definitions. There was then a practice of shifting use, as in Shakespeare's *Lear*:

> Allow not nature more than nature needs,
> Man's life's as cheap as beast's . . .
>   . . . one daughter
> Who redeems nature from the general curse
> Which twain have brought her to.

That nature, which contemns its origin,
Cannot be border'd certain in itself. . . .
　. . . All shaking thunder
Crack nature's moulds, all germens spill at once,
That make ungrateful man. . . .
　. . . Hear, nature hear; dear goddess, hear. . . .

In these examples there is a range of meanings: from nature as the primitive condition before human society; through the sense of an original innocence from which there has been a fall and a curse, requiring redemption; through the special sense of a quality of birth, as in the root word; through again a sense of the forms and molds of nature which can yet, paradoxically, be destroyed by the natural force of thunder; to that simple and persistent form of the goddess, Nature herself. This complexity of meaning is possible in a dramatic rather than an expository mode. What can be seen as an uncertainty was also a tension: nature was at once innocent, unprovided, sure, unsure, fruitful, destructive, a pure force and tainted and cursed. The real complexity of natural processes has been rendered by a complexity within the singular term.

There was then, especially from eC17, a critical argument about the observation and understanding of nature. It could seem wrong to inquire into the workings of an absolute monarch, or of a minister of God. But a formula was arrived at: to understand the creation was to praise the creator, seeing absolute power through contingent works. In practice the formula became lip-service and was then forgotten. Paralleling political changes, nature was altered from an absolute to a constitutional monarch, with a new kind of emphasis on natural laws. Nature, in C18 and C19, was often in effect personified as a constitutional lawyer. The laws came *from* somewhere, and this was variously but often indifferently defined; most practical attention was given to interpreting and classifying the laws, making predictions from precedents, discovering or reviving forgotten statutes, and above all shaping new laws from new cases: nature not as an inherent and shaping force but as an accumulation and classification of cases.

This was the decisive emergence of sense (iii): **nature** as the material world. But the emphasis on discoverable laws—

Nature and Nature's laws lay hid in night;
God said, Let Newton be! and all was light! (Pope)

—led to a common identification of Nature with Reason: the object of observation with the mode of observation. This provided a basis for a significant variation, in which Nature was contrasted with what had been made of man, or what man had made of himself. A "state of nature" could be contrasted—sometimes pessimistically but more often optimistically and even programmatically—with an existing state of society. The "state of nature," and the newly personified idea of Nature, then played critical roles in arguments about, first, an obsolete or corrupt society, needing redemption and renewal, and, second, an "ARTIFICIAL" or "mechanical" society, which learning from **Nature** must cure. Broadly, these two phases were the ENLIGHTENMENT and the Romantic movement. The senses can readily be distinguished, but there was often a good deal of overlapping. The emphasis on law gave a philosophical basis for conceiving an ideal society. The emphasis on an inherent original power—a new version of the much older idea—gave a basis for actual regeneration, or, where regeneration seemed impossible or was too long delayed, an alternative source for belief in the goodness of life and of humanity, as counterweight or as solace against a harsh "world."

Each of these conceptions of Nature was significantly static: a set of laws—the constitution of the world, or an inherent, universal, primary but also recurrent force—evident in the "beauties of nature" and in the "hearts of men," teaching a singular goodness. Each of these concepts, but especially the latter, has retained currency. Indeed one of the most powerful uses of nature, since 1C18, has been in this selective sense of goodness and innocence. **Nature** has meant the "countryside," the "unspoiled places," plants and creatures other than man. The use is especially current in contrasts between town and COUNTRY: **nature** is what man has not made, though if he made it long enough ago—a hedgerow or a desert—it will usually be included as **natural**. **Nature-lover** and **nature poetry** date from this phase.

But there was one further powerful personification yet to come: nature as the goddess, the minister, the monarch, the lawyer, or the source of original innocence was joined by nature the selective breeder: natural selection, and the "ruthless" competition apparently inherent in it, were made the basis for seeing nature as both historical and active. Nature still indeed had laws, but they were the laws of survival and extinction: species rose and flourished, decayed and died. The extraordinary accumulation of knowledge about actual evolutionary processes, and about the highly variable relations between organisms and their environments including other organisms, was again, astonishingly, generalized to a singular name. **Nature** was doing this and this to species. There was then an expansion of variable forms of the newly scientific generalization: "Nature teaches . . . ," "Nature shows us that. . . ." In the actual record what was taught or shown ranged from inherent and inevitable bitter competition to inherent mutuality or cooperation. Numerous **natural** examples could be selected to support any of these versions: aggression, property, parasitism, symbiosis, cooperation have all been demonstrated, justified, and projected into social ideas by selective statements of this form, normally cast as dependent on a singular **Nature** even while the facts of variation and variability were being collected and used.

The complexity of the word is hardly surprising, given the fundamental importance of the processes to which it refers. But since **nature** is a word which carries, over a very long period, many of the major variations of human thought—often, in any particular use, only implicitly yet with powerful effect on the character of the argument—it is necessary to be especially aware of its difficulty.

RECENT DEVELOPMENTS

Nature remains a central and centrally complex word. Indeed, the growth of the ecological movement, of Green parties and animal rights activism, and, perhaps most powerfully, concerns about global warming might suggest that it is even more central now than when the second edition of *Keywords* was published in 1983. Perhaps not surprisingly, there has been a significant increase in its frequency in the past thirty years. It is difficult, however, to discern a new sense of the word. Even the controversial Gaia hypothesis of the world as a self-regulating mechanism assumes a globally interactive **Nature** with which William Wordsworth would have been familiar.

Two competing if not entirely contradictory accounts of **nature** exercise impressive ideological dominance. On the one hand there is the **Nature** of the Romantics in which untamed natural vistas, the noble savage, and the innocent child function as antidotes to the artificiality and decadence of URBAN life; on the other there is Darwinian EVOLUTION endlessly creating and destroying. Behind both of these are older but not yet exhausted conceptions. Hobbes's "war of all against all" offers a less biological but more pessimistic buttress to Darwinian arguments, while elements of the perfectly ordered world of Christian Aristotelianism and the Enlightenment equation of Reason and **Nature** can be found flickering through Romantic accounts.

Yet further complications must be taken into account.

Consider the three major touchstones of Romantic **Nature**: (1) the noble savage (now INDIGENOUS peoples), (2) the innocent child, and (3) a generalized country-side expanded to take in all aspects of the globe untouched by urbanization and mechanization. All these benchmarks have been undercut by scientific and cultural developments of the past century. Anthropology has analyzed the noble savage as complicated in cultural beliefs and as stratified in social structures as modern HU-MANITY. Psychology, particularly psychoanalysis, has displayed a child, subject to a whole range of very adult murderous and sexual desires. Finally, the most important literature and films since World War I—for instance, Joyce, Eliot, and Woolf—have displayed modern humanity's most natural ENVIRONMENT as the city. Similarly, the determinist teleology that informs the commentaries of most nature documentaries (and everyday conversation) is at odds with the very complicated relation between genes and environment with which modern biology grapples.

Yet **nature** remains a powerfully appealing reference in contemporary cultural and ideological debate. From medieval times, **nature** has never ceased to take on the role of the divine, once often in opposition to the Christian God, now often as his successor. **Nature**'s role as the ultimate arbiter of both personal and social life is strengthened rather than weakened by its extraordinarily complicated semantics. **Mother** remains the second most frequent collocate for **Nature**.

See ARTIFICIAL, COUNTRY, CULTURE, ECOLOGY, ENLIGHTENMENT, ENVIRONMENT, EVOLUTION

NETWORK

The vast majority of keywords in English, and its conceptual vocabulary more gen-erally, derive from Latin. **Network**, however derives from two words central to the vocabulary of Old English, both of which are used frequently in contemporary lan-guage: *net*, a piece of openwork fabric forming meshes of a suitable size to catch fish; and *work*, whose primary meaning is labor or activity. While only of specialized use in Early Modern and Modern English, in the last fifty years **network** has become central to the vocabulary of transport, telecommunications, and computers and has developed meanings so crucial that there are serious claims that we are living in a **network society**.

The first recorded use of **network** in English dates back to 1530. This compound of *net* and *work* referred to a manufactured work in which threads or wires are interlaced in the fashion of a net: "Thou shalt haue garments of Imbrodred silke,

Lawnes and rich networks for thy head attyre" (R. Greene's *Frier Bacon*, 1594). By C18, **network** was being deployed in biology and the natural sciences to describe patterned forms of animal and plant tissue. It was also being used in physics in eC20 to describe an extended array of atoms bonded together in a crystalline or other substance.

By eC19, **network** had also acquired an immaterial sense, as in Emerson's pronouncement that "[t]heir law is a network of fictions" (1856). The decisive shift, however, came in mC19, when the sense of nodes linked to other nodes by numerous ties in a decentralized way was used to describe developments in transport, particularly railways, and electrical engineering. These senses developed to describe the new TECHNOLOGIES of broadcasting and, even more crucially, computing. It also became an important term to describe new developments in retailing with businesses developing **networks** of shops and branches.

The transfer of these senses to describe social relations is very late, with the *OED*'s first quotation dated 1884: "British India is a network of cliquism and favoritism"; and more than sixty years before its second: "I mentioned to him that you maintain a network of overpaid informers" (Evelyn Waugh, 1946). Both of these examples use **network** with a pejorative inflection and as the term proliferates in the postwar period this negative judgment is pronounced: **spy networks**, **terrorist networks**, **old boy networks** to take prominent examples. However, the growing importance of computers (and particularly the development of the Internet), together with the increasing disappearance of many traditional hierarchical social relations, saw **network** being used in much more positive senses. Indeed, it has recently become a crucial term to describe contemporary society: **global network capitalism**; **network society**; **network economy**.

In recent decades, many areas of the social sciences have explored **networks**, understood as either a technique for mapping and explaining interactions between social units or, more profoundly, as a form of organization that generates particular types of identities and interests. From the 1950s, uses of this understanding of the term developed in anthropology by scholars who pioneered studies on **social networks**, a rare phrase at the time. From the 1970s, **social network analysis** (SNA), with its charting of nodes and ties among actors, became popular in sociology and other fields, although there was (and remains) debate over whether SNA is a metaphor, a method, a theory, or something of all three. By the 1990s, in an influential argument Manuel Castells argued that a **network society** was on the rise, underpinned by new COMMUNICATION technologies, notably the mainstream commercialization of the Internet. Castells claimed that the **network society** is still a capitalist society, but one in which advanced firms process INFORMATION and knowledge.

Since the 1990s, the term **network** has also become commonplace within a range of managerial discourses. As suggested by some writers, there was something almost inevitable about this deployment in the digital era: "As an existing concept . . . , associated with a specific vocabulary, models of causality and mathematical models, and formed to offer an alternative to hierarchical algorithms, 'network' naturally enough finds itself mobilized by capitalism" (Boltanski and Chiapello, 2007). The **networked business** is claimed to produce major commercial benefits, including the ability to reach new customers, foster creativity, and enhance efficiency savings. This justification has been sharpened in comparison to the so-called bureaucratic model of business organization which, in the opinion of mainstream management theorists, is viewed as an unsuitable structure within a competitive commercial world. The appeal to **network** also tends to carry a moral inflection: if the hierarchical firm is characterized by dominant-dominated relations of power, the **network** is presented as a social configuration that encourages liberty, such as via the idea of **networked teams** that electronically unite workers across geographic spaces.

No analysis of the term **network** would be complete without returning to the related idea of **networking**. From the 1940s, this word originally carried a physical or technological sense when applied to radio and television broadcasting, before extending from the 1960s to information exchange, particularly in reference to computing. From the mid-1970s, the social sense of **networking** as the process of striving to make professional contacts and acquaintances emerged, although it would take until the 1990s for this meaning to become mainstream. For instance, in a search of titles in the US Library of Congress, the phrase **business networking**, when invoked in a social sense, does not return any results before 1991. Today, the appeal to **social networking** is often viewed as a significant, even crucial, activity for constructing and sustaining a professional career, a practice that has been given added legitimacy by the popularity of Internet services such as LinkedIn. Debates on **networking** have often been coupled with the idea of social capital, a notion originally coined by the sociologist Pierre Bourdieu, but now reapplied by many others in management studies, political science, and development studies.

The concept of **network** helps to encourage thinking on the visualization of relations that may be hidden in the social world. Yet the dominance of the **network** paradigm can also lead to the marginalization of other important spatial and group categories. As one analyst has expressed it, "What used to be easily referred to as relations within a 'culture,' 'community,' 'class,' or 'group,' is now indiscriminately being called a network" (Bourgouin, 2009). For instance, the value of the notion of social class derives from its historical connections to capital-labor relations, solidarity, and competitive struggle, themes that retain relevance for examining many sociopolitical problems. By contrast, the word **network**, partly due to its scientific legacy and sense as a comparatively neutral analytical tool, tends not to have the same degree of expressive potency. Yet, for some, this may be precisely why the phrase **social network** is so appealing: if social class is perceived to carry political or ideological baggage, the notion of **social network**, in a world of two billion Facebook users and 500 million daily tweets, appears as a relatively untainted reflection of today's developing world.

See BUSINESS, COMMUNICATION, TECHNOLOGY

OCCUPY

The recent spike in usage of the verb **occupy**, as well as its deployment across disparate sociopolitical spheres, should not lead us to believe that this hot-button word has only lately emerged as a critical—and critically debated—term. The history of both **occupy** and its noun form, **occupation**, reveals a matrix of often intersecting senses involving military action, labor, the investment of capital, and sexual relations. Its use to describe the taking of a building to make a political protest became widespread in the student movements of the 1960s. In recent years, following the Arab Spring of 2011, it became a generalized name for protests against economic INEQUALITY.

Occupy entered into English in eC14, from French *occuper* and Latin *occupāre*, "to seize (by force), take possession of, get hold of, to take up, fill, occupy (time or space), to employ, invest (money)." This Latinate polysemy prefigures a dispersion of valences from ME to the present. Early usage of the term revolved around an initial sense of "to keep busy, engage, employ (a person, or the mind, attention, etc.)." As such, and due to the verb's frequent passive formation and reflexive potential, the elasticity of the word ensured that from the start **occupation** would be tied to complex concerns over subject-object relations and borders.

These issues are manifest in the slippage between two senses of **occupy**, which the *OED* marks as being "in some contexts difficult to distinguish." There is a sort of ontological porousness between "to hold possession of; to have in one's possession or power; to hold (a position, office, or privilege)" and "to live in and use (a place) as its tenant or regular inhabitant; to inhabit; to stay or lodge in." Thus Chaucer, *c*1375, writes "This kyng was slawe And Darius occupieth his degree," while in *c*1387 Trevisa gives us "Bretayne was somtyme occupied wiþ Saxons." The verb *invade* (from L *invadere,* to go, walk) enters English in eC16, and we find Edward Hall in 1548 using a telling equivocation: "That he would inuade or occupie the territory of hys enemies." Does this *or* signify synonymy, or a difference in register? How to determine whether an event constitutes an *invasion* or an **occupation**, in the sense of "tak[ing] possession of (a place), esp. by force?"

Both World Wars of C20 played a role in separating out this distinction and generated a number of related compound terms. **Occupation army** appeared in mC19 with respect to France's military endeavors, and World War I ended with the institution of various nations' **occupying forces** in the Rhineland. The German **occupation** of a large swath of Europe is among the most ubiquitously cited examples of what E. S. Farrow refers to in 1918 as an **occupation army** that "remains in possession of a newly conquered country, retaining it as a kind of hostage." Thus, while to **occupy** may still refer to the actual seizure or invasion of a territory, its primary deployment in military matters indicates the subsequent holding of such space. The long-running debate over the status of Israeli Occupied Territories significantly complicates these issues. Diplomatic rhetoric declaring Israel an **occupying power**, or treating its **belligerent occupation**, fundamentally shifts the international discourse. In a 2002 breakdown of the semantic turbulence, Dore Gold called for the replacement of **occupied** with "disputed territories," shifting the balance of aggression versus self-defense, and reframing allegations of TERRORISM.

It is also intriguing to consider the notorious sense of **occupy**, which entered into usage during mC15, denoting the act of "having sexual intercourse or relations with." In 1598, Florio's *Worlde of Wordes* included, in its entry for *trentuno* (thirty-one), a sketch of the "punishment inflicted by ruffianly fellowes upon"

Italian prostitutes, the latter "occupide one and thirtie times by one and thirtie seuerall base raskalie companions." As the *OED* notes, "Throughout the 17th and most of the 18th cent., there seems to have been a general tendency to avoid this word, probably as a result of the use of the word in [this sexual sense]." According to the 1902 *New English Dictionary*, the number of available quotes dropped tenfold from C16 to C17, and one of two uses of **occupy** by Shakespeare hint at the aversion: "[T]hese villaines will make the word as odious as the word occupy, which was an excellent good worde before it was il sorted" (2 *Henry IV* 2.4.144–6). This micro-history is not merely an example of a word accruing a negative semantic register that must be purged and made obsolete before its restoration. In attending to recent uses of **occupy** and **occupation**, it must be considered whether this valence might be re-emerging with a certain subtextual weight.

The explosion of popular **occupy** movements across the globe, sparked in 2011, thus raises questions about its shifting of the verb's valence *and* the possible resonance of earlier negative senses of the term. Suspended between the semantic processes of pejoration and amelioration, this complicated political deployment of **occupy** might more aptly be read as an example of irony, an incongruity of semantic directions. It seems at once to shift the term's meaning to a more positive sense while not doing away with the history of adverse valences in order to energize use value and heighten rhetoric. Furthermore, in a troubling turn of events, the Occupy Wall Street movement was rebuked for inattentiveness to sexual abuse within its protest plots. Tamura Lomax decried its failure to provide "safe spaces" within a "rape culture that makes sexual occupancy permissible everywhere," while Darnell L. Moore quickly echoed these claims and referred to Lomax's statement as a call for men to "un-occupy [. . .] women's bodies."

In addition, the shift from **Occupy Wall Street**, to the **Occupy Movement**, to simply (#)**occupy** has muddied the waters considerably. The *New York Times* website, on October 18, 2011, ran a slideshow titled "Occupy (Fill in the Blank"). While a nod to the burgeoning movements across the globe, the headline also marks the flexibility of the verb as a signifier. This confusion also led to a 2011 *Times* op-ed inquiring, "Who Is Occupy Wall Street?" and a 2012 *Continent* essay, "What Does It Mean to Occupy?" In the latter, Tim Gilman-Ševčík and Matt Statler suggest that "[t]o occupy, occupying, occupation" beg the following question of **occupiers**: "are you willing to step into a different space, where the rule of law is unclear and evolving?"

OPINION

Opinion is a difficult word in modern English, despite apparent continuity with its root *opiniō* in Classical Latin. It is a prominent but unsettled term across fields including political science, marketing, and public relations, as well as in both academic and general understandings of human ideas, beliefs, and action.

Latin *opiniō* (with related pejorative adjective in post-classical Latin *opiniōsus*, cf. modern English **opinionated** meaning "dogmatic, obstinate or conceited") carried a range of senses: supposition that falls short of demonstration; general impression or repute; and report, including rumor. In expressions such as *opinione vulgi* (**opinion** of the people), mostly cited from Cicero but in widespread use, connection is implicit between *opinio* and wider Roman social institutions of DEMOCRACY and rhetoric.

Opinion comes into English (partly via Anglo-Norman and Middle French) with broadly the same senses, but is adapted (and then continues to adapt) to different and changing social structures. Three evolving emphases need to be distinguished.

(1) The epistemological meaning of conjecture, disputable belief, or conviction that goes beyond supporting evidence. This meaning contrasts with statements based on TRUTH and fact, especially where **opinion** signifies "feeling" as much as "thought." A closely related contrast is that between subjective and objective; and on some occasions qualification of **opinion** is offered by reference to a particular source of evidence, framework of ideas, or social authority. This broad sense (attested from the 1320s to the present day) gives rise to modern expressions including **a matter of opinion**, **to be of the opinion that**, and pejorative **mere opinion**. Note that this sense involves interplay, as it develops, between fundamentally different kinds of evidence and AUTHORITY. An increasingly dominant subjective or personal authority finds itself in tension with *dogma* or (taught) *doctrine*, and sometimes dismisses such frameworks as "received opinion." Tension between apparently subjective viewpoint and agreed doctrine is similarly reflected in a hybrid from lC14: **opinion** can denote "professional advice," such as a **medical opinion** or formal statement by a judge or other competent authority, with related more recent expressions **get an opinion**, "seek a medical diagnosis," and **second opinion**.

(2) A second strand of meaning extends the dimension of assessment and judgment into "reputation or public perception." This sense, now virtually obsolete, describes what is thought by one person of another: the (especially good)

estimation in which a person is held (because he or she represents something, or possesses some quality), a sense readily inflected toward favorable estimates of the self. In turn, a further meaning (now obsolete) for **opinion** develops: "conceit; arrogance; self-confidence" (with its then overdetermined links with **opinionated**).

(3) A third strand of meaning (also from lC14) involves attributed beliefs aggregated from individual views: the perception of a social group rather than of an individual. This sense, which contrasts with **opinion** as a matter of countable beliefs or views held by individuals, existed in Latin *opinione vulgi* and its equivalent in early Italian, and enters English usually with a specifying adjective, as in **common opinion**, **general opinion**, and **vulgar opinion**. In each phrase, **opinion** denotes what is thought or felt either by some designated group of people or by a whole population, hence from lC18 onward **public opinion**, an expression whose significance depends on social structures (not always present) which permit and have uses for such reports.

Tension exists among the three intersecting strands, both when used of individual and collective social opinion: whether **opinion** denotes limited perceptions or ideas (which, as merely subjective, may be dismissed as relatively unimportant); whether the word denotes ideas that, while disputable, are significant because they have the backing of some widely shared doctrine or ideology; or whether, as responses to social EXPERIENCE, **opinion** foreshadows new ideas and values in the making. Examples of each emphasis can be found, as well as equivocal statements between them, including in formulations linked to political positions that contrast PRIVATE and PUBLIC (or COMMON) belief and VALUE—emphases whose significance is increased by historical shifts they express from feudal social relations into modern capitalism, liberal ideology, and practical formation of a modern public sphere.

In *Areopagitica* (1644), John Milton writes that "where there is much desire to learn, there of necessity will be much arguing, much writing, many opinions; for opinion in good men is but knowledge in the making." In Thomas Hobbes's *Leviathan* (1651, Part I, Chapter XI), the clash between private and public in defenses of **opinion** as expression of emergent ideas is explicit when we are told that "[t]hey that approve a private opinion, call it opinion; but they that mislike it, heresy: and yet heresy signifies no more than private opinion." In the dedicatory epistle of John Locke's *Essay Concerning Human Understanding* (1690), implications from the "private" nature of **opinion**, in contrast with "common" belief, are challenged when it is argued that "new opinions are always suspected, and usually opposed, without any other reason but because they are not already common." Almost a century later, striking political contrast is to be found between Tom Paine's reliance on "general opinion" as political vindication, "[W]hen such a time, from the general opinion of the nation, shall arrive . . ." (*Rights of Man*, 1792, Part II) and Edmund Burke's reservation about the "coquetry of public opinion, which has her caprices, and must have her way" ("Letter to Thomas Burgh," January 1, 1780). Half a century on again, J. S. Mill's *On Liberty* (1859, Chapter II) foregrounds **opinion** in his exposition of liberty as protected by a marketplace of ideas: "If all mankind minus one, were of one opinion, and only one person were of the contrary opinion, mankind would be no more justified in silencing that one person, than he, if he had the power, would be justified in silencing mankind." In one political current, **opinion** signifies progressive momentum; at the end of C18, political reference is most likely to democratic impulses associated with the French Revolution and/or the US Constitution, as well as political mobilization within rapidly industrializing British society. In an opposing political current, **opinion** bears superficially the same meaning but connotes danger from masses made confident by open expression of collective experience and values.

In C20, **opinion** was increasingly used to describe collected data on patterns in public belief and attitude, in a current leading from Walter Lippmann's *Public Opinion* (1922), through the impact of George Gallup's *Public Opinion in Democracy* (1939), into a contemporary meaning of **opinion**, central to the practices of modern representative democracy, as "measured social distribution of ideas and values." Early development of this emphasis was linked to wider arguments during the 1920s over peacetime application to commercial and political activity of mass psychology and wartime propaganda techniques, as well as about the effect of such techniques on established conceptions of democracy. **Opinion poll**, meaning systematic collection of sampled opinion by means of surveys, develops as part of a cluster of compounds from eC20, including **opinion former**. From 1951, as **opinion** became more central to electioneering, policy forecasts, and marketing, the professional designation **opinion pollster** is also attested. Also in the same period, published formats that offer comment began to be known as **opinion columns**, and the writing in them as **opinion pieces**.

With variant meanings and emphases, **opinion** has now become a guiding concept in consultation processes, transaction ratings, and solicitation of feedback in most areas of public and commercial life. With easier means of data collection, by phone and online, and with broadcast and online media eager to incorporate user-generated comment, **opinion** has also become a form of entertainment with its own requirements of supply and demand: "if you have an opinion, call now. . . ." Across such usage, however, **opinion** continues to have unsettled implications. These arise partly because of the traditional contrast with *fact* and *knowledge*, and partly on account of the unresolved contrast between private and public. In suitable circumstances, accordingly, calling something an **opinion** can achieve any of the following: it can dismiss a given viewpoint as merely personal and subjective; it can assert an entitlement to that same viewpoint because it is personal and subjective; it can condemn a widely held view because it lacks appropriate evidence; or it can urge the merit of that same, widely held view because it reflects a PUBLIC reservoir of belief and value, irrespective of the evidence.

See COMMON, DEMOCRACY, EXPERIENCE, PRIVATE, PUBLIC, TRUTH, VALUE

ORGANIC

Organic has a specific meaning in modern English, to refer to the processes or products of LIFE, in human beings, animals, or plants. It has also an important applied or metaphorical meaning, to indicate certain kinds of relationship and thence certain kinds of society. In this latter sense it is an especially difficult word, and its history is in any case exceptionally complicated.

Organ first appeared in English, from C13, to signify a musical instrument; something like the modern **organ**, in this context, appeared from C14. It had fw *organe*, oF, from *organum*, L, rw *órganon*, Gk—an instrument, engine, or tool, with two derived senses: the abstract "instrument"—agency, and musical instrument. There was a later applied sense of *órganon*, which was repeated in all the derived words: the eye as a "seeing instrument," the ear a "hearing instrument" and so on, whence **organ** as a part of the body, in English from eC15. But the full range of meanings—musical instrument, engine, instrument (**organ of opinion**), and part of the body—was present in English in C16. **Organic**, appearing from C16, followed first the sense of engine or tool. North, translating Plutarch in 1569, wrote: "to frame instruments and Engines (which are called mechanicall, or organicall)." This is instructive in view of the later conventional contrast between **organic** and *mechanical*.

It is from the sense of **organ** as instrument or agency that **organize** and **organization** in their modern senses eventually developed, mainly from 1C18 and eC19 (compare the developments of *society* and *civilization*). But each word was used earlier with the distinct physical reference, as, from C17, was **organism**.

Organic followed a different course, and indeed by C19 could be used in contrast with **organized**. The source of its common specific modern meaning is the major development of natural history and biology in C18, when it acquired a dominant reference to things living and growing. **Organic chemistry** was defined in eC19, acquiring the later more specialized sense of the chemistry of compounds of carbon from c1860. It was this development in biology and the "life sciences" which laid the basis for the distinction between the former synonyms **organic** and *mechanical*.

The distinction was made in the Romantic movement, probably first in German, among the Nature Philosophers. Coleridge distinguished between **organic** and **inorganic** bodies or systems; in the **organic** "the whole is everything and the parts are nothing," while in the **inorganic** "the whole is nothing more than a collection of the individual parts." This has obvious connections with the developing sense of **organized** and of **organism**, but the distinction was profoundly influenced by the contrast with *mechanical*, in opposition to *mechanical* philosophy and, unquestionably, to the new significance of machines in the Industrial Revolution. When applied to social organization, **organic** moved towards a contemporary specialization of *natural*: an **organic** society was one that has "grown" rather than been "made." This acquired early relevance in criticism of revolutionary societies or proposals as ARTIFICIAL and against the "natural order" of things. It later acquired relevance to contrasts between primarily agricultural and primarily industrial societies. Carlyle still had the complex sense in mind when he wrote of "taming" the French Revolution, "so that its intrinsic purpose can be made good, that it may become organic, and be able to live among other organisms and formed things." Yet Burke, on the same subject, had used an opposite sense: comparing the English of 1688 with the French of 1789, he wrote: "they acted by the ancient organized states in the shape of their old organization, and not by the organic moleculae of a disbanded people." *Moleculae*, here, reminds us of a developing sense of *atomistic* to indicate relatively disorganized or disintegrating forms of society and social thought.

Through C19 and to mC20 **organic** was often used in social thought, mainly of a conservative kind. Leavis and Thompson, in *Culture and Environment* (1932), contrasted the "'organized' modern state" with the "Old England . . . of the organic community." R. J. White, in *The Conservative Tradition* (1954), argued that "it were better that a state should be a tree than an engine" and that "diffusion of power is the characteristic of organic life, just as concentration of power is the characteristic of mechanism." Bertrand Russell, in a different tradition, argued in *The Prospects of Industrial Civilization* (1923) that "a machine is essentially organic, in the sense that it has parts which co-operate to produce a single useful result, and that the separate parts have little value on their own account" (the latter distinction recalling that made by Coleridge) and that, consequently, "when we are exhorted to make society 'organic' it is from machinery that we shall necessarily derive our imaginative models, since we do not know how to make society a living animal." At some points, behind the modern controversy, the old metaphor of society as a *body*, with *members*, and hence an **organism** in an applied biological sense, seems to have some influence. Again, Durkheim distinguished between **organic** and *mechanical solidarity*, where **organic** carries the sense of functional interdependence. But the fundamental overlap of meanings, and the difficult modern relationship between **organic, organized, organization,** and **organism,** can tempt one to say that all societies are **organic** but that some are more **organic**—instrumentally planned or naturally evolving—than others.

Two other senses of **organic** still have effect. There is the modern specialized use of farming and of food, with a stress on *natural* rather than *artificial* fertilizers or growing and breeding methods. This is linked with general criticism of *industrial* society. There is also the wider sense, to describe a kind of relationship rather than, as in explicit social theory, a kind of society (cf. ECOLOGY). **Organic** has been widely used in discussions of ART and LITERATURE to indicate a significant relationship and interrelationship between parts of a work: **organic relation** or **organic connection.** This use, to indicate significantly or "integrally" connected or related, is evident in descriptions not so much of societies as wholes but of specific internal relationships: "an **organic** connection with the local community." The word is easier but still not easy to use in this more specific sense.

RECENT DEVELOPMENTS

Williams's entry emphasized the political distinction between an **organic** society thought to be "naturally evolving" and an ARTIFICIAL one, in which the relationships among parts were seen to be either arbitrary or imposed from without. Williams also noted that the term **organic** had become increasingly synonymous with *natural* in the fields of agriculture and food production.

This last usage has predominated since the 1970s, referring to foods produced without pesticides or artificial fertilizers. This sense is supported by the fact that its most frequent collocates include "food," "farming," "soil," and "matter." **Organic farming** emphasizes biodiversity, crop rotation, and multi-cropping (growing several crops together on the same field), while industrial farming depends on proprietary seeds, synthetic fertilizers, and genetically modified plants and animals. Proponents of **organic farming** argue that it produces healthier food and is more environmentally SUSTAINABLE. Proponents of large-scale, industrial farming point to the benefits of higher yields and cheaper production costs.

In the continuing debate over which agricultural practices are most appropriate, **organic** has become the opposite of *conventional*. In the labelling system of grocery stores, consumers can differentiate between conventional fruits and vegetables that have been genetically modified as opposed to those that have not. Most recently, **organic** is a common descriptor beyond food products, with common discussions of organic beauty products, organic makeup, organic moisturizers, and organic perfumes. As federal governments have become involved in defining what constitutes an **organic** product, charges of "greenwashing" have arisen; the environmental marketing claims of so-called **organic** products are not all equal.

See ARTIFICIAL, ECOLOGY, EVOLUTION, GENETIC, LIFE, NATURE, SUSTAINABLE

PERFORMANCE

Originally a word of fairly neutral connotation meaning broadly "the doing of an action or operation," **performance** has long been particularly closely associated with the theatre, to the extent that this has significantly colored many of its other uses; more recently, it has become a key term in the discourse of management, in the assessment of how well employees fulfill the requirements of their jobs. The tensions between these two poles of meaning are significant and ongoing.

The parent verb **perform** was borrowed from (Anglo-)French around 1300. By the end of C14, it shows the starting points of a broad range of senses, including: "to put (something) into effect," "to do what one has to do," "to carry out, execute, or accomplish (something)," "to cause or produce (a certain result)," "to carry out (a public function, rite, etc.)," and also (now obsolete) "to make or create (something)," "to complete (something)." Major later sense developments include "to carry out one's function"; (of a financial investment) "to give a good return"; and a cluster of related senses that have their starting point in lC16: "to present (a play)"; "to act (a role)"; "to act, give a performance"; and (developed from these in lC19) "to display bad temper, to misbehave." (The French verb is a formation from *par-*, *per-* (< Latin *per*>) and *fournir*, from which English *furnish* is also borrowed; *fournir* was borrowed into French in pre-literary times from another Germanic language.)

C20 developments include: "To have sexual intercourse (esp. satisfactorily)" and "Esp. of a child or a pet: to urinate or defecate," both developments from "to do what one has to do" and related uses, but frequently playing or punning on the theatrical senses, and probably sometimes perceived as extensions of those senses. This same punning is an important undercurrent of many contemporary uses of the word.

The derivative **performance** is found from lC15 in a set of meanings which mirror those of the verb, including "accomplishment, carrying out, or doing of something"; "quality of execution (especially against a standard or measure)"; "something done"; (now obsolete) "an achievement or creation"; "carrying out or fulfillment (of a duty, etc.)"; "performing or instance of performing a play or artistic work, or a ceremony, rite, etc." (Middle French *parformance* is very rare, and probably not the root of the English word.)

Although the core meanings of **perform** and **performance** have changed relatively little since the early modern period, their typical uses have changed considerably, in ways that are highly revealing of shifts in C20 society. In C19, uses typically center on the **performance** of machinery, on the fulfillment of tasks and duties, and on **dramatic** and **artistic performance**. In lC20, two major developments have occurred: first, the employment of **performance measures** in education has become more and more prevalent; and second, in the workplace trends from measurement of the **performance** of machinery and systems and trends from psychology and education have converged in the measurement and assessment of the **performance** of the individual worker in the workplace.

Among other cultural developments, two from the world of linguistics are significant. In the 1955 William James lectures at Harvard, J. L. Austin introduced the notion of **performative** uses of language. Against traditional philosophies of language that only understood LANGUAGE as referring to the world, Austin pointed to uses of language like "I promise," in which the utterance actually performs an action—the action of promising. This emphasis on the construction of an intersubjective world through symbolic action has led in the humanities and social sciences to the **"performative turn,"** which has brought a focus on human actions and behavior as **performance**.

In a separate development, an important distinction in linguistics was introduced in the 1960s by Noam Chomsky, between **performance** as actual linguistic usage as opposed to *competence* as a speaker's knowledge of a language; hence **performance grammar**, **performance error**, etc.

In other areas of cultural and intellectual life, **performance art** developed in the 1960s as ART that focused on the live relation between artist and audience, introducing a strong element of theatre into galleries and museums. The theorizing of gender in the 1990s, and particularly the work of Judith Butler, emphasized how GENDER could be understood as a continuous social **performance** rather than a simple biological given.

Contemporary collocations of **perform** and **performance** highlight the use of these terms in the workplace. In contemporary usage, *functions, tasks, duties*, and *obligations* are all frequently **performed**, as are *roles, miracles, calculations, experiments, exercises*, and *acts* (frequently sexual ones), as well as, less frequently, *feats, songs*, and *tricks*. People are *able* or *unable* to **perform** tasks, etc., which they are *asked, required*, or *expected* to **perform**. Frequent modifying adverbs are *effectively, efficiently, satisfactorily, adequately, successfully, regularly*, or *competently*. These adverbial modifiers point particularly clearly to the key role of **perform** in the contemporary discourse of management. The most frequent collocates of **performance** incline even more strongly in this direction. **Performance** is frequently modified by *high, poor, improved, improving*, or *excellent*; it may be *improved, measured, monitored*, or *assessed*. Important compounds include **performance standards**, **indicators**, **measures**, **criteria**, **assessment**, and **targets**. Not all uses by any means relate to **performance** by human beings, but even those which do not have shifted away from the physical machinery typically assessed in C19 uses. In contemporary use, *software* is very frequently assessed for its **performance**; and one of the most frequent of all compounds is **economic performance**. Frequent compounds belonging to particular fields are **academic performance** and **athletic performance**. **Sexual performance** is a very frequent collocation, and **performance anxiety** frequently has reference to sexual intercourse.

The modern study of **performance management** in the workplace has gone under that name only since the 1970s, although **performance appraisal** has some earlier currency, as does **job performance** (in the latter case back even into the first half of C20); in earlier use, **individual performance** refers more often to testing machinery than human individuals, as does **performance testing**. The collocation **performance standards** in early use typically belongs to the discourse of testing machinery and also to the discourse of psychology, while **performance measures** occurs in early use chiefly in the realms of psychology and EDUCATION. All these compounds have shifted significantly into the discourse of management in recent decades, where they have been joined by other expressions such as **performance-related pay**.

Perform and **performance** are in this way central to a modern discourse of assessment and measurement, especially in the workplace and especially with regard to how well people are considered to be meeting the requirements of their jobs or (more commonly) their roles—a further reminder of the somewhat uneasy links that exist between the lexicon of workplace management and the lexicon of theatre.

See ART, GENDER, LANGUAGE

POLITICAL

The problems posed by **political** result from a combination of the term's semantic shift over the last several centuries and the changing face of post-national politics that have become so important since mC20.

One hallmark of modern politics is its asymmetry. Whereas the **political** was formerly imagined as practically synonymous with the public sphere, and with conflicts among institutions or nation-states, now it can just as frequently designate conflicts between an individual and an INSTITUTION, or between a non-national group and an ideology (e.g., between G8 protestors and police in various countries, or between the Taliban and the "WEST"). This shift has affected the linguistic fortunes of the words **politics** and **political**, as the adjectival and nominal forms have developed different connotations over the last several decades.

The adjective **political** has developed to have two relatively exclusive meanings. **Political** has supplanted the now largely archaic adjectival form **politic**. Both forms derive ultimately from Greek *polis*, initially a city-state and then later, by extension, the body politic. In medieval usage, the adjective *politik* connoted that which was prudent, sensible, and sagacious, a meaning that continued even as the usual form migrated to **political**. The **political** as a realm of public speech was imagined as elevated and righteous, often contrasting the perceived benefits of constitutional governments against the characteristics of despotism or tyranny. In mC18, for instance, David Hume described the "security and protection, which we enjoy in political society" (1740), and a character in Oliver Goldsmith's novel *The Vicar of Wakefield* (1766) shudders lest this rarified sphere be degraded by expanding suffrage. From C16 onward, another set of meanings came to be attached to the term: against its more elevated connotations, **political** came to mean "cunning" or "temporizing." Today, the **political sphere** may more readily be imagined as contaminating the COMMON man rather than the other way around. To call someone "**political**" is rarely a compliment. The adjectival form that once connoted good government, which was synonymous with "judicious" and "insightful," now activates an altogether different set of connotations: "calculating" and, perhaps more of a piece with our political moment, "partisan." The crux of this semantic fall from prudence to mere expediency seems to lie in a correlative historical shift: **politics**, once viewed as a space of quasi-transcendental stability, is now viewed as an arena of profound contingency.

The adjectival form **political** has become weaponized in recent years, with more pervasive use of terms such as **political animal** and **political agenda**, together with the advent of **political correctness** and the PAC, the **political action committee** that has taken over American politics in the wake of the 2010 Citizens United decision. (What does it mean that "**political action**," rather than the government or an identifiable **political party**, is the primary engine of US politics now?) In the US, the noun **politics** seems to have been superseded in current usage by what we might call the "political plus noun" formula.

The metastasis of the "political plus" formulation reflects the shifting epistemological grounds on which political theory has traditionally taken its ETHICAL stand. While it is beyond the scope of this entry to summarize the main schools of C20 political thought, some brief remarks may help to clarify the linguistic situation. Long gone is the idea of the **political** as the Aristotelian idea of the inclination toward the *bonum apprehensum*, that thing that is good in itself, a teleological ethics effectively eviscerated by Thomas Hobbes and the ENLIGHTENMENT. The semantic shift of **political** might be viewed in light of Hannah Arendt's interpretation of the political *longue durée*, in which the past, with its defining public sphere of active citizenship—politics as the realm of prudent discourse—was eclipsed by a modernity that had begun to look inward rather than outward, intent on the private pursuit of happiness and WEALTH. Within this paradigm, increasing inwardness results in a fracturing of political realities. A nostalgic follower of Arendt would ask: where has all the substantive political engagement gone?—yet the definitions of PUBLIC and PRIVATE assumed by Arendt seem insufficient to describe the recent multiplication of **political**. In particular it does not engage with one of feminism's most insistent slogans: "the personal is political."

What has happened is less that politics has migrated from the public to the private spheres and more that the **political** can take place in many different arenas, with many different types of agents participating simultaneously. We have moved from the sphere of **politics** to **the political** because the language needs to describe the contingency of shifting assemblages of political actors that do not fall completely or easily within a particular domain of discourse. Those actors may include institutions (the European Union), individuals (a chancellor), non-governmental collectives (WikiLeaks, the IRA), or even non-human actors (global warming). In such a world, the **political**, with its ability to follow the dust of migrating geo-political animals, may seem a nimbler alternative to a more static, public sphere-identified **politics**.

See INSTITUTION, PRIVATE, PUBLIC

POPULAR

Popular was originally a legal and political term, from *popularis*, L—belonging to the people. An **action popular**, from C15, was a legal suit which was open to anyone to begin. **Popular estate** and **popular government**, from C16, referred to a POLITICAL system constituted or carried on by the whole people, but there was also the sense (cf. COMMON) of "low" or "base." The transition to the predominant modern meaning of "widely favored" or "well-liked" is interesting in that it contains a strong element of setting out to gain favor, with a sense of calculation that has not quite disappeared but that is evident in a reinforced phrase like **deliberately popular**. Most of the men who have left records of the use of the word saw the matter from this point of view, downwards. There were neutral uses, such as North's "more popular, and desirous of the common peoples good will and favour" (1580) (where **popular** was still a term of policy rather than of condition), and evidently derogatory uses, such as Bacon's "a Noble-man of an ancient Family, but unquiet and popular" (1622). **Popularity** was defined in 1697, by Collier, as "a courting the favour of the people by undue practices." This use was probably reinforced by unfavorable applications: a neutral reference to "popular . . . theams" (1573) is less characteristic than "popular error" (1616) and "popular sickenesse" (1603) or "popular disease" (C17–C19), in which an unwelcome thing was merely widespread. A primary sense of "widely favored" was clear by 1C18; the sense of "well-liked" is probably C19. A 1C19 American magazine observed: "they have come . . . to take popular quite gravely and sincerely as a synonym for good." The shift in perspective is then evident. **Popular** was being seen from the point of view of the people rather than from those seeking favor or power from them. Yet the earlier sense has not died. **Popular culture** was not identified by *the people* but by others, and it still carries two older senses: inferior kinds of work (cf. **popular literature, popular press** as distinguished from *quality press*); and work deliberately setting out to win favor (**popular journalism** as distinguished from *democratic journalism*, or **popular entertainment**); as well as the more modern sense of well-liked by many people, with which of course, in many cases, the earlier senses overlap. The sense of **popular culture** as the culture actually made by people for themselves is different from all these. It relates, evidently, to Herder's sense of *Kultur des Volkes*, 1C18, but what came through in English as *folk-culture* (cf. *folk*) is distinguishable from recent senses of **popular culture** as contemporary as well as historical. The range of senses can be seen again in **popularize**, which until C19 was a political term, in the old sense, and then took on its special meaning of presenting knowledge in generally accessible ways. Its C19 uses were mainly favorable, and in C20 the favorable sense is still available, but there is also a strong sense of "simplification," which in some circles is predominant.

Populism, in political discussion, embodies all these variations. In the US the Populists (People's Party), from 1892, were in a *radical* alliance with *labor* organizations, though the relations between **populism** and *socialism* were complex. The sense of representing **popular** interests and values has survived, but is often overridden by either (a) right-wing criticism of this, as in *demagogy*, which has moved from "leading the people" to "crude and simplifying agitation," or (b) left-wing criticism of rightist and fascist movements which exploit "**popular** prejudices," or of leftist movements which subordinate socialist ideas to **popular** (**populist**) assumptions and habits.

In mC20 **popular song** and **popular art** were characteristically shortened to **pop**, and the familiar range of senses, from unfavorable to favorable, gathered again around this. The shortening gave the word a lively informality but opened it, more easily, to a sense of the trivial. It is hard to say whether older senses of **pop** have become fused with this use: the common sense of a sudden lively movement, in many familiar and generally pleasing contexts, is certainly appropriate.

Recent Developments

While **popular**'s frequency remained level over the last half-century, both **popular culture** and **populism** have risen dramatically in the last twenty years. **Popular culture** in the early history of the word **popular** would have been for many an oxymoron, but it has shed almost all its former pejorative force. Most current uses of the phrase are either neutrally descriptive or warmly approving. The opposition between *folk culture* and **popular culture** (*folk* referring to traditional and pre-industrial forms, **popular** referring to forms dominated by commerce and new-fangled technologies) has all but disappeared. Not only did *folk* appropriate the modern technology of rock music (most strikingly, Bob Dylan). Even more importantly, the technological means of production (electric guitars, amplifiers, cameras, editing suites, etc.) have become easily affordable: since the early 1960s almost any group of young people could form their own rock 'n' roll band, and in the past decade consumers easily become producers, equipping their own film studio from their telephone and laptop and setting up their own television station on YouTube. So the attempt to oppose *traditional* and MODERN forms of entertainment has lost much of its pertinence. The questions of VALUE that animated that earlier debate still challenge thought. There is a deep ambiguity written into **popular**. This opposes the sense of **popular** as something applied *to* the people against the sense of something approved *by* the people. Between *apply* and *approve* is the shift between conceiving the people as passive object or active subject. The distinction between authentic folk art and meretricious commercial culture has undoubtedly lost its relevance. However, there remains an important distinction between entertainment that is produced predominantly for money and entertainment in which the producers identify with the audience.

If **popular culture** has mostly shed the pejorative meanings that historically have attached to words deriving from the Latin word for people, **populism** continues to be mainly a negative term. While terms like CONSERVATIVE, SOCIALIST, and LIBERAL are often used as terms of self-ascription, **populist** is almost entirely used to describe opponents and has curiously little specific content. Politicians as different as Venezuela's radical socialist Hugo Chávez and Turkey's religious conservative Recep Tayyip Erdoğan have been labelled **populists**. The ultra-conservative Tea

Party is called **populist**, as is the leftist Occupy Wall Street. The fluidity of meanings around **populist** can explain why Barack Obama wants to deny Donald Trump the name of **populist**; for Obama, a **populist** must represent the people. One may, however, be forgiven for thinking that Obama has missed the point of **populism**: the **populist** always claims to represent the people *against* a system that has failed them and its elites, who have robbed them. Ordinary democratic politicians seek power to represent their electorate within the system; **populism** promises to drain the swamp. For opponents of **populist** politics, it is politics applied to a gullible and unthinking people, who have no role except to be fooled. This usage continues the semantic tradition of the people as mob: fickle, stupid, and dangerous. It is worth noting a new role for the media in contemporary **populism**. A more definite meaning is discernible in the ever more frequent collocation **economic populism**, which simply designates an economic policy that favors the majority of the population. This renders an already confusing word more confusing because this is the use of **populism** to which Barack Obama is appealing.

Populism is often discussed alongside NATIONALISM, and in very recent discourse, both are discussed alongside "xenophobia" and "racism." One unique feature of English in the US, Great Britain, Canada, and Australia is discussion of **populism** alongside "conservatism" and "conservatives"; that discourse of **populism** and conservatism is largely absent from English in the rest of the world.

See ART, COMMON, CULTURE, DEMOCRACY, NATIONALIST, POLITICAL, SOCIALIST

PRIVATE

Private is still a complex word but its extraordinary historical revaluation is for the most part long completed. It came into English from fw *privatus*, L—withdrawn from public life, from rw *privare*, L—to bereave or deprive (English *deprive* has kept the strongest early sense). It was applied to withdrawn religious orders, where the action was voluntary (C14) and from C15 to persons not holding public or official position or rank, as still in **private soldier** and **private member** (in Parliament). It acquired the sense of secret and concealed both in politics and in the sexual sense of **private parts**. It acquired also (and this was one of the crucial moments of transition) a conventional opposition to PUBLIC, as in **private house**, **private education**, **private theatre**, **private view**, **private hotel**, **private club**, **private property**. In virtually all these uses the primary sense was one of *privilege*; the limited ACCESS or participation was seen not as deprivation but as advantage (cf. *exclusive*). This favorable sense developed mainly from C16 and was still being rapidly extended in C19, even while **privation** retained its old sense of being deprived and **privateer** its sense (from the original **private man of war**) of seizing the property of others. PRIVILEGE meanwhile went with **private**; originally, in *privilegium*, L—a law or ruling in favor of or against an individual, it became a special advantage or benefit.

But this general movement in **private** (the association with PRIVILEGE) has to be set alongside an even more important movement, in which "withdrawal" and "seclusion" came to be replaced, as senses, by "independence" and "intimacy." It is very difficult to date this. There is a positive use in Ridley (1549): "the privits of my hart and conscience." There was a common sense of privileged intimacy with some powerful or important person, and this allowed overlap with a developed uncalculating sense, as in **private friends**. In C17 and especially C18, seclusion in the sense of a quiet life was valued as **privacy**, and this developed beyond the sense of solitude to the senses of decent and dignified withdrawal and of the **privacy of my family and friends**, and beyond these to the generalized values of **private life**. This development was deeply connected with corresponding changes in the senses of *individual* and FAMILY.

Private life still has its old sense, in special distinction from *public life* ("what he is in private life"), but it is the steady association of **private** with *personal*, as strongly favorable terms, that now seems predominant. In certain contexts the word can still be unfavorable—**private profit**, **private advantage**—but the association with personal independence is strong enough to permit the extraordinary description of large joint-stock corporations as **private enterprise** (where the chosen distinction is not from PUBLIC but from STATE). **Private**, that is, in its positive senses, is a record of the legitimation of a bourgeois view of LIFE: the ultimate generalized privilege, however abstract in practice, of seclusion and protection from others (*the public*); of lack of accountability to "them"; and of related gains in closeness and comfort of these general kinds. As such, and especially in the senses of the rights of the *individual* (to his **private life** or, from a quite different tradition, to his *civil liberties*) and of the valued intimacy of *family* and friends, it has been widely adopted outside the strict bourgeois viewpoint. This is the real reason for its current complexity.

RECENT DEVELOPMENTS

Williams's statement that **private life** is increasingly to be equated with the *personal* rather than understood in opposition to the PUBLIC has been validated by a number of developments since he wrote. First, social media has allowed individuals to make public many details of what they would still see as their **private lives**, but now might be better understood as their personal lives, to an extent inconceivable fifty years ago. Second, **privacy** need no longer involve seclusion. Important legal decisions have interpreted the **right to a private life**, under the European Convention on Human Rights, to mean that individuals may maintain their **privacy** even in public spaces. This holds even for public figures if they are acting in their **private capacity**. For example, Princess Caroline of Monaco was held to have a **right to privacy** and hence to protection from press intrusion even when sunbathing on a very public beach (*von Hannover v Germany*, 2004). Conversely, since Williams wrote, new limits to individual **privacy**, both legal and pragmatic, have also evolved, in the latter case largely because of new technologies. Legally, the courts have ruled that a right to a **private life** must cede to other rights such as freedom of expression, if it is in the public interest; therefore a newspaper could invoke public interest to expose the behavior of a role model, naming an athlete who was having an affair. Pragmatically, it has become nearly impossible to prevent the dissemination of information courts have deemed **private**. In one recent example, the anonymity of a celebrity involved in an extramarital threesome continues to be legally protected in the UK even though he has been widely identified on social media.

Digital technologies have also facilitated the exploitation by **private individuals** of **private assets** for commercial gain. The *sharing economy*, not yet in the *OED*, is defined as "assets or services . . . shared between private individuals, either free or for a fee, typically by means of the Internet." As exemplified by companies such as ride-sharing services Uber and Lyft or the "online marketplace and hospitality service" Airbnb, this new practice means welcoming strangers into your **private** dwelling or vehicle. The company controls the app that makes possible the marketplace in which "peer to peer" transactions take place. In this model of **private** ENTERPRISE the entrepreneur provides the invisible hand. The claim of peer **privacy** upsets long-established models, imposed by the state, of public regulation for taxis and hotels. Even more trouble for the relations between the state and its citizens arises from the claim made on behalf of "privacy as a defense against government abuse," contesting what "the surveillance state" claims as necessary for SECURITY ("Privacy in the Age of Surveillance," 2014). This issue became inescapable after the revelations made by Edward Snowden in 2013 concerning data-gathering by the National Security Agency of the US, with the cooperation of other governments and of telecommunication companies. **Privacy** here does not contrast to *publicity*, since the state's gathering and hoarding of **private data** were conducted with great secrecy and were intended to remain unknown. The *OED* in its current 2007 entry does not recognize **private** as contrasted to the STATE, rather than the PUBLIC.

See ACCESS, COMMON, FAMILY, PRIVILEGE, PROPERTY, PUBLIC, SECURITY, STATE

PRIVILEGE

Increasingly within social, political, and economic discourses, **privilege** is used to interrogate the ways in which structural and systemic inequality operate. This newer usage does not displace the word's traditional positive meanings that allude to a group's or individual's RIGHTS, honors, and advantages. Presently, **privilege** communicates how economic and class politics, complicated by intersections of various IDENTITIES, especially RACE, GENDER, CLASS, SEXUALITY, can precipitate forms of social exclusion and limitations.

The noun **privilege** derives from the classical Latin *privilegium*, and the French *privilege* and enters into English around C12. In Latin, the noun *privilegium* refers to a "bill or law . . . against or . . . in favour of an individual, special right, privilege, prerogative, claim having special rights, privileged claim. . . ." In this early usage, the special right or favor alluded to was granted through Ecclesiastical Law by a Papal ordinance, as used by John Wycliffe, "Dignities and *pryvelegies* þat ben now grauntid bi þe pope" (1425). This reference to ecclesiastical law can be compared to other uses such as the C12 Anglo-Norman *privilegie, privelege, privilie*, used to mean "advantage granted to or enjoyed by an individual," for instance in the quote attributed to William Bonde, "To suche other, as he hathe graunted suche speciall priuilege" (1526).

In *Keywords*, Raymond Williams included an entry for *under*privileged but not **privilege**. In the entry, Williams defines **underprivileged** by contrasting it with the *OED* sense of the mass noun: "the fact or state of being privileged," which ties economic status to social rank. That fact of such **privilege** inflects an elitism that Samuel Richardson censures when he comments on "A . . . man, who wants to assume airs of privilege, and thinks he has the right to be impertinent" (1753).

Williams notes that **underprivileged** "is sometimes used . . . as a euphemism for *poor* or *oppressed*" and that such usage makes **underprivileged** "a kind of special case, to indicate those falling below an assumed normal level of social existence." Thus, this use of **underprivileged** assumes that **privilege** is the norm, and EQUALITY would mean securing **privilege** for all. This is significantly different from the *OED*'s senses of **privilege**, which suggest that **privilege** is anything but normal, but is rather special, advantageous, or exclusive. Senses of **privilege** used in recent times elaborate the word's evolution within a discourse of social and economic discrimination. For instance, George Orwell champions the virtues of a classless society as one that exists with "no privilege and no bootlicking," for him its most attractive feature.

A further sense marks the path toward its current use as a term of critique: "a special advantage, benefit, or favour (bestowed by God, providence, chance, etc.)." This can be seen in examples such as Thomas Sherlock's "To be the Children of God is the greatest privilege under the Gospel" (1754), and John Grange's "What make you then of beautie by this (quoth she?) Plato defined it lady (quoth he) to be a priuiledge of nature" (1577). This sense distinguishes between Williams's understanding of **privilege** vis-à-vis **underprivileged** and broadens the usage of the word to encompass other markers of a hierarchy within a social structure that may be unrelated to CLASS.

Predating Williams's *Keywords*, in 1975 post–civil rights America, public intellectual and activist Theodore W. Allen, who was also invested in working-class politics, includes race, or what he terms "white skin privilege" in his analysis of class and economic disparity—or for him what marks differences between the **privileged** and **underprivileged** in the sense that Williams uses it. In other words, Allen's work focuses on the ways in which structures of inequality identified in class and economic terms are actually predicated on racial discrimination that limits financial access for non-whites. Allen published a pamphlet titled *Class Struggle and the Origin of Racial Slavery: The Invention of the White Race*, where he argues that the American class struggle is inevitably tied up in the legacy of racial slavery. Allen contends that "[t]he 'white race' social control formation, racial slavery, the system of white supremacy, and white racial privileges were ruinous to the class interests of working people. . . ." According to Allen, white skin is leveraged as a form of **privilege** "bestowed by providence, chance, etc.," which was used divisively to create a rift among different races of people even while they belong to the same social class. Unlike Williams, Allen's understanding of **privilege** does not seem to posit **underprivileged** as the opposite of **privilege** in working-class terms; instead, it is a complete *lack* of **privilege** that separates working-class blacks from working-class whites, and thus race is seen as the marker of **privilege**.

Like Allen and Williams, other C20 social critics such as W. E. B. Du Bois, Peggy McIntosh, and Kimberlé Crenshaw have sought to account for certain unearned advantages afforded specific social groups. Du Bois's landmark work *The Souls of Black Folk* (1903) notes the ways in which being on the wrong side of the "color line" subjects the American Negro to "having the doors of Opportunity closed roughly on his face" (Chapter 1). White Americans are spared "psychological wage" of that subject position, but in addition, or perhaps by virtue of that fact, they are able to leverage opportunity and through their **racial privilege** become **privileged**. Peggy McIntosh further expands the sense of special advantage to include male **gender privilege** wherein male gendered bodies access social mobility and visibility in ways that female gendered bodies cannot. Kimberlé Crenshaw further complicates this notion of "special advantage, benefit, or favour" by suggesting matrices of **privilege,** or intersected identities, whereby, for example, one group or class of people may enjoy certain group **privileges,** but still be subordinated to other groups **privileged** in more significant ways. Nowadays in potentially fraught social encounters, the reminder to **"check (y)our privilege"** when engaging with others encourages recognition of our individual contexts of **privilege.**

Some objections to the uses of the word in sociopolitical contexts claim that **privilege** is not bestowed by chance of birth; it is earned. However, as a critique, **privilege** stresses existing structural impediments that deny various forms of ACCESS to particular groups. Whatever benefits accrue to **privileged** groups remain unattainable within prevailing unequal social, political, and economic structures. **Privilege** has become contested precisely because of the discrepancy between discerning how **privilege** may be understood as an unearned, unfair advantage within social, economic, and political contexts and the ubiquity of types of **privilege,** earned or bestowed.

See ACCESS, CLASS, EQUALITY, GENDER, RACE, RIGHTS, SEXUALITY

PROPERTY

Property is a central concept in social relations, not only in CAPITALISM. What makes the word **property** a keyword, as well as the notion of **property** a difficult concept, is that its technical senses in fields including law and social theory (as well as, now less influentially, in logic) interact with and complicate the word's more general senses. Even in the broad meaning of ownership, **property** denotes a fundamental social relation or degree of socially approved control: between human beings and land (**"real" property**); with tangible belongings (chattels); and increasingly with intangibles, including financial investments and ideas (**intellectual property**). But use of the term is not always attitudinally neutral. **Property** is sometimes used descriptively, to categorize whatever is owned; sometimes approvingly, to naturalize the social relations that underpin capitalism; and sometimes pejoratively, for instance when deployed in wider criticism of capitalism (e.g., Pierre-Joseph Proudhon's "Property is theft!" 1840). In serving such referentially broad and attitudinally contrasting functions, **property** acts as a lightning rod in efforts to delineate, test, and contest boundaries of ownership and commodification.

    Property comes into English in lC14 from Anglo-Norman *properté* and Middle French *propreté*, with their own antecedents in Latin *proprius* and *proprietas*. Some of the polysemy now associated with **property** existed in the Latin antecedents. Adjectival *proprius* meant "particular" or "peculiar," and conveyed distinctiveness of the self, for instance in contrast with *alienus*, meaning "other" or "foreign" (cf. English *alienation*), and with *communis*, "common" or "shared." The noun *proprietas* conveyed an analogous sense of "characteristic," and was often combined with *rerum* (of things). But *proprietas* is also cited with an overt "ownership" sense, and was also commonly used to convey aptness or suitability, reflected in English *proper* and *propriety*, as well as in some senses of **property** itself.

    In English, **property** is attested from lC14 in four of its main later senses outlined in the *OED*:

(1) As an attribute, characteristic, or quality; effectively an application to a part of something of an overall characteristic quality, hence character or nature.

(2) As the quality of being proper or appropriate; fitness or suitability (e.g., in relation to dress and manners, or use of words). This sense, now obsolete (with no recorded use after 1740), allows a connection between the favorable sense of aptness or suitability and the neutral sense of "attribute."

(3) As an appurtenance or adjunct; something belonging to a thing. While now obsolete in the straightforward "adjunct" meaning, this sense allows a shift of emphasis for **property** in the direction of the word's later dominant meaning: that of possession and ownership. Especially when used as a mass noun, **property** in this sense conveys "that which one owns"; possessions collectively; a person's goods or wealth. Shifts of emphasis and attitude in this sense continue between lC14 and C18, but crucially during C17 (when a traditional system of property rights was gradually displaced by more

comprehensive market relations that allowed such rights to be seen as almost unlimited, exclusive possession).

(4) As the abstract enjoyment of RIGHTS: the general fact or basis of possessing something or being owned. This sense is found especially but not only in legal discourse, and indicates title to the use or disposal of something: proprietorship. **Property** in this context is a general relation between people, rather than between people and things: a right held by one person to exclude someone else from something, or, in the case of common property, an individual's right not to be excluded from something. In political discussion, the scope of this meaning poses a major challenge in efforts to define, justify, or challenge the social institution of **property**, explored for example in Locke (who set out a case for an individual right of unlimited APPROPRIATION, influencing the French and American revolutions), in critiques mounted by Rousseau, Proudhon, Marx, and others, and fully into contemporary social theory.

Shifts of meaning and emphasis in the interactions among the four senses described in the preceding contribute to a major historical realignment of economic and social relations. The relevant shifts in meaning are found not only in **property** itself, but in other words in the same semantic field, including for instance MARKET and *estate*. A significant narrowing of one meaning of **property** itself (attested from eC18) is toward the sense of a piece of land under one ownership: a landed "estate," then later any residential or other building (with or without associated land) or separately owned part of a building (such as an apartment). The notion of a **property owning democracy** became a key element in postwar Conservative ideology, particularly in Margaret Thatcher's policy to sell publicly owned housing to existing tenants. Indeed, the phrase became a shorthand for the disposal of other public assets in the form of shares, along with encouragement to the electorate to view themselves less as a public enjoying relational rights and obligations in a society (even in a "commons") and increasingly as customers and CONSUMERS.

Many compounds involving **property** date from middle years of C19, and relate to changing attitudes associated with this larger social trend: **property class; property mark; property market; property owner;** and **property qualification,** important historically in struggles over eligibility to vote. **Property speculator** dates from roughly the same period, bringing later **property developer.**

In contemporary use, **property** is often indeterminate or ambiguous between its general meaning and technical senses that the word has acquired in legal and political discourse. Many speakers consider **property** as a matter of consumable things. However, in law and social theory **property** is typically less concerned with things exclusively owned than with defined rights indicating an enforceable but specified claim to use of or benefit from something. Physical ownership or occupancy, in the popular view, can simply presume as already in place a completed system of property as a social institution. In theoretical discussion, by contrast, it is common for that view to be dismissed as merely a misunderstanding, rather than acknowledged as an alternative meaning, fueling powerful aspirations also prompted by the complex history.

Spread of the (individualistic) "exclusionary possession" sense can put pressure on the "simultaneous rights and obligations" (social) sense in varying contexts. Potential misunderstandings may, for instance, surround the scope of what **property** should be able to denote: land, objects, labor; in some societies and historical periods, also slaves, servants, and wives; a threshold triggering electoral franchise; and an indefinite range of intangibles (from copyright, trademark signs, and image rights through to claimed ownership in synthetic cell material and the human genome). Misunderstandings may also arise as regards the degree of ownership enjoyed (e.g., as presumed **private property**), by comparison with specified and limited entitlement. Struggles over these two dimensions of the meaning of **property** combine in fields as various as stem cell research, global markets in genetically modified seeds, media content, and software downloading, as well as in disputes over postwar reparation. Such troubles may become especially acute in countries such as China, where a transition is underway toward a system of private "ownership" embedded within a state command economy.

With the increased reach of BRANDS and branding, contemporary questions raised by **property** as possession also begin to link up with older meanings of **property** as attribute, character, and identity. In a convergence between the notion of CELEBRITY and a perception that people "are what they own," the literary and theatrical sense of **property**, applied to people as well as to inert **props** from the 1940s, opens up the possibility of not simply being a person *of* property but in an enlarged personal-branding market becoming oneself a property, even a **hot property**.

See APPROPRIATION, BRAND, CAPITALISM, CONSUMER, MARKET, PRIVATE, RIGHTS

PUBLIC

Public is a keyword both as adjective and noun in the rise and development of European nation-states, constantly veering in meaning between the population as constituting an organized political body and the population as participants in the cultural and ideological life of a COMMUNITY and its subdivisions. It is always in some kind of opposition to PRIVATE across a whole range of meanings, as the *OED* notes at the very beginning of its entry. Some of these complexities can be briefly indicated by a trivial example. Speakers of American English are often astonished that the phrase **public schools** in British English refers to fee-paying schools because in American English **public schools** refers to schools funded by the state. However, the sense in which **public** means funded by the state rather than *privately* funded is a relatively recent development. The **public** in British English **public schools** dates back to medieval times and distinguished schools that were open to all from *private* Church schools, which limited their intake to pupils intending to make a career in the Church.

Public is derived from one of the keywords of Roman political vocabulary. The Latin *Publicus* is defined by the *OED* as "of or belonging to the people as a whole, common to all, universal, of or affecting everyone in the state, communal, authorized, provided, or maintained by the state, available to or enjoyed by all members of a community." The word is derived from *populus*—the people—but influenced by the Latin word for adult men, *pūbes*. Thus *publicus* genders etymologically the social and political world. *Res publica*, literally "public things," names the Republic—the realm of the state itself. A key difficulty of the term hinges upon the limits of its referent: who exactly belongs to **the public** or even **the American** or **British public** is often unclear, and rarely made explicit. Its meanings track the growth of a bourgeois political sphere. Within that sphere it is challenged from lC18 on by *people,* a word that encapsulates a more active role for the general population in political life. Its recent developments that see it multiply into different **publics** is closely linked to the development of communications technology.

It is borrowed into French from Latin from C13 and into English in C14 and C15 from both French and Latin. The earliest uses of **public** show the sense "Open to general observation . . . ; existing, performed, or carried out without concealment," and this is still frequent in collocations like **public appearance** and **public apology**, as well as the expressions **make public** and **go public**. This sense gives rise to the slightly later meaning "in the public eye; prominent, well-known," as in **public figure**, and the more recent **public intellectual**. In this kind of use, **public** is very clearly the opposite of *private*, one of its most common collocates, in the sense "hidden, secret."

Another major sense in which **public** and *private* are antonymous, which is slightly later in English, is defined by *OED* as "Authorized by, serving, or representing, the community; carried out or made on behalf of the community by the government or State." This is intended in many collocations that tended to be more frequent in the past, such as **public meetings** or **public offices**, but in modern times it shades into the sense "Of, relating to, or designating the business, government, or service of a community or nation," often broadly synonymous with STATE or *governmental*, for example in **public spending** or **public sector**.

In many contexts it is difficult to make a clear distinction between the "state, governmental" sense and the sense "Of or relating to the people as a whole; that belongs to, affects, or concerns the community or the nation." There is relatively little ambiguity in expressions like **public good** (particularly frequent in C19) or **public space(s)**. On the other hand, **public money** (or earlier, **monies**) may be the property of the nation, but in practice it is managed by government; **public libraries** and other **public services** are intended to serve communities, but are state-funded and therefore subject to governmental legislation. Jeremy Bentham's gloss of acts "which may be termed public offences or offences against the state" (1780) shows exactly this complexity, but also highlights the similarly problematic nature of terms like *state* and *nation*. David Cameron in 2015 (repeating Margaret Thatcher in 1983) perhaps tries to downplay the same connection in asserting that "[t]here is no such thing as public money—there is only taxpayers' money."

The emergence in C16 of the meaning "the community or people" for the noun **public** raises a difficulty inherent in many of the adjectival uses: who exactly does **public** refer to, and where are the boundaries of the term? This is a particularly pertinent question in the use of the term with the definite article, i.e., **the public**, but also arises in modified uses like **American** or **British public**, or the still more specific **reading public**, **educated public**, or **viewing public**. In political or media discourse, there is rarely any interrogation of who is or is not included in the group referred to as **the public**, and statements about what "the public thinks" or **public opinion** are commonplace; these formulations imply that people are a homogenous mass rather than a collection of individuals with diverse views. Scientific and survey methods of capturing the **public opinion** proceed from the assumption that the aggregation of individual beliefs constitute public thoughts by conceiving of **the public** as an individualized mass.

The modified form **general public** is no less problematic a category in its lack of a clearly defined referent, but it suggests something more than simply "most people." While one semantic problem of **public** is that its reference is too inclusive, there is also almost always a hidden sense of exclusion. If **the public** thinks something and you do not, then you are effectively excluding yourself from the national community. This deeply buried meaning is most evident in an archaic medieval use where **public** referred to Christian Europe. Anyone outside the borders of Christendom could not be considered a member of the public.

In order to carry out the tasks of **public administration, public employees** or **public servants**, individuals "serving the public in a professional capacity" and "employed by local or central government" are utilized. Public administration may also include the maintenance of **public places** that are "open or available to all members of a community, or all who are legally or properly qualified" and are usually "provided by local and central government for the community and supported by rates or taxes." In this sense we might think of the **public streets, public parks,** and the **public library** that Williams utilized in developing *Keywords*. Finally, there is also **public assistance,** "financial or other" that is "provided to those in need out of public funds by the community or the State." Provided by various agents and with varying associations with PRIVILEGE, such assistance may include **public housing** and **public healthcare**. In each case, the notion of **public** is contrasted with *private* and primarily associated with the work of the government to provide for its people.

The administration of government comes to exist by the consent of the people in order to protect RIGHTS and promote **public good**. Individuals' pursuit of self-interest would include participation in **public life** as a **public person** seeking to influence **public affairs** through **public deliberation**. **Public** in these collocations is conceived of as an entity distinct from the state and the FAMILY. While some suggest this **public sphere** declined throughout the Industrial Revolution as technical discourses eclipsed public deliberation, it should be noted that women were never members of **the public** before C20.

Historically, the noun form **(the) public** is a mass noun, but in recent times it is also used with the indefinite article or in the plural as a count noun. Across a range of discourses (**public relations**, political science, and psychology) it is now common to talk about **publics**, groups of people who have some common characteristic or are concerned with a specific interest. The development of social media and **digital publics** in the last decade has intensified this pluralization of publics.

See COMMON, COMMUNITY, PRIVATE, STATE

QUEER

The adjective **queer** poses etymological problems. Its sense of "strange, odd, peculiar, eccentric" is given an initial *OED* date of 1513; thus John Bale in 1550 writes of chronicles that "contayne muche more truthe than their quere legendes." There is then another sense, recorded as obsolete, with a date of 1567: that of **queer** as "bad; contemptible, worthless; untrustworthy, disreputable." In this sense the word is used with reference especially to vagabonds and criminals, and eventually also applied to counterfeit coins and banknotes. This bad **queer** (in early use often occurring as *quire*) seems to have been a different word, of unknown origin, from the strange **queer**, itself of uncertain origin, with which it gradually became identified after the end of C17.

The merging of the more or less distinct words is subsequently important. Strange **queer** continues through into contemporary English, acquiring in the course of C18 an associated sense of feeling "out of sorts; unwell; faint, giddy." The *OED* quotes from a 1750 novel: "All on a sudden, my Wife complained she was sick, and both myself and Sir Thomas found ourselves very queer and qualmish." The major development is use of the term in the specific sense of, or relating to, homosexuals or homosexuality. The *OED* dates this from eC20, with an initial quotation from *The Los Angeles Times* in 1914 that characterizes a club as "composed of the 'queer' people," where "the 'queer' people have a good time"; followed by a 1915 quotation from Arnold Bennett describing "[a]n immense reunion of art students, painters, and queer people. Girls in fancy male costume, queer dancing, etc. . . ."

If context points to the specific, homosexual sense, the sense of "strange, odd, peculiar" is still present, both inasmuch as the equation of homosexuality and peculiarity is at stake and inasmuch as the appearance of the word **queer** may be taken one way or the other. The word appears a number of times in Radclyffe Hall's *The Well of Loneliness* (1928), for example, but its use in particular instances might be read one way or another, or, more significantly and importantly, both ways at once. Stephen, the central figure, is "a queer kid" who discovers in the course of the novel what her queerness involves: "the queer compositions" she shows her father are strange, as is "the queer vital strength" of the hand of a woman she holds, both uses proleptically indicative of the queerness being discovered. "He's in Paris; it's too queer" is merely *strange*, though the effect of the frequency of **queer** in the novel pulls it nevertheless toward queer **queer**. The *Los Angeles Times* fixes the homosexual reference by putting **queer** in inverted commas; Bennett leaves the one-way-or-the-other reading just possibly open to those of his readers who lack the familiarity of knowledge that would enable the particular homosexual sense. Today, of course, the general currency of homosexual **queer** makes the reception of that sense more or less inevitable and, indeed, can be at the expense of earlier ambiguities, overriding or insistently overlaying strange **queer**.

The *OED* has two entries for **queer** as a noun. The first is derived from the "bad" **queer**, and means "forged or counterfeit money." The second has two separate senses. The first shows uses with *the*, i.e., things that are "queer" in various senses, taken collectively. It is specified as rare, has a late initial date of 1826, and brings us back to strange, peculiar **queer**, with a quotation from Walter Scott: "His appearance bordered . . . upon what is vulgarly called the queer." The second is that of a homosexual, in the first instance a male homosexual. The initial date given is 1894, referring to the infamous letter sent by the Marquess of Queensberry to his son Lord Alfred Douglas in which he anathematizes "The Snob Queers."

In *OED* the derogatory force is noted with which the adjective and noun **queer** could be used in respect of homosexuals. The merging of strange and bad **queer** senses made available a term of abuse and offensive judgment. Though the history of its use from the start by homosexual people and communities themselves is complex, making it more than simply abusive, only recent decades have seen the reclaiming of **queer** as a positive and empowering term of identification and IDENTITY. The *OED* cites a 1992 piece from *The Nation* referring to an advertisement as "thoroughly offensive to queer readers," where what is offensive is not **queer** as an identification of a section of the readership but rather the advertisement itself.

At the same time, **queer** has been extended beyond reference to a particular homosexual identification. The term now calls into question both sexual identities and solid gender roles. The sense of **queer** as strange comes to the fore here, as the word refers to those who reject the terms of heteronormativity. Thus, the *OED* records the derivative **queerdom** as "the state or condition of being homosexual; homosexuals collectively," from 1961, but then has a quotation from 1994 that defines **queerdom** as "a polymorphously perverse, all-inclusive left-of-centre community." This later use relates to the development of **queer theory**, itself with an initial *OED* date of 1990: an approach to social and cultural study that challenges or deconstructs accepted notions of SEXUALITY and GENDER, goes against acceptance of heterosexuality as normative and the assumption of fixed terms of male and female. As a 2003 *OED* quotation from the *Times Literary Supplement* puts it, "The overriding priority for queer theory is to get rid of the idea that some kinds of people, and some forms of sex, are more natural than others."

Contemporary development of **queer** becomes in these circumstances a site of contention, raising questions as to whether the word can be effectively separated from the history of derogatory and derisive usages, as well as questions regarding the effects of its general extension into an academic all-inclusiveness at the expense of specific cultural-political use in relation to particular identified groups.

Queer as a verb is a late development, and carries a sense of "to make a fool of, ridicule; swindle, cheat" (1781), as well as "to put out of order; to spoil" (1818), hence **to queer a pitch** (1846), originally with reference to spoiling the business of a street vendor or performer. The *OED* gives no sense or quotation relating **queer** as verb to the homosexual senses of adjective and noun **queer**, although this is current—as, for example, in the title of a book of gay musicology: *Queering the Pitch* (1994).

See GENDER, IDENTITY, SEXUALITY, TRANS

RACE

Race is one of the most difficult words in the language. Its meanings and uses have made it unavoidably a keyword. **Race**, as a former chairman of Britain's Commission for Racial Equality put it, is one of "the most divisive and potent flashpoints" in Western societies; this even when **race** is largely regarded as devoid of any demonstrable non-ideological value. In a 1950 Statement on Race, UNESCO advised that the word should no longer be used of human groups. Other official bodies followed suit; the French Parliament declared that it did "not recognize the existence of any so claimed race" and began legislation to remove the word from the French Constitution. Getting rid of words and their consequences, however, is not easy. Scientifically there may be no such thing as **race** but that, as a character says in Toni Morrison's *God Save the Child* (2015), has "little to do with day-to-day experience."

Race with the *OED*'s meaning "group of people connected by common descent" entered English in C16 from Middle French *race*, linked to C14 Italian *razza*, meaning kind, species; in the same period, the word entered a number of other European languages—Spanish *raza* 1438, Portuguese *raça* 1473. The etymology is uncertain: it has been seen as derived from Latin *ratio*, but also from Latin *generatio*. Its range of senses in the mid-1550s as set out by *OED* share overall reference to matters of descent and origin of human beings: the people of a family stemming from a common ancestor, "Ofspring of eche race" (*a*1547); a tribe, nation, or people regarded as of common stock: "the Englishe race" (1572); a group of several tribes or peoples taken as forming a distinct set: "the race of the Tartares" (1612); the class of humans: "the humane race" (*c*1580). These separate senses are not easily distinguishable: what variously unites them are concerns with *lineage, blood, stock*; all these words used from C14 with reference to lines of descent. **Race** was used too of plants and animals, notably horses ("the race of horses and other beastes," 1561).

In mC18, Nathan Bailey's *Dictionarium Britannicum* (1730) has **race** as "Lineage, or Generation, proceeding from Father to Son; a Family." Twenty-five years later, Samuel Johnson's *Dictionary of the English Language* (1755), gives: "1. A family ascending; 2. Family descending; 3. A generation; a collective family; 4. A particular breed" (quoting *Paradise Lost*: God created humankind in order "a better race to bring"). Not recognized in the Bailey/Johnson entries is the insistent C17 sense of **race** with regard to peoples as distinct *kinds*. Colonial expansion, encounters with different peoples, and the establishment of the slave trade led to the concern to study and classify the races of humankind. If recognition of a *human* species was supported by the evidence of intraspecific reproduction (reproduction only between individuals of the same single species), it remained to account for the plurality of (supposed) human races: descended from a unique line of descent, the biblical Adam-and-Eve couple, or from separate lines, as physical features such as skin color were taken to suggest. In the terms introduced in C19, was this *monogeny* (one common pair of ancestors) or *polygeny* (several independent pairs of ancestors), and *how many* races were there? From C18 on, classifying **races** was a much debated issue. J. F. Blumenbach's highly influential work on the "natural variety of mankind," *De generis humani varietate nativa* (1776), identified four **races**, five in its second edition (1781). Such distinctions led to hierarchization (higher and lower races) or incommensurability (distinct, entirely separate races).

"Race is everything," declares a character in Benjamin Disraeli's *Tancred* (1847), warning against mixing blood. Of the numerous **race** compounds listed by *OED*— **race aversion, race blood, race character, race conflict**, etc.—almost all date from C19. The words *monogeny* and *polygeny* themselves appear in 1865 in the recently founded British *Anthropological Review*. From mC19, the proposed "science" of **race** was physical anthropology (1841), concerned with the development of human biological and physiological characteristics. Endeavors to substantiate **race** and **races** as "natural" were countered by accounts of it as socially constructed, challenging beliefs in *given* races and resulting **racism** (1903; subsequently superseding **racialism** 1902). The scientific development of genetics left "racism without races": no "natural" races, only social representations of certain aspects of GENETIC variation; *genetic ancestry* is not **biological race**. Moreover, genetics emphasizes variation *between individuals* rather than *between groups*, and studies not **races** but *populations*.

The history of **race** as an oppressive term of discrimination has also known its APPROPRIATION as—its reversal into—an assumed value of identity. African-American **race man** (1896) and **race woman** (1915) were and are positive terms for black men and women who supported BLACK causes and who, to quote Zora Neale Hurston, "kept the glory and honour of their people before them" (1942). The contemporary critic Henry Louis Gates, Jr. describes himself as a **race man**: "a person of letters who writes about African-American culture" (1991).

If **race** is discredited, **racial**, belonging to or characteristic of a group, is more readily employed. Entering the language in mC19, the word was tied to belief in **races**; notably a superior—white—**race**, to be preserved through **racial hygiene**. Subsequently it has come to be used in compounds suggesting rather the negative consequences of such beliefs—**racial prejudice, racial discrimination**, etc.—or the aim of their overcoming—**racial equality, racial harmony**, etc.; the word occurs mainly in contexts involving or relating to **racial minorities**. In these uses the idea of **race** is still present; **racial** contains **race** that is its implicit or explicit basis, with **racial profiling** (1989) an obvious example of the latter.

UNESCO's Statement on Race advised that *ethnic groups* should be preferred to **races**, and *ethnic* and *ethnicity* have since gained considerably in frequency of use. The word *ethnic* comes partly from Greek *ethnikos* derived from *ethnos*, nation, people, place of origin; partly from post-classical Latin *ethnicus*, pagan, heathen. It is with this meaning that *ethnic* is recorded in English from lC15; "halfe an Ethnicke, halfe a Christian," says one of Ben Jonson's characters of another (1631). This is the only meaning recorded by Samuel Johnson's *Dictionary* (1755): "Heathen; Pagan; not Jewish; not Christian." In the course of C19, this limited sense faded and *ethnic* came broadly to designate people of actual or perceived common descent, and then of shared national or cultural IDENTITY: their *ethnicity* (1920). The same period saw the appearance of *ethnology* (1787), concerned with the overall understanding of the development of human society and CULTURE, and *ethnography* (1831), the study of different peoples, societies, and cultures.

While *ethnic groups* may be identified in terms of nationality, the term most often refers to particular groups within a nation or crossing national boundaries, typically forming *ethnic minorities* (1919). Frequently *ethnic* appears in contexts of conflict: *OED*'s earliest example concerns "ethnic struggles" (1849); its second links *ethnic* to **race**: "old ethnic Hates that stirred long race-wars" (1870); ending in *ethnic cleansing*, recorded in 1991 with reference to events during the breakup of Yugoslavia. Such conflicts may be characterized as *multi-ethnic* (1941) rather than **multiracial** (1903), though the two terms are often used synonymously. *Ethnic* is proposed as distinct from **race**, yet common uses suggest their continuity. Ethnic identifications, that is, easily overlap with racial ones; indicatively, the second, 1989 edition of *OED* used **race** and **racial** in its definitions of *ethnic* ("having common racial . . . characteristics," "peculiar to a race," "a racial or other group") before removing them online in 2014. Anticipating UNESCO, biologist Julian Huxley and anthropologist Alfred Haddon had proposed in *We Europeans* (1935) "the noncommittal term *ethnic group*" precisely to end reference to human groups as **races**; *ethnic* has not proved altogether the noncommittal term they hoped.

If *ethnic* identifies groups and people in respect of cultural characteristics and factors such as religion, art, dress, music, food, this is often external "from outside"; its meaning equivalent to *non-Western*. *OED* quotes a US newspaper in 1965 defining *ethnic* as having "come to mean foreign, or un-American or plain quaint." Equally, *ethnic* is assumed "from within," an acknowledged *ethnicity* (1920), defined by aspects of shared history and culture.

Ethnic and *ethnicity*, however, are never just free of the **racism** of **race**. *Ethnicism* (1945), consciousness of or emphasis on ethnic identity, has been regarded as the cultural form of **racism**, essentializing groups and thereby providing another framework for racial attitudes. This is *ethnic absolutism*, a term proposed by the British cultural critic Paul Gilroy in 1993 to refer to versions of ethnic and national difference that serve as some fixed idea of the identity of a culture. Such absolutism, however, is effected not only from outside to fix some "other" group as *ethnic*, but from inside, claims made on some essentialist version of an ethnicity, an *ethnic identity*.

The history of **race** is complex. Ideas of **race** have been discredited and the word accordingly made problematic, to be used only with caution. At the same time, **race** and **racial** remain current in everyday language use, alongside *ethnic* and its cognate word forms, often distinct from **race** and **racial** but often close nevertheless.

See BLACK, CULTURE, DIVERSITY, GENETIC, IDENTITY

REALISM

Realism is a difficult word, not only because of the intricacy of the disputes in art and philosophy to which its predominant uses refer, but also because the two words on which it seems to depend, **real** and **reality**, have a very complicated linguistic history. The earliest **Realists**, in English, were at a great distance from anything now indicated by the term, for the philosophical school known as **Realist** was primarily opposed by the *Nominalists*, who themselves might in post-mC19 terms be classed as **realists** of an extreme kind. The old doctrine of **Realism** was an assertion of the absolute and objective existence of universals, in the Platonic sense. These universal Forms or Ideas were held either to exist independently of the objects in which they were perceived, or to exist in such objects as their constituting properties. Redness, for the nominalists, was merely a (confusing) name for a number of red things; for the conceptualists it became a generalizing mental idea; for the **Realists** it was an absolute and objective Form independent of red objects or essentially constituting such objects. It is very striking, and very confusing, that this **Realist** doctrine is what we would now call extreme *idealism*.

That use may be said to have faded. From eC19 quite different senses of **realist**, and the new word **realism** in a more modern sense, can be said to have overlain and suppressed it. But this is not wholly true. Our common distinction between *appearance* and **reality** goes back, fundamentally, to the early use—"the reality underlying appearances"—and this has significantly affected many arguments about **realism**. **Real**, from the beginning, has had this shifting double sense. It is from fw *real*, oF, *realis*, 1L, from rw *res*, L—thing. Its earliest English uses, from C15, were in matters of law and property, to denote something actually existing. There was a connected and persisting later use for immovable PROPERTY, as still in **real estate**. The sense of something actually existing was transferred to general use, from 1C16, in an implicit or explicit contrast with something *imaginary*: "Is't reall that I see?" (*All's Well That Ends Well*, V, iii); "not Imaginary, but Reall" (Hobbes, *Leviathan*, III, xxxiv). But at the same time there was an important sense of **real** as contrasted not with *imaginary* but with *apparent*: not only in theological arguments about the "real presence" of Christ in the materials of communion, but also in wider arguments about the true or fundamental quality of some thing or situation—the **real** thing, the **reality** of something. This use is still very common, if often not noticed as such, in phrases like "refusing to face the real facts of his situation" or "refusing to face reality." Since the use to indicate something tangible, palpable, or factual was also strongly continued, it can be seen that there is almost endless play in the word. A **Realist** in the pre-C18 sense of the word took **real** in the general sense of an underlying TRUTH or quality; in the post-eC19 sense in the (often opposed) sense of *concrete* (as from C14 opposed to abstract) existence.

Realism was a new word in C19. It was used in French from the 1830s and in English from the 1850s. It developed four distinguishable meanings: (i) as a term to describe, historically, the doctrines of Realists as opposed to those of Nominalists; (ii) as a term to describe new doctrines of the physical world as independent of mind or spirit, in this sense sometimes interchangeable with *naturalism* or *materialism*; (iii) as a description of facing up to things as they **really** are, and not as we imagine or would like them to be—"let us replace sentimentalism by realism, and dare to uncover those simple and terrible laws which, be they seen or unseen, pervade and govern" (Emerson, 1860); (iv) as a term to describe a method or an attitude in art and literature—at first an exceptional accuracy of representation, later a commitment to describing **real** events and showing things as they actually exist.

It is not surprising that there should have been so fierce and often so confused a controversy, especially over sense (iv). Senses (i) and (ii) can now normally be disregarded: (i) because it is now an isolated and specific historical reference, (ii) because for all practical purposes this sense has been taken over by *materialism*. Sense (iii) is still very important in everyday use. In the Emerson example the familiar play of **real** is evident: the laws may be seen or unseen. But the use has come through as "facing facts," as in the characteristic new mC19 adjective **realistic**: "could not be reconciled to life by any plain view of things, by any realistic calculations" (Seeley, 1869). What matters is that in this sense most people hold that their own views of any matter are **realistic**. But there is an evident range of application, from the older sense of being based on a true understanding of a situation, to a now common sense which shares the implicit impatience of one sense of *practical*. "Let's be realistic" probably more often means "let us accept the limits of this situation" (*limits* meaning *hard facts*, often of power or money in their existing and established forms) than "let us look at the whole truth of this situation" (which can allow that an existing **reality** is changeable or is changing). Thus though **realistic** (cf. *reasonable*) is an immensely popular word among businessmen and politicians, it has acquired some consequent tone of limited calculation, and is then often contrasted, from both points of view, with *idealistic*.

Sense (iv) remains the most difficult. It does not end but only begins a controversy in art and literature when it is said that the purpose is "to show things as they really are." There is a surviving sense of the old *idealism*, as in Shelley's lines on the Poet in *Prometheus Unbound*:

He will watch from dawn to gloom
The lake-reflected sun illume
The yellow bees in the ivy bloom,
Nor heed nor see, what things they be;
But from these create he can
Forms more real than living man,
Nurslings of immortality.

Here the stress must fall not only on **real** but on *forms*: a poetic creation which is indifferent and certainly not tied to the objects of observation, but which **realizes** immortal essences or entities. (This use of **realize** began in C17, and was common from mC18: "an Act of the Imagination, that realizes the Event however fictitious, or approximates it however remote" (Johnson, *Rambler*, 60; 1750). The term is popular in modern criticism, to refer to the *means* and *effect* of bringing something vividly to life.) But this is the kind of use which was eventually distinguished from **realism** and which indeed allowed a contrast between **realism** and other words in this complex, as in Swinburne's contrast of "prosaic realism" and "poetic reality" (1880). Again and again, from positions of this kind, **realism** has been accused of evading the **real**.

The difficulty is most acute when we see that **realism** in art and literature is both a method and a general attitude. As the latter it is distinguished from *romanticism* or from *Imaginary* or *mythical* subjects, things not of **the real world**. The use to describe a method is often a term of praise—the characters, objects, actions, situations are **realistically** described; that is, they are lifelike in description or appearance; they show **realism**. It is often also a term of blame or limitation, in these senses: (a) that what is described or represented is seen only superficially, in terms of its outward *appearance* rather than its inner **reality**; (b) in a more modern form of the same objection, that there are many **real** forces—from inner feelings to underlying social and historical movements—which are either not accessible to ordinary observation or which are imperfectly or not at all represented in how things appear, so that a **realism** "of the surface" can quite miss important **realities**; (c) in a quite different objection, that the MEDIUM in which this REPRESENTATION occurs, whether language or stone or paint or film, is radically different from the objects *represented* in it, so that the effect of "lifelike representation," "the reproduction of reality," is at best a particular artistic convention, at worst a falsification making us take the forms of REPRESENTATION as *real*.

Objections (a) and (b) have been countered by a specialized sense of **realism**, which has used *naturalism* as the form to which these objections can properly be made, but then preserves **realism**—sometimes in even more specialized forms such as **psychological realism** or **socialist realism**—to include or to emphasize hidden or underlying forces or movements, which simple "naturalistic" observation could not pick up but which it is the whole purpose of **realism** to discover and express. This depends on the old play in the senses of **real**, but it has been important not so much in an idealist sense, which would now normally avoid **realism** as a term, as in senses deriving from dynamic psychology or from *dialectical* as opposed to *mechanical materialism*. **Reality** is here seen not as static *appearance* but as the movement of psychological or social or physical forces; **realism** is then a conscious commitment to understanding and describing these. It then may or may not include **realistic** description or *representation* of particular features.

Objection (c) is directed primarily at **realistic** in the sense of *lifelike*. **Realist** art or literature is seen as simply one convention among others, a set of formal REPRESENTATIONS, in a particular MEDIUM to which we have become accustomed. The object is not **really** lifelike but by convention and repetition has been made to appear so. This can be seen as relatively harmless or as extremely harmful. To see it as harmful depends on a sense that (as in *mechanical materialism*) a pseudo-objective *version* of reality (a version that will be found to depend, finally, on a particular phase of history or on a particular set of relationships between men and between men and things) is passed off as **reality**, although in this instance at least (and perhaps more generally) what is there is what has been made, by the specific practices of writing and painting and film-making. To see it as **reality** or as the **faithful copying of reality** is to exclude this active element and in extreme cases to pass off a *fiction* or a *convention* as **the real world**.

This is a powerful argument against many of the claims of **realism** as accurate *representation*, but it is an accident of the way that the argument has gone, in relation to this one sense of **realism**, that it can be taken either way in relation to **realism** as a whole movement. Thus it could be made compatible with the sense of **realism** that was distinguished from *naturalism*, and especially with that sense of a conscious commitment to understanding and describing real forces (a commitment that at its best includes understanding the processes of consciousness and composition that are involved in any such attempt). More often, however, the argument has been linked, in particular intellectual formations, with the idealist modes of *formalism* and of *structuralism*, where the strength of attention to the detailed practice of composition, and especially to the basic forms and structures within which composition occurs, goes along with or can be used to justify an indifference to the forces other than literary and artistic and intellectual practice which it was the purpose of the broader **realism** (even at times naively) to take into radical account. The historical significance of **realism** was to make social and physical **reality** (in a generally materialist sense) the basis of literature, art, and thought. Many marginal points can be made against the methods historically associated with this purpose, and from a frankly idealist position many radical points can be made against the purpose itself. But what has most often happened, recently, is that the marginal points have been extended, loosely, as if they were radical points, or that making the marginal points has been so absorbing that the radical points at issue, from a materialist or an idealist standpoint, have been in effect ignored.

It is hardly necessary to add that the critical attention which is necessary in most cases of the use of **real**, **realistic**, and **reality** is at least equally necessary in the case of this extraordinary current variation in uses of **realism**.

RECENT DEVELOPMENTS

In choosing **realism** rather than **reality** or **real** as his head word for this entry, Williams acknowledged the most politically important debate about aesthetics of his lifetime. From the 1930s on, Soviet ideologues had argued that **realism** was the only progressive form, and the publication of Lukács's *The Meaning of Contemporary Realism* in 1957 had divided modern literature into a socially positive **realism** and a decadent and subjective *modernism*. By the time Williams published *Keywords*, however, this debate had already been overtaken by the poststructuralist emphasis on the formal organization of a TEXT, which ignored all questions of reference. Williams refers to this development but minimizes its importance. While coinages such as **magical realism**, **dirty realism**, and **hyperrealism** show that **realism** remains a key term in literary debates, its importance in an academic setting declined dramatically from the early 1970s on. In long retrospect it may seem that the opposition between *modernism* and **realism** is largely mistaken in its key terms. None of the great "modernist" writers used a term of the much later Cold War to describe themselves. Indeed, when Virginia Woolf asks, "Have I the power of conveying the true reality?" she makes clear that her experiments are at the service of a deeper investigation of **reality** than that allowed by the Victorian novel.

Reality replaces **realism** as the keyword from the 1960s on. This is largely due to the importance of hallucinogenic drugs in this period, which offered an experiential challenge to the deeply embedded Western notion of a single fixed, objective **reality**. In the same period various philosophies of science were abandoning notions of science as a unified REPRESENTATION of **reality**. By the 1980s with the growth of IDENTITY politics there was a tendency to place **reality** in scare quotes and claim that it was simply a subjective choice rather than an objective fact: "that's what you call 'reality.'" This use originated on the left, but it was very quickly taken up on the right. In 2004 Karl Rove, George W. Bush's spin doctor, gave a famous interview in which he mocked the journalist interviewing him as part of "what we call the reality-based community," which Rove defined as people who "believe that solutions emerge from your judicious study of discernible reality." . . . "That's not the way the world really works anymore," he continued. "We're an empire now, and when we act, we create our own reality. And while you're studying that reality— judiciously, as you will—we'll act again, creating other new realities, which you can study too, and that's how things will sort out. We're history's actors . . . and you, all of you, will be left to just study what we do."

The dominant traditions in both analytic and continental philosophy of lC20 emphasized the extent to which **reality** was always part of a complicated set of linguistic and non-linguistic practices. It may be that the reduction of those sophisticated positions to the pure assertions of power that one reads in Rove's quote is one reason why in the past decade important movements in both analytic and continental philosophy have wanted to stress not only the existence of **reality** but also its independence from our forms of thought and LANGUAGE. While the two traditions summon up very different versions of **reality**, the analytic appealing to the most banal common-sense view of **reality** and the continental to a surrealist world in which **reality** could always and immediately be completely different, both are concerned to stress the difference between **reality** and *thought*. This historical imperviousness of **reality** to thought is witnessed in the recent widespread coinage: **reality checkpoint**.

One important new use links **reality** to a certain kind of television: **reality show**, **reality television**, and **reality TV** in which nonfictional subject matter is used primarily for entertainment rather than INFORMATION. The development of these genres exemplifies the ever growing power of the IMAGE as part of contemporary **reality**.

See CREATIVE, EXPERIENCE, IMAGE, INFORMATION, REPRESENTATION, TRUTH

RELATIVISM

Relativism was not an entry in Raymond Williams's *Keywords*, though his account of *subjective*—and its concomitant *objective*—is relevant. In recent decades, however, it has gained currency as a keyword in contemporary thinking and debate regarding the foundations and nature of knowledge and TRUTH, as well as more widely in cultural studies and in common parlance.

Itself a recent word, **relativism** depends on **relative**, derived through Middle and Old French from Latin *relativus*, which appears as a noun at the end of C14, with a grammatical use to refer to words relating to an antecedent (so in the Prologue to the Wycliffite Bible, before 1397: "A relatif . . . may be resoluid into his antecedent with a coniunccioun copulative"); an equivalent adjectival use follows, particularly in respect of "pronownes relatives" (1530). There is an accompanying development of **relative**, both noun and adjective, in a variety of senses of relating. So, for example: "Having relation to the matter in hand; pertinent, relevant" (1579: "declarations relatiue"); "A person who is related to another or others by blood or marriage" (1650: "The sons and the parents, friends and relatives . . ."); "Having application or reference *to*; relating to" (1563: "Our Sauiour . . . willeth vs to do this in remembrance of him, which is relatiue to the whole action . . ."); "Existing or possessing a specified characteristic only in comparison to something else; not absolute or independent" (before 1500: "hope relative" as opposed to "determinacion substantyve"); and so on. It is this latter use of **relative**, with an attendant philosophical sense (1818) contrasting the **relative** with the *absolute*, that underpins the particular appearance of **relativism** in C19.

The *OED* dates **relativism** from 1865, as referring to "Any theory or doctrine asserting that knowledge, truth, morality, etc., are relative to situations, rather than being absolute"; with **relativist**, as one who holds the doctrine of **relativism,** preceding it in 1857. The first quotation in *OED* is from the Cambridge philosopher John Grote's *Exploratio Philosophica*: "The notion of the mask over the face of nature is . . . what I have called 'relativism.' If 'the face of nature' is reality, then the mask over it, which is what theory gives us, is so much deception, and that is what relativism really comes to." Behind Grote's refusal of what he names **relativism** is a concern to resolve questions of knowledge. Knowledge involves relations with the objects known, but to recognize this is not, therefore, for Grote to call the achievement of knowledge into question. The *OED* also quotes the American philosopher

Charles W. Morris in 1934 who, recognizing that "qualities of the object may yet be relative to a conditioning organism," talks of "objective relativism."

That the qualities of the object may be relative to a conditioning organism can be taken as a statement regarding the human in general; that knowledge is determined, for example, by the nature of our sensory apparatus. Thus for Kant we can have knowledge of space, time, and causation only because these are forms imposed by our minds upon experience. Objects and events as they are in themselves are shaped by the nature of our cognitive faculties: the noumenal world lies behind our phenomenal world. The *OED* has an 1857 example for *subjectivism* which talks of "the doctrine of Kant, that all human knowledge is merely relative; or rather that we cannot prove it to be absolute."

The collocations **cognitive relativism** and **epistemological relativism** (neither presently recorded in the *OED*) acknowledge current debates in philosophy and the philosophy of science concerning the status, foundation, and production of knowledge, and appear in various forms involving some conception of TRUTH as relative to an epistemic framework, whether specific to HUMANITY or to a particular COMMUNITY.

This emphasis on frameworks of perception and judgment across a range of areas has given the keyword-ness of **relativism**. The *OED* records **ethical relativism** with a first date of 1889 and includes a 1937 quotation from the sociologist Talcott Parsons: "[Durkheim] was forced to define normality with reference to the social type alone, thus ending in a complete ethical relativism." Such **relativism** refuses ETHICAL theories that see moral criteria as transcending specific cultures or specific historical periods. This refusal goes beyond the empirical recognition that different cultures and societies have different moralities, and it can end in the claim that different moralities are of equal VALUE or validity.

The same 1937 work by Parsons also includes a discussion of **historical relativism** (a collocation first recorded in 1893), "the theory that there can be no objective standard of historical truth, as the interpretation of data will be affected by subjective factors characteristic either of the historian or of the period in which the historian lives"; more widely, this is the view that our opinions overall are defined by our historical situation. **Cultural relativism** (1924) is then the more or less thoroughgoing derivation from this way of thinking. A clear example in *OED* is from the anthropologist F. M. Keesing in 1958: "The scientific habit of looking at each people's standards and values objectively, seeing them as 'relative' to the particular view of life fostered within the culture concerned, has led some thinkers to a philosophic position often called 'cultural relativism.'" Anthropology's study of different cultures and the postwar expansion of the human sciences has largely contributed to the contemporary hold of **relativism**, nourishing ideas that cultures should be treated equally and that transcultural judgments are not to be made, or, if made, are no more than an imposition of external values, usually viewed as those of a Western cultural hegemony.

Relativism in this modern history has links with several other words with which it is often confused. Thus it can be equated with *subjectivism* (1845), described by the *OED* as the theory that all our knowledge is merely "subjective and relative," denying the possibility of objective knowledge and in its extreme version making the truth of any judgment relative to the individual judging; *perspectivism* (1910), which the *OED* traces to the work of Nietzsche and which holds that knowledge is inevitably partial and limited by the individual perspective from which it is viewed, with objectivity impossible. The *OED*'s first quotation comes indeed from a translation of a work by Nietzsche: "Fundamentally our actions are in an incomparable manner altogether personal, unique and absolutely individual— . . . but as soon as we translate them into consciousness, they do not appear so any longer. . . . This is the proper phenomenalism and perspectivism as I understand it"; *skepticism*, referring to the doctrine of the Greek Skeptics and the opinion that real knowledge of any kind is unattainable (*a*1651; *skeptic* 1587), but also, beyond that historical reference, to (1646) an attitude of doubt regarding some assertion or supposed fact, or of doubt regarding knowledge in general or some particular area of knowledge (*skeptic* in this wider sense, 1615). Though all these may be (and often are) taken as forms, or used as synonyms, of **relativism**, they can be differentiated: **relativism** does not necessarily involve reduction to a subjective point of view, and is not necessarily an individual *perspectivism*; while *skepticism*'s doubt as to the possibility of truth is not by definition shared by **relativism**, which in many of its forms does not give up truth, but simply sees it as relative to the agreed norms of the culture within which truth statements are made.

Relativism today is a difficult word precisely because the term has spread widely and with conflicting and confusing uses. It runs from precise philosophical debates through to ideas of a postmodern world in which there are no foundations other than those relative to cultural contexts and orders of language. The phrase **"it's all relative"** is recorded from 1812 but has become commonplace today to express the many ways in which **relativism** is now itself taken, paradoxically, as a fundamental truth.

Mention should be made of the specialist use of **relativism** and its related terms to refer to theories of **relativity** developed in physics at the beginning of C20: Einstein's "special theory of **relativity**," 1905; and "the general theory of **relativity**," 1916. Recognition of motion as implying relativity of either place or time was there before Einstein, and the word **relativity** in that sense has an *OED* initial date of 1858. Popular accounts of **relativity** and its hold on the cultural imagination have allowed for its vague association with, and supposed support for, **relativism**, despite having nothing to do with it.

See CULTURE, ETHICAL, EXPERIENCE, HISTORY, OPINION, TRUTH, VALUE

RELIGION

Religion is recorded in English from C13 and has since had a central, and often conflictual, currency in social and POLITICAL discourse, not least today when the conjunction and confusion of **religion** and RACE, for example, has had damaging consequences. At the end of 2016, moreover, **religion**—the "faith economy"—was reported as having a higher value than the combined revenues of the top ten US technology companies.

The word comes from Latin *religio*, indicating devoutness, regard for sacred things. The etymology of the Latin word is uncertain but commonly linked to *relegere*, to go through again, read again; thus **religion** as the careful observance of rites and teachings. Alternatively, it is linked to *religare*, to secure, attach; thus **religion** as binding people in belief in God. Borrowed from Middle French *religioun*, meaning a community of beliefs grounded in the recognition of some divine power or powers, **religion** enters English in C13, its first senses relating to belonging to a religious order (*c*1225) and conduct indicating belief in and reverence for God, gods, or similar superhuman power (*c*1225); the adjective **religious** enters at the same time with the same semantic range. The sense of a particular system of faith and worship, the word's common use today, is recorded from 1325, allowing for the distinction of plural **religions**. A character in Ben Jonson's *The Staple of News* (1631) has "friends . . . of all religions" who provide him with "puritan news . . . protestant news . . . pontifical news."

That list of religions underlines the initial uses of **religion** as predominantly within the known context of the Christian religion. In eC18, Nathan Bailey's *Dictionarium Britannicum* (1730) defined **religion** as: "a general Habit of Reverence towards the divine Nature, by which we are both enabled and inclined to worship and serve God." A few years later, Samuel Johnson's *Dictionary of the English Language* (1755) had **religion** as: "1. Virtue as founded upon reverence of God, and expectation of future rewards and punishments. 2. A system of divine faith and worship as opposite to others." The basis for both definitions is Christianity, that being the *accepted* faith "opposite to others."

Bailey provides separate entries for **natural religion** (*OED*, 1622) and **revealed religion** (*OED*, 1673), marking the increasing concern with the epistemological status of religion, the concern to specify what kind of knowledge it is and how that knowledge is acquired: for the former, belief is based on reason and observation; for the latter, it is given through divine revelation. Enlightenment practice of science as "the study of the phaenomena of nature" (1779) gave rise to arguments regarding the compatibility of *science* and **religion** that continue in today's "science-versus-God," EVOLUTION or creation controversies.

When John Milton in *Paradise Lost* (1667) described God falsely adorned with "gay religions," his reference was to the heathen deities of the Old Testament. Encounters through travel and trade with different peoples and cultures, with ensuing colonial expansion, brought a missionary urge to lead those peoples into **the religion**, along with questions as to whether or not their beliefs and practices could properly be called **religion**. The C19 development of anthropology brought the study of "religion in primitive culture" (1873, the focus of the second volume of Edward B. Tylor's influential *Primitive Culture*); the manifestations of religion in different cultures across the centuries were regarded as stages in a progressive evolutionary development. **Religion** is then taken as the term for a universal experience involving "sets of beliefs that go both beyond the self and the natural world" (UNESCO, 1997). Different religions are thus particular cultural systematizations of that (posited) transcultural experience explained in functional terms as creating social cohesion, as "community building." Against which, the critique of religion developed in C19 described it as a form of social control, the alienating projection of essential human aspirations onto some divinity; this at the same time that historical studies of contemporary Christian religion were placing it, like all religions, solely within the human sphere. Hence the appeal of a **religious humanism** (1850), a **religion of humanity** (1852), free from supernatural belief but retaining essential personal and community moral values that had been regarded as depending on such belief. With this humanization came an increasing emphasis on **religion** as a matter of subjective inner experience of FAITH, rather than of any institutionalized belief-system. This is the **personal religion** identified by William James in *The Varieties of Religious Experience* (1902), defining **religion** as: "the feelings, acts, and experiences of individual men in their solitude, in so far as they apprehend themselves to stand in relation to whatever they may consider the divine."

The sense of **religion** as SPIRITUAL devotion is used figuratively from lC16/eC17, its object transferred from God to the material world, notably to money and commerce: "gain is his Religion" (1606). Over the following centuries, this figurative secularization includes indiscriminately a multitude of the aspects of a world in which "the new religion is consumerism" (*Independent*, November 3, 1993), in which anything can be an object of devotion; witness the proliferation of "X-is-my-religion" blogs, where X is sex, food, shopping, football, this or that commercial brand. True Religion, indeed, is the brand name of an American clothing company.

The SECULAR appropriation of **religion** and related word-forms is particularly evident in the case of **religiously** and **religiosity**, both of which enter the language in C14; the former meaning reverently, devoutly; the latter religious feeling or belief. From C16, **religiously** renewing with certain senses of Latin *religio*, is used also to mean faithfully, scrupulously; the *OED*'s initial example concerns men who "somewhat relygiouslye and preciselye observe the elegauncie of the Latyne speche" (1534). Likewise, **religiosity** retains its first meaning of religious feeling but becomes characteristically pejorative, indicating affected or excessive manifestations of such feeling: "A feverish state of what might better be called religiosity, than religion" (1829).

The word FAITH used for a **religion** appears in late C14: "him that is of the faith of Jesus Christ" (1384). Hence today, *faith schools* (1883) are those providing teaching in conformity with the tenets of a particular religion. Etymologically, *faith* derives from Latin *fides*, with meanings involving trust, loyalty, belief. In accordance with which, it is recorded from C14 as referring to the spiritual capacity for belief, for apprehension of the divine—what the theologian Reginald Pecock in his *Book or Rule of Christian Religion* called "a knowingal virtue" (1443). *Faith*, that is, refers both to belief, the essential component of religion, and to the religion itself overall. In the latter use, *faith* is now invariably identified by a modifying word— *Muslim faith, Christian faith*, etc.

The related words *sect* and *cult* refer initially to groups within a religion. The former is from Latin *secta*, used in respect of a class of persons, a school of thought. This use carries over into English in lC14 for groups of people linked by some quality or activity: "sects of great ones" (1608), "a sect of writers" (1616). Its use for orders of religious belief and their followers is also found from lC14, applied to groups within a religion that differ in aspects of belief—"this new secte of Lollardie" (1390). Generally with negative connotations, it indicates heretical views, deviations from orthodoxy—"manye untrewe sectis of Cristen men" (*c*1449); not that the orthodoxy cannot itself be opposed as no more than a sect: "The oppressive sect which calls itself the Church of England" (1840). The word *cult* derives from Latin *cultus*, with senses of reverence, veneration, adoration, and appears in eC17 with the now obsolete sense of paying reverential homage to a deity: "a divine cult and worship" (1613). *OED*'s first example of its use for a particular form of worship is from the Quaker William Penn, insisting that "not every circumstantial difference or Variety of Cult be Nick-named a new Religion" (1679). As that suggests, *cult* too is often negative, now commonly applied to groups with quasi-religious beliefs and practices regarded as weird, disturbing, dangerous: "the free-love cult . . . has been added to Chicago's roster of freak religious societies" (1905); "Charles Manson['s] . . . hippie cult followers" (1969). Anthropology adopted *cult* for the veneration by "primitive" cultures of figures or objects: "the ancient cult of the God of the Gardens" (1781). From lC18, this use embraces contemporary non-anthropological references—*the Wordsworth cult, the cult of Wagner*—and from C20 is widely used as an attribute for a range of cultural phenomena—*cult figure, cult book, cult movie*. The expressions *cult of personality* (1898) and *personality cult* (1927) interestingly recognize collective adulation of public figures; in the case of the former, adulation particularly of political leaders that plays an essential role in the establishment of authoritarian regimes.

Over 150 million Americans are members of *faith congregations*, almost half the population. These congregations may in many cases be **religions**, but *faith* is now the key word for an experience of belief, unconstrained by the institutionalized orders of established religions; this simultaneous with the increasing turn to **personal religion**, inner faith (the two are not incompatible, are for many complementary). Along with which the question of **religion** as a matter of identity has become fundamental, most evidently with the tensions within societies around the place of religions and their beliefs and practices, tensions that become acute when a **religion** is cast as a racial term—as, for example, MUSLIM now so readily is.

The vast majority of new words that have been added to *Keywords for Today* are words that have become newly prominent. **Religion**, however, is a word, like SOUL and SPIRITUAL, that would have been considered prominent in the language from the Middle Ages to the end of C19 but which Williams chose to ignore. This lack of attention is evident throughout Williams's work; it seems part of his critique of **religion** as a form of social control. Yet Williams's own fundamental, materialist belief in "human evolution, to mean the general growth of man as a kind" (*The Long Revolution*, 1961), despite making no reference to a transcendent order, could be considered itself **religious**, following the analysis of EVOLUTION. If this evolutionary humanist socialism counts as a **religious** belief, it helps to explain why the extraordinary revival of theocentric religion since the last quarter of C20 has proved so difficult for SOCIALIST thinking.

See FAITH, FUNDAMENTALISM, INSTITUTION, SECULAR, SPIRITUAL

REPRESENTATION

The verb **represent** is recorded in English from lC14. The various senses that developed in the course of C15 include: bringing clearly and distinctly before the mind: "þe ymage of þe crucifix hangynge on the cros, which represente to þe þe passioun of crist" (*c*1400); presenting to the eye, as in a painting, where something is "representid and purtraid" (*a*1425); to symbolize, stand for (*c*1450); applied to language: "Wordes . . . be but ymages representing the things that the writer or speaker conceiueth in his minde" (1529); and some quality, fact, or abstract concept: "Ymagis þat representen pompe and glorie of oþ worlde" (*c*1380). Initial uses relating to government are largely tied to ideas of symbolization—the king in his sovereign body stands for, **represents** the nation; the noun **representation** appears in C15 with the same range of senses. The history of **represent** and **representation** in English is then marked by a shift in which **represent** and **representation** become modern POLITICAL terms with reference to systems in which the interests of the governed are **represented** to those who govern them by chosen **representatives**. Absent from the word's early English uses, this sense is absent too in its etymology: from C12 French *représenter*/C13 *représentation*; themselves derived from Latin *repraesentare* and *repraesentatio*, with meanings of making present, displaying, but not that of people representing others (the ancient Greeks had no word corresponding to Latin *repraesentatio*). Our emergent political sense—impelled by the English Civil War and the conflict between king and Parliament—takes the latter no longer as the **representation** of a *pregiven* authority which it embodies, but as itself having authority *by virtue of* its foundation in **representation**: the authority to govern on behalf of those represented established by election or some other form of selecting **representatives** (1635, **representative** in the sense of a member of a legislative body or assembly).

Further senses follow: giving an account of something: "When Darius had spoken theis wordes, the representacion of the present perill so amased them all, that they were not able to shew there aduise" (1553); stating facts, arguments, reasons, a sense noted as recent as in lC17: "The King . . . in answer to their Representation (that's ye word now), told them that too much time had already been lost" (1679). The theatrical sense gains currency from lC16, *OED*'s first quotation again notes this as of recent usage: "The order and maner of our playes, which he termed by the name of representations" (1589).

From lC17, **representation** is central in accounts of "human understanding," the workings of the mind, with **representation** here defined by *OED* as: "a mental image or idea regarded as an object of direct knowledge and as the means by which knowledge of objects in the world may indirectly be acquired"; with first examples from Locke's *Essay Concerning Human Understanding* (1690). If, however, knowledge is possession of **representations** that correspond to material facts of reality, questions arise regarding the accuracy of such representations and how we can know them to be accurate (*OED*'s "direct"/"indirectly" pair acknowledges the problem). Used as the keyword in theories of knowledge, **representation** brought with it epistemological difficulties. Difficulties arose too with the word's use in aesthetic and political contexts. In the arts the desire to produce faithful representations of reality was accompanied by concerns as to how this could be achieved, as to the validity of the forms and conventions in any (artistic) representation. In politics the problems were those of the means by which representation was to be established and for whom.

With **representation** comes **misrepresentation**, recorded from 1641 with the meaning incorrect representation of facts, opinions, someone's character, etc.; the word is often pejorative, suggesting falsification, willful misleading—Samuel Johnson's *Dictionary of the English Language* (1755) says simply: "Account maliciously false." Today the UK Misrepresentation Act of 1967 is aimed at untrue statements of facts in contracts or commercial negotiations. The major social/political use is illustrated by John Stuart Mill in his *Considerations on Representative Government* (1861) where he talks of classes of people being "either unrepresented or misrepresented"; a parliamentary democracy may leave people **unrepresented** (1681), because not eligible to vote; **misrepresented** (1796), because having no representative from their class or minority and so not present, not made present.

The terms of **political** and, more widely, **social representation** have been the insistent focus of contemporary actions, debates, and struggles. Rudyard Kipling's "The White Man's Burden" (1899), the asserted colonialist duty of civilizing other populations, is now overturned in **the burden of representation**, the duty felt by populations and minorities to represent themselves, with *burden* suggesting the personal weight of the demands entailed. For Henry Louis Gates, Jr: "'the burden of representation' [is] the homely notion that you represent your race, thus that your actions can betray your race or honor it" (1995).

The idea of such a burden points to two strands in recent developments in uses of **representation**. Conceived in terms of political and other social forms, it can be experienced as a constraint on individual identity, pulling away from particularity, enclosing an individual in some category, against which categorization Chester Himes asserts: "[he is] not at all like any other Negro American writer on earth, or any other writer of whatever nationality or race" (1955). Recently, identity politics has seen struggles by particular groups—particular identities—for recognition and **representation** in respect of those self-identified groups. At the same time, the modern valorization of individual experience and the valorization of this as the core of a person's identity can effectively cast **representation** as an alienating reduction of IDENTITY, then opposed by the assertion of **self-representation**—"I'm . . . just the best to represent me" is a common social media claim. Social media indeed play a fundamental part in what has been seen as **the end of representation** as technological advances have allowed an instantaneous worldwide circulation of words and images without any foundation, any stability of the represented on which it has conventionally been taken to depend. **Representation** as *simulacra* is one popular statement of this: **representation** precedes and determines the real, with no longer any distinction between *reality* and its **representation**. The frenzied and perpetually transient individual turn of social media is then a symptom of this—along with which go challenges to traditional ideas and practices of **representative** DEMOCRACY. OPINION and *participation* increasingly substitute for **representation**—through polls as political validation, online petitions, and so on.

The different senses brought together in **representation** and their overlapping underpin its complex history as a keyword: ideas of depiction (this picture represents the White House), statement (representing that something would be wrong), standing in for (representing someone at a meeting). All these senses are there to a greater or lesser degree in any use of the word, in any representation.

Representation is always *of* and *to* and *for*, all of which have been taken as problematic, subject to critical debate and challenge.

See ART, DEMOCRACY, IDENTITY, IMAGE, OPINION, POLITICAL, REALISM

RESPECT

Respect has been in common usage since lC14 from the Latin *respectus*, the "action of looking round or back, consideration, regard." However, political nuances stem from the *OED*'s "senses relating to deference or esteem," which first appear in eC16. The noun form is followed closely by the verb form, "to value or esteem," in lC16. This use took on strong connotations of religious and state AUTHORITY, and was used primarily within the context of hierarchical relationships, as in "respect your elders." Apart from this definition of **respect** as esteem based on hierarchical relations stands a second use, **respect** as "don't harass." This shorthand comes from an *OED* verb definition "to refrain from harassing or obstructing (a person)," which first appeared in mC18. The dictionary cites Richard Pococke's *A Description of the East, and Some Other Countries* (1745): "In the excursions which [the English] make for pleasure they are commonly respected by the Arabs, Curdeens and Turcomen, there being very few instances of their having been plundered by them."

The second use of **respect** aligns with individualist ENLIGHTENMENT rhetoric that argued that individual subjects had RIGHTS independent of any religious or state authority. However, **respect** as "don't harass" is not present in any of the most iconic Enlightenment documents, or those from the American or French revolutions. This would suggest that the second verb form of **respect** was not yet common enough to be used comfortably, without fear of it being mistaken for the older form. C18 revolutionaries wouldn't have used **respect** to argue for better treatment because the word still maintained strong connotations of religious and state authority, the very authority they were fighting.

During C18 **self-respect** also changes. It sheds its negative connotation and becomes distinctly positive. **Self-respect** before lC17 was used to indicate selfishness or self-conceit. However, in eC19, the term's positive connotation is recognized in the *OED*: "Proper regard for the dignity of one's person or one's position." Robert Burns makes use of the term's polysemy in his "Despondency: An Ode" (1786). In the poem, the hermit's "self-respecting art" is used to indicate the self-indulgence of such a lifestyle. However, the word is also used to highlight Burns's despondency in society, suggesting that the hermit has regard for his own dignity and that Burns does not.

Because of its early alignment with state and religious authorities, **respect** has always been heavily conscious of CLASS and status. Williams uses the term (somewhat indistinct between the two meanings set out in the preceding) in his *Keywords* entry on DEMOCRACY: "to have democratic manners or feelings, is to be unconscious of class distinctions, or consciously to disregard or overcome them in everyday behaviour: acting *as if* all people were equal, and deserved equal respect, whether this is really so or not." This suggests that Williams bears some skepticism that **respect** can be implemented across class lines, but this skepticism might be remedied with a more concrete distinction among usages of **respect**.

One cannot remark upon **respect** in contemporary culture without reference to Aretha Franklin's "Respect" (1967), adapted from Otis Redding's "Respect" (1965). In it, Franklin emphasizes that she is not asking for much: "All I'm asking is for *a little* respect." She is not asking to be esteemed above others, but merely the proper treatment owed to her, indicating her alignment with the second use of **respect**. Franklin makes significant changes to the lyrics, incorporating African-American vernacular like "propers" (proper respect) and "TCB" (taking care of business). These words speak to the politically charged undercurrents of the song, calling out misogyny in the civil rights movement, and in society at large. Jerry Wexler, producer of the Franklin version, once remarked in an interview that "Respect" was "global in its influence, with overtones of the civil rights movement and gender equality. It was an appeal for dignity."

Huey Newton, cofounder of the Black Panther Party, utilized the polysemy of **respect** in his "Fear and Doubt" (1967), a widely read political essay of the Black Panther movement. "He [the African-American man] is asked to respect laws that do not respect him." In this essay, Newton remarks on the irony of giving deferential treatment to a system of police violence that will not refrain from harassing African Americans. The overlap and deliberate blurring between these two meanings has allowed authorities significant political maneuvers around the term. The argument against a corrupt legal system is still borne out nearly fifty years later in the Black Lives Matter protests, and it still utilizes the rhetoric of **respect**.

The Black Lives Matter website articulates their members' conception of **respect** as absence of harassment, but it also engages the charges that its members fail to show respect as proper esteem. The website begins by saying, "All people should be treated with dignity and respect, regardless of how one looks or speaks."

It continues to articulate both a rejection of state-defined **disrespect** and a rejection of **respect** as enforceable by the state. "[W]e reject the idea that asking officers questions about why one is being stopped or arrested, about what one is being charged with, constitutes either disrespect or resistance. [. . .] We reject the faulty idea that disrespect is a crime, that black people should be nice or civil when they are being hassled or arrested on trumped-up charges."

Additionally, this demand for the police to be held in high esteem is the foundation of most pro-police rhetoric. This is epitomized in the animated sitcom *South Park* with Erik Cartman's catchphrase "respect my authoritah," a parody of over-zealous police forces.

The demand for equal **respect** is set up in stark contrast to the Black Lives Matter movement's opinion of what Evelyn Brooks Higginbotham calls a **politics of respectability** (1994), now more commonly **respectability politics**. This term refers to attempts by marginalized groups, most often black Americans, to enforce norms in their communities that are congruent with mainstream culture, thus making their group more "respectable." This desire to PERFORM **respectability** is not new. The aspiration to **respectability** was already important for many Victorians, but **respectability politics** as a term only came into public use eC21, and maintains distinct ties to black communities. Contemporary debates around respectability politics can be traced to writers W. E. B. Du Bois and Booker T. Washington, and the disagreements have continued into popular discussion of President Barack Obama's expressions of his blackness. Critics of respectability politics suggest that **respect** should not be contingent on assimilation, aligning with **respect** as absence of harassment. Those who might be described as adherents, however, suggest that esteem based upon assimilation is a small price to pay for better treatment in mainstream culture.

The polysemy of **respect** has allowed for a slippage that makes the word a placeholder for the ideology of the speaker. To a crowd of likeminded individuals, petitions for **respect** (either absence of harassment or esteem for authorities) are prudent and sensible. To onlookers who disagree, petitions for respect can be combated as entitled and obstinate. The still lively history of this word's contention indicates a complex argument about how members of our culture assign worth to individuals. Moreover, the reactionary aggression to certain calls for **respect** shows the word's importance in constructing our understanding of the world—deciding whom we deem worthy and unworthy of **respect**.

See AUTHORITY, EQUALITY, RIGHTS, VALUE

RESPONSIBILITY

Responsibility and the related adjective **responsible** are important terms in law, philosophy, and politics, as well as in more general non-technical use. For example, they are difficult words in news reporting and discussion of avoidable disasters, crimes, accidents, and alleged medical or corporate negligence. Understandably, victims and relatives often wish to hold to account those judged to be responsible, in circumstances where whoever was responsible is not considered to have acted responsibly. Part of the challenge in seeking to hold people to account in this way is that, in present-day English, while both **responsibility** and **responsible** have strands of meaning that intersect with *duty* and *accountability*, they also show partial synonymy with morality terms like ETHICAL and elusive descriptors of standards such as *reasonable*. At the same time, **responsibility** may also convey a concept of moral agency, associated both with clinical and philosophical assessments of mental capacity and culpability.

According to the *OED*, the noun **responsibility** is first attested in English in mC17, derived from adjective **responsible**, from around a century earlier. Etymologically, both forms can be traced to a French legal term that carried senses approximating to "answerable, accountable," with the French term ultimately derived from the past participle form of classical Latin *respondere*: "answer, reply (in a formal or official capacity)." Early citations of **responsible** in English, as with its French counterpart, show frequent legal use, particularly in relation to money: a **responsible** person is one who is financially trustworthy and capable of fulfilling financial obligations. By C18, both the French and English words show the complex range of related senses that characterize their use in modern times.

In a change from its earliest uses in English, however, the adjective **responsible** tends now to be most frequently followed by the preposition *for*. **Responsible for** *x* tends to account for the majority of occurrences. This pattern is found from mC17, and shows the development of the sense "having an obligation to do something, or having control over or care for someone." The resulting concept has two facets: legal and philosophical treatments of **responsibility** distinguish between **prospective responsibility** and **retrospective** or **historic responsibility**. The first involves creating and allocating duties and obligations: if, for example, an employee is given responsibility for health and safety in a workplace, or a government minister has responsibility for Education, he/she is expected to perform or oversee specific tasks as they arise, i.e., the **responsibilities** of the job. **Retrospective responsibility**, by contrast, is closely related to liability, and concerns the failure of a person or group of people to do something that they were expected to do: if a person is **held responsible**, he/she is blamed for an event or situation. This relatively clear distinction between prospective and retrospective responsibility nevertheless masks potential ambiguity regarding the required role of a responsible party, who may directly cause things to happen, or have only a more distant, overseeing role. A murderer who is **responsible** for several deaths has caused them, and can be said to be **directly responsible** or to have **sole responsibility**. On the other hand, a director of a bank who is **responsible** for the bank's failure may not have done anything him/ herself to cause the failure, but has been negligent in supervising employees whose actions are to blame: the director is **ultimately** or **indirectly responsible**, or may be held to have **overall responsibility**. Without use of modifiers in a given context, it is not always clear which meaning is intended. For example, after an investigation into the fixing of interest rates by banks in June 2012, the UK Chancellor of the Exchequer George Osborne said in a statement that "[t]hose responsible should be held responsible"; in itself, however, this did not indicate whether lower-level bank employees such as traders, or higher-level employees such as the CEO, or both, should be inferred.

Alternatively, **responsible** can occur with the preposition *to*. Such use specifies the institution or individual imposing the duties, and in this way makes explicit the relevant aspect of hierarchy or social structure. For example, a head teacher may be **responsible to** a board of governors. In constructions without *to*, an unspecified higher authority or body is merely implied. The British notion of **responsible government** relates to a government answerable to Parliament, while **parental responsibility** is less clear, and may be considered to be responsibility *for* children but *to* both those children and society more generally.

A key element of the current meaning of **responsibility**—one that distinguishes it from partial synonyms like *accountable* and *liable*—is its association with morality and morally correct behavior. "Moral obligation" appears to have emerged as an identifiable sense during C18, and is often intended where **responsible** and **responsibility** occur without any following prepositional phrase *for/to*: a person or body considered morally virtuous might be described as **responsible** or as having a **(strong) sense of responsibility**. This meaning overlaps with *ethical* and with *moral*. In fact, a notion of morality colors many uses of **responsibility** and **responsible**, with frequent collocates reflecting the popular idea that not only individuals (who might show **personal responsibility**) but also governments and corporations have a duty to behave in a morally prudent way, even if there may be no clear consensus as to what this means in practice. It is generally recognized that **legal** and **moral responsibility** may not coincide, although it is a widespread conception that one should inform the other.

Corporate responsibility cuts institutionally and politically across these various threads of meaning. It is not restricted to legal or financial obligation but has moral entailments as well, and is often viewed as a LIBERAL concern. Pressure groups such as the Corporate Responsibilities Coalition, an alliance of UK voluntary organizations, trade unions, and companies set up in 2001, actively campaign for legislation to protect the rights of workers, communities, and the environment. **Social** and **collective responsibility** and **responsible citizenship** place the needs and priorities of the group above those of the individual, and also often imply attention to environmental concerns, as the *Responsiblecitizen* website illustrates: its guide to responsible citizenship identifies three strands—of legal, social, and moral obligation—noting that moral obligations are "harder to pin down because different people have different moral codes. But one place we can all start is in helping the environment." The phrases **financial responsibility** and **fiscal responsibility**, on the other hand, have very different resonances, and are associated with CONSERVATIVE ideals to the extent that they valorize restraint on public borrowing and public spending. **Responsibility** is also found as a count noun in the expression **rights and responsibilities**, a phrase that is used by political groups on both left and right (as well as by non-political organizations and individuals), and is particularly associated with discussion of the welfare state.

A specific development in the meaning of **responsibility** that bridges the senses "accountability, blameworthiness" and "moral obligation" can be seen in the legal phrase **diminished responsibility**. This is a defense that can be invoked where an individual is not in possession of full mental agency and cannot be held to be fully in control of his/her actions; the equivalent plea in US military law is **lack of mental responsibility**. The underlying idea of **responsibility** as *agency* has its origins in mC18, and has been explored in philosophical discussion of responsibility that investigates the role of free will in an individual's actions. **Responsibility** in this sense is central to clinical opinions about mental and behavioral disorders. For example, in The Hare Revised Psychopathy Checklist, widely used as a tool in legal and clinical diagnoses, one attribute of a psychopath is "failure to accept responsibility for own actions"; another is "a tendency to transfer responsibility to others," part of the condition labelled "dependent personality disorder" in the World Health

Organization's *International Classification of Diseases and Related Health Problems* (10th edition).

Across these various meanings, **responsibility** is a vague and increasingly difficult term, whose meanings are complicated by often occurring in contexts and collocations that play off one meaning against another. Yet the word's importance is beyond doubt. The present cultural importance of **responsibility** seems greater than ever, apparently motivated by anxiety regarding what values underpin social order, a concern reflected in newly coined expressions and not least by calls during the past decade—a period of serious financial collapse and recession—for a **responsibility revolution** in business.

See ETHICAL, RIGHTS

RIGHTS

Widespread use of **rights** (the plural of **right**, as used in combinations such as **women's rights, civil rights, workers' rights, gay rights, human rights**, and **equal rights**) results in a contemporary **rights discourse** that takes specialized form in law but is frequently contested in public discourse. The word **rights** commonly enters into such different contrasts (e.g., with "might," "wrong," and "left"), and engages such a spectrum of human activities (from simply staying alive to exercising varying degrees of economic monopoly), that contemporary debate is easily obfuscated by divergent and potentially conflicting uses of the term.

The singular noun **right** comes into OE (in forms including *riht, rihtan*) from a precursor in several Northern European languages. The word's later semantic development was then influenced, the *OED* suggests, by meaning changes in Anglo-Norman and Old French *dreit* as well as Middle French *droit*. From its earliest uses in English, **right** had a cluster of meanings related to religious, hereditary, and socioeconomic position in the prevailing social order; these meanings have evolved and intersected, sometimes reflecting, sometimes contesting, and sometimes leading social change at different historical moments.

The first sense in the *OED* conveys a broad, "moral," or "justice" meaning: "That which is considered proper, correct, or consonant with justice," with an implication that what is just is also honorable, wise, and consistent with laws of NATURE ordained by God. A related sense is then that of "something proper for, or incumbent on, a person to do; one's duty." Only in later developments of this broad sense, in response to increased individualism, is stronger contrast drawn between the potentially contrasting "personal entitlement" and "social obligation" dimensions of **right** that resurface in modern political arguments about the need for greater interconnection between **rights** and RESPONSIBILITIES.

Alongside this wide "moral value" meaning of **right**, *OED* defines a narrower, more concrete meaning: that of specific entitlements and obligations available under the changing economic and legal system of feudalism and in the social and legal systems which replaced it. The force of **right** in this sense lies in the justifiability of any specific claim on grounds other than force, relying on law in the first instance as the basis of legitimacy. Considered as a category, **rights** in this sense acquired their specialized form as the essential means by which a legal person's position within the social formation was defined through a combination of rights, duties/obligations, and powers.

While still based on a mythology of "ancient rights and liberties," **rights** were increasingly restricted from C14 by an accumulating body of common law. Such law curtailed earlier, presumed freedoms, but left what can be seen as **residual rights** in the gaps between areas that had been legally defined. More abstractly, **rights** continued to be understood, through to C17, as part of a system of **natural rights** including a presumed *divine right of kings*, or absolute sovereignty dented only by limitations such as those associated with the Magna Carta (1215). As belief in natural law gradually receded, however, following bitter political experiences including the tyrannicide of Charles I in 1649, commitment to **natural rights** was increasingly challenged, including by further Parliamentary restriction on sovereign powers imposed in the 1688 Bill of Rights.

What most clearly makes **rights** a keyword, however, is the series of shifts in philosophical and political thought from C17 to C19 which connect the word with social activism leading to American independence and the French Revolution. Early conceptions of **rights** had either referred, as noted earlier, to ancient origins and existence "from time immemorial," or been traced to Roman law formulation of civic values held to be common across classical civilizations (*ius gentium*). With increased questioning of legitimacy based on **natural rights**, however—by the end of C18, Jeremy Bentham's "nonsense on stilts"—social thinking from Hobbes and Locke to Rousseau and Paine shifted emphasis from subjection to absolute sovereignty, through notions of consent (terrified and one-off in Hobbes, more continuous in Locke), to Rousseau's social contract. These changes paved the way for justly celebrated statements of **general**—*sacred, inalienable, human, indivisible*—**rights**, such as Thomas Jefferson's assertion in the American Declaration of Independence in 1776 that [all men] "are endowed by their Creator with certain unalienable Rights, [that] amongst these are Life, Liberty, and the pursuit of Happiness," or Lafayette's formulation (assisted by Thomas Paine) in the French National Constituent Assembly's Declaration of the Rights of Man and of the Citizen. The social thinking associated with such declarations involved a fundamental political shift: away from *implied* or *residual* **rights**, which continued in common law, toward articulation of **rights** as propositions conceived by viewing any particular "good" from the standpoint of its beneficiary. This shift led to a surge in such declarations of **rights**: already in 1789, for example, Jefferson (as American ambassador in Paris) wrote to James Madison that "[e]verybody here is trying their hands at forming declarations of rights."

This fundamental C18 and eC19 movement from local and specific toward universal, and from implicit toward declared, put in place the main conditions for emancipatory political conceptualizations underpinning social activism during C19 and C20, in fields ranging from **women's rights**, through US **civil rights** and more general **equal rights**, to **sexual rights** and wider **human rights**. The more recent history of **rights discourse**—ranging from the international, such as the Universal Declaration of Human Rights (1948), to detailed specification of **consumer rights**—combines the notions of an underpinning baseline entitlement with direct statement in the form of general or "universal" propositions.

Broad statements of **rights** appear to many to promise an entitlement more profound than any historical (hence political or administrative) construction of social order offers, based on values that are in some way intrinsic. Especially among the disenfranchised, and those who align themselves with them, arguing in terms of **rights** may accordingly trump asymmetries embedded in law and power in the struggle toward some (perhaps equally complicated) notion of what is FAIR or just. Contrary to such a view, packages of claimed **rights** are often dismissed, even ridiculed, as utopian and emptily inspirational, on the grounds that they leapfrog expediency and a necessary balancing of entitlement against obligation, and promote absolutes that only make sense if modulated (and in that process inevitably limited and potentially compromised) by reference to the complexities of specific historical and political circumstances.

The resulting tensions are directly political, involving continuing struggles between haves and have-nots. Some tensions, however, arise from complexities in the word **rights** itself. Confusion may arise, for example, because of a naturalizing overlap between the word's general "justice and reason" meaning and its more technical, legal "entitlement" meanings. There are also perplexing associations between **rights,** as entitlement, and values sponsored by **right** as correctness, as well as **right** or **Right** meaning politically CONSERVATIVE (the uppercase form giving rise to the wider political sense, based on an originally trivial fact from the French Revolutionary period when conservatives were seated physically to the right in the National Assembly as compared with liberals seated to the left). The complications politically from the word **rights** can be significant, potentially confusing socially oriented emancipatory rights, often concerned with collective **human rights,** with arguments from reactionary libertarianism (e.g., the advocacy of the **right to bear arms**). Such confusion can make balancing more difficult when **rights** clash. Relating positions on **rights** to political positions is also complex. For example, in the US the political right draws heavily on the language of **individual rights,** though both liberals and conservatives extensively employ a **rights** discourse (albeit one with further splits on the right between libertarian and religious factions on what the **rights** they are referring to actually are). In the UK, by contrast, the political right tends to be dismissive of **rights** (e.g., with respect to the European Convention on Human Rights). The general situation, accordingly, means that positions adopted by the right on **rights** cannot be taken for granted. Nor are the tensions confined to right-wing politics. For example, the present period challenges Marx's 1840s critique of "the so-called rights of man" as a "right of selfishness"— "nothing but the rights of egotistic man, of man separated from other men and from the community."

See CONSERVATIVE, DEMOCRACY, EQUALITY, FAIR, LEGITIMATE, LIBERAL, RESPONSIBILITY

RISK

In the last half-century, **risk** has become a ubiquitous term covering almost all areas of human activity, and **risk management** is practiced in almost every major institution. From its very beginnings, the term is linked to notions of financial investment and becomes central to development of finance capitalism as the revolution in financial data, actuarial practices, and futures trading at the end of C19 sees **risk taking** as a way of mitigating the effects of risk. Currency and price stability are linked to wild speculative risk. But **risk** is equally important in the growth of social insurance: "By placing the burden and the risk upon many shoulders it is lessened for each" ("Studies in Social Christianity and What to Do," 1914). The steady growth of the frequency of **risk** through the history of capitalism accelerates dramatically from the 1960s onward as technical advances in computing combine with ideologies of safety and SECURITY.

The etymology of the term **risk** is complex. According to the *OED*, the word entered English in 1621. Derived from the French *risque*, which first appeared in mC16, the term referred to danger or inconvenience. **Risque** was the dominant spelling through C17, but in C18 English and French spellings were used interchangeably. In C19, however, the Anglicized **risk** became the accepted spelling in English. The French term was probably derived from the older Italian word *risco*, which referred to the possibility of harm or adverse consequence. A longer history suggests that the post-classical Latin *resicum* or *risicum*, meaning a danger or hazard, represents the main root. Since at least C13, **risk** was deployed in nautical contexts to specify damage to merchandise when transported by sea (see also the Spanish *riesgo*). This may prove the ultimate root of the word, which found a logical home referring to the perils of navigating around rocks, crags, and cliffs. For instance, the term *risco* is found in the trade contracts of Genoese merchants. It is also possible that **risk** entered Greek or Latin via the Arabic *rizq*, a notion with meanings that include not only fortune, luck, destiny, and chance, but blessings and provisions granted by God.

In C17, **risk** became associated with the possibility of loss, injury, or unwelcome circumstances. It developed as a count noun or something to be quantified, as in phrases such as **to run a risk** or **to take a risk**. By C19, the term began to be used in relation to a person or thing, either with regard to a good or bad outcome (as the phrase **worth the risk**) or, in keeping with the dominant negative connotation again, some kind of threat. At the same time, as indicated by its earlier use in maritime discourse, the notion of **risk** was increasingly used in the context of the development of financial CAPITALISM, such as new insurance markets around Lloyd's of London (founded in 1686). In this particular sense, **risk** refers to the degree to which an individual or property is exposed to harm causing financial loss or failure. Such a way of thinking continued in C19 and eC20 with a series of compound phrases, many of them reflecting the vocabulary of financial evaluation and investment, such as **risk-free** (1830), **risk-rate** (1835), **risk-bearing** (1851), **risk-taker** (1875), **risk analysis** (1926), **risk capital** (1927), and **risk aversion** (1938). Another, particular, sense of **risk** was also found in mathematics from C19 where, among other meanings, it could refer to the probability of an error in a calculation.

Since the 1950s, **risk** has become an increasingly commonplace term within government, BUSINESS, and everyday conversation, to the extent that the sociologist Ulrich Beck has argued that since the end of the first Industrial Revolution we have lived in a **risk society**. The related compound expression **risk assessment** has become a normal phrase within both public and private organizations. While its core meaning has remained broadly stable, the word **risk** has continued to evolve along two major paths. The first path is conceptual spreading. The word has now become attached to multiple subjects including, but by no means limited to, SECURITY, health, workplace, geopolitics, MARKET, regulatory, data, and the ENVIRONMENT. Among the more important reasons for these extensions, one can note the development of more litigious and media-saturated cultures, with a preoccupation for citizen safety and the need to allocate RESPONSIBILITY in episodes of perceived wrongdoing. Elsewhere, certain debates around moral individualism, notably in the neoliberal period since the 1980s, have involved the promotion of an ideal, self-governing subject who, at least partially, manages the risks of welfare costs on their own. Other more specific reasons for the increased use of the term include advances in actuarial studies (particularly via computing); the application of probability theory to many areas (such as agriculture and engineering); and quality-control accounting in fields that require high reliability (such as the chemical and nuclear industries).

These technical discourses of **risk** have fed a tendency to present declared risks as knowable and manageable, particularly by institutions of authority. **Risk agendas** now aim to classify and control uncertainties or, perhaps more precisely, to create the appearance of manageability. By the turn of C21, an entire field of **risk management** had emerged to debate and advise organizations on how to define and govern their objectified risks. In the UK, for instance, the BSE (or "mad cow") disease crisis in the 1990s prompted the government to develop a new discourse around **risk communication** as a way of shaping public expectations on legitimate state conduct. Many of these institutional applications of the word use methods of quantification as a presumed basis for rational measuring, decision-making, and forecasting. Reliance on such models and techniques demonstrates the legitimating power of scientific expertise and the need for organizations to appeal to such forms of knowledge. Within a world where BRANDS matter, **reputational risk** has become an associated phrase that contains a similar managerial sense; that is, public perceptions are read as potential sources of risks in themselves. In short, the institutionalization of **risk management** is often part of a desire to guard against blame through systems of accountability and, at the very least, to act as if one could know and handle the risks under scrutiny.

While **risk** is often linked to something that should be guarded against or potentially avoided, the term can also have an attractive quality when associated with entrepreneurship, other forms of investment, or gambling activity. Again, this general pattern is long-standing, although the precise phrases **risk and reward** or **risk versus reward** are not found prior to the 1950s. In the modern financial industry, other terms have surfaced to debate the often tense and ambiguous relationship between precautionary and adventurous spirits of behavior. Such expressions include **risk appetite** (in US English, **risk tolerance**) or, simply, a dichotomy between **risk on** versus **risk off** to signal a kind of mood or feeling of financial players. Overall, the appeal to the notion of **risk** represents a way in which social actors struggle to define, order, and govern REALITY. Since the designation of something as a **risk** tends to enhance its profile, the term shares some overlap with the concept of (in)SECURITY. While some risks may be more acknowledged or even tolerated than others, the process of risk categorization is not preordained or apolitical but, rather, often reflects how those in powerful positions shape the wider historical and sociocultural context.

See BUSINESS, MARKET, REALISM, RESPONSIBILITY, SECURITY

SECULAR

The terms **secular** and **secularism** have come to life as keywords in the last forty years, largely because of their contrastive relationship with *religious* and RELIGION. These contrasts have been precipitated by such historical events as the presidency of Jimmy Carter (1977–81; the first modern president avowedly a born-again Christian); the papacy of John Paul II (1978–2005); and the Iranian Revolution (1979). The meaning of **secular** was relatively uncontested in the early and middle

Cold War era ("Godless Communism" was not called **secular**), but the word has gained energy and complexity in debates provoked by the new age since Thatcher, Reagan, the end of the Soviet Union, the crisis in India provoked by militant Hinduism, and the rise of Islamism. The denotation of **secular** is an issue around the world, for example in both South Asia and the Middle East, as well as the United States and the European Union, especially in relation to new immigrants. Within English-language political and intellectual debates, Edward Said's "Secular Criticism" (1983) marks one major beginning.

Secular comes from Latin adjective *saecularis*, from *saeculum*, "generation" or "age." The Latin poet Horace wrote his *Carmen Saeculare* in 17 BCE at the request of the Emperor Augustus to mark the inauguration of a new age. Within medieval Latin Christianity, *saecularis* designated what pertained to "the world," in contrast to the Church. The implied contrast is between what is of an age and what is eternal: the timed versus the timeless. *OED* citations offer hardly any instance of the now conventional binary pairing *sacred*/**secular**, though for **secularization** can be found the quotation "He resented the secularization of revenues set apart for a . . . sacred purpose" (1888).

The *OED* presents **secular** as arising (with a first attestation in 1290) to capture a distinction within the community of Christian clerics: regular or religious clerics lived in monastic seclusion, while **secular** clergy lived in the world. The *OED* second sense is equally early in its first citation (in fact, from the same collection of English Saints' lives): this sense no longer denotes a distinction within the Church but a distinction between religion or the Church and the world of affairs, a "seculer court" (*c*1290). In this usage, the **secular** could still be closely affiliated with the Church. As early as 1380, John Wycliffe wrote of "the seculer arme of þe chirche," the means by which the Church could physically punish offenders.

The sense of the **secular** as contrasted with the SPIRITUAL first appears in *OED* in a moment from *Paradise Lost*. Because the clergy dominated formal education, a minor but intriguing transferred sense developed that referred specifically to lower-class autodidacts, as attested in the quotations: "Oft haue I obserued . . . a secular wit that hath liued all daies of his life by what doo you lacke, to bee more iudiciall . . . than our quadrant crepundios" (Thomas Nashe, 1589), and "Hang him poore snip, a secular shop-wit!" (Ben Jonson, 1631).

A more specialized sense arises in later C15 applying to the arts: "neither in holi scripture nor in seculare litterature vnlerned" (Thomas More, 1529), clearly related to the later usages by Nashe and Jonson. A Victorian characterization of classical

Greek education states that it was not entrusted to priests (generally the case in England at the earlier time) "but to the professors of the secular arts—rhetoric and gymnastics" (1835).

Another specialized sense, relating to educational policy, has become important in the last 150 years, and especially controversial recently. It implies "the exclusion of religious teaching from education," or from that part of it provided at PUBLIC expense.

There is a further sense in the *OED* that contrasts the temporal or worldly with the realm of eternity or the spirit rather than organized religion. Richard Hooker, in a 1597 attestation, asserts that "[r]eligion and the feare of God as well induceth secular prosperitie as euerlasting blisse in the world to come." Perhaps this is more Protestant; it is certainly Weberian.

The verb **secularize**, first attested in C17, follows the same pattern. Its first usages involve transfer from ecclesiastical or clerical status to civil status. But by C18 it has taken on a sense more moral than legal. Samuel Johnson's *Dictionary of the English Language* (1755) gives as its second sense, "to make worldly."

All of these senses of **secular** were well established when G. J. Holyoake raised the concept to a new pitch by his polemical formulation of *Secularism* in his book of that title published in 1854 and in his journal, *The Reasoner*. He coined the term **secularism** after spending six months in prison as the last man to be punished in this manner for public blasphemy. *OED* summarizes Holyoake's view as "The doctrine that morality should be based solely on regard to the well-being of mankind in the present life, to the exclusion of all considerations drawn from belief in God or in a future state," or as Gladstone put it in 1876, "the positive and exclusive claims of the purposes, the enjoyments, and the needs, presented to us in the world of sight and experience." As early as 1890, the *Times* noted what has become a regular topic for recent debate, "characteristic . . . secularist intolerance." In C20, the adjective **secular** has assumed major importance when related to the larger, non-institutional form of this worldview, which has at least since C19 been taken by some opponents and some advocates as equivalent to *materialism* (*OED* **secularity**, last attested in 1882).

This context of Victorian debate opened the way to the sense of **secularization** that has been a crucial part of Western discourse for the last 150 years. Whereas **secularization** initially meant no more than conversion of property or governance from church to CIVIL use (as in **secularization of the administration**, attested 1864), by the 1860s, in the wake of the term **secularism**, uses are sometimes directed to the history of the arts and culture that crucially "prepared the way for that general secularisation of the European intellect" (Lecky, 1865). It is worth noting that in French there is a related term *laïcité* (etymologically related to the English term *lay*) which embodies an entire philosophy of the neutrality of the STATE in regard to matters of religion. It was the most important ideological underpinning of the Third Republic, established in 1870, and remains a crucial element of contemporary debates in France, particularly in relation to Islam. It is not too paradoxical to say that *laïcité* is the secular religion of republican France.

In recent usage, an important development as yet unregistered by the *OED* has been that the **secular** is now contrasted not simply to *religion*, the *church*, or the *spiritual*, but to any and all forms of what Kenneth Burke called "God-terms" (*Rhetoric of Religion*, 1961). So, for instance, in the work of Edward Said, **secular** writing is opposed to NATIONALIST writing, even though the nation-state had earlier been itself a major instance of the **secular**.

See CIVIL, RELIGION, SPIRITUAL, STATE

SECURITY

Security is a key term of the modern STATE and its apparatuses. Britain's intelligence agencies are called the **security services**, and one can trace modern American history through the establishment of Social Security (1935), the National Security Agency (1952), and the Department of Homeland Security (2002). If **security** in many of its modern meanings is linked to the modern state, it also gains much of its force in opposition to **insecurity**, which becomes a key term of modern psychology in the first half of C20 for describing subjective states of mind. Given that **security** also has important meanings in both finance and computing, it is a word with an unusually broad range of reference and whose senses play on a set of political assumptions that are rarely explicit.

It comes into the language via both Middle French and Anglo Norman *securite*, both derived from the classical Latin *securitas*, from the prefix *se*—*without* and the noun *cura* meaning *care*. Its initial meanings refer to an objective state, "freedom from care, anxiety or apprehension" and "confidence in one's safety or well-being." At this stage **security** is related to near-synonyms *rest, peace, ease, surety, carelessness*, and *serenity*, as well as *certainty* and *certitude*. The original Latin root has a sense of "complacent negligence, carelessness" and from C16 to C18 this "overconfidence, complacency" appears to be the dominant meaning of the word. This meaning became archaic as it came into contradiction with new senses crucial both in the developing forms of capitalist finance and in the modern definition of a nation. This archaic meaning was replaced by the phrase "**a false sense of security**."

From C15 on, **security** has been used in a wide variety of new forms of finance, with a text of 1606 pithily observing that "without good securitie they will lend Nobody mony." The *OED* defines this sense as "property, etc., deposited or pledged by or on behalf of a person as a guarantee of the payment of a debt." As capitalist forms of finance developed from C18 on, **security** multiplied its meaning in a wide variety of financial instruments called **securities**. As John Stuart Mill observed in his *Principles of Political Economy* (1848), "He buys from the State what are called government securities; that is, obligations by the government to pay a certain annual income." The complexity of these financial instruments is central both to the booms and busts of capitalism and in addition to the narrow and specific sense of Franklin D. Roosevelt's Securities Exchange Act of 1934 and the Social Security Act of 1935; **economic** and **financial security** become the centerpiece of many a political party's electoral programs. This tendency is particularly marked when the neoliberal consensus that follows the fall of the Berlin Wall means that computerization and globalization make **job security**, which is first recorded in 1926, an increasingly frequent term.

Important as these economic uses are, they are arguably dwarfed by the way in which the nation-state constitutes itself in terms of **security**. The *OED* provides this definition: "The safety or safeguarding of (the interests of) a state . . . against some internal or external threat, now esp. terrorism, espionage, etc." The first examples go back to lC16, and George Washington in 1783 succinctly expresses the soon-to-be dominant meaning: "I cannot hesitate to contribute my best endeavours towards the establishment of the national security." From C19, this notion of **security**, very closely linked to borders and the necessity of securing borders, becomes a major rhetorical trope in international politics as Europe redraws its own internal maps. The importance of this use is especially clear in the European refugee crisis of the second decade of C21. If borders must be made secure, so too must some of the internal population.

However, **security** becomes a key political term with the notion of increased threats to the state, both external and internal. The establishment of the National Security Agency at the height of the Cold War conjures a world of spies and nuclear bombs, but now the Department of Homeland Security introduces us to the world where our enemy is the person sitting next to us on a plane. This particular subsense reveals the underlying pragmatic tension in **security**: clandestine activities aimed at preserving and defending the state may not ensure the safety of individuals or the people at large. The relatively frequent collocation of **security** with *intelligence* (in the sphere of espionage) across the range of global Englishes suggests the international adoption of **security** with this sense.

Security has attracted adjectives since lC16 with the introduction of compounds such as **public security** and **state security**. The last two decades have many new compounds: **national security**, **airport security**, **domestic security**, culminating in **biometric security**. As computers have gained in social and economic importance, questions of **cybersecurity** have become crucial to questions of privacy and secrecy. In almost all the modern state-related meanings, **security** effectively talks about the security of the "haves." The thought that this system might be incredibly damaging to the have-nots, that the system itself might be **insecure**, is semantically impossible.

New developments of **security** show the extent to which the meanings of **security** are now at the center of much political debate. The use of **campus security** to cover every kind of assault from rape and murder to engagement with unwelcome ideas raises crucial questions about the relations between free speech and **personal insecurity**. The demand that has emerged from these debates for **psychological security** might seem a contradiction in terms in a world riddled with insecurity. In the field of global politics, the attempt since the 1974 World Food Conference to argue for **food security** marks an attempt to produce a definition of **security** that is both GLOBAL and universal and which focuses on the security of the have-nots rather than the haves.

See RISK, STATE, TERROR, WELL-BEING

SEXUALITY

The word **sexuality** is first recorded in English at the end of C18. It is based on the adjective **sexual**, and ultimately on the noun **sex**. **Sex** came into the English language in lC14 as a borrowing partly from French and partly from Latin; for most of its history in English, its primary, default meaning has been "Either of the two main categories (male and female) into which humans and many other living things are divided on the basis of their reproductive functions"; until recently, it also commonly referred to such differences in their social and cultural aspects— uses in which GENDER is now the much more usual term. Already in C16 phrases such as "the fair sex" and even "the sex" are found referring specifically to women in literary and general discourse. The earliest uses of the corresponding adjective **sexual** (another borrowing from Latin) in eC17 are also specifically in the meaning "characteristic of or peculiar to the female sex; feminine" (uses which survived until eC19). However, **sex** and **sexual** were also important terms in the language of science, in reference to the reproductive differences between male and female animals and humans, and to their reproductive behavior. From this specialist discourse, expressions such as **sexual intercourse** (mC18) gradually worked their way into general usage; as Raymond Williams astutely noted in his entry for **sex** in *Keywords*, "this seems to be a case . . . of the relatively learned or scientific word being adopted and generalized in the period in which it became more acceptable to speak or write of such matters at all openly."

Such a process appears to have happened at least twice in the interesting history of the derivative noun **sexuality**. This is an abstract noun formed on the adjective **sexual**, probably on the model of post-classical Latin *sexualitas*. This Latin word was probably also coined not earlier than the second half of C18, and, although it may not actually have been used by the great Swedish naturalist Linnaeus, it occurs early with reference to his work on biology, and especially botany. The corresponding English sense is defined by the *OED* as "The quality of being sexual or possessing sex. Opposed to asexuality *n*." The earliest example for this sense comes from the third edition of John Walker's *Elements of geography, and of natural and civil history* (1797): "The Linnaean system . . . is founded on the sexuality of plants." This sense has remained in use by biologists ever since; the areas of contestation and ambiguity in the word's contemporary use stem from its application to humans.

The earliest sense in *OED* used in reference to humans is attested in 1833, and defined as: "Sexual nature, instinct, or feelings; the possession or expression of these." **Sexuality** as so defined is something usually assumed to be inherent in all normally functioning human beings, although usage differs considerably according to the user's standpoint on a number of social and cultural issues. This sense has long been found in general as well as technical use; *OED*'s earliest example is from a collection of traditional tales from Scotland, Andrew Picken's *Traditionary Stories of Old Families* (1833): "This, like most matters of love and sexuality, became the bitter bottoming of many sorrows."

Before looking at this sense in further detail, the second major sense of **sexuality** as applied to human beings should be considered. This sense is first attested in 1897, and is defined in *OED* as "a person's sexual identity in relation to the gender to which he or she is typically attracted; the fact of being heterosexual, homosexual, or bisexual; sexual orientation." This use probably arose on the model of the words **homosexuality** and **heterosexuality**. It is not common in the first half of C20, and appears to have taken some time to break through into non-technical use. However, a use with this meaning in a *New York Times* book review from 1958, quoted by *OED*, points toward a characteristic pattern of contemporary usage: "Torn between his love for an intelligent, sympathetic French girl, Solange, and a haunting attraction to his top sergeant . . . he is held captive by . . . a brutal reality demanding that he define his own sexuality or face damnation."

Two of the most frequent collocations of **sexuality** in general corpora of contemporary English tend to be (i) **human sexuality** and (ii) modified by a possessive pronoun, e.g., **their sexuality, his sexuality, my sexuality**. The collocation **human sexuality** correlates closely with the meaning defined as "Sexual nature, instinct, or feelings; the possession or expression of these." The word is used with this meaning by people with a wide variety of different social, political, moral, and religious standpoints, and these differing standpoints will affect how different individuals conceptualize **human sexuality**. The term labels a concept that is at the center of a key battlefield in contemporary social and cultural debate. However, the mapping between word and concept is itself relatively uncomplicated: what is at issue is how different individuals define or conceptualize "sexual nature, instinct, or feelings," as well as, crucially, what they take to be "normal," "natural," or part of the expected or accepted spectrum of human feelings and behavior.

In the case of use modified by a possessive pronoun, e.g., **their sexuality, his sexuality, my sexuality**, use of the word **sexuality** may map to either of *OED*'s main senses, "Sexual nature, instinct, or feelings; the possession or expression of these" or "A person's sexual identity in relation to the gender to which he or she is typically attracted; the fact of being heterosexual, homosexual, or bisexual; sexual orientation." However, there is an interesting tension among these uses. When used in the second meaning, the construction typically refers to a particular **sexual** IDENTITY to which a person is (usually if not uncontroversially) taken to belong categorically; uses typically refer to **recognition, suppression, repression**, or **acceptance of one's sexuality**. Overwhelmingly, usage refers to **homosexuality**: if a man is described as "hiding his sexuality," this nearly always means that he is hiding the fact that he is gay (however this is construed), not that he is hiding his **heterosexuality**.

But alongside this usage, **sexuality** modified by a possessive pronoun is also used frequently in the meaning "sexual nature, instinct, or feelings." Examining contemporary usage shows that, for instance, "he/she [struggles/attempts/is obliged/is forced/is expected] to suppress/repress his/her sexuality" is found frequently in reference to gay people who attempt to "suppress" their sexual identity, but also not uncommonly in reference to heterosexual men who attempt to "suppress" or "control" their sexual instincts in a particular behavioral situation. Such uses are often, but not always, from contexts with clear echoes of psychoanalytical discourse, e.g.,: "Early on, he had learned to repress his sexuality in response to his rejecting wife" (from Anne C. Heller's *Ayn Rand*, 2009); or "Eugène Rougon . . . attempts to repress his sexuality by finding other means of powerful sexual sublimation. He thus achieves the pinnacle of success . . . by avoiding the charms of a *femme fatale*" (from A. Gural-Migdal and R. Singer's *Zola and Film*, 2005, 35).

Individuals (or perhaps, different individuals) are thus conceptualized as possessing a **sexuality** in two distinct but overlapping meanings: one is a matter of group membership (**heterosexual, homosexual, bisexual**); the other a question of sexual urges or instincts and how these affect behavior. The expression **sexual orientation** exists as a synonym in the first meaning, but **sexuality** appears to be the term preferred by many (perhaps because of connotations it carries of an inherent, non-volitional quality). In the second meaning, **sexual instinct** is perhaps the likeliest substitute, but occurs only relatively rarely; however, the richly developed vocabulary of **sexual desire** and *lust* is only a small step away. Coexistence of the two meanings in parallel constructions is surprising, since the danger of ambiguity is real and the meanings occur in a semantic area that is generally regarded as highly sensitive, where ambiguity may lead to intense embarrassment or social difficulties. Whether the two meanings continue to coexist, and continue to occur in such similar constructions, may be revealing about changing social attitudes in coming decades.

See GENDER, IDENTITY, LOVE, MARRIAGE, QUEER, TRANS

SOCIALIST

Socialist emerged as a philosophical description in eC19. Its linguistic root was the developed sense of *social*. But this could be understood in two ways, which have had profound effects on the use of the term by radically different POLITICAL tendencies. *Social* in sense (i) was the merely descriptive term for *society* in its now predominant sense of the system of common life; a *social reformer* wished to reform this system. *Social* in sense (ii) was an emphatic and distinguishing term, explicitly contrasted with *individual* and especially *individualist* theories of society. There has of course been much interaction and overlap between these two senses, but their varying effect can be seen from the beginning in the formation of the term. One popular form of sense (i) was in effect a continuation of LIBERALISM: reform, including radical reform, of the social order, to develop, extend, and assure the main *liberal* values: political freedom, the ending of privileges and formal inequalities, social justice (conceived as equity between different individuals and groups). A popular form of sense (ii) went in a quite different direction: a competitive, *individualist* form of society—specifically, industrial capitalism and the system of wage-labor—was seen as the enemy of truly *social* forms, which depended on practical cooperation and mutuality, which in turn could not be achieved while there was still *private* (*individual*) ownership of the means of production. Real freedom could not be achieved, basic inequalities could not be ended, social justice (conceived now as a just social order rather than equity between the different individuals and groups produced by the existing social order) could not be established, unless a society based on PRIVATE property was replaced by one based on *social* ownership and control.

The resulting controversy, between many groups and tendencies all calling themselves **socialist**, has been long, intricate, and bitter. Each main tendency has found alternative, often derogatory terms for the other. But until *c*1850 the word was too new and too general to have any predominant use. The earliest use I have found in English is in Hazlitt, "On Persons One Would Wish to Have Seen" (1826), where recalling a conversation from *c*1809 he writes: "those profound and redoubted socialists, Thomas Aquinas and Duns Scotus." There is then a more contemporary use in the English Owenite *Cooperative Magazine* of November 1827; its first recorded political use in French is in 1833. On the other hand, *socialisme* seems to have been first used in French in 1831, and in English in 1837 (Owen, *New Moral World*, III, 364). (A use of *socialismo* in Italian, in 1803, seems to have no connection with the later development; its meaning was quite different.) Given the intense political climate, in France and in England in the 1820s and 1830s, the exact dates are less important than the sense of a period. Moreover, it could not then have been known which word would come through as decisive. It was a period of very intense and rapid political argument and formation, and until well into the 1840s other terms stood level with **socialist**, or were indeed more common: *cooperative, mutualist, associationist, societarian, phalansterian, agrarianist, radical*. As late as 1848 Webster's *Dictionary* (US) defined **socialism** as "a new term for agrarianism," although in France and Germany, and to a lesser extent in England, **socialist** and **socialism** were by then common terms. The active verbs, **socialize** and *socialiser*, had been current in English and French from around 1830.

One alternative term, *communist*, had begun to be used in France and England from 1840. The sense of any of these words could vary in particular national contexts. In England in the 1840s *communist* had strong religious attachments, and this was important since **socialist**, as used by Robert Owen, was associated with opposition to religion and was sometimes avoided for that reason. Developments in France and Germany were different: so much so that Engels, in his *Preface* of 1888 looking back to the *Communist Manifesto* which he and Marx had written in 1848, observed:

> We could not have called it a *Socialist* manifesto. In 1847, Socialism
> was a middle-class movement. Socialism was, on the continent at least,
> respectable; Communism was the very opposite.

Communist had French and German senses of a militant movement, at the same time that in England it was being preferred to **socialist** because it did not involve atheism.

Modern usage began to settle from the 1860s, and in spite of the earlier variations and distinctions it was **socialist** and **socialism** which came through as the predominant words. What also came through in this period was a predominance of sense (ii), as the range of associated words—*cooperative, mutualist, associationist* and the new (from the 1850s) *collectivist*—made natural. Though there was still extensive and intricate internal dispute, **socialist** and **socialism** were, from this period, accepted general terms. *Communist*, in spite of the distinction that had been made in the 1840s, was very much less used, and parties in the Marxist tradition took some variant of *social* and **socialist** as titles: usually *Social Democratic*, which meant adherence to **socialism**. Even in the renewed and bitter internal disputes of the period 1880–1914, these titles held. *Communism* was in this period most often used either as a description of an early form of society—*primitive communism*—or as a description of an ultimate form, which would be achieved after passing through **socialism**. Yet, also in this period, movements describing themselves as **socialist**, for example the English Fabians, powerfully revived what was really a variant of sense (i), in which **socialism** was seen as necessary to complete *liberalism*, rather than as an alternative and opposed theory of society. To Shaw and others, **socialism** was "the economic side of the democratic ideal" (*Fabian Essays*, 33) and its achievement was an inevitable prolongation of the earlier tendencies which *Liberalism* had represented. It is interesting that opposing this view, and emphasizing the resistance of the capitalist economic system to such an "inevitable" development, William Morris used the word *communism*. The relative militancy of *communist* had also been affected by the example of the Paris Commune, though there was a significant argument whether the correct term to be derived from that was *communist* or *communard*.

The decisive distinction between **socialist** and *communist*, as in one sense these terms are now ordinarily used, came with the renaming, in 1918, of the Russian Social-Democratic Labour Party (Bolsheviks) as the *All-Russian* Communist Party (Bolsheviks). From that time on, a distinction of **socialist** from *communist*, often with supporting definitions such as *social democrat* or **democratic socialist**, became widely current, although it is significant that all *communist* parties, in line with earlier usage, continued to describe themselves as **socialist** and dedicated to **socialism**. Each tendency continues to deny the title to its opponents and competitors, but what has really happened is a resurfacing, in new terms, of the originally variant senses of *social* and thence **socialist**. Those relying on sense (ii) are right to see other kinds of **socialist** as a new stage of *liberalism* (and thus to call them, often contemptuously, *liberals*), while those relying on sense (i), seeing a natural association between *liberal* values and **socialism**, have grounds for opposing **socialists** who in their view are enemies of the *liberal* tradition (where the difficulty, always, is in the alternative interpretations: (a) political freedom understood as an *individual* right and expressed socially in competitive political parties; (b) *individualism* understood as the competitive and antagonistic ethos and practice of capitalism, which *individual* rights and political competition merely qualify.

Some other associated political terms provide further complications. There is the significant development, in mC19, of *anarchy* and its derivatives in new political senses. *Anarchy* had been used in English from C16 in a broad sense: "this unleful lyberty or lycence of the multytude is called an Anarchie" (1539). But this specific political sense, often interpreted as opposition to a single ruler—"*Anarchism* . . . the being itself of the people without a Prince or Ruler" (1656) (where the sense is close to that of early *democracy*)—was on the whole less common than the more general sense of disorder and chaos. Yet in 1791 Bentham defined the *anarchist* as one who "denies the validity of the law . . . and calls upon all mankind to rise up in a mass, and resist the execution of it," a sense again near that of early *democrat*. What was really new from mC19 was the positive adoption of the term by certain groups, as a statement of their political position; most of the earlier descriptions were by opponents. *Anarchism* and *anarchist*, by 1C19, represented a specific continuation of earlier senses of *democracy* and *democrat*, but at a time when both *democracy* and, though less widely, **socialism** had acquired new general and positive senses. *Anarchists* opposed the *statist* tendencies of much of the **socialist** movement, but stressed *mutuality* and *cooperation* as the principles of the self-organization of society. Particular *anarchist* groups opposed particular tyrannies and governments by *militant* and VIOLENT means, but this was not a necessary or universal result of *anarchist* principles, and there was in any case a complicated overlap between such policies and **socialist** definitions of *revolution*. Yet the persistent general senses of disorder and chaos were relatively easily transferred (often with obvious injustice) to *anarchists*: the variant senses of *lawlessness*—from active criminality to resistance to laws made by others—were in this context critical. *Militant*, meanwhile, had been going through a related development: its early senses in English were stronger in the context of dedicated activity than in the root *military* sense, and the predominant use, to 1C19, was in religion: *church militant* (from eC15); "our condition, whilst we are in this world, is militant" (Wilkins, *Natural Religion*, 251; 1672); "the Church is ever militant" (Newman, 1873). The word was effectively transferred from religious to social activity during C19: "militant in the endeavour to reason aright" (Coleridge, *Friend*, 57; 1809); "a normal condition of militancy against social injustice" (Froude, 1856). The further development from political to industrial *militancy* came in C20, and much of the earlier history of the word has been forgotten, except in residual uses. There has also been a marked association—as in *anarchism*—with senses of disorder and of VIOLENCE. *Solidarity*, in its sense of unity in industrial or political action, came into English in mC19, from fw *solidarité*, F, 1C18. *Exploitation* appeared in English from eC19, originally in the sense of profitable working of an area or a material, and from mC19 in the sense of using other persons for (selfish) profit; it depended in both senses on fw *exploitation*, F, 1C18.

Nihilist was invented by Turgenev in *Fathers and Sons* (1862). Its confusion with *anarchist* has been widespread. *Populist* began in the United States, from the People's Party, in the early 1890s; it spread quickly, and is now often used in distinction from socialist, to express reliance on popular interests and sentiments rather than par-ticular (*principled*) theories and movements. *Syndicalist* appeared in French in 1904 and in English in 1907; it has gone through varying combinations with *anarchism* (in its stress on *mutuality*) and with **socialism**.

The widest term of all, the *Left*, is known from C19 from an accident of parlia-mentary seating, but it was not common as a general description before C20, and *leftism* and *leftist* do not seem to have been used in English before the 1920s. The derisive *lefty*, though it has some currency from the 1930s, belongs mainly to the 1950s and after.

RECENT DEVELOPMENTS

The most striking development in the meaning of **socialist** since the second edition of *Keywords* in 1983 was historical and not linguistic. In the late 1980s and early 1990s, the Soviet Union and its satellite states collapsed with a speed and thor-oughness that few had foreseen. Soviet Communism had been the most powerful promoter of the sense of **socialism** as the organization of society on a collective rather than individual basis. There had been many **socialists** who opposed the il-liberalism of Soviet Communism while nonetheless arguing for the social owner-ship of the means of production. However, the total collapse of the Soviet model meant that many social democratic parties now abandoned any commitment to a **socialist** transformation of the economy. The debate which had opposed those who argued for social justice within a capitalist economy and those who argued that social justice was only possible with a socially transformed economy (a debate that had dominated the left since its inception) was as speedily terminated as the Soviet Bloc. Typical of a global change was the British Labour Party's decision in 1995 to drop Clause 4 of its constitution with its commitment to the social ownership of "production, distribution, and exchange." Indeed, one might have been tempted to argue until quite recently that **socialist** itself was an archaic term with its frequency dropping precipitously in the two decades after 1990.

However, since 2015 a variety of political campaigns, Bernie Sanders in the US, Jeremy Corbyn in the UK, and Jean-Luc Mélenchon in France, have seen a renewed use of the term. In the US, which had never developed a meaningful **socialist** party and where the word had often carried very pejorative senses, a significant number of Sanders supporters identified themselves as **socialist** in the 2016 presidential campaign. By and large this new **socialism** is a **socialism** of social justice rather than economic transformation, yet social movements such as environmentalism, feminism, and animal rights have demanded transformations of the economic that go beyond simple notions of social ownership.

Militant, like **socialist**, has become much less frequently used, while *activist* has increased at a very striking rate, particularly in the last two decades. *Activist* covers a much larger range of social movements, and it also places an emphasis on direct action, a legacy from the 1960s. Finally, in the past decade and particularly around the Occupy Wall Street movement of 2011, *anarchist*, with its refusal to recognize existing power structures, has proved an increasingly popular political identification on the left.

See CAPITALISM, DEMOCRACY, LIBERAL, POLITICAL, POPULAR

SOUL

The word **soul** has a long history in the language with shifting nuances and contentions of meaning that involve complex theological and philosophical debates, as well as a variety of uses in other contexts. Its currency today reflects an extension into areas related to self and IDENTITY no longer understood with direct reference to any religious sense of **soul**, though the word is never entirely free of its religious heritage.

The etymology of the word is relatively straightforward. **Soul** derives from OE *sáwol*—spiritual and emotional part of a person, animate existence, life—itself from Old High German *sêula, sêla*; English and German today have **soul** and *Seele*, with cognates in other Germanic languages (Swedish *själ*, Danish *sjael*). French has *âme*, with cognates in other romance languages (Spanish *alma*, Italian *anima*). The derivation here is from classical Latin *anima*, which translates classical Greek *psyché*; both of which have senses of breath, air, vital principle of life. The nature and mode of existence of *psyché* much concerned Greek philosophers who commonly distinguished three souls—vegetative, animal, rational; with humans combining the essential qualities of the souls of plants and animals with the soul possessed by them alone, the **rational soul** (*a*1398 *soule racional*). In English this tripartite division became something of a commonplace—"I scorn it with my three souls," swears a character in Ben Jonson's *Poetaster* (1601).

Soul with the sense of LIFE, the principle of animate existence, enters English in C14. "Soul and Life in the Scripture, do usually signifie the same thing," notes Hobbes in 1650. It could be used for countable lives: "Erthe and soulis that thereon dwelle" (Chaucer, *c*1430); as in certain usages it still is—ships sink with so many **souls** aboard, where **souls** instead of *passengers* or *people* intensifies the loss. The important sense of **soul** that comes through from Old English in C13 is that of what *OED* describes as the principle of intelligence, mind, and the essential, SPIRITUAL part of a person distinct from the *physical*; a late C14 quotation gives a succinct definition: "a soule is a bodiles substaunce ruling a body." Understanding the relation of **soul** to *body* is fundamental: "My sensis, and my saull I saw, Debait a deadly strife" (1599); soul-body debates indeed were a medieval genre, popular again in the 1600s following the Reformation and Puritan emphasis on strenuous examination of one's spiritual condition—an example is Andrew Marvell's "A Dialogue between the Soul and the Body" (*c*1652). The need to preserve the soul's integrity from **soul wrack** (1595) and **soul destruction** (1619) during its life in the body is reflected in many such C16/17 **soul** compounds: **soul surgeon** (1593), **soul chirurgery** (1654), and many others. The compound **soul-searching**—adjective (1591), noun (*a*1651)—refers in this context precisely to the necessity for knowing "how it is with our precious and immortall souls. . . . The benefit of this soul-searching, will abundantly recompence our pains" (*a*1651).

The assimilation of the work of the Greek philosophers in the writings of the Church Fathers ensured the place of **soul** in Christian theology with meanings bearing on the spiritual reality of a person understood in his relation to God, to faith. At the same time, it has, over the centuries, known developments in use and meaning in which its basis in RELIGION is both drawn on and to a greater or lesser degree set aside. When President Obama, after the death in police custody of a young African American, urged **soul-searching** as an obligation—"We have some soul-searching to do" (2015)—the soul to be searched was more a personal and social matter of conscience and moral feeling than one of any religious soul, though the presence of the latter was still felt to a greater or lesser degree by his listeners. From C17 uses of **soul** more or less separated from any direct religious reference became common: either with a modifying adjective to indicate some quality—"mean dull souls" (1635), "active sauls" (1721); or without adjectival modification, likewise indicating possession of a particular character or nature: "Those fellowes haue some soule," says Iago appreciatively of people like him (*a*1616). Unmodified uses of **soul** are rarely negative; much of its meaning indeed has come to lie simply in its emphatic force as a term of appreciation, not least when applied to things: a station wagon, was "in less than perfect condition, but . . . had soul" (1991). Increasingly from late C18, **soul** stands for the emotional core, the innermost part of a person's being: "there is an internal landscape, a geography of the soul; we search for its outlines all our lives" (Josephine Hart, 1991). What such a use means is not readily definable, no longer held within a determining religious framework, this indefinableness being intrinsic to the effect of meaning sought. Byron writes of "an indefinable *je ne sais quoi* . . . which pretty women—the sweet souls—call *Soul*" (1823). Women in particular reflect intensity of **soul**: "I never saw so much soul in a lady's eyes," declares Lovelace in Richardson's *Clarissa* (1748); this becoming a linguistic automatism of romance-fiction: "He looked at her . . . deep, deep into her soul" (2002, from Sue-Ellen Welfonder's romance *Knight in My Bed*). The C19 words **soulful** (1837, nightingales "fly to sing their soulful songs in far lands"), **soulfully** (1841, two individuals "corporeally two, but soulfully one"), and **soulfulness** (1842, "Those eyes . . . wherein such soulfulness has birth") likewise largely repeat this sense of depth of **soul**, with the depth a matter of emotional intensity, suggestive often of melancholy, of sadness.

The American Black community has used **soul** to name an essential quality and experience of its life and CULTURE, expressed in the first instance in its music. The phrase **soul music** had been used from C19 to qualify music felt as coming from the soul or rising above the given world: "That wondrous soul-music of which the purified tones now belong to more exalted spheres" (1829). W. E. B. Du Bois in his *Souls of Black Folk* (1903) had described a "double consciousness" of African Americans: "An American, a Negro; two souls, two thoughts," recognizing thereby a distinct cultural identity—a **soul**—to be acknowledged and enabled. The compound **soul music** was not used in Du Bois's book, though each chapter began with musical notation of bars from spirituals—"music which welled up from *black souls* in the dark* past." The African-American context for **soul music** and the identification of cultural **soul** was jazz; *OED*'s first recorded example of **soul music** is from a newspaper report of "the fine jazz and soul music played by J. Nimrod Jones' crack orchestra" (1920). Used of jazz and other forms of African-American music, it subsequently narrowed to a particular form, called simply **soul**, exemplified by the "Memphis soul" of Otis Redding, one of whose albums indeed was a *Dictionary of Soul* (1966). Responding to the emergence of this music, the US entertainment magazine *Billboard* in 1969 replaced its *R&B* charts with **Soul** charts. As an adjective, **soul** extended beyond music to recognize membership or specify components of African-American culture: **soul brother** (1957), **soul sister** (1967), earlier uses of which (C18/19) had been to designate generally kindred spirits; **soul food**, from C13, food for the soul, spiritual nourishment, from 1960s gains specific reference to

Black American food, with **soul** then used as something of a quasi-ethnic term, and as such potentially problematic in the ways it may objectify and annex cultural forms. The title of a recent book, *Soul Thieves: The Appropriation and Misrepresentation of African American Popular Culture* (2014), for example, declares at once the essential ownership of **soul** and its extension today—the "APPROPRIATION"—beyond its original cultural application. Like so many other **soul** expressions, **soul thief** also had an early religious existence: "These Soule-thiefes . . . put out the Candle of knowledge, the Scripture" (1618; the thieves here are Papists).

The history of the word **soul** shows its extension from meanings dependent on and developed within a religion to meanings bound up with reference to some essential quality or reality of person or community rather than to any religious ground of being. At the same time, these are not exclusive: individual agents of their own personal religions are often at the same time believers filling the congregations of the multitude of today's proclaimed public religions.

See CULTURE, IDENTITY, LIFE, RELIGION, SPIRITUAL

SPIRITUAL

"Spiritual but not religious" is an increasingly common self-description, yet the noun **spirit**, from which the adjective **spiritual** derives, functions as a central term for some 500 million Charismatic Christians, one of the world's largest religious groups. The tension between these two usages captures the challenge of **spiritual** today. Both **spiritual** and *religious* describe *sacred* or *non-secular* matters, but the terms have become contested and used to express different attitudes toward organized religion since the rise of the New Age movement in Western societies in lC20.

Spiritual comes from the Latin adjective *spīrituālis*, from the Latin noun *spīritus*, meaning "breathing, breath, air, etc." *Spīritus* was itself frequently deployed as a translation of *rūaḥ* from the Hebrew Bible and *pneuma* from the Greek New Testament, and this specific biblical use figures strongly in the world's earliest uses in English. First documented in English in eC14, the noun **spirit** and adjective **spiritual** already had a range of different meanings and associations in lC14. John Wycliffe's Bible translation (early version, *a*1382) from the Latin Vulgate provides the strongest evidence of these words' polysemy in early English usage; the *OED* identifies three subsenses of **spiritual** and eighteen subsenses of **spirit** in the Wycliffe Bible alone.

From C14, **spiritual** has implied a distinction from the material or corporeal. Such uses reflect understandings of **spirit** as "[t]he animating or vital principle in man (and animals); that which gives life to the physical organism, in contrast to its purely material elements; the breath of life." Since lC14, **spirit** has often been deemed synonymous with SOUL, but the possession of a *soul* or **spirit** is typically restricted to humans. Both senses regard the **spirit** as an immaterial entity separate from the physical *body*, a distinction that became especially significant in philosophical and scientific discourses from C17 onward.

Since mC14, **spiritual** has also meant "Of, belonging or relating to, concerned with, sacred or ecclesiastical things or matters, as distinguished from secular affairs; relating to the church or the clergy; ecclesiastical." A separation between the **spiritual** and the SECULAR is found as early as Wycliffe (*c*1380, "Þei meyntenen þis cursed þefte boþe bi seculer power and spiritual swerd"). Due to the influence of Lockean and Enlightenment thought, the division of the two spheres became more distinct in C18, as evident in the following *OED* citation: "The duties of life, which are either spiritual or secular" (1738).

New branches of meaning, which were not directly concerned with the sacred or ecclesiastical, emerged in C18 and C19. In eC18 a new sense denoted "Of or relating to, emanating from, the intellect or higher faculties of the mind; intellectual." During the Romantic period in eC19, another sense of **spiritual** arose to describe someone or something "[c]haracterized by or exhibiting a high degree of refinement of thought or feeling." Contemporary feelings of **spirituality**, which are generally regarded as personal experiences of the sacred outside of organized religion, hark back to the work of romantic philosophers and poets, such as Rousseau, Novalis, and Wordsworth, for whom NATURE was a source of the **spiritual**.

The *OED* presents **spiritual** and *religious* as closely related, but it does not yet capture the tension that has developed between the two terms since lC20. Considerable overlap still exists between the adjectives; *religious* matters may be called **spiritual**, as distinguished from *secular* affairs. Over the past few decades, however, it has become increasingly common to differentiate between *religious* and **spiritual**.

Religious is usually associated with INSTITUTIONS and systems of practice and belief and now carries a negative connotation in many contexts. For example, *religious extremism* and *religious fanaticism*, collocations commonly found in contemporary news media and political discourse, have been identified as responsible for GLOBAL terrorism. Even in less extreme cases, however, *religious* often carries negative implications of blind faith or strict adherence to dogma. **Spiritual**, in contrast, is less bound to rules and institutions, more a state of mind than a discipline of practices. The term enjoys positive connotations, owing to its historical association with intellect, wit, and refinement of thought or feeling.

Tension between **spirituality** and RELIGION is especially evident in the ambiguous phrase **spiritual but not religious**. Corpora show that use of the phrase increased during the 1990s and the first decade of the 2000s. According to a 2012 Pew Research Center study, nearly one-fifth of Americans surveyed reported no religious affiliation, but thirty-seven percent of the unaffiliated claimed to be "spiritual but not religious" (SBNR). The rise of identification with the label has been attributed to disillusionment with organized religion and other institutions, as well as a strong global interest in other forms of **spiritual** practice and FAITH. Under the influence of neoliberal corporate capitalism, **spiritual** practices like yoga, meditation, and alternative healing have been appropriated from Eastern religious traditions and marketed to Western consumers. The preference for these and other individualized, eclectic forms of commercialized **spirituality** over organized *religion* is a feature of the New Age movement that arose in Western societies in the 1960s and 1970s.

Critics on the left have argued that New Age **spirituality**, with its focus on personal self-growth, is removed from politics and social activism. Yet for the interfaith Network of Spiritual Progressives (NSP), which includes religious believers and atheists who identify as **spiritual but not religious**, combining **spirituality** with political and social activism is central. Seeking to bring a **spiritual** political movement to the progressive world, the NSP regards as **spiritual** "all those whose deepest values lead them to challenge the ethos of selfishness and materialism that has led people into a frantic search for money and power and away from a life that places love, kindness, generosity, peace, non-violence, social justice, awe and wonder at the grandeur of creation, thanksgiving, humility and joy at the center of our lives." Such expressions of the new **spirituality** movement cannot be reduced to commercialized forms of **spiritual** practice.

Throughout the word's long history, discussions of the **spiritual** have typically focused on human experiences of the sacred. The discovery that chimpanzees exhibit certain ritualistic behaviors that remind human observers of *religious* practices, however, has raised the question of the **spirituality** of non-human ANIMALS. Conclusions about whether non-human animals are **spiritual** beings depends on how one understands the term, but the possibility of animal **spirituality** calls for a re-examination of human **spirituality** and the way we relate to other species.

As a result of the individualization and rebranding of *religion* as **spirituality**, **spiritual** is more difficult than ever to define. **Spiritual** has commonly encompassed organized *religion*, but, since lC20, it has broadened to include more *secular* matters, sometimes to the point of excluding *religion* completely. Nonetheless, the increasing use of **spiritual** and **spiritual but not religious** as labels of self-identification attests to a widespread and ongoing search for meaning and fulfillment between the *sacred* and the *secular*.

See ANIMAL, FAITH, NATURE, RELIGION, SECULAR, SOUL, WELL-BEING

STATE

The noun **state** is first found in English in C13. It shows multiple inputs that have merged to give the single word **state**, although these inputs are all ultimately related to one another. It partly shows a shortening, by a process of initial vowel loss, of English *estate*, which is in turn borrowed from Anglo-Norman and Old French *estat* (modern French *état*), which is the usual French development of Latin *status*. In addition, English **state** also partly shows a borrowing directly from Latin *status*. The Latin word is a verbal noun formed on the root of *stāre*, to stand. (It also gives rise to English **status**.) Additionally, in (relatively rare) senses related to a verbal or written statement the noun **state** may also show some input from the verb **to state**, which was itself formed (by conversion) from the noun.

The word is highly polysemous, showing a large number of separate dictionary senses, which in turn often show a number of different nuances. Most of the senses fall into three major groups. The earliest group of senses relates to a "condition or manner of existing," whether a temporary immaterial condition, or a physical or essential condition; here belong uses such as **the state of the roads**, a person's **mental state**, a **state of equilibrium**, etc.; here too belong idiomatic uses such as **in a disordered state**. Another group of senses, recorded from C14 onward, relate to status or rank; some of these uses, such as **marital state**, are now more commonly represented by uses of (ultimately related) **status**; others are now more typically realized by the form **estate**, such as the traditional division of the body politic into the three **states** of clergy, nobility, and commons. This last group of uses (particularly in its application to the government of the Netherlands, formerly referred to as the States General) shows interesting points of connection and overlap with the third major group of senses, which will form the main focus of the following paragraphs. These uses, again recorded in English from C14 onward, denote various types of commonwealth or polity, either as a collective unit (hence coming close in meaning to *nation* or COUNTRY) or specifically as the body politic within a nation (hence close in meaning to *government*). The first of these groups of senses, "condition or manner of existing," build clearly on meanings already shown by classical Latin *status*, as do uses relating to the status or standing of an individual; uses relating to divisions of the body politic, or to the body politic as a whole, or to a national unit under a single authority, all reflect developments shown by Old and Middle French *estat* (modern French *état*).

Definitions of **state** as polity differ greatly according to historical and social context, and also according to political perspective. An important (more-or-less binary) division is between **sovereign states** and **federated states** that form part of a larger federal union (such as the constituent states of the US). The 1933 Montevideo Convention on the Rights and Duties of States, signed by sovereign states of the Americas, says that a **state** has "a) a permanent population; b) a defined territory; c) government; and d) capacity to enter into relations with the other states," and also that "the federal state shall constitute a sole person in the eyes of international law." Additionally, **state** is used to denote the central AUTHORITY within such a polity, typically distinguished from *government* in denoting those functions and agencies that remain in existence regardless of which particular set of politicians (or others) form the administration. In this use, the **state** (often spelled with a capital initial) is typically distinguished from *civil society*.

The typical collocation patterns in both of these senses are interesting, particularly in how they contrast with those of near-synonyms such as *nation, country, land*, or (in the central authority sense) *government*. Uses of **state** denoting a polity seldom show the positive emotional engagement of *nation, country*, or *land*—conflict between states is a topic for international lawyers, but the discourse of patriotism seldom invokes loyalty to one's **state**. In technical discourse, a CULTURE may be a possession of a **nation-state**—i.e., of a unit that is a sovereign state with a national IDENTITY—but in popular discourse aspects of cultural identity are attributed to the *nation* or *country*. Where strong emotions are associated with uses of **state**, it is more typically negative ones directed against a central authority, as reflected by such collocations as **state security apparatus**, **state oppression**, or **state terror**. **Statism** and **statist** are seldom used as positive terms, typically being deployed by those critical of a situation where the state is perceived to play too great a role. In Britain the pejorative **nanny state** is frequently employed by those hostile to welfare spending or social regulation. Interestingly, in discussion of spending by the state, attributive use of **state**, as in e.g., **state expenditure**, is often avoided by those in favor of such expenditure, the more positive (or at least neutral) PUBLIC being preferred; those opposed to such expenditure are more likely to draw on pejorative expressions such as **state handouts**.

Distinction between the **state** and other elements of the polity has a very long history, most notably in the separation of Church and **state** in the British intellectual tradition extending to Locke and beyond. Today, in contexts of globalization and neoliberalism, public/private partnerships, competing models for school and health funding, or the spread on quasi-governmental organizations or agencies, the boundaries of the **state** and its activities may seem blurred as seldom before, especially in Anglophone societies such as the UK and the US.

See AUTHORITY, COUNTRY, CULTURE, IDENTITY, NATIONALIST, PUBLIC

SUSTAINABLE

Sustainable is an adjective that has shown a relatively recent rise to importance. The oldest (eC17) and rare sense of the word, which relates to being endured or borne, is now obsolete. An additional meaning signaling defensibility and validity, recorded from lC17, though still in use, is hardly frequent. It is, therefore, in the third *OED* sense of "capable of being maintained or continued at a certain rate or level" that it re-emerged in public discourse in the 1970s, particularly to describe (economic) development and growth.

By the 1980s the currently dominant use relating to the impact of human activity on the ENVIRONMENT and natural resources becomes common. Often articulated in its nominalized form as **sustainability**, this explicitly relates to **environmental** and **natural resource sustainability** as broadly conceived. The special uses of the word **sustainable** include some of the most common phrases in the fields of economics, environmental science, and agriculture: **sustainable growth**, **sustainable energy**, **sustainable agriculture**, and **sustainable ecology**.

Sustainable clearly derives from the verb **sustain** with recorded use dating from *c*1300, but only appears to reflect a few of the verb's many meanings. "To support, maintain, uphold" and "to maintain (a person, etc.) in life and health" as well as "to supply or satisfy (a person's needs, wants, etc.)" are the key senses carried forward in the adjective. Among the meanings that have been directly "lost" in the adjectival form is "To advocate or support as valid, correct, or true; to uphold or affirm the justice or validity of," and yet this ethical element is contained in the bio-psycho-social **sustainability** movement.

Pre-sustainability environmentalism by pioneers such as Rachel Carson (*Silent Spring*, 1962) and Aldo Leopold (*A Sand Country Almanac*, 1949) gradually led to the United Nations taking up this issue and globalizing its rhetoric. The still current and oft-quoted, if overly broad, definition of **sustainability** comes from this impetus and the UN's Brundtland Commission in 1987, which states that "sustainable development is development that meets the needs of the present without compromising the ability of future generations to meet their own needs."

The Rio Earth Summit of 1992 marked the GLOBAL ascendancy of the concept of **sustainable development** when *Agenda 21* was recognized by 178 governments. In this document, CULTURE was included under the umbrella of **sustainability**, which led to conceptualizations such as **sustainability cycles**. However, as even the UN Commission on Sustainable Development noted in 2013, there has been a signal lack of success "in fully integrating economic, social and environmental dimensions of sustainable development into its work and outcomes."

Among the more important movements of our times is the so-called **sustainability revolution**, which "offers the possibility of a much broader coalition for positive change both within and among societies. Rather than pitting 'tree-huggers' against lumberjacks—so often the trope of environmental discourse—**sustainability** seeks a context in which the legitimate interests of all parties can be satisfied to a greater or lesser extent, always within the framework of concern for equity" (Andres Edwards, *The Sustainability Revolution*, 2005). Note, however, that despite these protestations, the local is still the site of contestation, and the search is for a win-win situation—satisfying the LEGITIMATE interests of all parties—which in the context of systematic historical discrimination and resource extraction is untenable.

One may legitimately ask, if the term is of relatively recent and unambiguous origin, and less than complex in its current usage, why should it be considered a keyword? The *OED* entry is uncomplicated because it fails to nuance the value coding of this mainstream current usage of **sustainable**, which carries geopolitical overtones that are crucial to understanding both the strengths and weaknesses of the concept itself. Moreover, the hidden yet powerful sense of a moral imperative in **sustainable** makes it a unique contemporary term that bridges the popular and technical domains.

The *OED* entry on **sustainability** holds that the earliest recorded use of the word in relation to the environment is from 1980. From that time until 2000, usage increased dramatically, but this hardly matched the increase of **sustainable**. **Sustainable** is self-consciously both a global *and* a local buzzword. At the super-macro end it is vague and general, while in its micro application it is COMMUNITY-oriented and directive to third-world governments, often as tied to Bretton Woods loan imperatives or development "grants."

Sustainability as a concept is used to occupy the moral high ground, not only for the present generation but also for future ones. ETHICAL imperatives in this discourse go beyond the narrowly human in order to encompass all life forms and eco-systems, even in a planetary sense. Yet, this universality is achieved precisely at the expense of disaggregating culpability and denying the need for a global accountability. Hence, sustainable ecosystems are conceived as global, and, therefore, specifically "Northern" overconsumption is dissimulated as a universal problem, while at the same time **sustainable development** becomes an imperative only for economically exploited nations.

The origin and etymology of **sustainable** demonstrates a remarkable continuity and consonance across the spectrum of European languages. Most comprehensive in this respect, as echoed in the other languages, is the classical Latin *sustinēre*, which meant "to hold up, support, to maintain, preserve, to uphold, to keep from failing or giving way, to support with food or resources, to withstand, to bear the weight of, shoulder, to play the part of, to submit to, endure, to tolerate, to hold back, to put off, [and] defer." Today, its range and ubiquity are equally overarching.

However, the current hegemony of **sustainable** as a global goal effaces both Northern RESPONSIBILITY and reparation for past exploitation, as well as willfully confuses maldistribution and overconsumption at the center with enforcement of austerity at the periphery. The newest global metanarrative of **sustainability** is a pious platitude that demands unequal and skewed responses from the global North and South, and yet its domination of international discourse and technical forums as the progressive grand NARRATIVE of globalization par excellence has left developing nations with few alternatives to compliance.

See ECOLOGY, ENVIRONMENT, RESPONSIBILITY

TECHNOLOGY

Technology was used from C17 to describe a systematic study of the arts (cf. ART) or the terminology of a particular art. It is from fw *tekhnologia*, Gk, and *technologia*, mod. L—a systematic treatment. The root is *tekhne*, Gk—an art or craft. In eC18 a characteristic definition of **technology** was "a description of arts, especially the Mechanical" (1706). It was mainly in mC19 that **technology** became fully specialized to the "practical arts"; this is also the period of **technologist**. The newly specialized sense of *science* and *scientist* opened the way to a familiar modern distinction between knowledge (*science*) and its practical application (**technology**), within the selected field. This leads to some awkwardness as between **technical**—matters of practical construction—and **technological**—often used in the same sense, but with the residual sense (in *logy*) of systematic treatment. In fact there is still room for a distinction between the two words, with **technique** as a particular construction or method, and **technology** as a system of such means and methods; **technological** would then indicate the crucial *systems* in all production, as distinct from specific "applications."

Technocrat is now common, though **technocracy**, from *c*1920, was a more specific doctrine of *government* by technically competent persons; this was often anti-capitalist in the US in the 1920s and 1930s. **Technocrat** now is more local, in economic and industrial management, and has overlapped with part of the sense of *bureaucrat*.

RECENT DEVELOPMENTS

Use of the keyword **technology** has increased sharply over the past fifty years. This rise in relative frequency follows the advent of the personal computer in the 1980s and the growth of computer science and **information technology** (IT). Since lC20, computers and developments in **information technology** have dramatically changed the ways in which people around the world communicate with each other, collect information, and conduct business.

Two senses of **technology** cited in the *OED* and referenced by Williams remain active: (i) "The branch of knowledge dealing with the mechanical arts and applied sciences" attested from lC18, and (ii) "The application of such knowledge for practical purposes, esp. in industry, manufacturing, etc." from eC19. The noun **technology** and its plural form **technologies** now commonly describe not only a branch of knowledge or its practical application, but also the products themselves. Gadgets such as fully waterproof smartphones, robotic chefs, and self-driving trucks, for instance, are considered examples of the most recent **new technologies**.

Although **technology** denoted "[a] discourse or treatise on an art or arts" from eC17 to mC19, this sense is now obsolete, and many perceive ART and **technology** as at odds with each other. Beginning in lC20, national science programs and education councils were established in the US to promote EXCELLENCE in the disciplines of science, **technology**, engineering, and math (known as STEM since 2001). The perceived conflict between the liberal arts and a STEM education has been a contested topic of debate in eC21. For some, STEM education is the future, but for others pitting the arts and humanities against science and **technology** creates a false dichotomy. When introducing the iPad 2 in March 2011, Steve Jobs described Apple's strategy for success as one that integrates the arts with **technology**: ". . . technology alone is not enough—it's technology married with liberal arts, married with the humanities, that yields the results that make our heart sing."

See ART

TERROR

Terror comes into English in lC14, partly from Middle French *terreur*, and partly directly from Latin *terror*. The word means both "the state of being greatly frightened" and "the cause of that state," an ambiguity that is central to its future political meanings. In Early Modern English, **terror** comes to stand for a state of fear provoked on the very edge of the social. That state is associated with the god Pan and the fear that grips men when they feel themselves removed from any social contact. It also stands for death itself.

The political meanings of **terror** date from the period March 1793 to July 1794, when the use of organized intimidation became an instrument of policy for the Jacobins and Robespierre. Interestingly, the announcement of **terror** as public policy was as much an attempt to claim the breakdown of social order as a government policy as it was a deliberate attempt to cause that breakdown. Throughout the first half of C19, "a state of affairs in which the general community live in dread of death or outrage" was the dominant political meaning, and was still the most important meaning for the first edition of *OED*. It is worth remembering that most POLITICAL **terror** during C20, from the German genocide in the Herero War of 1904–05 to the gulags of Stalin's Soviet Union and the terror bombing by the Allied air forces during World War II, has been **state terror** (to be distinguished from **state-sponsored terrorism**, discussed later).

The invention of dynamite in 1866 by Alfred Nobel was the crucial technological condition that gave us modern terrorism. Although both **terrorism** and **terrorist** were joined in relation to the Jacobins, widespread use of these modern nouns comes when small groups of political dissidents attempt to use violent explosive force against an existing state to bring about political change. Three more or less distinct stages in this process can be sketched. The first, up until 1914, sees particularly in Russia the growth of a kind of terrorism which describes itself as such, and which believes that the social order is so rotten that a single act of VIOLENCE aimed at the center of power will bring about a revolutionary transformation. Some sense of this is captured in the phrase **little terror**, which begins to be used at this time to describe difficult young children. This first wave of terrorism found unprecedented historical success when the assassination of the Archduke Ferdinand in Sarajevo in 1914 occasioned what John Maynard Keynes called the "European Civil War."

In the aftermath of that war, the Irish, who had participated in this first chapter of terrorism, developed a terrorist campaign targeting the police, a campaign that described itself as part of a military struggle for national liberation. This conception of **terrorism**, the model for a host of imitators, is captured in the slogan "one man's terrorist is another man's freedom fighter." The focus of definition for **terror** passes from the act of terrorism itself to the status of the terrorist and whether he or she is authorized by an alternative and unrecognized legal AUTHORITY. Thus, Michael Collins and the Irish Republican Army claimed their actions as legitimized by the Irish Republic that Pearse had proclaimed on the steps of the Post Office on Easter Monday 1916. Similarly, Umkhonto we Sizwe (or MK), translated as "Spear of the Nation," authorized its violence in relation to the African National Congress, an authorization accepted by George W. Bush when he signed a bill removing the ANC from the US terror blacklist. In this period, use of **terrorism** and **terrorist** becomes widespread—note for example the decision made by British colonial authorities in the Malayan emergency of the 1950s to always refer to "Communist terrorists" and never just "Communists."

This second stage culminated in the terror campaigns of the National Liberation Front or FLN (one of which is famously represented in Gillo Pontecorvo's *Battle of Algiers*) that led to Algerian independence in 1962. The Algerian experience became the constant reference point for a new wave of terrorism in the aftermath of the Six-Day War of 1967, when a variety of Palestinian groups adopted terrorist tactics now taken onto an international stage. This was also the start of **state-sponsored terrorism**, as different Arab states supported different Palestinian groupings.

A full history of **terrorism** would need to reflect continuously on both the development of weapons and communication TECHNOLOGY. The new phase, for instance, was marked by plastic explosives (the expression *car bomb* is added to the language in this period) and the ability (most famously in Munich in 1972) to get the world's instant attention through television screens. In the 1980s, with the failure of Arab NATIONALISM to deliver either SOCIALIST or CAPITALIST success for its peoples, a new form of **Islamic terrorism** began to develop. This new variety of **terrorism** claimed its authority not from a political but from divine authority. This appearance of the divine was one of the conditions of the emergence of the *suicide bomber* (another was further sophistication of the technology of plastic explosives). These developments culminated in the attacks of September 11, 2001.

In the aftermath of the September 11 attacks, George W. Bush announced his "War on Terror," thus, as Terry Jones remarked, becoming the first world leader to declare war on an abstract noun. The political effects of this use of **terror** have prompted widespread questioning of the term and of the nature of **terrorism** itself.

Distinguishing between **terrorist** and **non-terrorist acts** of violence in terms of the acts themselves is problematic, and if we follow the Hobbesian arguments of the German legal philosopher Carl Schmidt that at the root of every state's LEGITIMATE use of violence is an illegitimate use of violence, it is difficult to produce a distinction in terms of legal authority. The linguistic effects of Bush's war are difficult to gauge, but it could be argued that Bush completed a process begun by Robespierre and that a word initially used to describe EMOTIONAL states experienced at the very margins of the social is now limited entirely to describing emotional states experienced at the very heart of social and political life.

See EMOTION, POLITICAL, VIOLENCE

TEXT

In the beginning was the word, now there is [the] **text**. The meanings of this widely used and problematic term follow a MEDIA transformation that has taken place over the past century, from script through print to COMMUNICATION by words-on-screen. As *scripture* (written language with the authority of God), **text** canonized the fixity of writing over the ephemerality of oral tradition. From the 1300s into the later C20, in consequence, **text** served special functions and had great significance in the discourses of RELIGION and EDUCATION, where it conveyed AUTHORITY as well as narrowness (the latter embodied in a doctrine of literalism). Around 1970, however, **text** left the pulpit and schoolroom and bloomed with new vigor in fields including linguistics, cultural studies, and digital INFORMATION processing. Within the new, interdisciplinary field of **textual studies** in particular, **text** dramatically changed its valence and connotative weight. It accrued still greater authority while becoming a principle of production rather than of fixity after production. In current usage, **text** is a digital commodity: the stuff of innumerable everyday transactions. It is also exactly what doesn't last, except in the ether of the Internet, where clustered words float like debris from exploded planets.

The most significant of the related but distinct meanings that make up the term's history are all first cited in the *OED* from lC14, supported by quotations largely from Chaucer and Langland. The etymology of the term is French from Latin, from the root "to weave." This etymology continues to shape phrasings such as the "thread of an argument," or the act of "spinning a tale." But the root sense, which was revivified in some later C20 usages, is not especially apparent in the earlier history.

The primary sense in the *OED*, cited from *Gawain and the Green Knight*, is that of "The wording of anything written or printed; the structure formed by the words in their order; the very words, phrases, and sentences as written." Related citations (from C16–C18) show key accompanying terms: Plato's followers offer "all kind of violence to his Text" (1678); Swift asks Stella to keep "strictly to the Text" (1728); and Luther understands Scripture "barely and symply after the texte of the letter" (1560).

Close to this primary meaning is a related sense: "The very words and sentences as originally written," either "in the original language, as opposed to a translation or rendering" or "in the original form and order, as distinguished from a commentary, marginal or other, or from annotations. Hence, in later use, the body of any treatise, the authoritative or formal part as distinguished from notes, appendices, introduction, and other explanatory or supplementary matter." Further specialization, clearly implicit in the earlier citations, leads to the meaning: "The very words and sentences of Holy Scripture; hence, the Scriptures themselves; also, any single book of the Scriptures." This sense, now obsolete, is evidenced from Langland's C14 work *Piers Plowman* (1393): "Ich theologie þe tixt knowe." It is this sense which captures the wording in a sermon by John Donne (1620), dear to literary critic Frank Kermode: "It is the Text that saves us; the interlineary glosses, and the marginal notes, and the *variae lectiones*, controversies and perplexities, undo us."

From Scripture as a whole, a narrowing development in **text** moves from whole to part: "A short passage from the Scriptures, esp. one quoted as authoritative, or illustrative of a point of belief or doctrine, as a motto, to point a moral, or esp. as the subject of an exposition or sermon." The next step in the word's developing meanings, analytically, then involves not narrowing but extension, from the Bible to other valued writings, indicating: "A short passage from some book or writer considered as authoritative; a received maxim or axiom; a proverb; an adage." This wider meaning is illustrated in the *OED* from Chaucer's *Manciple's Tale*, 1386: "But for I am a man not textueel I wol noght telle of textes neuer a deel." This enlarged sense of **text** as authority, extended from Scripture, provides the basis for such crucial, familiar usages as **text-book**, dating from later C18.

From such notable Renaissance projects as Erasmus's edition of the New Testament onward, for centuries scholarly editing played an important role in consolidating the word **text**. In the *OED* account, however, it is only in eC19—in the wake of such endeavors as Wolf's Homer and the Higher Criticism of the Bible, as well as documentary Historicism with its emphasis on *Quellenkritik* (source criticism)—that we find the first citation for a prominent, modern sense of **text**: "The wording adopted by an editor as (in his opinion) most nearly representing the author's original work; a book or edition containing this; also, with qualification, any form in which a writing exists or is current, as a good text, bad text, corrupt text, critical text, received text." Terms related to this new meaning, including **text-critic/critical/criticism**, are all attested only from eC20.

By mC20, the linguistic collocation **text-frequency** had appeared in descriptions of statistical analysis of the wording of texts; and as early as c1970 **text-processing** is cited as a task for computers. The field of **text linguistics** (from German) expanded the self-understanding of linguistics from its earlier, primary concern with the level of the sentence to discourse, but with the complication for disciplinary self-understanding that linguistics had until then been fundamentally about speech, not writing. That complication concerning the proper object of linguistics has had the apparently odd effect that, in order to constitute its object, text linguistics requires **textualization**—a word widely recognized but which is not in the *OED* or SpellCheck.

A 2009 draft addition to the *OED* expands the notion of **text** further, beyond language: "A non-textual subject regarded as open to analysis or interpretation using methods of literary criticism, semiotics, etc." Cross-reference highlights a transferred, figurative sense at work in this extension, requiring an enlarged meaning of the phrase *to read*, quite remarkably extended beyond **textuality** to the **non-textual** and yet evidenced from lC14 in Chaucer's *Physician's Tale*, l. 107: "In hir lyuyng maydens myghten rede As in a book euery good word or dede That longeth to a mayden vertuous." This strand of the *OED* account suggests that the apparently modern cultural studies sense of **text** may have been already latent contemporaneous with other uses of **text** referred to earlier, in some form of coexistence between more SECULAR and religious usage.

The term **cultural text** is cited in *OED* from 1970 (*Icons of Popular Culture*); and in 1972 Clifford Geertz asserted in his influential close reading of a Balinese cockfight that "cultural forms can be treated as texts, as imaginative works built out of social materials." In the *OED* citations, this is the first collocation of *imaginative* with **text**, as Geertz's cultural anthropology finally brought together Romantic literary theory with Romantic historicism. Also in the 1970s, Roland Barthes (in an influential essay "From Work to Text") put forward a series of theses that made **text** the living, generative counter-term to the dead-letter of the "work" [*oeuvre*, from L *opus*]. Negative associations accrued by **text** over its history, as literal, restrictive, petrified monument, were transferred to *work*, and **text** took on all the plus-values. This revaluation was joined by Jacques Derrida, whose statement *"il n'y a pas de hors-texte"* (1967) led to versions of **textualism** and **textualist** quite different from those cited in the *OED*, which refer only to Biblical Scripture. The *OED* does, however, cite Gayatri Spivak's introduction to her translation of Derrida, which uses the term **textuality** in this new meaning. In a more traditional framework, one thing outside or beyond the text might be **context**, which historians especially seek to set up in opposition to **text** without appreciating that **context** is not a contrast term but an amplification of **text**, as was argued throughout the literary critical debates of mC20.

Alongside these more technical debates in **text-based** or **textual studies**, the usage most common in contemporary culture, especially through the related verb **to text**, is likely to rise and wane in tandem with the (SMS) generation of TECHNOLOGY to which it relates. Interestingly, in this meaning **text** proves to have had a longer recent prehistory than is generally realized: the term is attested from 1977 in relation to a technology not associated with mobile phones: ARPA, the predecessor of the Internet.

See AUTHORITY, COMMUNICATION, CULTURE, INFORMATION, LITERATURE, MEDIA

THEORY

The word **theory** derives from the same Greek root as *theatre* and stresses the visual element in contemplation in both its medieval French and post-classical Latin developments. It comes into English in lC16 but the link to any visual sense, as in Lancelot Andrewes: "Saint Luke . . . calleth the Passion . . . a Theorie or Sight. . . . Of our blessed Saviovr's whole life or death, there is no part but is a Theorie of it selfe, well worthy our looking on," does not survive C17. Indeed, **theory** and **theoretical** in modern English have lost any reference to sight, unlike a related word, *speculation*, which still retains a clear reference to the visual sense. When **theory** enters English in the Renaissance, it is from the beginning linked to modern conceptions of science, either as a general description of scientific thinking or as a particular example of such thinking. It is also from the beginning opposed to *practice*, again both very specifically as the way that a **scientific theory** is tested in a laboratory or by other kinds of observation and very generally as an opposition between thought and action. The opposition between **theory** and *practice* dates back as far as Aristotle. In C19 the opposition between **theory** and *practice* develops a pejorative sense of **theory** captured in a phrase like "That's all very well in theory." Indeed, once one takes **theory** out of its specific scientific and mathematical uses, it might be hazarded that this pejorative use may now be dominant, particularly in speech.

Theory shows a marked increase in frequency in recent decades, and one can speculate that this is in part due to the renewed controversy about the **theory of** EVOLUTION in the United States, where attacks on the teachings of Darwin in schools has become a signature of the new Christian FUNDAMENTALISM. However, what is certain is that the last fifty years have seen the development in the HUMANITIES of a whole new area of reflection called **Theory**. The *OED* identifies the first use of this sense in 1982 and characterizes it as follows: "An approach to the study of literature, the arts, and culture that incorporates concepts from disciplines such as philosophy, psychoanalysis, and the social sciences; *esp.* such an approach intended to challenge or provide an alternative to critical methods and interpretations that are established, traditional, and seen as arising from particular metaphysical or ideological assumptions." It is striking how little content there is in this very long definition and that the *OED* holds it to be an example of its first sense, "The conceptual basis of a subject or area of study," where one might argue that this recent development of **theory** is an entirely new sense and relates to the impact of psychoanalysis, linguistics, and Marxism on academic thought, particularly in Paris in the more politically charged 1960s. A more accurate definition might be: "Work in the humanities drawing on psychoanalysis, Marxism, and linguistics to interrogate fundamental social and political concepts as a contribution to a project of social liberation."

This new sense of **theory** develops originally in relation to **theory** in its scientific sense under two different aspects. The first is the appeal to linguistics as the model for explanation in the social and human sciences. Under the name of structuralism, this approach became of great significance particularly in anthropology and literary criticism in the 1950s and 1960s. The aim was to find systematic patterns within cultural artifacts that would enable them to be described and analyzed with scientific precision. The ambition to use these analyses to provide a general **theory** of CULTURE was punctured by the advent of deconstruction, which not only stressed that there were infinite patterns to be analyzed, but also argued that any particular choice of pattern was always as dependent on the analyst as it was on the object analyzed.

If attempts to produce the structural analysis of NARRATIVE, for example, found their basis in an appeal to a notion of **scientific theory** borrowed from the natural sciences, there was another powerful definition of **theory** available within the Marxist tradition. Here **theory** was related to *practice*, not as hypothesis to experiment in a rigorously controlled laboratory, but as political assumptions that were proved or disproved in social practice. While it is easy to separate out these two conceptions theoretically, in Paris of the 1960s they were often run together in a triumphalist account of a new humanities that would leave behind the class-based dilettantism of traditional scholarship. As experimental scientific **theory** and as putative political movement, both aspects had crashed and burned by the early seventies. Only then did the new use of **theory** blossom in the English-speaking American academy.

Two things could be noticed about this new sense of **theory** which was to dominate the American academy for at least twenty years. First was that it had no relation to traditional definitions of practice either within controlled laboratories or class-based politics. Practice was conceived in terms of IDENTITY politics and the university. The second was that the original appeal to the scientificity of linguistics, Marxism, and psychoanalysis evaporated. **Theory** functioned as a way of ignoring **theories**. Anecdotally this tendency found expression in the Sokal affair of 1996, when a natural scientist published a spoof article in the journal *Social Text* that argued for the social construction of science in the most extravagant and ludicrous terms.

To grasp the extent to which scientific explanation in general has lost prestige over a period when technological advances have never been more striking is a paradox that is not to be resolved linguistically. However, it is worth noting that the major mathematical sense of the word: "The body of knowledge relating to the properties of a particular mathematical concept; a collection of theorems forming a connected system," stresses the notion of a connected system. It is just such a connected system that was the great fantasy of philosophy of science in the first part of C20, and developments both in science and philosophy of science since then have emphasized that science is a discontinuous set of **theories** and practices for which it is not possible to produce a fully coherent account.

See NARRATIVE, TEXT

TRANS

In Latin the preposition **trans** served as a much-used prefix in many words that entered English as early as C11. Defined as "across, through, over, to or on the other side of, beyond, outside of, from one place, person, thing, or state to another," **trans** is a word that is constantly in motion, transitioning and translating compounded words from their original meanings into new terms. Its use in English as an independent prefix, applied to words that had not already been prefixed in Latin, dates to C16 or earlier. As a noun it has been used by poets such as Emily Dickinson, Hart Crane, and Ezra Pound as a familiar shortening of **translation** and, starting mC20, in auto talk as short for **transmission**.

Its recent usages as an adjective make it a keyword that engages complex matters of GENDER and SEXUALITY, which stretch across, through, and beyond binary understandings. The first *OED* citation dates from 1973: "He describes encounters with people from a variety of backgrounds and sexual predilections—hetero, homo, bi, and trans." The adjective was formed by pulling back the prefix from such prior compound terms as **transvestite, transsexual**, and **transgender**.

Our contemporary understanding of **trans** as a marker of **gendered** IDENTITY exists as a catch-all for the many different ways in which **transgender** identity has been linguistically represented within Western culture. The first documented term in this cluster is **transvestite,** derived from German *Transvestit,* coined by German sexologist Magnus Hirschfeld from **trans** plus Latin *vestitus,* clothed. Hirschfeld's *Die Transvestiten* appeared in German in 1910, and **transvestite** is first cited in English the next year. This technical term for "A person . . . who derives pleasure from dressing in clothes appropriate to the opposite sex" was originally applied only to men, but usage over C20 enlarged its scope. Citations for the technical term precede such vernacular usages as *drag queen* (1941) and *drag king* (1972). From the beginning, the emphasis on "pleasure" marked this **trans**-activity as chosen. The term relates to a perceived transgression of gendered modes of behavior and sexuality, which marks the term with deviance, as perceived, named, and demonized by the dominant culture. While some have argued that **transvestite** subverts gender norms, other have argued that it only reinforces them.

Transsexual was already used in German by Hirschfeld as early as 1923, with the sense "having physical characteristics of one sex and psychological characteristics of the other." It entered English, via Latin, in D. O. Cauldwell's article "Psychopathia Transexualis" (1949). Cauldwell was especially concerned with those who wished to change their bodies so as to live as members of the gender they had not been assigned at birth. Christine Jorgensen, the first **trans woman** to receive sexual reassignment surgery in the 1950s (and the subject of the 2015 Oscar-nominated film *The Danish Girl*), together with her surgeon Dr. Harry Benjamin, injected the term into popular knowledge. The NHS today defines **transsexual** as "someone who uses hormones and/or surgery to correct their gender identity from the identity given at birth." This ongoing focus on biological features of gender, from Cauldwell to today, has led some people to avoid **transsexual** entirely, in favor of terms that focus more on the social and cultural features of gender.

Transgender is just such a term; **transgender** relates to **transsexual** just as *gender* often relates to *sex*, the former emphasizing social and cultural features, the latter emphasizing biological ones. Since its first citation (1965 as **transgenderism**), it was explicitly defined as gender-related rather than sex-related. **Transgender** has come to dominate this discursive field, as the identifying name for "a person whose identity does not conform unambiguously to conventional notions of male or female gender, but combines or moves between these," according to the *OED*. Just as **transgender** emphasizes the social and cultural over the biological, transgender communities have criticized a preoccupation with surgery and genitals in discussing **transgender** issues, and this criticism is now echoed in diversity training in many institutions.

Trans in its present iterations represents a wide range of identities across social, cultural, and biological elements of gender, including *genderqueer* and *non-binary* identities (cf. GENDER and QUEER). Reflecting the standardization of the term, the NHS defines **trans** as "an 'umbrella' term for all people who cross traditional gender boundaries—whether that is permanently or periodically." As the word opens up to a variety of different meanings dependent on context, online communities as well as LGBT rights organization Stonewall have taken to employing **trans***, using the asterisk as a stand-in for any of the many identity markers **trans** may prefix, as a way to call attention to the multiplicity of **trans** identity. Some discussions of **trans** identities point to the existence of **trans** people and culture throughout history and around the world, including *hijras* in South Asia, among many others. *Cisgender* was coined as the contrastive term to **transgender** in the mid-1990s. *Cis* derives from Latin meaning, "on this side of" and is used in opposition to **trans**. Added to the *OED* in June 2015, *cisgender* plays an important POLITICAL role for the COMMUNITIES that use it: "Using the word 'cisgender' is . . . an educational tool. To simply define people as 'non-trans' implies that only transgender people have a gender identity," says Basic Rights Oregon, an LGBT Rights group, continuing, "Referring to cisgender people as 'non trans' implies that cisgender people are the default and that being trans is abnormal." This push for the visibility of **trans** identity, and the visible negotiation of **trans** terminology, is part and parcel with larger political efforts by the **trans**, genderqueer, and gender non-conforming communities to counter years of silence, political and social invisibility, and VIOLENCE done to queer and **trans** bodies. This push for visibility operates in sources like the *OED* and the *Washington Post*, which have increased the use of gender-neutral pronouns as well as the use of Mx as mode of written address to some **trans** individuals, including non-binary and genderqueer individuals.

While LGBT stands for *lesbian, gay, bisexual,* and **trans(gender)**, the amalgamation of those four terms has often been contentious. For example, the major gay rights organization Stonewall, founded in 1989, maintained a strict distinction between sexual orientation and gender identity for many years, and only extended its advocacy work to trans people in 2015, arguing that "homophobia, transphobia, and sexism are inextricably linked." In the US, some state laws (such as in Colorado) prohibit discrimination based on sexual orientation, and define *sexual orientation* to include gender identity, thus covering trans people.

Anti-trans sentiment and violence are often termed **transphobia** (1993), parallel to *homophobia* and *islamophobia*. In 2016, South Carolina, North Carolina, Tennessee, and Georgia all introduced anti-**transgender** legislation that legitimated anti-**trans** discrimination. This wave of legislation and the increased media attention to violence done to **trans** bodies have increased conversations around cis PRIVILEGE, and the ways in which **trans** issues have come to represent a newly visible Civil Rights frontier.

See GENDER, IDENTITY, QUEER, SEXUALITY

TRAUMA

Once a relatively straightforward term, **trauma**, with its broadened psychological sense, has been contested and intensely politicized over the past few decades. Like VICTIM, the word **trauma** has been used by individuals and groups to make the extent of their suffering known and to advocate particular POLITICAL agendas. **Trauma** has become generalized so that almost any negative experience may now qualify as **traumatic**.

Trauma is borrowed into English from the Greek *trauma*, meaning "wound." The *OED* entry, which has not yet been fully updated, currently lists two main senses of **trauma**. The first, attested from lC17 onward, denotes "A wound, or external bodily injury in general; also the condition caused by this." The earliest recorded use of **trauma** in this sense appears in Steven Blankaart's *Physical Dictionary*

(1684): "*Trauma*, . . . a Wound from an external Cause." Originally used primarily in medical contexts concerned with wound pathology, **trauma** came to signify not only physical, but also psychological wounds beginning in lC19 as a result of developments in psychiatry and psychoanalysis. The second sense recorded in *OED* is "A psychic injury, esp. one caused by emotional shock the memory of which is repressed and remains unhealed; an internal injury, esp. to the brain, which may result in a behavioral disorder of organic origin. Also the state or condition so caused." This second sense of **trauma** widened in mC20. In general use, the noun **trauma** and its adjectival form, **traumatic**, increasingly refer to anything perceived as distressing or emotionally disturbing.

Use of **trauma** rose steadily after 1890 but has increased even more dramatically since 1970. **Trauma's** prominence in psychiatric and political debates around 1970 was undoubtedly due to assertions that the **traumas** experienced by Vietnam veterans and victims of rape and child abuse were not merely physical, but psychological and enduring. The diagnosis of **post-traumatic stress disorder** (PTSD), a product of the anti-war movement in the United States, thus legitimized the struggles of Vietnam veterans and regarded them as **traumatized** victims of war, not as culprits. It was not until 1980, however, that the American Psychiatric Association officially recognized PTSD in the *Diagnostic and Statistical Manual of Mental Disorders* (*DSM-III*). Earlier terms for what is now known as PTSD include "shell shock," which was used during World War I but banned by the British Army in 1917, and "combat fatigue" in World War II. PTSD is still most immediately associated with the **traumas** of war, but the *DSM-5*, which identifies the trigger to PTSD as "exposure to actual or threatened death, serious injury or sexual violation," acknowledges a much wider range of potentially **traumatic** events, including but not limited to physical assault, sexual VIOLENCE, motor vehicle accidents, natural or human-made disasters, exposure to war, and terrorist attacks (cf. TERROR).

Both primary senses of **trauma** outlined in *OED* remain active, as some of the most frequently occurring collocations attest. **Head trauma, blunt trauma, abdominal trauma**, and **brain trauma** describe significant physical wounds or injuries sustained after an accident or assault. **Trauma insurance**, also called critical illness insurance, pays a lump-sum benefit for covered medical conditions like cancer, heart attack, and stroke. The synonymous collocations **psychological trauma** and **emotional trauma** denote damage to the psyche incurred after a distressing experience. **Psychological** or **emotional trauma** can arise as a result of or in the absence of **physical trauma**. Those who endure such physical or psychological injuries may be labeled **trauma patients**, **trauma victims**, or **trauma survivors**. Of the three terms, **trauma survivors** carries the most positive connotation, suggesting recovery and strength rather than weakness and vulnerability. **Trauma victims** might be preferred, however, when it is desirable to elicit sympathy and emphasize the innocence of those affected.

Trauma has recently become a contested term in public debate because its general definition now extends beyond specific medical or psychiatric diagnoses. Experiences no longer need to be life-threatening or able to cause serious injury in order to be considered **psychologically traumatic**. According to the nonprofit organization Global Trauma Research, "Emotional and psychological trauma is the result of extraordinarily stressful events that shatter your sense of security, making you feel helpless and vulnerable in a dangerous world." The term **trauma** has become oversimplified, as the recent practice of distinguishing between major events ("trauma with a capital T") and everyday occurrences that negatively impact daily life ("trauma with a lowercase t") indicates.

Trauma's expanded psychological sense and growing prominence in public discourse from mC20 onward can be attributed to the pervasive influence of psychology on society at large, which sociologist Philip Rieff termed "the triumph of the therapeutic" in 1966. Since mC20, **trauma** has been used figuratively and applied to crises in the economic sectors, for example: "the trauma of possible strike action" (1981); "the trauma of the 2008 financial crisis" (2012); "the trauma of Brexit" (2016).

Although now common practice, using **trauma** loosely or figuratively invites criticism. Karen Kelsky coined the label "Job Market PTSD," which she defined as "the state of being so traumatized by the academic job search that even when it is successful, [. . .] you cannot stop feeling anxious, inadequate, panicked and insecure." Some commentators criticized this use of **trauma** and PTSD as insensitive to veterans and rape victims; others wrote that it was validating and accurately described their experiences. After the massacre at Pulse nightclub in Orlando on June 12, 2016, Gersh Kuntzman, a liberal reporter for the *NY Daily News*, wrote that firing an AR-15 gave him "a temporary form of PTSD" but later apologized for his "inarticulate use of the term." While Kuntzman used PTSD to describe his impression of the power of such assault rifles, suggesting that they should be out of civilian hands, conservative news sites criticized him for reporting "his poor little traumatized emotions" and used the language of **trauma** to question his masculinity (*Conservative Review*, June 14, 2016).

Critics have blamed the concepts of **psychological** or **emotional trauma** for initiating a major change in campus culture at American and British universities. Supporters of trigger warnings and safe spaces wish to accommodate students with **trauma** history (e.g., physical assault, sexual violence, or oppression based on race, national origin, religion, gender, or sexual orientation). Those against trigger warnings and safe spaces argue that accommodating such claims of **psychological trauma** coddles students, limits free speech, and threatens academic FREEDOM. The campus rhetoric of **trauma** seems to overlook or oversimplify significant contributions in the field of **trauma studies**, which has theorized **traumatic** memory repression, flashbacks, and **traumatic recall** over the past few decades.

The Black Lives Matter movement and LGBTQ+ activist groups have employed **trauma**-informed discourse to highlight their social marginalization and to demand change. Some critics have cautioned, however, that the individualized language of **trauma** could actually impede large-scale efforts to fight against discrimination and achieve social and economic justice. Historian Robin D. G. Kelley has observed that "words such as *trauma, PTSD, micro-aggression*, and *triggers* have virtually replaced *oppression, repression*, and *subjugation*." For some, the individualized language of **trauma** risks dividing marginalized groups and potential political allies. Yet for many activist groups, **trauma** and activism are not in contradiction; rather, activism begins with recognizing and reclaiming oppression-based **trauma**.

Due to differences in perception, resilience, and life experiences, what one person considers **traumatic** might not be **traumatic** for another. This, together with **trauma**'s expanded and imprecise meaning in ordinary language, makes it difficult to determine who is more **traumatized**.

See EMOTION, TERROR, VICTIM, VIOLENCE

TRUTH

We are not strongly inclined to think of **truth** as having a HISTORY because its meaning appears to be both stable and self-evident: something is either **true** or it isn't. Yet historical fluctuation in both meaning and frequency over time suggests that the term tracks several wider social constellations with which it is associated. Its popularity is linked to how a society understands the complex relations between bodily insides and outsides, and between mind and matter, as well as the degree to which humans believe they have ACCESS to these respective realms. Related to this understanding of the relative accessibility of mind as opposed to material body, an ability to discern what is "**true**"—objectively rather than subjectively— has played (and continues to play) a determining role in the sometimes fraught relations among RELIGION, science, and politics. At the heart of these historical tensions lies continued debate over the degree to which inner conviction can (or should) be proven by outer demonstration.

The most significant semantic shift in **truth**—and a source of subsequent contestation—occurs early in its career. The medieval concept of *troth*, or fidelity, shifted in the late medieval period to mean "conformity to an exterior reality" or "actual existence." Old English *tríewþ* denoted good faith toward another or the tangible proof of that FAITH. Marital and martial fidelity are the usual referents up to C14. The word was often employed to gloss or translate Latin *pactum* (a military covenant) or *foedera* (an agreement established by means of a treaty). In C12 Middle English Laȝamon's *Brut*, it refers to military contracts: "Coel and Maximen cuðliche speken & freondscipe makeden, i-uastened mid treoðen" (5427), while the C13 romance *King Horn* uses it to refer to a marriage contract.

By lC14, the word had also come to mean "something that is true," with **trueness** judged as adherence to divine or legal precepts. The reforming Wycliffite movement emphasized **truth** as coextensive with knowledge of Christ and the Bible. The concept of **truth** as *fact* beyond a religious context arises, according to Richard Firth Green, in legal contexts where it came to suggest an accurate description of circumstance: a 1443 trade document requires legal witnesses to swear "upon a booke to sey þe trouth," and an entry in the *Rolls of Parliament* from 1436 asserts that jurors should endeavor to find the "naked trouth." As increasingly literate rather than oral standards of evidence and witnessing were instituted, the measurement of **truth** shifted from an intra-personal standard (what a person can know with surety concerning their own inner intentions) to an extrinsic standard (whether divine, biblical, or based on community standards). This shift suggests that **truth** had migrated from an interior experience of subjectivity to a more exteriorized, relational one by the end of the medieval period.

In the early modern period, the meaning "faithfulness" is largely eclipsed by that of "accuracy." Such usage suggests a changing attitude about the knowability of inner and outer states. The earlier medieval sense of the term suggests that what can be known resides inside a person, while what remains opaque is outside. By the end of C17, the opposite was largely true: what can be definitively known is that which can be measured with a tool rather than through mere introspection, an epistemological shift exemplified by the distance between, say, Montaigne's *Essays* and Descartes' cogito. This movement is the result of the term's increasing use in a scientific and descriptive prose that emphasized **truth** as something that could be verified through sensory observation. As such, it tended to describe a set of external, rather than internal, circumstances (as in the work of Francis Bacon and Robert Boyle). Occurrences of the term spiked in mC17 print, a surge that can be attributed to the pamphlet war attendant on the English Civil War, as well as the term's centrality to the Scientific Revolution.

Early modern print culture established a dichotomy that encouraged the Enlightenment conflict between SPIRITUAL and scientific **truths**, a tension that would remain significant throughout the modern period. As **truth** travelled from the realm of devotion to the domain of science and fact, the term became a partisan football in debates over the extent to which something that is "true" needed to be demonstrated logically or physically. Over time, science claimed **truth** as its exclusive possession, leaving *faith* (now semantically precipitated out of **truth**) to religion. Interestingly, the Anglo-Saxon **truth** has always been preferred (to judge from relative frequency of use in print) to the loan words *accuracy* and *veracity*, despite the term's increasingly narrow semantic range.

In eC20, **truth** lost ground to the **truth-claim**, beginning with William James's *The Meaning of Truth* (1909): "Good consequences [. . .] are proposed rather as the lurking motive inside of every truth-claim" (xiv. 273). The situational nature of **truth** was reinforced by pragmatics as practiced in linguistics, philosophy, and sociology. This contextual definition of **truth** was also popularized by later C20 sociologists concerned with the possibility of cultural REPRESENTATION. Such substitution signaled unease with the Enlightenment model of **truth** as demarcating an unbiased sense of objectivity that facilitated access to a transparently knowable "truth," something that could be measured or accurately described. Later this skepticism informed poststructuralist critiques of language and positivist history and, within science studies, bred a wary attitude toward the possibility of an unbiased knowledge of the natural world as independent of the human observer. This debate largely rendered redundant the smuggling of **truth** back and forth across the militarized border separating religion from science.

While both **truth** and "truth" remain unfashionable in academic circles, the word has seen resurgence in the realm of cultural politics during the last several decades. With the establishment in the wake of apartheid of the South African Truth and Reconciliation Committee (1995), **truth** became a tool for investigating human rights abuses as well as for nation-building. In the US, the term also became a conspicuous post-9/11 rationale for military action, as in George W. Bush's justification of the imminent invasion of Iraq on the basis of weapons of mass destruction in 2003: "We concluded that tomorrow is a moment of truth for the world. Many nations have voiced a commitment to peace and security, and now they must demonstrate that commitment to peace and security in the only effective way: by supporting the immediate and unconditional disarmament of Saddam Hussein."

The degree to which **truth** is subject to POLITICAL manipulation in the age of twenty-four-hour news cycles can be seen in the rise of **truthiness**, a term popularized by the US faux news pundit Stephen Colbert. **Truthiness** refers to a truth that a person claims to know intuitively, "from the gut," without regard to verifiable facts. As such, it gestures toward the wobbly nature of **truth** as accuracy, so suggesting how objectivity can circle back around into subjectivity while standards of evidence are lacking or subject to debate.

The recent revival of **truth** and derivative terms signals another episode in the word's history. Disintegration of a collective consensus about **truth** as denoting "conformity to facts"—a demise witnessed by the rise of **truthiness** and by ever more frequent reference to a **post-truth society**—shows that, in some circles at least, **truth** has regained the sense that **truth** can be an interior, subjective experience, a definition previously conspicuous only before the early modern period. Such a connotation may indicate a return to conflation of religion and politics that marked the pre- and early modern periods.

See EXPERIENCE, FAITH, POLITICAL, REALISM, RELIGION, REPRESENTATION

URBAN

The term **urban**, common since C19, has undergone something of a renewal in the last several decades. Presently the most common adjective for designating an entity "relating to a city," the word has accrued specific, sometimes contradictory, denotations. In locutions such as **urban planning**, it is synonymous with neutral terms denoting "life in a city," such as *civic* or *municipal*. In other phrases, such as **urban poverty** or **urban decay**, it has come to be synonymous with the blight associated with the "inner city." In certain US usages, the term has both latent and explicit racial overtones that associate it primarily with African American but also with Hispanic and Caribbean communities. Such racial politics are apparent in the way that the oppositional terms **urban/suburban** have largely come to replace the opposition between **urban**/*rural* in US usage, in part because the first contrasting pair is often used as shorthand for other binary oppositions including *non-white/ white* or *poor/middle class*. **Urban** can also be contrasted with adjectives such as *metropolitan* or *cosmopolitan* that have more positive connotations.

Urban came into English in C17 from Latin *urbānus*, meaning "of or pertaining to a city or city life," which derived, in turn, from Latin *urbs*, "city." The term appears only sporadically until the first half of C19, when it becomes common. This ubiquity was influenced by changing demographics. The spread of the railroad encouraged growth in industrial and manufacturing jobs, while newly mechanized farming techniques diminished the need for rural labor. These twin developments gave rise to more densely populated cities. The adjective **urban** is unusual in that it has no corresponding noun, unlike the semantically related *city/civic, metropolis/metropolitan*, or *municipality/municipal*. This fact may explain why the term soaks up other rhetorical colorings so readily. For example, in C19 **urban** came to connote movements of popular political unrest: "[H]is urban, or suburban brother, the man of the multitude, the unit of the mob" (1837); and "[G]overnment has . . . found a counterpoise to the vehemence of urban democracy" (1849). The related adjective **urbane** was used synonymously with **urban** until C19, when its meaning became restricted to "having the manners, refinement, or polish regarded as characteristic of a town." The term could be used either approvingly (as in "His manners were gentle, affable, and urbane," 1832) or disapprovingly ("In Eustace Chapuys, master of requests, he had a man of law, . . . urbane, alert, unscrupulous," 1873).

The rise of **urban** in popular speech was reflected in its increasing centrality to institutional and governmental initiatives beginning in C19. In the UK, the Urban District Council replaced the older "sanitary district" in the 1890s in order to respond to an increasing need for services in more heavily populated county centers; these districts were in turn largely abandoned in the 1970s in another wave of municipal reorganization. In the US, the "urban renewal" fund was first created in the 1950s to aid in the redevelopment of cities, and, in 1965, the Office of Housing and Urban Development (HUD) was created. These UK and US institutions witnessed the assumption that the city is the appropriate locus for discussion of social and economic challenges that face society as a whole. The centrality of the countryside as both the center of food production and the imaginative heart of the nation was being displaced. In the US, **urban development** became associated with an agenda of racial reparation, since HUD had responsibility for outlawing housing discrimination, one of the major provisions of the 1968 Civil Rights Act. This association is underscored by organizations such as the National Urban League (founded in 1910), whose mission is to "provide economic empowerment, educational opportunities and the guarantee of civil rights for African Americans."

The profession of **urban planning** came into being in the 1950s to combat the **urban decay** associated with city centers across North America and Europe. **Urban renewal** (recorded in US English from 1955) was initially euphemistic for "slum clearance." In the US, this movement was associated with "white flight" from the cities, and the concomitant establishment of suburban communities and "edge cities" (a space that concentrates business, shopping, and entertainment outside a traditional urban area in what had recently been a semi-rural area). As **urban planning** gained a foothold in university departments of human geography, as well as in the social sciences more widely, **urban renewal** has come to denote a more positive process.

The so-called New Urbanism movement associated with Jane Jacobs and other urban planners in the US and Canada has contributed to a revival of the fortunes of **urban** by associating city centers with positive ideas of DIVERSITY, EQUALITY, and the importance of communal PUBLIC space. This movement is designed to combat **urban sprawl** with its associated problems of separation, segregation, and inequality—problems underscored by a reliance on cars and a landscape marked by non-human-sized features (such as expressways and superhighways). In the UK, debate about **urban planning** in recent years has been fueled by the highly public pronouncements of Prince Charles, a vocal critic of postwar urban planning. Debates have focused on how to revitalize former city centers while preserving traditional architectural styles, a debate put to the test in Poundbury, the model "urban village" (underwritten by Charles) designed to mix residential and commercial properties on a human scale.

Over the course of the last two decades, the opposition **urban-suburban** (or the **urban-suburban-rural** triad) has largely come to replace the older paradigmatic contrast of *city-country*, the pair that Raymond Williams explored so suggestively in *The Country and the City* (1973). Even after the industrialization of

Britain, Williams argued, the ideological lure of the countryside remained strong, continuing to influence a self-representation of England to its own inhabitants out of all proportion to its dwindling reality. If the countryside appeared to offer an idyllic Eden, the city was troped as a modernist hub of alienation and loneliness. Williams argues that geographical space impacts not only our social structures but our interpretations of it, and that cultural representations of **urban** space signify social conflicts as well as social difference. His insights can, in turn, help us to understand this reconfiguration of opposite terms: what for Williams was largely about class and the effects of capitalism has now morphed into a discussion about race and the possibility of an integrated society. Unlike Williams's pairing, where COUNTRY functioned as an oftentimes idealized term, the **urban-suburban-rural** designation does not a priori value one of its elements over the others; one could argue that all three already feel fallen.

More recently, **urban** has been used in business to refer to BLACK or Hispanic culture, often obviating the need to mention race overtly. In moving beyond the nerd-chic of SUSTAINABLE **urban** planning, the term has come to designate a world populated by youthful consumers of media, services, and goods. Playlists of **urban contemporary** radio stations play almost exclusively hip-hop and rap music. In this usage, common in both US and UK, black culture is valued and, consequently, commodified ("Top DJs provide a tour through the best in urban black music with 'phat' servings of soul, hip-hop and drum 'n' bass" (*Independent*, October 26, 1996, 41); and "An all-night party that features the best in electronic and urban music, from drum 'n' bass and techno to hip-hop and house beats" (*Baltimore Sun*, September 25, 2003, 30T). Similarly, **urban sportswear** is a lucrative market that allows **suburban** YOUTH to aspire to **urban** cool: "His invention has been to take urban sportswear, meaning the oversized hip-hop clothes born of the disenfranchised and disaffected poor black rappers, and turn them into aspirational clothing for his generation" (*International Herald Tribune* [Paris], February 11, 2003).

These usages demonstrate how sometimes opposing meanings have accreted around the term **urban** over the course of C19 and C20. The word has served as a neutral term for a municipal area; a pejorative term for a poor and/or non-white population center; a movement associated with sustainable development; and, finally, a youthful, cutting-edge CONSUMER movement. These meanings do not necessarily succeed one another serially. Instead, several (sometimes contradictory) meanings can exist in a single cultural moment simultaneously.

See BLACK, COMMUNITY, COUNTRY, DIVERSITY, EQUALITY, PUBLIC, YOUTH

VALUE

Two factors make **value** an especially challenging word in modern English. First, during periods of social crisis or upheaval, **values** tend to be vigorously asserted (and attacks made on the presumed values of others). Second, disagreements over **value** are exacerbated by accentuated contrast between "relativity of values" (e.g., in perceptions of postmodernism), claims to authority based on "traditional values" (e.g., in religion), and unresolved arguments over **value freedom** (e.g., in relation to science). Difficulties with **value** inevitably run beyond the word itself into its tangled relations with questions of objectivity and subjectivity, intrinsic and extrinsic worth, and authority of interpretation. What makes **value** both distinctive and confusing, however, is the set of connections, as well as slippage, that the word facilitates among radically different kinds of social thinking.

The noun **value** comes into English from oF *value* (C13), the feminine past participle of *valoir*, "to be of worth" (cf. L *valere* and mL *valua*). In a variety of spellings, **value** is illustrated in *OED* from eC14. The noun starts off in English close to what we now think of as adjectival **valued**. The verb form **value**, meaning to estimate or appraise as being worth a specified sum or amount, is attested from roughly a century later; and the adjective **valuable**, which indicates a condition of having material or monetary value or being useful, is reported from eC17.

Across these related forms are found a cluster of senses. Principally there is the sense of an amount of some commodity that is considered an equivalent for something else, or a fair or adequate return. Typically the standard of estimation or exchange applied is that of material or monetary worth. This "amount," or "equivalent material worth" sense in the noun is accompanied by the sense conveyed by the verb of a process of assigning worth: a practice of evaluation. **To value** is to set an estimate of worth on something, to judge it at a specified rate, or more generally to set store by it or rate it highly.

Historical developments from this cluster of early senses are shaped by a transfer of meaning that takes place from a reified process involving judgment or relation ("*x* is worth or equivalent to *y*") to designation of the object of such a judgment: the thing worth having.

One line of development in **value** extends the relation or calculation of equivalence between respective fields. Translation between two currencies is variable, hence the need for estimation; it is also implicitly negotiable, if only because some statement of relation is necessary. This sense of "worth within a formal system of some kind" has affinities with the mathematical sense of value, as a figure or number representing a precise amount (e.g., "the value of the root" or "the values of these angles"). Use of this kind states "value" but typically serves to calculate transformations of value or analyze the place of a given value in a series or pattern. Formal characterization of **value** also extends to ranking cards and chess pieces according to conventions of games they are used in, and to music, where **value** signifies the relative duration of a note. In eC20, the same schema of equivalence within a formal system was proposed as explanation of how **value** varies in money, in Georg Simmel's *Philosophy of Money* (1900); it also serves as a basis for **linguistic value,** as functional identity dependent on differentiation within an overall system, in Ferdinand de Saussure's characterization of LANGUAGE.

The other line of development in **value** focuses on the object of worth, rather than on the process of estimation. It designates something as being **valuable** on account of its relative status according to some real or supposed usefulness, importance, or other criterion of esteem. The distance between this sense and the other sense can be seen in the number of arguments associated with **value**: from three-argument "we value x *at* y" or "we value x *as* y" (a subjective attribution of value), through two-argument "we value *x*" (i.e., with relation left implicit), to "*x* is a value" or "*x* is valuable" in the sense that it *could be, has been,* or *might be* judged to be of worth, or is inherently or intrinsically of worth.

Many objects have **value,** if worth is viewed in this combination of ways. There are instrumental and specialized values, including **entertainment value, emotional value, nutritional value**, and **news value. Value** can also be associated with mental or immaterial objects, including ETHICAL and SPIRITUAL principles. In such an extended meaning, **value** denotes anything considered to be of profound importance or significance. Examples include **family values, democratic values, religious values**, and **the value of poetry**, as well as **transcendent** and **ultimate values**, the last of which may appear not just different from but contradictory with the sense of socially constructed equivalence.

What is most interesting about the historical development of **value**, however, is how, during C18 and C19, senses of the word were linked to evolving arguments about the ends and worth of individual and social LIFE: the *summum bonum* and its basis in the good, the true, or the beautiful. Increasingly influential assertions were made of utility as a fourth possible domain of **value** alongside ethics, politics, and aesthetics, a new source of **value** often formulated in Utilitarianism as usefulness to the largest number of people. Such arguments affected the word's later development, in that C19 notions of *utility* combined Utilitarian perceptions of happiness, pleasure, and usefulness with a **market value** of usefulness to the purchaser or CONSUMER, to some extent marginalizing concern with other, potentially competing values.

From these complex interconnections, positions expressed by **value** go off in two divergent ways, with the result that value features in two different models of **value theory**: in axiology, in a philosophical context; and in the (Marxist) labor theory of **value**, which at its simplest views amount of labor as the currency in which to determine equivalence.

The continuing, classical philosophical debate questions whether **value** and related ideas of the *good* are objective or subjective, or intrinsic, teleological, or consequentialist. In contemporary discussion, **value** is usually replaced by plural **values**, to reflect critical arguments in anthropology and then sociology (and derived in part from Weberian debates over **value freedom**). In the other direction, value arguments in political economy centered increasingly on the relation analyzed by Marx between **exchange value** and **use value**, and how value functions in Marx's theory of **surplus value**. Following the main Marxist phase of **value theory**, however, neoliberal economic discussion has narrowed the argument from considering general structures of social exchange to individuals' cost-benefit calculations: producers or consumers estimating value in isolation from social relations and relying on market efficiency to achieve **value for money**, or VFM.

A cluster of recent combinations with **value** take this MARKET emphasis further. Alongside vague expressions like **delivering value**, there is (from the 1930s onward) **value added**, meaning an amount by which worth is increased at each stage of a chain of production. There is also (from the late 1980s) **value proposition**, used to describe the specific factor intended to drive consumer purchase decisions. Such commercial ways of conceiving **value** may seem imprecise but are subject to **value analysis** (from the 1950s onward). Following such analysis, too, market propositions may be revisited with **value engineering** (from 1973): "the systematic application of techniques and principles which aim at cutting production costs."

If **value** in these new combinations had no connection with wider issues of *worth* and *esteem*, then the word would have come to embody Oscar Wilde's caricature of the cynic as "a person who knows the price of everything and the value of nothing." What connects between *price* and **value**, however, is in some cases the polysemy of **value** itself, which links the relational, "exchange value" meaning with an implied "social good" or "personal WELL-BEING" meaning.

See CONSUMER, MARKET, WELL-BEING

VICTIM

Victim is an important word because it links often TRAUMATIC personal or group experiences in contemporary societies to frameworks that understand such experiences and respond to them through public policy, political advocacy, and in wider public debate. The etymology of **victim** is straightforward: the word comes from Latin *victima*. Its first sense is that of a sacrificial offering, and this strong sense is made stronger by the identification of *the* sacrificial offering and thus *the* victim as Christ. By C17, however, it has developed the more general meaning "a person who is put to death or subjected to torture by another; one who suffers severely in body or property through cruel or oppressive treatment." These strong meanings developed into a general sense of a passive recipient of misfortune. While in earlier uses such misfortune has been regarded as individual or random, there has been a concerted attempt in recent years to use the word as a route to POLITICAL empowerment as the status of **victim** becomes structural. Governments have also chosen to endow **victims** with an active role in addressing their misfortune; this is most evident in some criminal justice systems, where the issue then arises of whether such victims have been given a power to override not only the RIGHTS of offenders but also the ability of the STATE itself to administer justice.

These recent developments depend on more recent meanings recorded in the *OED*: "One who is reduced or destined to suffer under some oppressive or destructive agency," and "In a weaker sense: One who suffers some injury, hardship, or loss, is badly treated or taken advantage of, etc." The last of these meanings, the "weaker sense," accords most closely with contemporary legal definitions of a **victim** as "a person who has complained of the commission of an offence against themselves or their property" (Crown Prosecution Service). This wider definition encompasses, for example, the relatives of murder victims, including partners or parents when the victim is a child. Use of **victim** remained fairly steady over the past century and a half, but has increased massively over the last thirty years. This is almost certainly because individuals (and groups) have come to be identified as **victims** not because (or not only because) of what has happened to them, but rather because of who they are. One reflection of this change of emphasis is the recent widespread use of both **victimization** and **victimhood,** both of which are C19 coinages and show a remarkable increase in frequency after 1980. They both capture the notion, dating from the 1970s, that a **victim** might be an individual or group caught in what has been characterized as an "asymmetric power relationship." For example, the concept of **shared victimhood** became central to FEMINIST debate in the 1980s, with the result that domestic abuse, and the failure of the criminal justice system to deal with this problem effectively, came to be seen as a reflection of a prevailing, asymmetric power relationship rather than (or as well as) the result of an individual criminal act.

Increasingly the identity of a **victim** has been transformed from being inflicted to one voluntarily adopted. This is clear in the claim to **victim status** made by some groups as a means of establishing a claim to greater rights, stronger protection, or, in the case of affirmative action, preferential treatment. The notion of **victim status** has sometimes been described as providing the basis for IDENTITY politics. According to J. D. Mandle, in "How Political Is the Personal? Identity Politics, Feminism and Social Change," groups claiming victim status, including ethnic and religious minorities and disabled groups, among others, "made rights, status and privilege claims on the basis of a victimized identity." This increase in the use of **victim** as a political category has drawn harsh criticism. For example, there has been an argument that there has been a **victims' revolution** on US campuses, privileging appeasement of minority student groups in the interests of political correctness at the expense of freedom of thought and speech, sometimes making **victims** of those academics who do not adhere to a politically correct code.

The notion that **victimhood** arises from structural inequalities has also been rejected from other positions. Instead, it has been suggested that adopting **victim status** may lead individuals to a passive acceptance of their "victimhood." By the

1990s, some feminists were rejecting the idea of what was termed **victim feminism** for presenting women as passive and helpless in the face of male domination and aggression. One result of such reaction against the notion of women as victims has been preference for use of *survivor*, rather than **victim**, in describing those who have been subjected to male violence.

Over the last several decades, **victim** has acquired an active role in shaping contemporary attitudes toward crime, which may explain the word's increased frequency in use. The 1960s and 1970s saw increasing recognition of the needs of victims of crime. **Victim support** (attested from 1973) became the name for specific schemes, and **victim compensation** programs also began to be established at around the same time. Such initiatives continue, however, to see the **victim** in the traditional sense, as the passive object of a criminal act. From the 1980s onward, by contrast, **victims** have increasingly been viewed as important actors in the criminal justice system in their own right. On the left, arguments were advanced that the criminal justice system not only often overlooked the plight of the victim but that traditional punishments did little to assist either the individual victim, or the community, or indeed the offender. This view lies behind the widespread introduction of restorative justice schemes in many developed countries, allowing the victim to both interrogate the perpetrator and at times to dictate the recompense made. But this placing the victim at the center of criminal justice might also be traced to a rise in popular punitiveness, and the belief of some on the right that offenders have been accorded too many rights at the expense of the victims.

According to David Garland's *The Culture of Control* (2001), under the influence of popular punitiveness the **victim** is no longer seen as an "unfortunate citizen who has been on the receiving end of a criminal harm," but rather as a "representative character, whose experience is taken to be common and collective, rather than individual and atypical" (11). The consequence, for Garland, has been an erosion of the protection given to offenders, since in a zero-sum game any rights given to the offender are taken away from the victim; and a spate of laws have carried the names of victims: e.g., Megan's Law in the US; Sarah's Law in the UK. A Victim's Charter was also enacted by the UK government in 1996, setting out what victims might expect from the criminal justice system and introducing use of **victims' statements** before sentencing.

See IDENTITY, POLITICAL, RIGHTS, TRAUMA, VIOLENCE

VIOLENCE

Violence is often now a difficult word, because its primary sense is of physical assault, as in "robbery with violence," yet it is also used more widely in ways that are not easy to define. If we take physical assault as sense (i) we can take a clear general sense (ii) as the use of physical force, including the distant use of weapons or bombs, but we have then to add that this seems to be specialized to "unauthorized" uses: the **violence** of a "terrorist" but not, except by its opponents, of an army, where "force" is preferred and most operations of war and preparations for war are described as "defense"; or the similar partisan range between "putting under restraint" or "restoring order," and "police violence." We can note also a relatively simple sense (iii), which is not always clearly distinguished from (i) and (ii), as in "violence on television," which can include the reporting of violent physical events but indicates mainly the dramatic portrayal of such events.

The difficulty begins when we try to distinguish sense (iv), **violence** as threat, and sense (v), **violence** as unruly behavior. Sense (iv) is clear when the threat is of physical violence, but it is often used when the real threat, or the real practice, is unruly behavior. The phenomenon known as "student violence" included cases in senses (i) and (ii), but it clearly also included cases of sense (iv) and sense (v). The emotional power of the word can then be very confusing.

It is a long-standing complexity. **Violence** is from fw *violence*, oF, *violentia*, L—vehemence, impetuosity—ultimately from rw *vis*, L—force. **Violence** had the sense of physical force in English from 1C13, and was used of hitting a priest in 1303. From the same period we hear, in what seems a familiar tone, that the world is in a state

Of filthe and of corrupcion
Of violence and oppression.

But this use is interesting, because it reminds us that **violence** can be exercised both ways, as Milton insisted of Charles I: "a tedious warr on his subjects, wherein he hath so farr exceeded his arbitrary violences in time of peace" (1649). There has been obvious interaction between **violence** and *violation*, the breaking of some custom or some dignity. This is part of the complexity. But **violent** has also been used in English, as in the Latin, for intensity or vehemence: "marke me with what violence she first lov'd the Moore" (*Othello*, II, i); "violence of party spirit" (Coleridge, 1818). There was an interesting note in 1696: "violence ... figuratively spoken of Human Passions and Designs, when unruly, and not to be govern'd." It is the interaction of this sense with the sense of physical force that underlies the real difficulties of senses (iv) and (v); a sense (vi), as in "violently in love," is never in practice misunderstood. But if it is said that the state uses force, not only in senses (i) and (ii) but more critically in sense (iv)—the threat implied as the consequence of any breach of "law and order" as at any one time or in any one place defined—it is objected that **violence** is the wrong word for this, not only because of the sense of "authorized" force but because it is not "unruly." At the same time, questions of what it is to be "unruly" or "not to be govern'd" can be sidestepped. It is within the assumption of "unruly," and not, despite the transfer in the word, of physical force, that loud or vehement (or even very strong and persistent) verbal criticism has been commonly described as **violent**, and the two steps beyond that—threat to some existing arrangement, threat of actual force—sometimes become a moving staircase to the strong meanings of **violence** in senses (i) and (ii).

It is then clearly a word that needs early specific definition, if it is not (as in yet another sense, [vii]) to be done **violence** to—to be wrenched from its meaning or significance (from 1C16).

RECENT DEVELOPMENTS

Since Williams wrote, it remains true that the simple meaning of **violence** as physical assault is inflected by the political and legal standing of the agent of that physical assault. However, awareness of this complication has grown, as evidenced in a 2002 World Health Organization report. The WHO defines **violence** as "the intentional use of force or power," while admitting that the use of *power* expands on the conventional definition of the word. The further complexity that physical assault itself shades into the threat of assault has perhaps intensified with the widespread linking of *hate speech* to **violence**.

In general, the notion of assault has been expanded as, for example, in the same 2002 WHO report, in which it is not simply injury or death that is threatened by **violence** but also "psychological harm, maldevelopment or deprivation." **Domestic** and **sexual** have become among the most frequent collocates for **violence**, with the growing recognition of the role of assault both within the home and in a wide variety of sexual relations.

In one of his most famous quotes, Gandhi said that "poverty is the worst form of violence." In the last fifty years, the terms **structural violence** and **systemic violence** have been developed to describe the social causes of premature death and avoidable disability.

See TRAUMA, VICTIM

WEALTH

Wealth was formed, perhaps by analogy with *health*, from the associated words *well*, adverb, fw *wel* or *well*, OE, and *weal*, noun, fw *wela*, OE. It indicated happiness and prosperity but, if the question arose, it could clearly be specialized to either. The modern sense is clear enough in:

> For here es welth inogh to win
> To make us riche for evermore. (1352)

But the wider meaning is evident in the need to distinguish "worldly welthe" (1340), and "nullus est felicior" (no man is more happy) was translated in 1398 as "no man hath more welth." In *c*1450 there was "with-oute you have I neither joye ne welthe" and in Wyatt (1542) there was the clear sense of happiness: "syns every wo is joynid to some welth." **Commonwealth,** from *common weal, commonweal*, and **common wealth,** had the general sense of the WELL-BEING of the COMMUNITY before it developed into a special but related sense of a kind of social order. It was still also possible to write "for the welth of my soul" (1463).

Wealthy was more often used in the general sense (from C14) until perhaps mC15, and specialization to the wealth of a country seems earlier than that to the wealth of a man. From 1C16 **wealth** was used in a surviving sense to indicate abundance of something: "wealth of saumon"; wealth of examples. In C17 and C18 the word acquired not only a more definite association with money and possessions, but a strong subsidiary deprecatory sense. The political economists from Adam Smith (who in his best-known work used as a title the already well-known C17 phrase **wealth of nations**) sought to distinguish between **wealth** in a man and the **wealth** of a society. The former had sufficient and often derogatory association with possessions to require a distinction of the latter as production: cf. "a man of wealth . . . implies quantity . . . a source of wealth . . . quantity is not implied . . . products" (1821). But on the whole **wealth** and **wealthy** have come through in individualist and possessive senses, with a predominant reference to money. Other words such as *resources* have been found for the other economic meaning. The general reference to happiness and WELL-BEING had been so far lost and forgotten that Ruskin (*Unto this Last*, iv, 26) was forced to coin a word to express a sense of the unhappiness and waste which followed from some kinds of production. These led, in the specialized sense, to **wealth**, but there was need for the opposite term, *illth*. This recalls the original formation, however oddly it may now read, and there was some precedent in *illfare* (see *welfare*) which was used occasionally between C14 and C17 and briefly revived in C19 and C20.

Recent Developments

Since the publication of Williams's *Keywords*, **wealth** has continued to be associated with an abundance of money and financial assets possessed by an individual or a community. The sense of **wealth** indicating the "condition of being happy and prosperous" (*OED*) is now best expressed by WELL-BEING, a term that implies favorable physical, social, emotional, and economic conditions.

Although the relative frequency of **wealth** has remained stable, collocations such as **wealth management, wealth creation, wealth inequality,** and **wealth gap** are increasingly visible in public discourse. **Wealth management** describes the delivery of services designed to enhance an affluent individual's financial situation, i.e., it focuses on improving the financial SECURITY of haves, not have-nots. **Wealth creation** aims to reduce poverty and foster self-reliance by giving people the opportunity to make investments and create **wealth** on their own, but, according to critics such as David Harvey in *A Brief History of Neoliberalism* (2005), neoliberalism has worsened inequality under the guise of reform, FREEDOM, and **wealth creation.**

The increase in the relative frequency of **wealth inequality** and **wealth gap** since *c*1990 reflects the greater sense of urgency with which the issue of the uneven distribution of money and resources has been taken up in English-speaking political discourse. For example, income and **wealth inequality** in the United States were central issues addressed in the 2016 presidential campaign of US Senator Bernie Sanders. Negative connotations of **wealth** become evident in the use of the collective noun **the wealthy** and the phrase "the **wealthiest** one percent," both of which emphasize the growing gap between a small number of extremely wealthy individuals with political and economic power and the other 99% of Americans.

See COMMON, ENTREPRENEUR, WELL-BEING

WELL-BEING

Although the concept has existed for centuries, **well-being** has only recently become a contested term at the forefront of public debates concerning governmental program development, organizational culture in the workplace, and GLOBAL prosperity and progress. **Well-being**'s complexity, in this context, stems from its association with favorable physical, social, emotional, and financial conditions simultaneously at individual and societal levels. A steady increase in relative frequency of the term **well-being** over the past few decades may be attributed to the influence of the field of positive psychology and related efforts to inquire beyond measures of *material welfare* such as GDP in order to examine other factors that may significantly affect the *health* and *happiness* of populations.

Well-being first entered English in mC16 as a translation of the Italian term *benessere*. The word also derives from Spanish *bienestar* and post-classical Latin *bene esse*, both of which are documented from mC13. As modification of the gerund of "to be" coupled with generalized adverb "well" implies, **well-being** differs from mere *being* as a matter of quality or degree. Earliest examples cited in *OED* highlight a disparity between **well-being** and *being*: "I will not nowe speake of the profit that the worlde hath by women beeside the bearinge of children, for it is well inoughe declared howe necessarye they be, not onlye to oure beeinge, but also to oure well beeinge" (Castiglione, *Courtyer*, 1561); and "Some are so necessary that the whole can haue no being without them: some are very necessary partes to the well being of an whole, and yet not so necessary but that it may haue a being without them" (Lever's *Arte of Reason*, 1573). The distinction between that which is essential for life and that which is not essential but improves the LIFE of a person or COMMUNITY explains the tendency to treat **well-being** and *quality of life* synonymously.

The *OED* Third Edition (December 2014) identifies three senses of **well-being**: (1) "With reference to a person or community: the state of being healthy, happy, or prosperous; physical, psychological, or moral welfare"; (2) "With reference to a thing: good or safe condition, ability to flourish or prosper"; and (3) "In plural: Individual instances of personal welfare." **Well-being** only rarely appears in the plural form suggested in sense (3), and, although the word does apply to things as outlined in sense (2), the present significance and complexity of the term in PUBLIC discourse primarily relate to sense (1). In contemporary contexts, **well-being** typically implies favorable conditions, though this is not always the case, as is attested by the recent practice of distinguishing between **high well-being** and **low well-being**.

Well-being has sparked heated debates because, as the *OED* entry reveals, the word conveys a range of associations which open up the term to interpretations that represent distinct interests. While common collocations such as **subjective** and **personal well-being** describe an individual's cognitive and affective evaluation of his or her own *quality of life*, other frequently occurring collocations, such as **collective, societal, cultural, organizational, relational**, and **communal well-being**, refer to the overall satisfaction and engagement of a particular group or society as a whole. Such uses indicate that **well-being** has come to embody a tension between an individual's own *pursuit of happiness* and governmental or institutional attempts to develop policies that promote the *material, social*, and *emotional welfare* of entire communities. In *On Liberty* (1859), John Stuart Mill emphasized individuality as one element of **well-being**: "Each is the proper guardian of his own health, whether bodily, or mental or spiritual. Mankind are greater gainers by suffering each other to live as seems good to themselves, than by compelling each to live as seems good to the rest." The complexity of the term, together with an unwillingness to impose one vision of the good life on all members of a society, helps to explain why nations have generally concentrated on improving the *economic welfare* of citizens but mostly left more subjective aspects of **well-being** to individuals themselves.

Some of the most frequent collocations consisting of nouns which follow **well-being—well-being index, indicators, measures, outcomes**, and **survey**—attest to the recent emergence of initiatives that aim to quantify and compare **well-being** across populations. Since the late 1960s, economists and sociologists have studied non-material factors alongside income and GDP in order to arrive at a more comprehensive picture of *quality of life* in communities around the globe. Yet since no consensus exists regarding the precise definition of **well-being**, the methods used to measure what researchers now generally call **subjective well-being** (SWB) and **objective well-being** (OWB) vary considerably. The **Global Well-Being Index** developed by Gallup-Healthways offers GLOBAL comparisons based on five criteria: "Purpose: liking what you do each day and being motivated to achieve your goals. Social: having supportive relationships and love in your life. Financial: managing your economic life to reduce stress and increase security. Community: liking where you live, feeling safe and having pride in your community. Physical: having good health and enough energy to get things done daily." Due to the wide range of factors that may influence **well-being**, not to mention cultural and individual differences in life priorities, researchers involved in such analysis face a major challenge in identifying key **well-being indicators** and assigning suitable weights to each category.

With Britain and France appearing to lead the way, national governments around the world show considerable interest in **well-being** because of its potential to inform policymaking across economic, social, moral, environmental, and public health domains. The development of programs that promote overall **well-being** demonstrates that governments are concerned not only with improving the economy and the financial *welfare* of citizens, but also with increasing the odds that their citizens will live happy, fulfilled lives. Skeptics dismiss such **well-being policies** as creations of a "nanny state" and question the extent to which a government should interfere with personal choice in their efforts to make people happier and healthier.

In the workplace, the focus of HR (human resources) has also shifted in recent years from learning and development to **well-being**, with employers now investing more in their employees' health and happiness. **Well-being agendas** have been created and implemented in light of the claim made in positive psychology that humans can learn how to become happier and more fulfilled. Such agendas are designed to remedy cases of employee stress, absenteeism, and turnover, all of which became increasingly prevalent during the 1980s and 1990s as a result of technological innovations and global economic recession. The turn to **well-being** to solve these problems within CORPORATE culture in this context appears to reflect a desire to maximize productivity while preventing burnout. Inevitably, critics assert that such corporate actions to increase job satisfaction and engagement blur necessary boundaries between the professional and personal lives of employees.

Although **well-being** connotes good physical and psychological *health*, the word presumes a broader, preventative model of *health*, i.e., conditions that enable a person to thrive, rather than merely a state of freedom from illness or pathology. **Well-being** researchers have accordingly also studied the impact that neoliberal policies, such as Thatcherism in Britain in the 1980s, have had on *health*, social inequality, and **subjective well-being**. National **well-being agendas** represent a possible shift in objectives from unchecked economic growth toward stability and signify a potential broadening of the sense of *welfare*. According to Raymond Williams, in his keyword analysis of *welfare* (1976/1983), the extended sense of *welfare* "as an object of organized care or provision" replaced older words like *charity*, which had by eC20 "acquired unacceptable associations." In eC21, **well-being** circumvents such negative overtones of *welfare*, which are especially evident in collocations such as *welfare dependency, welfare schemes, welfare queens,* and *welfare fraud*. A major challenge associated with the concept **well-being** in present manifestations is that the word's range of possible meanings and tendency to become laden with modifiers can convey the impression that **well-being** itself is an empty concept.

See LIFE, SECURITY, WEALTH

WEST

West (including **western** and **westernize**, as well as related terms such as the cluster of words around *occidental*) has operated as a crucial and contested term of value connected to large geopolitical and cultural issues since at least C18. It remains live in our time, as witnessed by Donald Trump's Warsaw speech (July 2017): "The fundamental question of our time is whether the west has the will to survive." The current complex uses of **west** carry cross-emphases arising from a history of what Edward Said called "imaginative geography," beginning from *The Persae* by Aeschylus. A different but no less definitive **east-west** split was produced by the division of the Roman Empire in C3 and then later of Christianity in C11.

Within the cultures of Europe, the explorations and conquests of the century following Columbus established a new sense of the globe. John Donne wrote of "The Western Hemispheare, the land of Gold, and Treasure, and the Eastern Hemispheare, the land of Spices and Perfumes" (1631), implying London's centrality as recipient but not source of either gold or spice. Between the Atlantic and Pacific Oceans lie the Americas; and a whole series of distinctive and important usages arose concerning the "West" of the United States, including one of the major genres of Hollywood, the **Western**. D. H. Lawrence found in the frontier romances of James Fenimore Cooper an image of the characteristic American-as-**Westerner**: "hard, isolate, stoic, and a killer." Yet Cooper's frontier, set at the time of the French and Indian Wars/Seven Years' War, was barely west of New York City. What counts as **West** is always relative.

As recently as June 2011, *Wikipedia* stated that "*Western culture*, sometimes equated with *Western civilization* or *European civilization*, refers to cultures of Indo-European origin." Yet this equation would include, within the West, the cultures associated with such major Indo-European languages as Hindi (India), Urdu (Pakistan and India), and Farsi (Iran), which long patterns of usage do not simply exclude but rather construe as the "Other" of the West.

Since the terror attacks of September 11, 2001, **west** has tended to operate as a contrast term to "Islamic" culture. During the 1990s, debates over globalization often circulated around what were referred to as "Asian values," especially values associated with Singapore, China, Korea, and Japan, in contrast to those of the **West**. In the decades of the Cold War, the **West** had been opposed to an "East" of Communism in the USSR and its satellites, while for much of the first half of C20, the "**West**" contrasted primarily to Germany in relation to the great wars of 1914–18 and 1939–45. Over the "long nineteenth century" of British imperial dominance, the term **West** operated within a dynamic characterized by Said as that of "Orientalism." (He cited Kipling, 1892: "East is East and West is West, and never the twain shall meet.") This in turn was the period in which the *OED* was produced. Even as that work registers all the C20 uses mentioned in the preceding, the fundamental definitions of its original entry for this word, published in 1926, seem to participate in Orientalist structures as well as making them analytically visible, as for instance with the *OED* sense "Of or pertaining to the Western or European countries or races as distinguished from the Eastern or Oriental."

The etymology of **west** is not complex. The word is related to similar Germanic forms with similar meaning. But an important dimension of value may be cued by a wider Indo-European (IE) resonance: it has long been assumed that **west** is related (albeit problematically) to Gr *hesperos* and L *vesper*, terms that refer both to the direction **west** and to a time of day: evening or sunset. The

C19 scholar Max Müller influentially connected **west** with a solar-mythological value-structure assumed to be deeply ingrained in IE; that value-structure was more recently critically explored by Jacques Derrida, as "White Mythology." The influential eC20 work of the German Oswald Spengler is known in English as *The Decline of the West*, but its German title might also be translated as "Sunset of the Evening-land." This temporal-mythological dimension colors important early citations such as one from R. Fanshawe's (1655) translation of the Portuguese Renaissance epic of exploration and conquest, *Lusiad*: "But now he fears that Glorie's neer it's [*sic*] West, In the black Water of Oblivion"; and a citation from Dryden's *Indian Emperor* (1667), "I in the Eastern parts and rising Sky, You in Heaven's downfal, and the West must lye." It represents quite a shift that the prestige of the European ENLIGHTENMENT has allowed western values to appear those of the bright side.

The phrase **western ideals**, along with close variants such as **western values** and **western culture**, is not specifically registered in the *OED*. But this collocation does appear in a telling *OED* citation provoked by the Russian Revolution, from a 1918 edition of the *Times*: "The greatest question in the world to-day is whether Russia is to be abandoned, or whether she is to be saved; whether Western ideals are to prevail in the country whose potential power will be the balance in history."

Cold War discourse defined an opposition between Western religious morality and "godless Communism." But RELIGION has not always counted as **western**. In 1880, writing for the widely circulated *Atlantic Monthly*, William James claimed, "Not to fall back on the gods, where a proximate principle may be found, has with us Westerners long since become the sign of an efficient . . . intellect." This pragmatic empiricist perspective has seemed to many others, as well as James, to characterize **Western** CIVILIZATION. Yet it is not easy to find citations. Those nowadays who care to address **western values** or **civilization** or **culture**, to judge from *Wikipedia*, tend to do so in opposition to *multiculturalism*, which they associate with SECULAR, RELATIVIST values broadly like those espoused by James. **Western culture**, in this representation, is marked by "rationalism" (claimed as a classical Greek heritage) and (sometimes "Judaeo-) Christian" norms and practices; unlike James, it seeks higher authority. Yet another aspect of the **West** that is not captured in this emphasis on heritage is the identification of the **West** with the MODERN, as contrasted with the *East* as traditional or antiquated. This dualism shows strikingly in the 1870 Phi Beta Kappa address by Oliver Wendell Holmes, *Mechanism in Thought and Morals*:

"To occidentalise and modernise the Asiatic modes of Thought which have come down to us."

The range of meanings discussed here shows especially in uses of **westernize**. The *OED* does not register the existence of a counterpart "easternize"; and *orientalize* seems mainly limited to C19. However, in *OED* citations the derived terms **westernizer** and **westernizing** show this process as active over more than a century in Russia, Turkey, China, Japan, and the Arab world. Especially piquant, in light of contemporary geopolitics, is a *TLS* citation from 1935 concerning Afghanistan: "French and English incursions . . . entered . . . from the East and . . . carried Dravidian ideas with them against that tide of Westernizers of whom Alexander was one of the earliest."

For some decades, thinking politically about *East* and **West** has been challenged from the left by the substitution of *North-South* (*rich-poor, industrial-nonindustrial, developed-underdeveloped* societies and economies). The "global South" has been held to be a more significant division of the world. Yet it is equally shaped by the transfer of geography into a metaphor of value.

See CIVILIZATION, CULTURE, EUROPEAN, MODERN

YOUTH

Contemporary adult society takes an ambivalent attitude toward **youth**, which is seen as both a state to be envied and as a population to be feared. The desire to capture or retain "**youth**" has long been part of the human condition. In striking contrast, however, **youth** has also been seen as at best irresponsible and, at worst, as posing a threat to the social order if left untutored or unrestrained. Conveying in this way contradictory messages about a key formative stage in the lives of successor generations, the word **youth** encapsulates a complex conceptualization which surfaces in a changeable mix in any contemporary debate on what being **young** might mean or what wider significance such a phase of personal and social life may have.

The noun **youth** has been part of the English language since earliest times, having relations in other Germanic languages such as Dutch *jeugd* or German *Jugend*. The *OED* comments that its first two senses "often blend together": (1) "The fact or state of being young; youngness," as for example in the phrase, "in the bloom of youth"; (2) "The time when one is young; the early part of life; more specifically the period from puberty till the attainment of full growth, between childhood and adult age." Neither meaning fixes exact ages to **youth**. According to the United Nations, definitions of **youth** change in different "demographic, financial, economic and social settings . . ."; it nevertheless proposes that age is the easiest way to define **youth**, and fixes on the years between fifteen and twenty-four. In the UK, by contrast, **Youth Courts** deal with young people between ten and eighteen, while in New Zealand the age range is twelve to sixteen. In the first *OED* meaning, it should be noted, **youth** need not apply only to humans. The word also has wide-ranging and suggestive metaphorical power (e.g., when, in 1850, the *Morning Post* referred to Canada and other colonies as formerly "in their youth," but at that historical moment on their way to maturity). In such metaphorical senses, as with human **youth**, actual age is variable and perhaps irrelevant.

In sense (2), **youth** is often used interchangeably with *adolescence*, and is understood as a period of physical change. Increasingly in C20, the period of bodily change is viewed as being also marked by psychological development. But the psychology of **youth** was from its earliest construction problematic. The pioneering psychologist G. Stanley Hall, whose books include *Youth: Its Education, Regimen and Hygiene* (1906), claimed that **youth**, particularly in males, involves a need to learn both discipline and control in order to offset physical and psychological changes (often related to sexuality). His work influenced the later rise of the field of **Youth Studies**, which put forward the idea of specific **youth cultures** and **subcultures**. For some researchers, such as those of the Chicago School, such subcultures might commonly manifest themselves in criminality, for example in the form of **youth gangs** (in marked contrast with institutionalized **youth clubs** or **youth movements**). In the 1960s, by contrast, **youth** came to be viewed not only as a period of potential alienation from mainstream culture, but as also a time of countercultural creativity and attraction to anti-establishment political movements. More recently again, recognition of **youth** as a period marked by cultural difference has been increasingly seized on as a marketing opportunity, evidenced by the number of companies that claim to specialize in **youth marketing**.

Two further senses, "A quality or condition characteristic of the young" and "personified, or vaguely denoting any young person or persons," can be grouped together. Each rests on an assumption that generalization is possible once **youth** is viewed as a distinct period. *OED* examples show the possibility of either positive or negative connotations: **youthful freshness** and **youthful vigor,** as compared with **youthful folly** and **youthful rashness.** Conceptually these attributes may be two sides of the same coin; the quality of **youthfulness** is invoked not only to explain, but also to mitigate blame for less positive behaviors. Another collocation, **youthful appearance,** seems to have only a positive meaning and has long been one of the key attractions of **youth. Youthful appearance** is also, in contrast to many other **youthful** characteristics, seen as predominantly female and of course, like **youth culture,** has been heavily commodified.

The further sense "Young people (or creatures) collectively," and the concrete sense "a young person," are also closely related. The *OED* suggests that the latter meaning is used especially of young men, but it is arguable that both meanings are heavily gendered and male (and have been so since at least C19). For example, while the Nazi Party established its Hitler Youth, this was an entirely male organization; the female equivalent was known as the League of German Girls. While **youth** as a characteristic may be seen as both positive and negative, and the period of **youth** as time for growth to maturity, phrases such as **the youth** and **youths** are typically viewed in a negative way, by both government and many in the general population, as constituting a social problem. There is evidence that young people between fourteen and eighteen are more likely to offend than other age groups. Anxiety about **youth** and **the youth** in contemporary society also appears far more general. In the words of Henry Giroux, "Youth are no longer at risk but considered the risk" (*Z Magazine*, 1999).

The idea that **youths** pose a particular RISK to society is not new. There have been a succession of moral panics about **youthful behavior** since at least C19, which saw the conceptual construction of the youthful *hooligan* as a particular social threat. But anxiety about **youthful misbehavior** has intensified in recent years. One example of this is the reaction of both public and government in the UK to the murder in 1993 of the child Jamie Bulger by two ten-year-old boys. Although child murderers were and remain extremely rare, the result of the killing was a moral panic which saw, according to one criminologist, the introduction "of ever more repressive youth justice policies" which were designed, in echoes of G. Stanley Hall, to "re-install discipline, decency, standards and order" in young people and which have resulted twenty years later in a system of "youth justice which is the most repressive in Europe" (Barry Goldstone, *Guardian*, February 11, 2013).

In response to such developments, which as with most criminal justice policies have had greatest impact on the poor and racial minorities, some young people (again predominantly male) have chosen to reclaim the terms **youth** and **the youth** as markers of their marginal social status. As Tupac sang in 1994, "They got money for wars, but can't feed the poor. Say there ain't no hope for the **youth** and the truth is it ain't no hope for the future." Or as the band NWA put it in 1989, "Since I was a youth, I smoked weed out; Now I'm the mother fucka that ya read about." Others have incorporated **youth** into the names of their "gangs," such as "Villa Youth," although they are more likely to call themselves *Boys* or *Boyz*. Perhaps the apotheosis of the commonly held view of **youth** and **the youth** as posing an undifferentiated social threat was the recent invention, and then widespread adoption by shop owners, of the "Mosquito MK4." The Mosquito is a "sounder" which emits a very high tone that can only be heard by people under twenty-five years old; the tone, according to its manufacturer, becomes "highly annoying" but is "completely harmless." Serving to "disperse groups of teenagers" who are "loitering in an anti-social manner," the Mosquito is marketed in a manner that conflicts with many other forms of commercialization of **youth**: as a "Youth Deterrent."

See CULTURE

Appendix 1

Sources of Lexical Data

A t the core of every entry in this book is a dialogue between the history of each word as it is presented in the *OED*, and each contributor's reading in social and cultural history. This same methodology is at the core of all of the entries in Williams (1976) and Williams (1983) (i.e., Williams's original *Keywords* volume and its expanded revision). However, the period since 1983 has seen both major changes to the *OED* and the emergence of large electronic corpora of texts as a new tool for investigating historical change in the language.

The *Oxford English Dictionary* is the major historical dictionary of English. For each word it presents an etymology, dealing with the history of the word before it entered English and subsequent influences either from other languages or within English, followed by an identification of each of the main strands of meaning shown by the word, presented as a series of separate senses, each with its own set of illustrative quotations; the first illustrative quotation given for each sense is the earliest documentary evidence available for that sense, and hence the "first date" for that sense. The remaining illustrative quotations for each sense have been selected to reflect different nuances of meaning and use, and also, so far as is possible in a small set of examples, to convey something of the breadth of contexts in which the sense is found; some uses are "canonical," from the most significant writers, others are intentionally much more from everyday discourse. (Of course, the *OED* also presents many other categories of information, such as pronunciations, and detailed listings of spelling variants found in the history of a word, but these are in most cases less central to the concerns of this book.)

The first edition of the *OED* was published in fascicles between 1884 and 1928, subsequently arranged into ten volumes (actually taking up twelve very large printed books, closely printed with three columns to each page). A first single-volume *Supplement* was added in 1933, and while Williams was working a fuller supplement was in preparation, published in four volumes (working progressively from A to Z) in 1972 (A–G), 1976 (H–N), 1982 (O–Scz), and 1986 (Se-Z): thus, some of this supplementary material (depending on its position in the alphabet) was available to Williams for some of the entries in Williams (1976), and more for the new entries in Williams (1983). Crucially, all of the supplements did precisely what is suggested by the word *supplement*: they added new words, lemmas (i.e., compounds, derivatives, and phrases), and senses, and they added new illustrative quotations for some existing senses, as well as providing explicit comment on some of the existing text; however, the main text of the dictionary remained unchanged, in the twelve large, closely printed books containing material first published 1884–1928. Thus, the dictionary with which Williams was engaging was in large part a product of late Victorian and very early 20th-century British scholarship. Williams shows his awareness of this in comments in his 1976 Introduction.

For each entry in *Keywords* (1976 and 1983), Williams takes information from the *OED* as his starting point. Although this is made explicit only in the Introduction, the information on etymologies and on the dates of first appearance of particular meanings that is given in Williams's entries is nearly all drawn from the *OED*; what is unique to *Keywords* is the selection of particular *OED* evidence to cite and the encapsulation of key information in a tightly focused essay (most of the *OED* entries for the words in question run to many thousands of words of text), and then the bringing of this evidence into dialogue with illuminating and often critical perspectives from Williams's own deep reading in and understanding of social and cultural history.

This basic approach remains at the core of all the new entries in this volume, and of the short update sections at the end of entries reproduced from Williams's volume. There have been major changes in the interim, though, to the *OED*. Since the first edition and various supplements were brought together in 1989 on paper and subsequently electronically as the integrated Second Edition, much more material has been added to existing entries as "additions": these essentially continue the model of the supplements. However, the integrated digital version of the dictionary made it possible to begin much more fundamental revision of the existing text, and since 2000 the fruits of this have been appearing online as part of *OED Online*. These revised and updated dictionary entries reconsider and where necessary revise all parts of the existing text, including etymologies, definitions of each sense, and illustrative quotations; as well as adding a great deal of new information for more recent periods, they also very frequently involve significant changes to the documentation and interpretation of the earlier history of each word, often involving earlier dates for particular words, lemmas, or meanings, and reconsideration of the circumstances in which a word first entered English. At the time of writing in early 2017, approximately 40 percent of the existing dictionary has been revised in this way, collectively constituting the Third Edition of the *OED*, or *OED3*. In fact, in this revision process many of the words featured in *Keywords* have been selected as priorities for revision, precisely because of their complex and interesting histories: therefore, much more than 40 percent of the material in this volume now corresponds to *OED* entries that have been fully revised as part of *OED3*.

Therefore, most of the information on etymology and meaning history presented in the new entries in this volume reflects *OED* entries that have been fully revised as part of *OED3* within the past seventeen years. Of the words newly added for this volume, only *appropriation, brand, corporate, depression, diversity, enterprise, excellence, fundamentalism, independent, indigenous, secular, spiritual, text, trauma, victim,* and *youth* have yet to be revised in full for *OED3* at the time of writing; these remaining entries are all likely to undergo full *OED3* revision during the lifetime of this book, and readers comparing these *Keywords* entries with the corresponding *OED* entries may therefore find that the *OED* has since incorporated revised dating of senses, or definitions, or etymologies, or has added new lemmas (compounds, derivatives, or phrases) or senses. Additionally, *OED Online* takes advantage of electronic publication to make (mostly smaller) updates to already revised entries, which may sometimes affect, for instance, first dates, where an earlier quotation becomes available and is added.

Of the words in this book that are inherited from Williams's volumes, only *common, elite, equality, experience, institution,* and *wealth* still await *OED* revision. However, the text reproduced here from Williams has not been altered in light of *OED* revisions; instead, the most significant changes are taken account of in the appended update sections for these entries.

These changes in the *OED* also intersect with the other major change in lexical information available to researchers since Williams's work: namely the advent of electronic corpora, and of very large text databases that make it possible to gauge word frequency, and even changing word frequency over time.

A *corpus* is a collection of texts that is sampled in order to represent a particular population of language users. Corpora may be highly specialized, such as a corpus of face-to-face conversations among London teenagers in 2017, or much less specialized, such as a collection of tens of thousands of documents printed in the 16th and 17th centuries. If the relationship between the corpus and the sampled population is clear, then the corpus *represents* the population; in that case, investigating the corpus can yield conclusions about the population, and such conclusions can be corroborated statistically. Obviously, then, any corpus is limited by what it does and does not represent, and many language users are woefully unrepresented in corpora. Nonetheless, even without statistical analysis and clearly representative samples, corpora can yield important factual evidence, illustrating the ways that words can be or have been used in particular contexts. While corpora inform the entries in this volume, these entries are not corpus studies: only very general claims are made in relation to corpus evidence, and specific corpora and corpus methods are not cited.

In the past quarter-century, electronic corpora have revolutionized lexicographical work on contemporary English. Corpora, ever increasing in size and in their sensitivity to different text types, language varieties, and registers, make it possible for lexicographers and researchers working on contemporary English to reflect actual usage with much more confidence, making decisions about which words and meanings to include, and how to define them, that are informed by quantitative and qualitative data of actual language use—that is to say, we can see how often words or constructions are used, and we can see real-life examples of how they are used.

In particular, collocational patterns, whether in terms of formal constructional information (such as which nouns are commonly the subjects or the objects of a particular verb) or simply in terms of which words typically occur near one another, make it possible for lexicographers and researchers to make decisions that are much better informed by representative linguistic evidence. (For some examples of this approach in this book, see the entries *artificial, civil, elite, fundamentalism, genetic, organic, sexuality, well-being*.) Of course, any corpus is dependent on the quality and breadth of the data that go into it, and even today English usage in many parts of the world, and in many types of discourse, is much less well represented in electronic resources than anyone would like.

In recent years, the corpus revolution has also begun to embrace historical data, so that, however tentatively, lexicographers and other researchers can begin to identify changes in the typical behavior of words over time. Changing collocational patterns are often revealing of changes either in core meaning or in connotation. These new tools are currently being exploited for ongoing research projects like the *OED*, and have also been drawn upon extensively for this book. (See, for example, the entries presented here for *education, environment, fair, gender, marriage, performance, public*.) Often, comparing the behavior shown by words which at first sight seem near synonyms can be particularly revealing (see, for example, the entry for *ethical*, comparing its collocational behavior with that of *moral*, or *freedom*, which is compared with *liberty*). Change is most typically measured in terms of the relative frequency of particular words or collocations, rather than their absolute presence in or absence from the historical record. Some of the historical and contemporary corpora most amenable to use by interested beginners in this area have been developed by Mark Davies at Brigham Young University; for instance, the *Corpus of Historical American English* (*COHA*) has a user-friendly interface, allowing it to be easily explored for insights into changing patterns of collocation over the past two centuries (especially in terms of which words immediately precede or follow the researcher's chosen keyword); comparing this data with contemporary information from the present-day *Corpus of Contemporary American English* (*COCA*) or the *Corpus of Web-Based Global English* (*GloWbE*) via the same interface can be particularly illuminating. Where changes in the frequency of individual words are concerned, the Google Ngram Viewer can also provide a simple, powerful tool for investigating change in modern English.